ZAGAT®

New York City
Nightlife
2011/12

EDITOR
Curt Gathje

Published and distributed by
Zagat Survey, LLC
4 Columbus Circle
New York, NY 10019
T: 212.977.6000
E: nynightlife@zagat.com
www.zagat.com

ACKNOWLEDGMENTS

We thank Jason Briker, Phil Carlucci, Bernard Onken, Troy Segal, Steven Shukow and Ian Turner, as well as the following members of our staff: Danielle Borovoy (assistant editor), Brian Albert, Sean Beachell, Maryanne Bertollo, Reni Chin, Larry Cohn, Nicole Diaz, Kelly Dobkin, Alison Flick, Jeff Freier, Matthew Hamm, Justin Hartung, Marc Henson, Natalie Lebert, Mike Liao, James Mulcahy, Polina Paley, Chris Walsh, Jacqueline Wasilczyk, Art Yaghci, Sharon Yates, Anna Zappia and Kyle Zolner.

The reviews in this guide are based on public opinion surveys. The ratings reflect the average scores given by the survey participants who voted on each establishment. The text is based on quotes from, or paraphrasings of, the surveyors' comments. Phone numbers, addresses and other factual data were correct to the best of our knowledge when published in this guide.

Maps © Antenna International™
except for p. 183 and front panel of foldout map
copyright Zagat Survey, LLC

© 2011 Zagat Survey, LLC
ISBN-13: 978-1-60478-357-5
ISBN-10: 1-60478-357-5
Printed in the
United States of America

Contents

Ratings & Symbols	4
About This Survey	5
What's New	6
Most Popular	7
Key Newcomers	9
Most Visited	10
Top Ratings:	
Appeal	11
Decor	17
Service	18

DIRECTORY

Names, Locations, Contact Info, Ratings & Reviews	20

INDEXES

Locations	172
Maps	183
Special Appeals:	
After Work	186
Art Bars	186
Bachelor/ette Parties	187
Beautiful People	187
Bottle Service	187
Cabaret	188
Celeb-Sightings	188
Cheap Drinks	188
Closings	188
Coffeehouses	189
Comedy Clubs	189
Commuter Oases	189
Cool Loos	189
Dance Clubs	189
Dinner Cruises	190
Dives	190
DJs	191
Drag Shows	191
Drink Specialists	
Beer	191
Champagne	192
Cocktails	192
Martinis	192
Rum	192
Sake/Shochu/Soju	192
Scotch/Single Malts	192
Tequila	193
Vodka	193
Whiskey	193
Wine Bars	193
Wine by the Glass	193
Euro	193
Expense-Accounters	194
Eye-Openers	194
Fireplaces	194

First Date	195
Foreign Feeling	
Asian	195
French	195
German	195
Indian	195
Irish	195
Latin	196
Moroccan	196
Russian	197
Frat House	197
Games	197
Gay	202
Happy Hour	202
Hookahs	203
Hotel Bars	203
Jazz Clubs	205
Jukeboxes	205
Karaoke Bars	207
Lesbian	207
Live Entertainment	207
Mature Crowds	207
Meat Markets	208
Music Clubs	208
Newcomers	209
Nightclubs	210
NY State of Mind	210
Old New York	210
Outdoor Spaces	211
Photo Booths	214
Piano Bars	214
Punk Bars	214
Quiet Conversation	214
Roadhouses	214
Romantic	215
Smoking Permitted	215
Speakeasy-Style	215
Spoken Word	215
Sports Bars	216
Strip Clubs	216
Suits	216
Swanky	217
Theme Bars	217
Tiki Bars	217
Tough Doors	218
Trendy	218
Views	218
WiFi Access	219
Wine Chart	220

Ratings & Symbols

Zagat Top Spot	Name	Symbols		Zagat Ratings			
				APPEAL	DECOR	SERVICE	COST

Area, Address & Contact

Z Tim & Nina's ⊘   ▽ 23 | 5 | 9 | $5

W 50s | 4 Columbus Circle (8th Ave.) | 1/A/B/C/D to 59th St./ Columbus Circle | 212-977-6000 | www.zagat.com

Review, surveyor comments in quotes

Open from sunset to sunrise, seven days a week, this "deep dive" bar with a bathroom and phone booth across the street looks most like a LES tattoo parlor; however, "dirt-cheap" prices, a "freeflowing tap and unlimited mega-pretzels" draw "spaced-out crowds" of "multi-pierced patrons"; please be careful not to "trip on any of the customers on the way out", but don't worry about tripping over the staff – they're seldom to be seen.

Ratings

Appeal, Decor & **Service** are rated on a 30-point scale.

0	-	9	poor to fair
10	-	15	fair to good
16	-	19	good to very good
20	-	25	very good to excellent
26	-	30	extraordinary to perfection
▽			low response	less reliable

Cost

The price of a typical single drink.

| I | below $7 | E | $11 to $14 |
| M | $7 to $10 | VE | $15 or above |

Symbols

Z   highest ratings, popularity and importance

⊘   no credit cards accepted

About This Survey

This **2011/12 New York City Nightlife Survey** is an update reflecting significant developments since our last Survey was published. It covers 1,007 bars, clubs and lounges in the five boroughs, including 90 important additions. We've also indicated new addresses, phone numbers and other major alterations. Like all our guides, this one is based on input from avid local consumers – 5,719 all told. Our editors have synopsized this feedback, highlighting representative comments (in quotation marks within each review). To read full surveyor comments – and share your opinions – visit **ZAGAT.com,** where you'll also find free nightlife and restaurant news, special events, deals, reservations, menus, photos and lots more.

ABOUT ZAGAT: In 1979, we started asking friends to rate and review restaurants purely for fun. The term "user-generated content" had not yet been coined. That hobby grew into Zagat Survey; 32 years later, we have over 375,000 surveyors and cover airlines, bars, dining, fast food, entertaining, golf, hotels, movies, music, resorts, shopping, spas, theater, tourist attractions – and even doctors – in over 100 countries. Along the way, we evolved from being a print publisher to a digital content provider, e.g. **ZAGAT.com** and Zagat mobile apps (for iPad, iPhone, Android, BlackBerry, Windows Phone 7 and Palm webOS). We also produce marketing tools for a wide range of corporate clients. And you can find us on Twitter (twitter.com/zagat), Facebook and just about any other social media network.

THREE SIMPLE PREMISES underlie our ratings and reviews. First, we believe that the collective opinions of large numbers of consumers are more accurate than those of any single person. (Consider that our surveyors bring some 546,000 nights' worth of experience to this survey. They also visit nightspots year-round, anonymously – and on their own dime.) Second, there are many parts of the equation when choosing a nightspot, thus we ask surveyors to separately rate appeal, decor and service and report on cost. Third, since people need reliable information in a fast, easy-to-digest format, we strive to be concise and we offer our content on every platform – print, online and mobile. Our Top Ratings lists (pages 17–18) and indexes (starting on page 172) are also designed to help you quickly choose the best place for any occasion.

JOIN IN: To improve our guides, we solicit your comments; it's vital that we hear your opinions. Just contact us at **nina-tim@zagat.com.** We also invite you to join our surveys at **ZAGAT.com.** Do so and you'll receive a choice of rewards in exchange.

New York, NY
June 22 , 2011

Nina and Tim Zagat

What's New

WHAT'S BREWING: Beer had quite a year, with suds-centric spots surfacing all over town the same way that wine bars multiplied during the aughts. The beer hall concept – already in progress at **Bohemian Hall, Radegast Hall, Standard Biergarten** and **Studio Square** – picked up steam at **Bierhaus, Bier International** and **Spritzenhaus** (a mega-rooftop version atop **Eataly** is also in the works). And a slew of more modest venues – **Banter, The Draft, Idle Hands, Keg No. 229, Park Avenue Tavern, Snap, Taproom No. 307, Three Monkeys** and **The Windsor** – rolled out exotic beer lists. Why all the interest in hops? Some called it a lingering effect of the recession, given beer's cheaper cost compared to wine or spirits. Meanwhile, wine bars kept on opening with **Anfora, Aria, Brooklyn Winery, The Immigrant** and **Vyne** making their debuts. Likewise, the tiki bar genre, a nightlife perennial, was interpreted this year at **Hurricane Club, Lani Kai** and **Riff Raff's**.

 LOOK, UP IN THE SKY: The drinking-under-the-stars craze showed no signs of let-up. New rooftop bars included **Above 6, Gansevoort Park, Jimmy, Le Bain, Upstairs** and **XVI,** not to mention the particularly atmospheric Gramercy Park Hotel roof, **Gramercy Terrace,** formerly a private venue and now open to all. Its vine-wrapped trellises and wicker furniture recall NYC's last rooftop boom a century ago, when the lack of air conditioning made outdoor imbibing popular.

GOODNIGHT, NURSE: Nothing is forever in fast-moving Gotham, and this year the curtain came down on favorites like **Bogart's, Carnival, Clo, Comix, Divine Bar, Don Hill's, The Eldridge, ESPN Zone, Pussycat Lounge, Sin Sin, Su Casa** and **Wet Bar.** (For our entire list, see page 188.) The year also saw the end of two long-running weekly parties: 1984 night at the **Pyramid Club** and Beige at **B Bar**; the latter had been in progress for 16 years, some kind of a nightlife record.

RANDOM NOTES: Party-hearty Williamsburg got a wake-up call when a local community board proposed a moratorium on all new liquor licenses for the area; the matter has been tabled – for now . . . The full-out dance club (somewhat of an endangered species in NY) got a boost with the arrival of two newcomers, **District 36** and **System,** although **Love,** an unassuming Villager with a hard-core fan base, shuttered . . . The latest candidates for the toughest-door-in-town award were **The Bunker, Kenmare, Lavo, Mister H** and **Mulberry Project**; for now, the **Boom Boom Room** atop the Standard Hotel seems to be the most impregnable fortress . . . Landmark Watch: **Chumley's,** closed after its building collapsed in 2007, is slowly being reconstructed, but the rebuild is so thorough that it appears little of the original will be preserved . . . Finally, they dusted off the chandelier at **McSorley's,** and it made the *New York Times.*

New York, NY
June 22, 2011

Curt Gathje

Most Popular – Manhattan

1. 230 Fifth
2. Campbell Apartment
3. 1 Oak
4. Brother Jimmy's
5. Four Seasons Hotel Bar*
6. P.J. Clarke's
7. McSorley's
8. Hudson Hotel Bar
9. Boat Basin
10. Ginger Man
11. B. B. King Blues Club
12. Algonquin Blue Bar
13. Pegu Club
14. W Union Sq. Living Rm.
15. Brandy Library
16. Employees Only
17. Flûte
18. Whiskey Blue
19. Angel's Share
20. Apothéke*
21. King Cole Bar
22. Empire Hotel Rooftop
23. PDT
24. Blue Note
25. D.B.A.
26. Ulysses
27. Bemelmans Bar
28. Cafe Carlyle
29. W Times Sq. Living Rm.
30. Bubble Lounge
31. Bar Veloce
32. Flatiron Lounge*
33. Death & Co
34. Frying Pan*
35. Oak Bar
36. Blarney Stone
37. Jekyll & Hyde*
38. Monkey Bar*
39. Rose Bar*
40. Ritz-Carlton Star Lounge
41. 40/40
42. Blind Tiger Ale House
43. Milk & Honey
44. Dizzy's Club
45. Pravda
46. Ava Lounge
47. Stone Rose*
48. Stout
49. Pete's Tavern
50. Ace Hotel Lobby Bar

Most Popular – Brooklyn

1. D.B.A. Brooklyn
2. Brooklyn Brewery
3. Brooklyn Bowl
4. Waterfront Ale House
5. Clover Club
6. 200 Fifth
7. Radegast Hall
8. Brooklyn Inn
9. Apartment 138
10. Beauty Bar
11. Union Hall
12. Alligator Lounge
13. Barcade
14. Bell House
15. Bembe
16. Gate*
17. Knitting Factory*
18. Brooklyn Social
19. Barbès
20. Angry Wade's

* Indicates a tie with place above

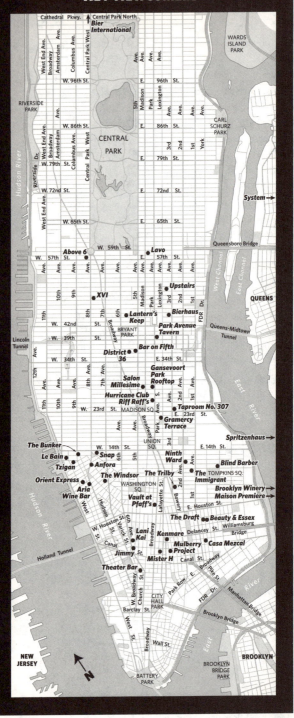

KEY NEWCOMERS

Bier International

Above 6 · Lavo

System →

XVI · Upstairs

Lantern's Keep · Bierhaus

Park Avenue Tavern

District 36 · Bar on Fifth

Gansevoort Park Rooftop

Salon Millesime

Hurricane Club · Riff Raff's

Taproom No. 307

Gramercy Terrace

Spritzenhaus →

The Bunker · Snap · Ninth Ward

Le Bain · Blind Barber

Tzigan · Anfora

Orient Express · The Windsor · The Trilby · The Immigrant

Aria Wine Bar · Brooklyn Winery →

Vault at Pfaff's · Maison Premiere →

The Draft · Beauty & Essex

Lani Kai · Kenmare · Casa Mezcal

Jimmy · Mulberry Project

Mister H

Theater Bar

Vote at ZAGAT.com

Key Newcomers

Our editors' favorites among this year's arrivals. See a full list on page 209.

SKY-SCRAPERS
Above 6
Gansevoort Park Rooftop
Gramercy Terrace
Jimmy
Le Bain
Upstairs
XVI

BEER BLASTS
Bierhaus
Bier International
Draft
Park Avenue Tavern
Snap
Spritzenhaus
Taproom 307
Windsor

DOOR SCENES
Bunker
Kenmare
Lavo
Mister H
Mulberry Project
Tzigan

TIKI
Hurricane Club
Lani Kai
Riff Raff's

IN VINO VERITAS
Anfora
Aria Wine Bar
Brooklyn Winery
Immigrant

INSTANT HITS
Beauty & Essex
Bierhaus
Hurricane Club
Spritzenhaus

TRANSPORTERS
Blind Barber
Casa Mezcal
Maison Premiere
Ninth Ward
Orient Express
Theater Bar
Vault at Pfaff's

CHA-CHA-CHA
District 36
System

HOTEL HIDEAWAYS
Bar on Fifth
Lantern's Keep
Mister H
Salon Millesime
Trilby

Coming soon, some interesting new projects that are in various stages of readiness: **Westway,** the new West Village project from the Jane Hotel Lobby Bar team, originally planned as a postmodern strip club, has jettisoned the stripping idea to get its liquor license; the latest iteration of longtime Latin dance palace, **The Copacabana,** this time set in Times Square's former **China Club** digs and equipped with a retractable roof for open air dancing; **Le Baron,** the long-in-the-making Chinatown spin-off of the exclusive clubs in Paris and Tokyo, brought to you by nightlife impresario/graffiti artist André Saraiva; **La Birreria,** a sprawling rooftop beer garden perched above Eataly with a view of the Empire State Building and all-seasons access thanks to a retractable roof; **Silver Lining,** a TriBeCa bar-cum-jazz room from cocktail kingpin Sasha Petraske (**Little Branch, Milk and Honey**); and a yet-to-be-named mixology den in the Financial District from the Death & Co folks.

Most Visited

BY GENDER

FEMALE
1. 230 Fifth
2. Brother Jimmy's
3. P.J. Clarke's
4. Boat Basin
5. Hudson Hotel Bar
6. Campbell Apartment
7. Ginger Man
8. Empire Hotel Rooftop
9. B. B. King Blues Club
10. 1 Oak

MALE
1. Brother Jimmy's
2. 230 Fifth
3. P.J. Clarke's
4. McSorley's
5. Ginger Man
6. 1 Oak
7. Blarney Stone*
8. Campbell Apartment
9. B. B. King Blues Club
10. Hudson Hotel Bar

BY AGE

TWENTIES
1. 230 Fifth
2. Brother Jimmy's
3. Ginger Man
4. 1 Oak
5. Crocodile Lounge
6. Tonic
7. Village Pourhouse*
8. Frying Pan
9. Joshua Tree*
10. Boat Basin

THIRTIES
1. 230 Fifth
2. Brother Jimmy's
3. P.J. Clarke's
4. Ginger Man
5. Boat Basin
6. Hudson Hotel Bar
7. 1 Oak
8. Campbell Apartment*
9. McSorley's*
10. Empire Hotel Rooftop

FORTIES
1. 230 Fifth
2. P.J. Clarke's
3. Brother Jimmy's
4. Campbell Apartment
5. Hudson Hotel Bar
6. McSorley's
7. B. B. King Blues Club
8. Four Seasons Hotel Bar
9. Ginger Man
10. Jekyll & Hyde

FIFTIES
1. P.J. Clarke's
2. B. B. King Blues Club
3. Algonquin Blue Bar
4. Blue Note
5. Blarney Stone
6. Four Seasons Hotel Bar
7. Campbell Apartment
8. Brother Jimmy's
9. Pete's Tavern*
10. Jekyll & Hyde

Top Appeal

28 Madam Geneva	Four Seasons Hotel Bar*
27 Dizzy's Club	Angel's Share
Raines Law Room	Death & Co
Bemelmans Bar	Terroir*
King Cole Bar	Jane Hotel Lobby Bar
Brooklyn Bowl	Bar Pleiades
PDT	Bembe*
Plaza Athénée Bar Seine	Feinstein's at Loews
Cafe Carlyle	Ritz-Carlton Star Lounge
Louis 649	Frying Pan
Brandy Library	Dutch Kills
Village Vanguard	Radegast Hall
26 Top of the Tower	25 Salon de Ning
Bar Centrale	Pegu Club
Plunge	Manitoba's
Bateaux NY	Rose Bar
Mayahuel	Jazz Standard
Rockwood Music Hall	Sweet Afton
Smalls	Bohemian Hall
Cávo	Milk & Honey

BY CATEGORY

AFTER WORK/UPTOWN
- 27 Bemelmans Bar
- 25 Boat Basin
- 24 Buceo 95
- 23 Bar Italia
- Shalel Lounge
- 22 Uptown Lounge

AFTER WORK/MIDTOWN
- 27 King Cole Bar
- 25 Campbell Apartment
- Oak Bar
- 24 Hudson Hotel Bar
- Bookmarks
- M Bar

AFTER WORK/DOWNTOWN
- 27 Brandy Library
- 22 Church Lounge
- 21 Bubble Lounge
- 20 Ulysses
- 17 Jeremy's Ale House
- Eamonn's

ART BARS
- 24 Box
- 23 Nuyorican Poets
- 22 Nublu
- 21 Galapagos
- 20 Half King
- KGB

BEER SPECIALISTS
- 26 Radegast Hall
- 25 Bohemian Hall
- Studio Square
- Spuyten Duyvil
- Barcade
- Room*

BOWLING ALLEYS
- 27 Brooklyn Bowl
- 23 Frames
- 22 Lucky Strike Lanes
- 21 300 New York
- 20 Harlem Lanes
- Bowlmor

Excludes places with low votes, unless otherwise indicated

CABARETS

27 Cafe Carlyle
26 Feinstein's at Loews
25 Oak Room
   Metropolitan Room
24 Box
   Joe's Pub

COCKTAIL EXPERTS

28 Madam Geneva
27 Raines Law Room
   Bemelmans Bar
   King Cole Bar
   PDT
   Brandy Library

COMEDY CLUBS

22 Comedy Cellar
21 Carolines
20 Stand-Up NY
   Gotham Comedy
   Comic Strip
18 New York Comedy

DANCE CLUBS

25 Santos Party House
23 Cielo
   Swing 46
21 S.O.B.'s
18 Webster Hall
   Saloon

DIVES

25 55 Bar
22 Boat
21 Library
   Ace Bar
   Lakeside Lounge
   Jimmy's Corner

FRAT HOUSE

21 Tortilla Flats
   Ace Bar
   Half Pint
   Bar Great Harry
20 Whiskey River
   Stumble Inn

GAY

23 Ritz
22 Therapy
21 xes lounge
   Eagle
   Splash
   Monster

HOOKAHS

23 Karma
22 Le Souk Harem
19 Kush
16 Katra

HOTEL BARS

27 Bemelmans Bar
   King Cole Bar
   Plaza Athénée Bar Seine
   Cafe Carlyle
26 Top of the Tower
   Plunge

IRISH

25 Sweet Afton
24 Wilfie & Nell
23 McSorley's
   Lillie's
   Molly's
22 St. Dymphna's
   Swift

JAZZ CLUBS

27 Dizzy's Club
   Village Vanguard
26 Smalls
25 Jazz Standard
   55 Bar
24 Birdland

LATIN

23 Nuyorican Poets
22 Barrio Chino
21 S.O.B.'s
20 El Morocco
19 Zinc Bar
18 Agozar!

LESBIAN

20 Henrietta Hudson
19 Cubby Hole
18 Ginger's∇

MATURE CROWDS

27 Dizzy's Club
   Bemelmans Bar
   King Cole Bar
   Plaza Athénée Bar Seine
   Cafe Carlyle
26 Feinstein's at Loews

MEAT MARKETS

26 Plunge
24 Standard Biergarten
   Hudson Hotel Bar
23 230 Fifth

Grand Bar
22 Church Lounge

MUSIC CLUBS

27 Brooklyn Bowl
26 Rockwood Music Hall
25 Pete's Candy Store
Metropolitan Room
City Winery
Santos Party House

NIGHTCLUBS

24 1 Oak
23 Juliet Supperclub
SL
Avenue
22 Tenjune
21 Greenhouse

PIANO BARS

24 Brandy's
Marie's Crisis
21 Monster
20 Townhouse
Don't Tell Mama
20 Duplex

POOL HALLS

21 Fat Cat
20 Slate
19 Soho Billiards
17 Amsterdam Billiards

PUNK BARS

25 Manitoba's
19 Mars Bar
18 Ding Dong Lounge
15 Trash▽

QUIET CONVERSATION

27 Raines Law Room
Bemelmans Bar
King Cole Bar
PDT

25 Milk & Honey
24 Otheroom

ROOFTOPS

26 Top of the Tower
Plunge
25 Salon de Ning
24 Rare View
Hudson Hotel Sky Terrace
Empire Hotel Rooftop

SPEAKEASY-STYLE

27 Raines Law Room
PDT
26 Angel's Share
Death & Co
Dutch Kills
25 Milk & Honey

SPORTS BARS

23 Ainsworth
22 Lansdowne Road
21 Beer Garden
Stan's
Kinsale Tavern
20 Yankee Tavern

STRIP CLUBS

23 Rick's Cabaret
Penthouse Exec. Club
VIP Club▽
21 Flashdancers
19 Hustler Club
18 Scores

WINE BARS

26 Terroir
25 City Winery
24 Barcibo Enoteca
Xai Xai Wine Bar
Blue Ribbon Downing St.
Buceo 95

BY LOCATION

CHELSEA

26 Frying Pan
25 Ace Hotel Lobby Bar
24 1 Oak
23 Juliet Supperclub
Pierre Loti
Tillman's

EAST 40s

26 Top of the Tower
25 Campbell Apartment

24 Bookmarks
Mad 46
21 Whiskey Blue
20 Beer Bar/Cafe Centro

EAST 50s

27 King Cole Bar
26 Four Seasons Hotel Bar
24 Beekman Bar and Books
23 Monkey Bar

22 Vero
21 Redemption

EAST 60s
27 Plaza Athénée Bar Seine
26 Feinstein's at Loews
24 Club Macanudo
23 Regency Hotel Library Bar
20 O'Flanagan's
18 Subway Inn

EAST 70s
27 Bemelmans Bar
   Cafe Carlyle
26 Bar Pleiades
23 Bar Italia
22 Vero
   Lexington Bar and Books

EAST 80s
24 Brandy's
22 Auction House
   Uptown Lounge
20 Comic Strip
19 Genesis
18 Saloon

EAST 90s
21 Kinsale Tavern
19 Manny's on Second ∇
17 Brother Jimmy's

EAST VILLAGE
27 PDT
   Louis 649
26 Mayahuel
   Angel's Share
   Death & Co
   Terroir*

FINANCIAL DISTRICT
21 P.J. Clarke's
20 Ulysses
19 17 Murray
17 Jeremy's Ale House
16 Full Shilling
14 Blarney Stone

FLATIRON/ UNION SQUARE
27 Raines Law Room
25 Metropolitan Room

23 Lillie's
   Flûte
   Park Bar
22 W Union Sq. Living Rm.

GARMENT DISTRICT
23 Rick's Cabaret
   Metro Grill Roof
20 Australian
   Stout
19 Hammerstein Ballroom
   Stitch

GRAMERCY PARK
25 Rose Bar
23 Pierre Loti
   Molly's
22 Cibar
   3 Steps
21 Pete's Tavern

GREENWICH VILLAGE
24 La Lanterna
   Blue Note
23 8th St. Winecellar
22 Comedy Cellar
   Le Souk Harem
   124 Rabbit

LITTLE ITALY
25 GoldBar
24 Onieal's Grand St.∇
20 Southside∇
   Xicala∇*

LOWER EAST SIDE
26 Rockwood Music Hall
25 Milk & Honey
24 Box
   Ten Bells
23 Above Allen
   Living Room

MEATPACKING
26 Plunge
25 675 Bar
24 Boom Boom Room
   Standard Biergarten
23 SL
   Cielo

MURRAY HILL

- 25 Jazz Standard
- 24 Rare View
- 22 Vino 313
- 21 Ginger Man
- Pine Tree Lodge
- Stone Creek*

NOHO

- 28 Madam Geneva
- 24 Von
- 23 Temple Bar
- 22 Swift
- 21 Tom & Jerry's
- 19 Soho Billiards

NOLITA

- 23 Vig Bar
- 22 Pravda
- 20 Botanica
- 19 Spring Lounge
- 18 R Bar
- 17 Sweet & Vicious

SOHO

- 25 Pegu Club
- Thom Bar
- Room
- 24 SubMercer
- Crosby Bar
- Circa Tabac

TRIBECA

- 27 Brandy Library
- 26 Terroir
- 24 Ward III
- 22 Church Lounge
- Anotheroom
- 21 Bubble Lounge

WEST 40s

- 26 Bar Centrale
- 25 Oak Room
- 24 Birdland
- M Bar
- 23 Algonquin Blue Bar
- W Times Sq. Living Rm.

WEST 50s

- 26 Ritz-Carlton Star Lounge
- 25 Salon de Ning
- Oak Bar
- 24 Xai Xai Wine Bar
- Hudson Hotel Bar
- Champagne Bar at the Plaza

WEST 60s

- 27 Dizzy's Club
- 24 Barcibo Enoteca
- Empire Hotel Rooftop
- MO Bar
- 23 Stone Rose
- 22 Empire Hotel Bar

WEST 70s

- 25 Boat Basin
- 23 Shalel Lounge
- Beacon Theatre
- Bin 71
- 22 Wine & Roses
- 21 P&G Cafe

WEST 80s

- 21 George Keeley's
- 20 Dead Poet
- 19 Prohibition
- 18 4_20
- 17 Jake's Dilemma
- Brother Jimmy's

WEST 90s & UP

- 24 Buceo 95
- Smoke
- 21 Abbey Pub
- 19 Cleopatra's Needle
- Amsterdam Tavern
- Lion's Head

WEST VILLAGE

- 27 Village Vanguard
- 26 Smalls
- Jane Hotel Lobby Bar
- 25 55 Bar
- 24 Blue Ribbon Downing St.
- Otheroom

OUTER BOROUGHS

BRONX

- [22] An Béal Bocht
- [21] Stan's
- [20] Yankee Tavern

BROOKLYN: CARROLL GARDENS/BOERUM HILL/COBBLE HILL

- [25] Brooklyn Inn
  - Clover Club
- [24] JakeWalk
- [23] Apartment 138
  - Zombie Hut
- [22] Gowanus Yacht

BROOKLYN: HEIGHTS/DUMBO

- [24] Rebar
- [21] Galapagos
- [20] Floyd, NY
  - Waterfront Ale House
- [17] Eamonn's

BROOKLYN: PARK SLOPE

- [24] Sidecar
  - Union Hall

- [23] Barbès
- [22] Beer Table
  - Tea Lounge
- [21] Buttermilk

BROOKLYN: WILLIAMSBURG

- [27] Brooklyn Bowl
- [26] Bembe
  - Radegast Hall
- [25] Pete's Candy Store
  - Spuyten Duyvil
  - Barcade

QUEENS: ASTORIA/L.I.C.

- [26] Cávo
  - Dutch Kills
- [25] Sweet Afton
  - Bohemian Hall
  - Studio Square
- [22] Central

STATEN ISLAND

- [21] Beer Garden
- [20] Cargo
- [19] Big Nose Kate's

Top Decor

28 Bar Pleiades	Oak Bar
27 King Cole Bar	M Bar
Bemelmans Bar	Larry Lawrence
GoldBar	Oak Room*
Rose Bar	Club Macanudo
Plaza Athénée Bar Seine	Plunge
26 Brandy Library	Union Hall
Dizzy's Club	Feinstein's at Loews
Cávo	Madam Geneva
Four Seasons Hotel Bar	Boom Boom Room
Raines Law Room	Hudson Hotel Bar
MO Bar	Salon de Ning
Campbell Apartment	24 Bowery Hotel Bar
Louis 649	Bar 44
Ritz-Carlton Star Lounge	Hudson Bar and Books
Crosby Bar	Juliet Supperclub
Brooklyn Bowl	Pegu Club
Jane Hotel Lobby Bar	Death & Co
25 Champagne Bar at the Plaza	Mayahuel
Cafe Carlyle	Ace Hotel Lobby Bar

OLD NEW YORK

Bill's Gay Nineties	Oak Bar
Campbell Apartment	Old Town Bar
Ear Inn	Pete's Tavern
Globe	P.J. Clarke's (East Side)
Lenox Lounge	United Palace
Marie's Crisis	Village Vanguard
McSorley's	White Horse

OUTDOORS

Berry Park	Gramercy Terrace
Bookmarks	Jimmy
Cávo	Rink Bar
Delancey	Standard Biergarten
Empire Hotel Rooftop	Studio Square

ROMANCE

Auction House	Madam Geneva
Bookmarks	Maison Premiere
Bourgeois Pig	Milk & Honey
Dove	Shalel Lounge
La Lanterna	Temple Bar
Lani Kai	Weather Up

VIEWS

Above Allen	Press Lounge
Ava Lounge	Rare View
Boat Basin	Salon de Ning
Boom Boom Room	Top of the Strand
Chelsea Brewing	230 Fifth
Plunge	Upstairs

Top Service

<u>27</u> Barcelona Bar

<u>26</u> Raines Law Room
Louis 649
Cafe Carlyle

<u>25</u> Bemelmans Bar
Ritz-Carlton Star Lounge
Four Seasons Hotel Bar
Terroir
MO Bar
King Cole Bar
Brandy Library
Manitoba's
Milk & Honey

<u>24</u> Beer Table
Bar Pleiades
Plaza Athénée Bar Seine
Bar Centrale
Blue Ribbon Downing St.
Sidecar
Zampa*

Angel's Share
Feinstein's at Loews
Metropolitan Room
Sweet Afton*
Ward III*
In Vino

<u>23</u> Brooklyn Bowl
Buceo 95*
Jadis*
LelaBar*
Stone Creek*
Little Branch
Barramundi
Death & Co
Vino 313
Whiskey Tavern*
Mayahuel
Dizzy's Club
Emmett O'Lunney's
Riposo*

NIGHTLIFE
DIRECTORY

| | APPEAL | DECOR | SERVICE | COST |

Abbey, The
20 | 17 | 21 | M

Williamsburg | 536 Driggs Ave. (bet. N. 7th & 8th Sts.) | Brooklyn |
L to Bedford Ave. | 718-599-4400

Everyone's "welcome" at this "divey" Williamsburger that works when
you're in search of a "quick pint" or simply as a place to "get twisted";
the "relatively nondescript" digs are enhanced by Sunday movies, a
"decent pool table" and the ultimate crowd-pleaser – "fresh popcorn."

Abbey Pub
21 | 16 | 21 | M

W 100s | 237 W. 105th St. (bet. Amsterdam Ave. & B'way) | 1 to 103rd St. |
212-222-8713

This "unpretentious" "neighborhood joint" is a bona fide UWS "institution" where Columbia professors, grad students and "lots of locals" assemble to "take a load off"; it may be "worn down" but old-timers say the
"homey" atmosphere conjures up "what the West Side used to be."

Abilene
▽ 23 | 19 | 22 | M

Carroll Gardens | 442 Court St. (3rd Pl.) | Brooklyn | F/G to Carroll St. |
718-522-6900 | www.abilenebarbrooklyn.com

Saddle up and head to Carroll Gardens for "creative beer selections"
and a hotly contested game of Battleship at this "pleasantly grungy"
hipster haven, a "low-key" spot with a "Western vibe"; sidewalk seating
provides plenty of "people-watching" opportunities in the summer.

Above Allen
23 | 23 | 18 | VE

LES | Thompson LES Hotel | 190 Allen St., 7th fl. (bet. Houston &
Stanton Sts.) | F to Lower East Side/2nd Ave. | 212-460-5300 |
www.thompsonles.com

For "swanky" cocktailing Downtown, this greenhouselike "perch" with a
retractable roof atop the Thompson LES Hotel is a favorite among "pretty
people" who are as "stunning" as its bird's-eye view; most don't mind
the "higher price tags", although foes dub it a "wannabe cool" scene.

NEW Above 6
- | - | - | E

W 50s | 6 Columbus Hotel | 308 W. 58th St., rooftop (bet. 8th & 9th Aves.) |
1/A/B/C/D to 59th St./Columbus Circle | 212-397-0404

A sibling of Above Allen and A60, this new rooftop is located just off
Columbus Circle in the hotel that's home to Blue Ribbon Sushi Bar & Grill;
while it doesn't offer a jawdropping view – it mostly overlooks the
Time Warner Center – a retractable roof makes it an all-seasons affair.

Ace Bar
21 | 15 | 17 | M

E Village | 531 E. Fifth St. (bet. Aves. A & B) | L to 1st Ave. | 212-979-8476 |
www.acebar.com

All that's missing is a ball pit at this "kick-ass" East Village bar-cum-
"arcade" where "hipsters" and fratsters stave off adulthood for a few
hours as they cradle a "cold PBR" in one hand and roll Skee-Ball with the
other; those billiards, darts, pinball and video games sure are "fun",
but this "quirky dive" ices the cake with a wall of "vintage lunchboxes."

ⓩ Ace Hotel Lobby Bar
25 | 24 | 17 | E

Chelsea | Ace Hotel | 20 W. 29th St. (bet. B'way & 5th Ave.) | N/R to
28th St. | 212-679-2222 | www.acehotel.com

Simultaneously "old-school" and too cool for school, this "spacious"
bar/lounge in the lobby of the "urban hipster"–friendly Ace Hotel fea-

tures a coffered-ceilinged, faux college-study-hall setting equipped with "comfy couches", "laptops in the middle of the room" and even a "cute photo booth"; although "service is less than could be desired", the place sure "beats anything else" in its "no-man's-land" North Chelsea neighborhood.

Against the Grain

▽ 28 | 26 | 26 | E

E Village | 620 E. Sixth St. (bet. Aves. B & C) | F to Lower East Side/2nd Ave. | 212-358-7065 | www.grapeandgrain.net

This "intimate" annex of the adjacent Grape and Grain wine bar plies a "huge selection of beer" in "tiny" digs overseen by a "friendly", "well-informed" crew; the "delightful" candlelit ambiance makes it a "quintessential" East Village "date spot", while the "far-east location" keeps overcrowding to a minimum.

Agozar!

18 | 16 | 17 | M

NoHo | 324 Bowery (Bleecker St.) | 6 to Bleecker St. | 212-677-6773 | www.agozarnyc.com

Pair "delicious mojitos" with a "great" tapas selection at this "lively little" Bowery Cubano with a "fun" happy hour that's as sweet as its special sangrito cocktail; occasional live Latin music lends "authentic noise and overcrowding."

Ainsworth, The

23 | 22 | 19 | E

Chelsea | 122 W. 26th St. (bet. 6th & 7th Aves.) | N/R to 28th St. | 212-741-0646 | www.ainsworthnyc.com

The sports bar gets kicked "up a notch" or three at this "gigantic" Chelsea plasma-screen palace, an "upscale" "football heaven" with "TVs on every possible surface" and a surprisingly "cool crowd"; rustic pine-and-wrought-iron decor plus "nice spins on classic pub food" make it the rare ESPN zone that "even ladies can enjoy."

Algonquin Blue Bar

23 | 23 | 22 | VE

W 40s | Algonquin Hotel | 59 W. 44th St. (bet. 5th & 6th Aves.) | 7/B/D/F/M to 42nd St./Bryant Park | 212-840-6800 | www.algonquinhotel.com

"Pricey" cocktails are "served with panache" at this Theater District bar in the "historic" Algonquin Hotel, where "Dorothy Parker" once held court; today, it's an "old-world" (verging on "stodgy") magnet for "people over 40" seeking "business drinks" in "sophisticated" digs.

Alligator Lounge

19 | 14 | 19 | M

Williamsburg | 600 Metropolitan Ave. (Lorimer St.) | Brooklyn | G/L to Metropolitan Ave./Lorimer St. | 718-599-4440

"Free pizza with every drink" is the "gimmick" at this "too-good-to-be-true" Williamsburg dive that draws penny-pinching "hipsters" and "NYU kids"; just ignore the "kitschy decor, straight out of a *Swamp Thing* movie" – for "drinking on a budget, this place can't be beat."

Alphabet Lounge

18 | 14 | 17 | M

E Village | 104 Ave. C (7th St.) | L to 1st Ave. | 212-780-0202 | www.alphabetnyc.com

Being in a "bachelorette party kind of mood" helps at this East Village "dance party" where weekend "'80s nights" draw folks eager to "live out their glory days"; despite a "ridiculous" cover, "long bathroom lines" and "so-crowded-you-can't-move" conditions, this one usually "delivers."

| | APPEAL | DECOR | SERVICE | COST |

Amity Hall

| - | - | - | M |

G Village | 80 W. Third St. (Thompson St.) | A/B/C/D/E/F/M to W. 4th St. | 212-677-2290 | www.amityhallnyc.com

Beer is king at this Village hops hall from the suds-obsessed minds behind Half Pint, St. Andrews and Stout; their latest effort offers 40 craft drafts (along with countless bottles) in a midsize, two-story space that's equal parts weathered brick, flickering flat-screens and NYU frat cats.

Amnesia

| - | - | - | E |

Chelsea | 609 W. 29th St. (bet. 11th & 12th Aves.) | A/C/E to 34th St./ Penn Station | 212-643-6464 | www.amnesianyc.com

An old Way West Chelsea stalwart (fka Sol, fka Ruby Falls) gets a relaunch via this mammoth nightclub with 45-ft.-high ceilings, a big dance floor and a 1,000-person capacity; though there's been some minor cosmetic changes (relocating the bar, moving the VIP pen to the balcony), the general idea – partying large – remains the same.

Amsterdam Ale House

| - | - | - | I |

W 70s | 340 Amsterdam Ave. (76th St.) | 1/2/3 to 72nd St. | 212-362-7260 | www.amsterdamalehouse.com

Lightly revamped from its days as the Westside Brewing Co., this Upper West Side joint remains a no-frills, standard-issue pub now dispensing a more extensive list of suds; regulars like its cheap tabs, low-key mood and unpretentious crowd.

Amsterdam Billiards/Union Square

| 17 | 15 | 15 | M |

E Village | 110 E. 11th St. (4th Ave.) | 4/5/6/L/N/Q/R to 14th St./ Union Sq. | 212-995-0333 | www.amsterdambilliards.com

"Serious pool" shooters find it "easy to get a game" at this 25-table East Village parlor that's "bigger" and "brighter" than the norm; casual players "kick back and relax" in the "cool" bar area (despite the "overpriced" pops) or try their hand at darts or foosball.

Amsterdam Tavern

| 19 | 15 | 20 | M |

W 100s | 938 Amsterdam Ave. (106th St.) | 1 to 103rd St. | 212-280-8070 | www.amsterdamtavernnyc.com

Hoppy ales and creamy stouts fill out the "extensive beer menu" at this "friendly" UWS neighborhood tavern with a "chill" vibe and a "Columbia undergrad" following; even if it's "average in every way", the "peppy crowd makes up for any deficiencies."

An Béal Bocht

| 22 | 18 | 22 | M |

Bronx | 445 W. 238th St. (bet. Greystone & Waldo Aves.) | 1 to 238th St. | 718-884-7127 | www.anbealbochtcafe.com

Dublin comes to Riverdale via this "authentic", "homey" pub where the "warmth of Ireland" comforts "colorful locals" and Manhattan College types gripping pints of Guinness; "live music", open-mike nights and poetry readings make it a "solid" addition to the North Bronx's "practically nonexistent nightlife."

Anchor, The

| 18 | 15 | 16 | M |

Hudson Square | 310 Spring St. (bet. Greenwich & Renwick Sts.) | 1 to Houston St. | 212-463-7406 | www.theanchornyc.com

"When you can't get into Sway", there's always this "unpretentious", nautically decorated alternative across the street that's either "super-crowded" or "dead", depending on the night; the main drawbacks are the Hudson Square address ("practically in New Jersey") and bathroom lines "longer than those at a Prada sample sale."

NEW Anfora
- - - M

W Village | 34 Eighth Ave. (bet. Jane & W. 12th Sts.) | A/C/E/L to 14th St./8th Ave. | 212-518-2722 | www.anforanyc.com

Brought to you by the owners of nearby Dell'anima, this new West Village wine bar is intended as a holding pen for its ultrapopular sibling, offering a global vino list that includes sustainable and biodynamic varieties; a gray quartz bartop, exposed-brick walls and dark leather banquettes lend a modern feel, though its name has a more historic ring, referring to the terra-cotta pots used by ancient Greeks and Romans to store wine.

Angels & Kings
(aka AK-47)
17 | 16 | 16 | M

E Village | 500 E. 11th St. (bet. Aves. A & B) | L to 1st Ave. | 212-254-4090 | www.angelsandkings.com

Credit Fall Out Boy/co-owner Pete Wentz for the "emo feel" at this East Village saloon with a vaguely "Goth" look and a rock 'n' roller fan base; "celebrity mug shots" on the walls and "up-and-coming indie" musicians in the seats supply the atmosphere.

⚡ Angel's Share
26 | 22 | 24 | E

E Village | 8 Stuyvesant St., 2nd fl. (3rd Ave. & 9th St.) | 6 to Astor Pl. | 212-777-5415

A "pioneer of the cocktail resurgence", this "Prohibition-esque" East Villager is a "great date spot" thanks to its "meticulous" mixology; the "strictly enforced" rules against standing, noise and groups larger than four can be "annoying", but otherwise this "tucked-away gem" – "hidden behind a Japanese restaurant" – is simply "perfection."

Angry Wade's
16 | 13 | 18 | M

Cobble Hill | 222 Smith St. (Butler St.) | Brooklyn | F/G to Bergen St. | 718-488-7253

There's "always a good game on" at this "old faithful" Cobble Hill sports bar, which some dub Smith Street's "last true dive"; "cheap beer", a "crackling fireplace" and "free popcorn" keep its "mixed" crowd "drunk and happy."

Annie Moore's
17 | 15 | 20 | M

E 40s | 50 E. 43rd St. (bet. Madison & Vanderbilt Aves.) | 4/5/6/7/S to 42nd St./Grand Central | 212-986-7826 | www.anniemooresnyc.com

Desk jockeys jam this "major commuter" watering hole near Grand Central to "network" with fellow suits while keeping an eye on the convenient "televised train schedules" on the wall; though it's "more upscale than your typical Irish pub", jaded types sigh "cookie cutter" and ask "can you order a kit for this kind of bar over the Internet?"

Anotheroom
22 | 19 | 20 | M

TriBeCa | 249 W. Broadway (bet. Beach & N. Moore Sts.) | 1 to Franklin St. | 212-226-1418 | www.theroomsbeerandwine.com

"Cozy corners" made for "make-out" sessions lure seekers of "romance" into this "intimate" TriBeCa watering hole that's the "size of a closet", but still "chill" given the "dark lighting" and "low sound level"; though there's "no hard liquor", an "excellent" beer-and-wine list more than compensates.

Antarctica

| 17 | 13 | 18 | M |

Hudson Square | 287 Hudson St. (Spring St.) | C/E to Spring St. | 212-352-1666 | www.antarcticabar.com

As "expansive" as its namesake continent, this "unpretentious" dive is a "great bar to avoid the crowds" given its "lonely location" in Hudson Square; fans say that "cheap" cocktails served in "pint glasses" and a nightly name game ("you drink for free if your name gets picked") make it "worth the trek."

Apartment 138

| 23 | 21 | 20 | M |

Cobble Hill | 138 Smith St. (bet. Bergen & Dean Sts.) | Brooklyn | F/G to Bergen St. | 718-858-0556 | www.apt138.com

A "young", "hipsterish" crowd spends "quiet evenings" on the "pretty patio" of this "delightful" Smith Street bar/eatery in Cobble Hill that cossets "cool" cats with its "warm" vibe; a downstairs rec room equipped with foosball and old-school video games ratchets up the "fun" factor.

☑ Apothéke

| 25 | 24 | 21 | VE |

Chinatown | 9 Doyers St. (Bowery) | 6/J/N/Q/Z to Canal St. | 212-406-0400 | www.apothekenyc.com

"Spiffy" barkeeps in "white lab coats" shake cocktails in pharmaceutical "beakers" at this apothecary-themed barroom set in a "hard-to-find" former "opium den" in "forgotten Chinatown"; the mood's "mysteriously romantic", the "obscure" address "adds to the appeal" and the "magical" drinks are rumored to have "healing powers", but regulars warn that the "lofty" pricing means you'll be "coughing up" lots of dough.

Ara Wine Bar

| 20 | 19 | 20 | E |

Meatpacking | 24 Ninth Ave. (bet. 13th & 14th Sts.) | A/C/E/L to 14th St./8th Ave. | 212-242-8642 | www.arawinebar.com

"Comfy and cool", this "cute little" wine bar serving "affordable" vinos, cheeses and pizzas is a "nice change of pace" amid the "Meatpacking craziness"; owned by three siblings, it draws a "fun mix of people" looking for a "classy place to unwind."

Archive, The

| - | - | - | E |

Murray Hill | 12 E. 36th St. (bet. 5th & Madison Aves.) | 6 to 33rd St. | 212-213-0093 | www.thearchivebar.com

Murray Hill's former Under the Volcano gets an upscale redo via this bar/lounge with a grown-up vibe burnished by slate-gray walls, tufted banquettes and soaring ceilings; it's a decent Plan B when the scene at the Ginger Man across the street gets too frenetic.

Arctica

| 17 | 18 | 18 | M |

Murray Hill | 384 Third Ave. (bet. 27th & 28th Sts.) | 6 to 28th St. | 212-725-4477 | www.arcticabar.com

A "long and narrow" thing that seems to "stretch back for eternity", this polar-themed Murray Hill triplex is "typical for the neighborhood" – "not bad to watch a game" but the "appeal ends there"; a variety of private party spaces brings in corporate trade.

Ardesia — | — | — | M

W 50s | 510 W. 52nd St. (bet. 10th & 11th Aves.) | C/E to 50th St. | 212-247-9191 | www.ardesia-ny.com

The rapidly gentrifying Way West 50s is home to this "gorgeous", "LA-style" wine bar that showcases its well-curated bottle selection on a wall meant to suggest a Hell's Kitchen fire escape; by-the-glass selections and charcuterie options are scrawled on a floor-to-ceiling chalkboard.

🆕 Aria Wine Bar — | — | — | E

W Village | 117 Perry St. (bet. Greenwich & Hudson Sts.) | A/B/C/D/E/F/M to W. 4th St. | 212-242-4233

Nestled on a quiet West Village side street, this cozy new wine bar goes the rustic route with warmly lit, wood-and-tile decor; all the vino comes from lady vintners, backed up by a long list of classic cocktails scrawled on a floor-to-ceiling chalkboard.

Arlene's Grocery 20 | 12 | 16 | M

LES | 95 Stanton St. (bet. Ludlow & Orchard Sts.) | F to Lower East Side/2nd Ave. | 212-995-1652 | www.arlenesgrocery.net

Catch "local bands" at this "loud and proud" LES "rock 'n' roll beer joint" where "up-and-coming" acts put on shows in a "gritty" "dive-bar" setting; regulars relish Monday night's "phenomenal" live-band karaoke for the chance to watch hipsters "make fools of themselves."

Arrow ▽ 20 | 15 | 18 | M

E Village | 85 Ave. A, downstairs (bet. 5th & 6th Sts.) | F to Lower East Side/2nd Ave. | 212-673-1775 | www.arrownyc.com

"Hit-or-miss" East Village basement bar that's "sometimes empty, sometimes packed", but is usually "chill and undistracting"; the tile-floored, film noir–ish setting lures a seen-it-all crowd, but when "being cool is no longer bearable", you can always play "Big Buck Hunter."

Art Bar 19 | 18 | 18 | M

W Village | 52 Eighth Ave. (bet. Horatio & Jane Sts.) | A/C/E/L to 14th St./8th Ave. | 212-727-0244 | www.artbar.com

It's "all about the back room" at this 20-year-old West Village watering hole where a fireplace, "dim lights" and "vintage couches" are the launching pad for some mighty "heavy petting"; in front, it's a standard-issue bar that might be "past its prime."

Arthur's Tavern ⌀ 23 | 15 | 17 | E

W Village | 57 Grove St. (bet. Bleecker St. & 7th Ave. S.) | 1 to Christopher St. | 212-675-6879 | www.arthurstavernnyc.com

Although "a bit tattered" now, this circa-1937 Village jazz "institution" remains jammed with a "mixed crowd" of "tourists", "old-timers" and "neighborhood characters" listening to everything from bebop to blues and Dixieland; there's "no cover" and it's "cash only", but supporters say that "time just seems to slip away" here.

Athens Café 18 | 17 | 19 | M

Astoria | 32-07 30th Ave. (bet. 32nd & 33rd Sts.) | Queens | N/Q to 30th Ave. | 718-626-2164

"People-watching", "late"-night hours and "frappes that would hypno-tize the gods" are the draws at this longtime Astoria cafe; it may be "a bit worn out" in comparison to the more recent joints "popping up on

30th Avenue", but adherents stick to this "old reliable" because it "feels like Europe."

Auction House

22 | 22 | 19 | M

E 80s | 300 E. 89th St. (bet. 1st & 2nd Aves.) | 4/5/6 to 86th St. | 212-427-4458

In the UES land of "sports, wings and beer pong" lies this "unmarked", "velvet"-lined lounge, a "welcome change" in an "otherwise boring neighborhood"; given the "dark lighting", "erotic" artwork and "PDA"-worthy couches, romeos show up with someone they "want to seduce and just let the room do the work."

Australian, The

20 | 18 | 23 | M

Garment District | 20 W. 38th St. (bet. 5th & 6th Aves.) | 7/B/D/F/M to 42nd St./Bryant Park | 212-869-8601 | www.theaustraliannyc.com

"Foreign beers" meet "foreign accents" at this Garment District pub, an "Aussie home away from home" that also doubles as a sports bar for "rugby" watchers; "impeccably friendly" service and an agreeably "low-key" mood enhance its "real-deal" feel.

Automatic Slims

19 | 13 | 16 | M

W Village | 733 Washington St. (Bank St.) | A/C/E/L to 14th St./8th Ave. | 212-645-8660

"Hordes of frat boys" "not much out of college" populate this "jam-packed" West Village "hole-in-the-wall" known for its "fun, fun, fun" atmosphere; it's just the ticket for "bumping up against a hottie" or "dancing on the bar", but be prepared for "no ambiance" and "long lines" on weekends.

⧫ Ava Lounge

23 | 23 | 17 | VE

W 50s | Dream Hotel | 210 W. 55th St., 14th fl. (bet. B'way & 7th Ave.) | N/Q/R to 57th St./7th Ave. | 212-956-7020 | www.avaloungenyc.com

Resembling the "penthouse apartment you always wished you had", this "sexy" lounge atop the Dream Hotel is a "swank" little number crowned by a petite roof deck offering "beautiful" views of Broadway and the "giant Diddy billboard in Times Square"; true, it's "very expensive" and there's "a bit of a velvet-rope mentality" in play, but overall it's a "splendid" destination.

Avenue

23 | 21 | 19 | VE

Chelsea | 116 10th Ave. (bet. 17th & 18th Sts.) | A/C/E/L to 14th St./8th Ave. | 212-337-0054 | www.avenue-newyork.com

The latest from nightlife poo-bah Noah Tepperberg (Marquee), this "exclusive" West Chelsea "hot spot" promises the usual tight door and loose crowd of "models", "celebs", "Euros" and "more models"; its "swanky" duplex setting is done up with the expected banquettes, chandeliers and Oriental rugs, and though it's "less bottle servicey than most", the by-the-drink prices are stiff enough to leave you breathless.

Babel Lounge

- | - | - | M

E Village | 131 Ave. C (bet. 8th & 9th Sts.) | L to 1st Ave. | 212-505-3468 | www.babelnyc.com

East Village bar-hoppers sample the Middle East at this high-energy Alphabet City lounge offering "hookahs", exotic cocktails and "mixed" international dance tracks spun by nightly DJs; an outdoor patio adds to its allure.

| | APPEAL | DECOR | SERVICE | COST |

Back Fence
| | 19 | 10 | 14 | M |

G Village | 155 Bleecker St. (Thompson St.) | A/B/C/D/E/F/M to
W. 4th St. | 212-475-9221 | www.thebackfenceonline.com

"Stroll down nostalgia alley" at this sawdust-strewn Village "throwback"
where "aging boomers" and NYU youngsters sing along with "great
cover bands" performing on its "phone booth–size stage"; the "honky-
tonk vibe" extends to the "gruff" service and "peanut shells on the floor."

Back Room
| | 23 | 23 | 17 | E |

LES | 102 Norfolk St. (bet. Delancey & Rivington Sts.) | F/J/M/Z to
Delancey/Essex Sts. | 212-228-5098

"Cocktails are served in teacups" and beer in "brown paper bags" "à la
Prohibition" at this "speakeasy"-themed LES lounge that's "hidden" at
the end of a "sketchy alley" for authenticity's sake; "not as exclusive
as it used to be", the concept's "still fun", though a few find it "too
contrived" and "pricey."

Baker Street
| | 17 | 13 | 18 | M |

E 60s | 1152 First Ave. (63rd St.) | F to Lexington Ave./63rd St. |
212-688-9663 | www.bakerstreetnyc.com

An Irish pub named after a British address, this "generic" Eastsider
"comes alive on trivia night" and also during football games (both
American and international versions are broadcast); fun facts: it was
home to the first TGI Friday's in 1965 and also the location where the
flick *Cocktail* was filmed.

Banjo Jim's
| | 20 | 13 | 17 | M |

E Village | 700 E. Ninth St. (Ave. C) | L to 1st Ave. | 212-777-0869 |
www.banjojims.com

Alphabet City meets Appalachia at this "hippie-ish" music venue that
"gets packed" with fans of blue grass, folk rock and beyond; the nightly
string-pluckers can be enjoyed for no cover, making it "one of the
cheapest ways to see showcased talent" in these parts.

NEW Banter
| | - | - | - | M |

Williamsburg | 132 Havemeyer St. (S. 1st St.) | Brooklyn | J/M/Z to
Marcy Ave. | 718-599-5200 | www.banterbrooklyn.com

New South Williamsburg saloon dispensing an impressive selection of
craft suds (plus Irish whiskies and small-batch bourbons) in a tidy,
public-house setting lined with wooden booths and local artwork; the
flat-screens are tuned to European futbol, the hipster sport of choice.

Barbès
| | 23 | 17 | 19 | M |

Park Slope | 376 Ninth St. (6th Ave.) | Brooklyn | F/G to 7th Ave. |
347-422-0248 | www.barbesbrooklyn.com

"Varied live acts" from all over the globe draw a "diverse" audience to
this "cool little" South Sloper with a "bustling" front bar and a "kickin'"
rear performance space; a well-curated list of beers, tequilas and single malts accounts for the "great energy" and "camaraderie" in the air.

Barcade
| | 25 | 19 | 19 | M |

Williamsburg | 388 Union Ave. (bet. Ainslie & Powers Sts.) | Brooklyn | G/L to
Metropolitan Ave./Lorimer St. | 718-302-6464 | www.barcadebrooklyn.com

"Wall-to-wall '80s video games" lures "nerdy hipsters" into this Billyburg
blast from the past stocked with "retro" favorites like "Donkey Kong"

and "Ms. Pac-Man"; ok, you "won't get anywhere near" a joystick on busy nights, but that doesn't mean Game Over since there's an "impeccable draft selection" to work through.

Bar Carrera

APPEAL	DECOR	SERVICE	COST
21	19	20	E

E Village | 175 Second Ave. (bet. 11th & 12th Sts.) | 6 to Astor Pl. | 212-375-1555
G Village | 146 W. Houston St. (MacDougal St.) | 1 to Houston St. | 212-253-9500
www.barcarrera.com
Snack on Basque "small plates" while sipping sangria at this "cute" East Village wine bar (and its Greenwich Village sidekick of a more recent vintage); the "relaxing vibe" is inviting, though the "small" settings can be too "cramped" for claustrophobes.

Barcelona Bar

APPEAL	DECOR	SERVICE	COST
21	13	27	M

W 50s | 923 Eighth Ave. (bet. 54th & 55th Sts.) | C/E to 50th St. | 212-245-3212 | www.barcelonabarnyc.com
Hell's Kitchen "shot bar" with a "huge selection", some of which involve "costumes", "fire" and magic wands; although "perfect for a night of drunken revelry", it's also renowned for "extremely friendly" service – "come often enough and they'll name a shot after you."

⯐ Bar Centrale

APPEAL	DECOR	SERVICE	COST
26	23	24	E

W 40s | 324 W. 46th St., 2nd fl. (bet. 8th & 9th Aves.) | A/C/E to 42nd St./ Port Authority | 212-581-3130 | www.barcentralenyc.com
There's "decent" Broadway "celeb-spotting" in store at this "cool" Restaurant Row bar/lounge, an "unmarked" thing with "pricey" pops and a "clubhouse" feel; prime time here is "après-theater" when the stars slip in, the "velvet-rope" mentality goes into effect and "reservations" are necessary for entry.

Barcibo Enoteca

APPEAL	DECOR	SERVICE	COST
24	22	23	E

W 60s | 2020 Broadway (69th St.) | 1/2/3 to 72nd St. | 212-595-2805 | www.barciboenoteca.com
"Cozy", "matchbook-size" UWS wine bar (and Bin 71 sibling) offering an "incredible" strictly Italian vino selection that can be paired with "delectable" nibbles; it draws "more mature" types despite the "sardinelike" squeeze and "splurge"-worthy costs.

NEW Bar Downstairs

APPEAL	DECOR	SERVICE	COST
-	-	-	VE

E 40s | Andaz 5th Avenue Hotel | 485 Fifth Ave., downstairs (41st St.) | 7/B/D/F/M to 42nd St./Bryant Park | 212-601-1234 | www.andaz5thavenue.com
An unlikely location (opposite the NY Public Library's main branch) and a hard-to-find basement setting aren't keeping the crowds away from this new lounge in the Andaz 5th Avenue Hotel; like its Downtown sibling, Bar Seven Five, it eschews the traditional long bartop in favor of a more casual 'bar station' plopped down in the center of the room, and ups the ante with the most open open kitchen in town.

Bar 89

APPEAL	DECOR	SERVICE	COST
22	23	20	E

SoHo | 89 Mercer St. (bet. Broome & Spring Sts.) | N/R to Prince St. | 212-274-0989 | www.bar89.com
A "throwback to the '90s", this longtime SoHo lounge still ropes in "chicly dressed skinny people" with its "memorable" martinis, "deca-

dent" desserts and "open-air" setting; still, it's probably best known for those "ingeniously designed loos" with glass doors that magically "turn opaque" when occupied.

Bar 515
14 | 13 | 14 | M

Murray Hill | 515 Third Ave. (bet. 34th & 35th Sts.) | 6 to 33rd St. | 212-532-3300 | www.bar515.com

Smack dab in the middle of Third Avenue's "which-bar-is-which" territory, this "hard-core Murray Hill" "meat market" features "cookie-cutter decor", plenty of plasma screens and a crowd that's "under 30 and ready to party"; regulars nickname it "516", given all the "Long Island" peeps who pile in on weekends.

Barfly
16 | 13 | 17 | M

Gramercy | 244 Third Ave. (20th St.) | 6 to 23rd St. | 212-473-9660 | www.barflyny.com

"Cheap pitchers" and "greasy" pub grub draw "neighborhood" types to this by-the-numbers Gramercy sports bar that's an "ok place to watch the game, but not much else"; darts and a "pool table in the back" help spectators milk the clock during halftime.

Bar 41
▽ 23 | 19 | 21 | E

W 40s | Hotel 41 at Times Sq. | 206 W. 41st St. (bet. 7th & 8th Aves.) | 1/2/3/7/N/Q/R/S to 42nd St./Times Sq. | 212-703-8600 | www.hotel41.com

Times Square desk jockeys report that this area hotel bar "fills up fast" after the whistle blows given its modest dimensions; it's *the* place to go if you want to "meet an Ernst & Younger", but you'll have to work fast – it closes early, at midnight.

Bar 4
▽ 19 | 17 | 20 | M

Park Slope | 444 Seventh Ave. (15th St.) | Brooklyn | F/G to 7th Ave. | 718-832-9800 | www.bar4brooklyn.com

"Local yokels" settle into "overstuffed sofas" and chill out at this Park Slope lounge best known for its expansive martini list; though some yawn "bland", others praise its "relaxed feel" and "cool music" on open-mike nights.

Bar Great Harry
21 | 14 | 19 | M

Carroll Gardens | 280 Smith St. (Sackett St.) | Brooklyn | F/G to Carroll St. | 718-222-1103 | www.bargreatharry.com

A "beer snob bar without the snobbery", this Carroll Gardens bar is "fairly average" in the looks department and "above-average" when it comes to suds, with an "astonishing" selection of rotating craft brews and lots of other "hoppy tipples"; fans also like its "pooch"-friendly disposition.

Bar Italia
23 | 23 | 20 | E

NEW **E 60s** | 768 Madison Ave. (66th St.) | 917-546-6676
E 70s | 1477 Second Ave. (77th St.) | 6 to 77th St. | 212-249-5300
www.baritalianyc.com

"Hobnob" with Euro expats at this UES "slice-of-the-Mediterranean" enoteca with whitewashed decor, "pretty" sidewalk seating and "subtitled Italian movies" on the flat-screens; "theatrical" barkeeps pour 40 wines by the glass and occasionally shake things up with flair bartending; P.S. the Madison Avenue sibling opened post-Survey.

	APPEAL	DECOR	SERVICE	COST

Bar Nine

18 | 15 | 17 | M

W 50s | 807 Ninth Ave. (bet. 53rd & 54th Sts.) | C/E to 50th St. | 212-399-9336

"Budget-minded locals" who dig the feel of living-room drinking tout this "shabby-chic" Hell's Kitchen lounge decorated with "old couches"; "low lighting" and "cheap beer" enhance the "relaxed attitude."

Bar None

12 | 10 | 14 | M

E Village | 98 Third Ave. (bet. 12th & 13th Sts.) | L to 3rd Ave. | 212-777-6663 | www.barnonenyc.com

Straight from the "college-bar" checklist comes kamikaze shots and late-night "power hours" at this lager-soaked East Village "dump", a "hair-rocking" frat party for those who never want to grow old; brace yourself for a "seedy" scene with the scent of "stale beer and desperation" in the air.

Bar on A

19 | 14 | 18 | M

E Village | 170 Ave. A (11th St.) | L to 1st Ave. | 212-353-8231

Despite the "ever-shifting East Village scene", this 15-year-old neighborhood "hangout" is still "frequented by all kinds"; although it's "nothing exciting or extraordinary", there are random reports of "witty" barkeeps and "cool Sunday night burlesque."

NEW Bar on Fifth

- | - | - | VE

Garment District | Setai 5th Ave. Hotel | 400 Fifth Ave. (36th St.) | B/D/F/M/N/Q/R to 34th St./Herald Sq. | 212-695-4005

Swanky cocktailing comes to the Garment District via this slick new bar/lounge in the Setai Hotel where a cosmopolitan crowd and limestone-and-oak decor lend a *Lost in Translation* vibe; stiff pours make the stiff tabs easier to abide, and there's also live music from a three-piece combo.

☒ Bar Pleiades

26 | 28 | 24 | VE

E 70s | Surrey Hotel | 20 E. 76th St. (bet. 5th & Madison Aves.) | 6 to 77th St. | 212-772-2600 | www.danielnyc.com

The room's as lacquered as the crowd at this "elegant" black-and-white boîte in the Upper East Side's Surrey Hotel, where the "ritzy" mood matches the art-deco-meets-Coco-Chanel decor; courtesy of "brand-name" chef Daniel Boulud (proprietor of Café Boulud next door), it's named after a star cluster in the constellation of Taurus, an oblique reference to the astronomical prices.

Barracuda ⊅

19 | 15 | 16 | M

Chelsea | 275 W. 22nd St. (bet. 7th & 8th Aves.) | C/E to 23rd St. | 212-645-8613

"Slightly friendlier than the typical Chelsea gay bar", this "long-in-the-tooth" spot is "not particularly fresh" yet still reels in schools of "good-looking boys" on weekends; but sourpusses citing "lowscale" looks and "patchy" service recommend you "go to the East Village" instead.

Barrage

19 | 15 | 23 | M

W 40s | 401 W. 47th St. (bet. 9th & 10th Aves.) | C/E to 50th St. | 212-586-9390

A "recession-friendly" late-night happy hour energizes the "let-yourself-loose" atmosphere at this Hell's Kitchen gay bar populated by a crowd that "loves a good drink special"; otherwise, it's just a "local hangout" with notably "friendly" barkeeps.

Barramundi

21	20	23	M

LES | 67 Clinton St. (bet. Rivington & Stanton Sts.) | F/J/M/Z to Delancey/Essex Sts. | 212-529-6999 | www.barramundiny.com

Standing out as a "bright spot" on "dreary" Clinton Street, this "funky" LES bar is furnished with "tree-trunk tables", red leather booths and a deer head "rocking a Lady Gaga wig"; "heavy-handed" bartenders pouring "excellent" sangria and house-infused vodkas ratchet up the "fun" quotient.

Barrio Chino

22	18	20	M

LES | 253 Broome St. (bet. Ludlow & Orchard Sts.) | F/J/M/Z to Delancey/Essex Sts. | 212-228-6710 | www.barriochinonyc.com

"Holy mole!", the tequila selection sure is "awesome" at this "tiny" LES Mexican cantina where the chow comes with a Chinese accent; the Asian-inspired decor may seem a bit out of place, but after a few "seriously spicy margaritas", you'll barely notice.

Barrow Street Ale House

18	12	16	M

W Village | 15 Barrow St. (bet. 7th Ave. S. & W. 4th St.) | 1 to Christopher St. | 212-691-6127 | www.barrowstreetalehouse.com

This former 19th-century carriage house has evolved into a "better-than-average" West Village tavern, though regulars say it "looks better from the outside than it does from the inside"; despite "inept" service and "overcrowded" conditions on the weekend, "you could do worse in the area."

Bar Seven Five

-	-	-	E

Financial District | Andaz Wall Street Hotel | 75 Wall St. (Water St.) | 2/3 to Wall St. | 212-590-1234

One of the few drinking options for the nightlife-challenged Financial District, this sleek hotel bar/lounge in the Andaz Wall Street's lobby eschews the traditional long bartop by scattering several bar stations around the room, allowing more up-close-and-personal interaction with the cocktail shakers; pricewise, there's no recession going on here.

Bar Six

21	21	19	E

G Village | 502 Sixth Ave. (bet. 12th & 13th Sts.) | 1/2/F/L to 14th St./7th Ave. | 212-691-1363 | www.barsixny.com

Folks say *oui* to this "cozy" French-Moroccan bistro, a fair approximation of "Paris" that works for "romantic interludes" and even "day drinking"; the "convivial" vibe burnishes the "out-on-the-town-in-another-country" feel, while "outdoor seating" supplies "fun" Greenwich Village people-watching.

Bartini's Lounge

18	16	19	E

Forest Hills | 1 Station Sq., downstairs (71st Ave.) | Queens | E/F/M/R to Forest Hills/71st Ave. | 718-896-5445 | www.bartinislounge.com

Martini mavens have over 600 varieties to choose from at this wannabe-"trendy" Forest Hills lounge that's "trying for a Manhattan vibe", though locals say "they only succeed with the prices"; it's "ok for a neighborhood place", however, but "nothing more than that."

| | APPEAL | DECOR | SERVICE | COST |

Bar-Tini Ultra Lounge
`- | - | - | M`

W 40s | 642 10th Ave. (bet. 45th & 46th Sts.) | A/C/E to 42nd St./
Port Authority | 917-388-2897 | www.bar-tiniultralounge.com

Hell's Kitchen's erstwhile Tenth Avenue Lounge has undergone an "amazing transformation" and emerged as this "fun" gay bar targeted toward trendy tipplers; while not exactly 'ultra', its white-on-white color scheme and Day-Glo light show are close enough approximations of Vegas swank for the Chelsea Heights crowd.

NEW Bar 29
`- | - | - | M`

Murray Hill | 405 Third Ave. (bet. 28th & 29th Sts.) | 6 to 28th St. | 212-779-0306 | www.bar29nyc.com

This Murray Hill newcomer may be nothing special, but fills a need for those in the mood to shoot pool, toss back draft brews and watch tube sports; it's also a good Plan B when nearby Tonic gets too crowded.

☑ Bar Veloce
`22 | 20 | 21 | E`

Chelsea | 176 Seventh Ave. (bet. 20th & 21st Sts.) | 1 to 23rd St. | 212-629-5300

E Village | 175 Second Ave. (bet. 11th & 12th Sts.) | L to 3rd Ave. | 212-260-3200

www.barveloce.com

"*Bellissima*" enoteca duo vending an "unparalleled" selection of Italian wines and small plates for "large prices"; both exude a "sophisticated" "European feel", though the Chelsea spin-off has more space to move around in than the "tiny" East Village original.

☑ Bateaux New York
`26 | 23 | 19 | VE`

Chelsea | Chelsea Piers | Pier 61 (Hudson River & W. 23rd St.) | C/E to 23rd St. | 866-399-8439 | www.bateauxnewyork.com

Set sail on the Hudson from Chelsea Piers and marvel at the "sun setting behind the Statue of Liberty" on this "beautiful" glass-walled cruise ship offering dinner, dancing and "spectacular" harbor views; though the "live band" can be "entertaining", some sink it as "overpriced."

Bayard's Ale House
`19 | 18 | 22 | M`

W Village | 533 Hudson St. (Charles St.) | A/C/E/L to 14th St./8th Ave. | 212-989-0313

"Pretty similar to its former incarnation, the Sazerac House", this "neighborhood" West Village taproom offers a "decent draft selection" served in standard tavern digs; "better-than-average" bar food and "delightful" staffers supply some uplift.

Bayard's Blue Bar
`- | - | - | E`

Financial District | 1 Hanover Sq. (bet. Pearl & Stone Sts.) | 2/3 to Wall St. | 212-514-9454

"High-end" haunt set in the Financial District's historic India House decorated in a "swanky" nautical style; it's populated by "Wall Street professionals" who use their "bonus money from the federal government" to settle the "expensive" tabs; P.S. closed on weekends.

BB&R
`18 | 17 | 20 | M`

E 80s | 1720 Second Ave. (bet. 89th & 90th Sts.) | 4/5/6 to 86th St. | 212-987-5555 | www.bbrnyc.com

The kind of place where you "don't worry what the bathroom will look like", this "clean" and "friendly" sports bar vends "cheap" brew and "no-frills" pub grub on an "otherwise dry patch" of the UES; it "never seems to be crowded", maybe because of all that Second Avenue Subway construction outside.

☑ B. B. King Blues Club

W 40s | 237 W. 42nd St. (bet. 7th & 8th Aves.) | 1/2/3/7/N/Q/R/S to 42nd St./Times Sq. | 212-997-4555 | www.bbkingblues.com

They "put on a good show" at this Times Square music club where "known artists" perform in a "small"-ish setting with "amazing acoustics" and "unobstructed views"; admirers say that seeing your favorite act "up close" compensates for the "short sets", "touristy" patrons and "too-crowded tables."

Beacon Theatre

W 70s | 2124 Broadway (bet. 74th & 75th Sts.) | 1/2/3 to 72nd St. | 212-465-6500 | www.beacontheatre.com

Following a "ravishing" $16 million restoration, this UWS "music institution" has maintained its "rock 'n' roll spirit" during an 83-year run as one of the city's "premier concert venues"; whether for a jazz concert or "dad rock with the Allman Brothers", there's "not a bad seat in the house" – though a few nix the "newly inflated" drink prices.

☑NEW Beauty & Essex

LES | 146 Essex St. (bet. Rivington & Stanton Sts.) | F/J/M/Z to Delancey/Essex Sts. | 212-614-0146 | www.beautyandessex.com

Brought to you by the owners of Stanton Social, this LES instant scene may be more restaurant than nightspot, yet it does sport two bars – and offers free champers in the ladies loo; the spread-out, AvroKO-designed duplex includes a pawn shop at the entrance, a grand staircase with fur-lined walls and a noise level akin to an airport runway.

Beauty Bar

E Village | 231 E. 14th St. (bet. 2nd & 3rd Aves.) | L to 3rd Ave. | 212-539-1389
Bushwick | 921 Broadway (Melrose St.) | Brooklyn | J/M/Z to Myrtle Ave. | 347-529-0370 ⊄
www.thebeautybar.com

"Fun" salon/saloon hybrids offering a "martini-and-manicure" special that attracts a mix of "indie broads" and "prom queens"; though the "kitschy" "retro" settings complete with "old-fashioned hair dryers" and the "scent of nail polish" suggest something out of a "John Waters movie", aesthetes think the scene could use some "Botox."

NEW Bedlam

E Village | 40 Ave. C (bet. 3rd & 4th Sts.) | F to Lower East Side/2nd Ave. | 212-228-1049 | www.bedlamnyc.com

This latest incarnation of the revolving-door space on Avenue C (fka Hacienda, 40C, Batista) exudes a Victorian vibe via taxidermy, shelves of curios and walls papered with yellowed pages from scientific journals; the crowd's arty, the cocktails classic and the tabs moderate.

Beekman Bar and Books

E 50s | 889 First Ave. (50th St.) | 6/E to 51st-53rd Sts./Lexington Ave. | 212-758-6600 | www.barandbooks.cz

"Classy" "older" folk convene at this "intimate" Sutton Place–area lounge for "conversation" over expertly crafted Rob Roys chased with "complimentary potato chips"; vintage "James Bond" flicks on the telly add to its "old-school" feel, and puffers note that indoor smoking is no longer permitted here.

Beer Bar at Cafe Centro
20 | 14 | 16 | M

E 40s | 200 Park Ave. (45th St. & Vanderbilt Ave.) | 4/5/6/7/S to 42nd St./Grand Central | 212-818-1222 | www.cafecentrony.com

It's all about the "crazy busy" "outdoor scene" at this Grand Central–area venue, a warm weather "hot spot" beneath the Park Avenue viaduct where hordes of "after-work" types hoist beers "before taking the train home to mama"; the inside bar, on the other hand, has "no appeal."

Beer Garden
21 | 15 | 19 | M

Staten Island | 1883 Victory Blvd. (Westcott Blvd.) | 718-876-8900 | www.thebeergardensi.com

"Don't go looking to sit in a garden – there isn't one" at this Staten Island sports bar in Westerleigh that does offer "good bang for your buck" and a vibe that "feels like home"; "live music on weekends" keeps its "mid-30s" crowd amused.

☑ Beer Table
22 | 19 | 24 | E

Park Slope | 427B Seventh Ave. (bet. 14th & 15th Sts.) | Brooklyn | F/G to 7th Ave. | 718-965-1196 | www.beertable.com

They "treat beer like fine wine" at this Park Slope "cathedral" of "unusual" brews that attracts purists who worship the "potent" pilsners and eagerly await word on the day's draft selections; "service with a smile" compensates for the "too-pricey" tabs and "tiny", communal-tabled setting.

Belgian Room
- | - | - | M

E Village | 125 St. Marks Pl. (bet. Ave. A & 1st Ave.) | 6 to Astor Pl. | 212-533-4467

Like the name says, Belgian brews are the focus at this St. Marks Place suds specialist that also supplies traditional Flemish eats like moules frites; the low-lit setting is rather run-of-the-mill, save for a rear lounge area fitted out with a meandering white banquette.

☑ Bell House
24 | 20 | 17 | M

Gowanus | 149 Seventh St. (bet. 2nd & 3rd Aves.) | Brooklyn | D/F/G/N/R to 4th Ave./9th St. | 718-643-6510 | www.thebellhouseny.com

"Amazing" live entertainment is the draw at this "cavernous" Gowanus bar-cum-performance space with "excellent sightlines", a "great sound system" and a "so-hip-it-hurts" "Brooklyn-chic" following; ok, it's set "in the middle of nowhere" ("unless you need to buy some lumber"), but otherwise this joint is "doing lots of things right."

Belmont Lounge
19 | 18 | 18 | M

Gramercy | 117 E. 15th St. (bet. Irving Pl. & Park Ave. S.) | 4/5/6/L/N/Q/R to 14th St./Union Sq. | 212-533-0009 | www.belmontloungenyc.com

"Laid-back", longtime Gramercy lounge offering an "unpretentious" vibe and a "nice, chill" atmosphere; it's good both pre- and post-Fillmore, and a heated "outside patio" absorbs the overflow on busy weekends when the "twentysomethings" pile in.

❷ Bembe ⊘ | 26 | 16 | 19 | M |

Williamsburg | 81 S. Sixth St. (Berry St.) | Brooklyn | L to Bedford Ave. | 718-387-5389 | www.bembe.us

"Awesome" global rhythms supply the "party" vibe at this "small" but "lively" Williamsburg lounge plying "delicious drinks" as well as "different" music via "excellent DJs" and live percussionists; befitting its multicultural mien, the atmosphere is "informal and friendly", with the only potential sore spot being "on your dancin' feet."

❷ Bemelmans Bar | 27 | 27 | 25 | VE |

E 70s | Carlyle Hotel | 35 E. 76th St. (Madison Ave.) | 6 to 77th St. | 212-744-1600 | www.thecarlyle.com

The "old-world" charm starts with the "whimsical" Ludwig Bemelmans murals decorating this super-"sophisticated" Carlyle Hotel bar where "superb drinks" and an "excellent" pianist draw everyone from "Choaties" and "cougars" to "sugar daddies" and "society types"; most "feel rich just being here", though it helps to really be that way given cocktails "priced like Harry Winston diamonds."

Berry Park ⊘ | - | - | - | M |

Williamsburg | 4 Berry St. (bet. N. 13th & 14th Sts.) | Brooklyn | L to Bedford Ave. | 718-782-2829 | www.berryparkbk.com

Rooftop drinking comes to Williamsburg via this big beer specialist, a "cavernous" double-decker featuring a rough-hewn, picnic-tabled ground floor topped by an alfresco deck with "views of Manhattan" and McCarren Park; the European suds list has a decided German accent, and the giant flat-screen is usually broadcasting soccer.

Biddys Pub | - | - | - | I |

E 90s | 301 E. 91st St. (bet. 1st & 2nd Aves.) | 4/5/6 to 86th St. | 212-534-4785 | www.biddysnyc.com

"You'll feel like you're in Dublin" at this "low-key" Yorkville pub, a "little hideaway" where "charming" bartenders with brogues "know your name" *and* their way around a Guinness pour; predictably, patrons tend to "live on or around the block."

ⓃⒺⓌ Bierhaus | - | - | - | M |
(aka Hofbräu Bierhaus)

E 40s | 712 Third Ave., 2nd fl. (bet. 44th & 45th Sts.) | 4/5/6/7/S to 42nd St./Grand Central | 646-580-2437 | www.bierhausnyc.com

An out-of-the-box hit from day one, this big Bavarian beer hall atop a former OTB parlor features free-flowing Hofbräu, dirndl-clad, cleavage-flashing waitresses and dancing-friendly communal tables, but its secret weapon is easy access – it's two blocks from Grand Central; P.S. an expansion into the downstairs street-level space is in the works.

ⓃⒺⓌ Bier International ⊘ | - | - | - | M |

Harlem | 2099 Frederick Douglass Blvd. (113th St.) | 1 to Cathedral Pkwy./ 110th St. | 212-280-0944 | www.bierinternational.com

The beer-hall craze comes to Harlem via this newcomer offering a well-edited suds selection that includes both local and international varieties; the airy, unadorned setting ain't Bavaria – don't expect a back garden or oompah bands – but it is a first for the neighborhood and another sign of gentrification in these parts.

	APPEAL	DECOR	SERVICE	COST

Big Bar ⊄
▽ 27 | 17 | 24 | M

E Village | 75 E. Seventh St. (bet. 1st & 2nd Aves.) | 6 to Astor Pl. | 212-777-6969

"Irony" is alive and well at this satirically named, "studio apartment-size" East Villager whose shortage of square-footage is offset by "appealing" barkeeps, chill tunes and a "devilish red" lighting scheme; those on a low-frat diet rejoice that the crowd is "easygoing."

Big Nose Kate's
19 | 18 | 20 | E

Staten Island | 2484 Arthur Kill Rd. (St. Luke's Ave.) | 718-227-3282

This "Old West"–style saloon on Staten Island's south shore is a "cool place" to bend an elbow in "friendly" company; "decent" tap brews and cover-free live music on weekends make it a "fun neighborhood" hang.

Bill's Gay Nineties
16 | 14 | 19 | M

E 50s | 57 E. 54th St. (bet. Madison & Park Aves.) | 6/E to 51st-53rd Sts./Lexington Ave. | 212-355-0243 | www.billsnyc.com

Although more likely to be raided today by "tourists" than Eliot Ness, this former speakeasy in Midtown shows its "Prohibition" roots with "throwback" pugilist prints on the walls and a lawn "jockey" statue out front; it may lie somewhere between "rickety" and "seedy", but die-hard fans say "you'll have a good time here whether you want to or not."

NEW Billy Hurricane's
- | - | - | M

E Village | 25 Ave. B (bet. 2nd & 3rd Sts.) | F to Lower East Side/2nd Ave. | 646-692-6216 | www.billyhurricanes.com

Targeted to frat boys and those fond of them, this rowdy East Village roadhouse has an offhanded New Orleans theme and features over-sized drinks, patio-furniture seating and Christmas-tree-light illumination; its bare-bones downstairs sibling, Idle Hands, is less hectic, specializing in beer and bourbon.

Billymark's West ⊄
▽ 16 | 8 | 24 | I

Chelsea | 332 Ninth Ave. (29th St.) | A/C/E to 34th St./Penn Station | 212-629-0118 | www.billymarkswest.com

Cheap "stiff drinks" keep this "lovable dive bar" popular with a "colorful" crowd ranging from "postal workers" to local "Chelsea art scene" types; ironic regulars dub it "BMW's", touting its jukebox, pool table and video games, not to mention bartenders who become "your best friend" as the night wears on.

Bin No. 220
▽ 20 | 19 | 19 | E

Seaport | 220 Front St. (bet. Beekman St. & Peck Slip) | 2/3/4/5/A/C/J/Z to Fulton St./B'way/Nassau | 212-374-9463 | www.binno220.com

"Quaint" wine bar on an "isolated" stretch of the Seaport featuring a "well-curated list" of labels plus a small selection of "more-than-acceptable finger food"; add in "knowledgeable" staffers, and it's a "classy addition" to the "sea of fried-fish places" in the neighborhood.

Bin 71
23 | 20 | 22 | E

W 70s | 237 Columbus Ave. (bet. 70th & 71st Sts.) | 1/2/3 to 72nd St. | 212-362-5446 | www.bin71.com

A "great selection" of vinos and vittles served by a "friendly" crew can be sampled (if "luck is on your side" and you "get a seat") at this "terrific" but "teeny-tiny" UWS wine bar; while there's additional seating "outdoors in warm weather", a better backup plan may be to try its "sister establishment, Barcibo Enoteca", a few blocks down.

Birdland

24 | 18 | 20 | E

W 40s | 315 W. 44th St. (bet. 8th & 9th Aves.) | A/C/E to 42nd St./ Port Authority | 212-581-3080 | www.birdlandjazz.com

"Roomy" is the word on this "hall-of-fame" Theater District "institution", a "classic" supper club showcasing "top-notch" jazz and serving a "quasi-Cajun" menu for hungry hep cats; a few wail at the "premium" pricing, but most feel it's "worth it for the wonderful music"; P.S. it's cheaper if you can "get a seat at the bar."

Bitter End

20 | 14 | 15 | M

G Village | 147 Bleecker St. (bet. La Guardia Pl. & Thompson St.) | A/ B/C/D/E/F/M to W. 4th St. | 212-673-7030 | www.bitterend.com

Best known for the '60s-era legends who performed here – think Dylan, Van Morrison, Joni Mitchell – this "mainstay" Village music club is "not what it used to be", though still a "fair shake" for hearing "your good friend's band"; despite "grubby" looks and too many "unknown acts", fans still feel it "should be a city landmark."

Black & White

18 | 13 | 15 | M

E Village | 86 E. 10th St. (bet. 3rd & 4th Aves.) | 6 to Astor Pl. | 212-253-0246

"Good DJs" ply a "punk"-centric soundtrack while "young NYU hipsters" chill out at this "dark" East Village den; doubters declare it's "nothing to really crow about", which may explain how the occasional "celeb" drops in without drawing much attention.

Black Bear Lodge

18 | 17 | 17 | I

Gramercy | 274 Third Ave. (bet. 21st & 22nd Sts.) | 6 to 23rd St. | 212-253-2178 | www.bblnyc.com

"Frat" packers plow through "cheap buckets of beer" in "rustic" comfort at this Gramercy bar decked out like a "ski lodge" right down to the "carpet", "fireplace" and "wooden" everything else; it's usually a "total sausagefest", so "girls get lots of free drinks" here.

Black Door

19 | 18 | 19 | M

Chelsea | 127 W. 26th St. (bet. 6th & 7th Aves.) | 1 to 28th St. | 212-645-0215

This "cool" yet "approachable" Chelsea "neighborhood" bar is done up in a "classic", vaguely vintage style (i.e. "stamped tin ceilings") and is just the ticket for "first dates" and "low-key" after-work drinks; for "birthday celebrations" and such, the back room is "more lively."

BlackFinn

16 | 14 | 16 | M

E 50s | 218 E. 53rd St. (bet. 2nd & 3rd Aves.) | 6/E to 51st-53rd Sts./ Lexington Ave. | 212-355-6607 | www.blackfinnnyc.com

Spend that "first year out of college" in familiar territory at this "trusty" Midtown "frat"-tacular, a "spacious" double-decker funhouse where meatheads meet up "after work"; though it's "meh" in many respects, the "open-bar" flat rate is a "deal."

Black Horse Pub

∇ 16 | 13 | 18 | M

Park Slope | 568 Fifth Ave. (16th St.) | Brooklyn | R to Prospect Ave. | 718-788-1975 | www.blackhorsebrooklyn.com

Airy Park Slope pub featuring British-Irish eats washed down with tap brews, as well as bargain boozing via five-buck pints; it distinguishes itself from the pack by offering a "full English breakfast" along with "EPL footy action on the telly."

Black Mountain Wine House   ▽ 28 | 27 | 24 | M

Carroll Gardens | 415 Union St. (Hoyt St.) | Brooklyn | F/G to Carroll St. | 718-522-4340 | www.blackmountainwinehouse.com

From the "roaring fireplace" to the "farmhouse" bric-a-brac on the walls, "atmosphere is the draw" at this "cozy" Carroll Gardens wine bar with "all the charm of an upstate cabin"; "friendly" staffers dispense a "well-edited list" of vintages that can be paired with "tasty" nibbles.

Black Rabbit   24 | 24 | 20 | M

Greenpoint | 91 Greenpoint Ave. (bet. Franklin St. & Manhattan Ave.) | Brooklyn | G to Greenpoint Ave. | 718-349-1595 | www.blackrabbitbar.com

A working fireplace and "private tables" lure locals into "Guinness and good conversation" at this "comfy" Greenpoint pub; a patio and "fun theme nights" (think trivia games) make it "one to remember."

Black Sheep   18 | 14 | 19 | M

Murray Hill | 583 Third Ave. (bet. 38th & 39th Sts.) | 4/5/6/7/S to 42nd St./Grand Central | 212-599-3476 | www.blacksheepnyc.com

This "local" Irish *baa* and grill catering to the Murray Hill flock features the "typical" lineup that area "frat"-ernizers have come to appreciate: tap brews, plasma screens and pub grub; just so ewe know, some say after "happy hour" ends, the party often heads for the hills.

Blackstone's   18 | 15 | 20 | M

E 50s | 245 E. 55th St. (bet. 2nd & 3rd Aves.) | 6/E to 51st-53rd Sts./Lexington Ave. | 212-355-4474 | www.blackstonesbarnyc.com

"Play pool, watch a game" or simply "sprawl out" at this spacious Midtown pub-a-palooza catering to the "after-work" crowd; it may be "standard" issue overall, but it "beats the mayhem on nearby Second Avenue" thanks to "attentive" service and a glass-walled atrium in back.

Blarney Stone   14 | 10 | 17 | I

Chelsea | 340 Ninth Ave. (bet. 29th & 30th Sts.) | A/C/E to 34th St./Penn Station | 212-502-4656 ⊄

E 40s | 710 Third Ave. (bet. 44th & 45th Sts.) | 4/5/6/7/S to 42nd St./Grand Central | 212-490-0457

Financial District | 11 Trinity Pl. (Morris St.) | 1/R to Rector St. | 212-269-4988

Garment District | 410 Eighth Ave. (bet. 30th & 31st Sts.) | A/C/E to 34th St./Penn Station | 212-594-5100

W 40s | 307 W. 47th St. (bet. 8th & 9th Aves.) | C/E to 50th St. | 212-245-3438

"People of all races, creeds and clothing styles" frequent these "working-man" Irish dives, though they're renowned as a haven for ultra-"serious drinkers" drawn in by their "steam-table-and-cheap-brewskis formula"; like *"Cheers* gone wrong", they're "dark, dreary" and a "place where no one will ever find you."

Bleecker Heights Tavern   - | - | - | M

W Village | 296 Bleecker St., 2nd fl. (7th Ave. S.) | 1 to Christopher St. | 212-675-6157

"Built atop a Five Guys" burger joint, this hidden-in-plain-sight West Village bar remains something of a secret, but regulars say it's "fantastic" for "watching sports and hanging with friends"; brick walls, flat-screens and cheap suds are all part of its standard-issue scene.

Bleecker Street Bar

| 17 | 13 | 17 | M |

NoHo | 56-58 Bleecker St. (bet. B'way & Lafayette St.) | 6 to Bleecker St. | 212-334-0244 | www.bleeckerstreetbarnyc.com

It's "not much to look at", but with three pool tables, three dartboards and 10 TVs, this "no-frills" NoHo sports bar makes "passing the time" palatable; hey, "it's got drinks" too – "reasonably priced" ones at that – so "until something more fun" comes along, let the "chillaxing" begin.

NEW Blind Barber

| - | - | - | M |

E Village | 339 E. 10th St. (bet. Aves. A & B) | L to 1st Ave. | 212-228-2123 | www.blindbarber.com

Mashing up a barber shop and a barroom, this new East Villager milks its Beauty-Bar-for-guys concept by offering a free drink with every haircut; once the tonsorial parlor closes at 9 PM, the action shifts to its stealth back bar, a dark, speakeasy-ish thing that shakes fancy cocktails and also includes a canoodle-ready back parlor.

Blind Pig

| 18 | 14 | 19 | M |

E Village | 233 E. 14th St. (bet. 2nd & 3rd Aves.) | L to 3rd Ave. | 212-209-1573 | www.blindpigbar.com

East Villagers tout this "local" pen that "isn't much to look at" but offers a "friendly" atmosphere for "catching the game"; despite "affordable booze" and "TV screens everywhere", it's "never too crowded."

☒ Blind Tiger Ale House

| 23 | 16 | 20 | M |

W Village | 281 Bleecker St. (Jones St.) | 1 to Christopher St. | 212-462-4682 | www.blindtigeralehouse.com

A "beer lover's El Dorado", this "justifiably renowned" West Village suds specialist serves a "daunting" selection of craft brews; since it's "always crowded" – it "suffers from its fame" – hopsheads turn up during "off hours" to sample "more beers than you can wrap your liver around."

Blondies

| 18 | 13 | 17 | M |

W 70s | 212 W. 79th St. (bet. Amsterdam Ave. & B'way) | 1 to 79th St. | 212-362-4360 | www.blondiessports.com

"Rowdy, sudsy" UWS sports bar with a "ton of TVs" tuned to all the "big games", but also known for its "zesty wings" served by saucy "Brother Jimmy's-lite" bar maids; athletic supporters arrive well "in advance" on "college basketball nights" when "table reservations" are essential.

Blue and Gold Tavern ⌿

| 16 | 7 | 15 | I |

E Village | 79 E. Seventh St. (bet. 1st & 2nd Aves.) | 6 to Astor Pl. | 212-777-1006

"Discerning boozers on a budget" dig this "recession-proof" East Village "hole" with "zero ambiance", "dirt-cheap" drinks and "take-no-crap" bartenders; if you think the "ripped furniture" and "meatheads at the pool table" are sore sights, wait till you see the bathrooms.

NEW Blue Haven

| - | - | - | M |

G Village | 108 W. Houston St. (Thompson St.) | 1 to Houston St. | 212-505-3400 | www.bluehavennyc.com

The former Bar 108 has been lightly retooled into this new Village sports bar vending the usual liquids to a fratty following; flat-screens, pub grub and a back room dedicated to darts hint at its unpretentious, come-as-you-are approach.

⚡ Blue Note

24 | 17 | 17 | VE

G Village | 131 W. Third St. (bet. MacDougal St. & 6th Ave.) | A/B/C/D/E/F/M to W. 4th St. | 212-475-8592 | www.bluenote.net

At this "adult" Village jazz joint, "legends" take the stage to serve up "soulful" music in a room equipped with "incredible sightlines and acoustics"; despite "watery drinks", "so-so" American grub, "cramped, love-thy-neighbor" seating and too many "Japanese tourists", aficionados say this "history-filled" club is "unmatched" in its class.

Blue Owl

20 | 18 | 18 | E

E Village | 196 Second Ave., downstairs (bet. 12th & 13th Sts.) | L to 1st Ave. | 212-505-2583 | www.blueowlnyc.com

Cocktail-swilling night owls hoot about the "innovative" mixology showcased at this sub-street-level East Village nest with a "dimly lit", sorta-"speakeasy" atmosphere; some birds of play suggest the scene is "best on weekdays, when it's not crowded" and "stellar happy-hour" drinking abounds.

Blue Ribbon Downing Street Bar

24 | 20 | 24 | E

W Village | 34 Downing St. (bet. Bedford & Varick Sts.) | 1 to Houston St. | 212-691-0404 | www.blueribbonrestaurants.com

"Just what you'd expect from the Blue Ribbon team", this "tiny" West Village wine bar is a "charming" "jewel box" that's all about "high quality", from its "stellar" vinos, sakes and cocktails to the "amazing" American nibbles; since it's usually "standing room only", it's "best for two people" in the mood for "all-night conversation."

Boat

22 | 12 | 18 | M

Boerum Hill | 175 Smith St. (bet. Warren & Wyckoff Sts.) | Brooklyn | F/G to Bergen St. | 718-254-0607

Docked in Boerum Hill "since before Smith Street was hot", this "dark dive" nets a crowd "heavy on tattoos" who put aweigh "cheap" pops while feeding the "amazing jukebox"; though a "sparse" aesthetic generally prevails, the place still exudes a "strange appeal."

⚡ Boat Basin Cafe

25 | 18 | 15 | M

W 70s | W. 79th St. (Hudson River) | 1 to 79th St. | 212-496-5542 | www.boatbasincafe.com

It's "all about the river view" at this Hudson-hugging outdoor "oasis" on the Upper West Side, a warm-months-only option that's practically "mandatory" for "summertime schmoozing" and boozing; though the food and drink are only "average" at best, the alfresco setting "can't be beat" for "escaping the hubbub of the city" and "watching some sailboats."

Bob

21 | 13 | 14 | M

LES | 235 Eldridge St. (bet. Houston & Stanton Sts.) | F to Lower East Side/2nd Ave. | 212-529-1807 | www.bobbarnyc.com

"Great DJs" blasting beats thrill the "sweat"-soaked masses at this "awesome" LES "hip-hop" haven, a (literally) "hot" scene; just remember it's a "cramped" little space, which means "you'll be bumping and grinding with your neighbor whether you like it or not."

	APPEAL	DECOR	SERVICE	COST

☑ Bohemian Hall
| 25 | 15 | 15 | M |

Astoria | 29-19 24th Ave. (bet. 29th & 31st Sts.) | Queens | N/Q to 30th Ave. | 718-274-4925 | www.bohemianhall.com

Raise a "huge stein" of "Staropramen" to summer alongside "hundreds of others with the same idea" at this "fab" Astoria beer garden, essentially a "giant backyard party" where the Czech suds flow freely and cheaply; ok, the "lines are hell" and it's "not about decor", but "tasty sausages" and a "relaxed" mood compensate.

Boiler Room ⊭
| 18 | 13 | 19 | I |

E Village | 86 E. Fourth St. (bet. 1st & 2nd Aves.) | F to Lower East Side/ 2nd Ave. | 212-254-7536 | www.boilerroomnyc.com

"Dudes of all ages" "dress down" and turn up at this "divey" East Village gay bar, a longtime "no-nonsense" joint that's refreshingly "unpretentious"; some say it's got "no personality", but at least the crowd's "approachable" and, like the booze, "cheap."

Bongo
| 22 | 21 | 23 | E |

W Village | 395 West St. (W. 10th St.) | 1 to Christopher St. | 212-675-6555 | www.bongonyc.com

"Trendy" tipplers bang the drum for the "stellar cocktails" and seafood-centric eats supplied at this "fab" Way West Village "party pad" done up with "retro", *Brady Bunch*–meets–Eero Saarinen decor; granted, it's "not cheap", but then again the atmosphere is much "better than your own living room."

Bookmarks
| 24 | 23 | 20 | E |

E 40s | Library Hotel | 299 Madison Ave., 14th fl. (41st St.) | 7/B/D/F/ M to 42nd St./Bryant Park | 212-983-4500 | www.hospitalityholdings.com

The Library Hotel's "little-known" rooftop bar marks the spot where "tourists" and Midtown "business" types congregate in a "refined" setting that's "part alfresco, part glass-enclosed" and all about the "pretty view"; it "sure isn't cheap" and they're "aren't many books" around, but it's worth checking out when you want to "impress a date."

☑ Boom Boom Room
| 24 | 25 | 18 | VE |

(aka Top of the Standard)

Meatpacking | Standard Hotel | 442 W. 13th St., 18th fl. (bet. Washington & West Sts.) | A/C/E/L to 14th St./8th Ave. | 212-645-4646 | www.standardhotels.com

Still the most "exclusive" venue in town, this swanky penthouse lounge atop the Standard Hotel is open to all early evening until closing time, 10 PM, when the clipboard police take over; expect "opulent", "throwback-to-the-'80s" decor, staggering prices and "spectacular" skyline views through the "floor-to-ceiling windows"; P.S. "make sure to check out the bathroom."

Boss Tweed's Saloon
| 17 | 13 | 18 | M |

LES | 115 Essex St. (bet. Delancey & Rivington Sts.) | F/J/M/Z to Delancey/Essex Sts. | 212-475-9997 | www.bosstweeds.com

"Cheap drinks" are the draw at this "unkempt" LES "dive" named after the "corrupt Tammany Hall" politico; a small rear garden offers refuge when "smelly kickballers" and "college birthday partyers" elect to "overrun" the place.

	APPEAL	DECOR	SERVICE	COST

Botanica
20 | 12 | 18 | M

NoLita | 47 E. Houston St., downstairs (bet. Mott & Mulberry Sts.) |
6 to Bleecker St. | 212-343-7251

There's "no pretension" in the air at this NoLita "hole-in-the-wall" where "chill" cats throw back "cheap drinks" and plant themselves on "comfy/shabby" couches for "low-key" interludes; bonus frills include "good DJ sets" and Sunday night karaoke.

Bounce
17 | 15 | 18 | M

E 70s | 1403 Second Ave. (73rd St.) | 6 to 68th St. | 212-535-2183 |
www.bounceny.com

"Frat guys and the women who love them" show up at this "upscale" UES sports bar to "watch the game" on a surfeit of "flat-screens" while tackling "tubes of beer"; regulars say staffers don "skimpy outfits" to ensure their tips get an extra bounce.

Bourbon St.
16 | 13 | 16 | M

W 70s | 407 Amsterdam Ave. (bet. 79th & 80th Sts.) | 1 to 79th St. |
212-721-1332 | www.bourbonstreetnyc.com

The intended theme may be Mardi Gras, but it's more like "Frat" Tuesday at this perennially "packed" UWS joint where "college kids and cheap drinks" collide; sure, it's a "dive" with "undergarments hanging from the ceiling", but no one notices when the "50-cent beer" special is in effect.

Bourgeois Pig
23 | 23 | 19 | E

E Village | 111 E. Seventh St. (bet. Ave. A & 1st Ave.) | L to 1st Ave. |
212-475-2246 | www.bourgeoispigny.com

Masses mull over a "first-rate" roster of vinos and cheese-centric snacks at this "atmospheric" East Village wine bar, a velvety "Victorian"-style parlor equipped with "cuddly couches" and lit by "dim" chandeliers; the "decadent" doings are naturally "pricey", but "half-off bottles" twice weekly facilitate "seduction" on a budget.

Bowery Ballroom
23 | 18 | 18 | M

LES | 6 Delancey St. (bet. Bowery & Chrystie St.) | F to Lower East Side/2nd Ave. | 212-533-2111 | www.boweryballroom.com

Music mavens maintain "there's no place" like this LES concert venue, a "perfect-size" space ("large enough but still intimate") with "incredible acoustics", "good sightlines" and a "full calendar" of "top-notch" bands; for tipples with your tunes, bars on all three levels "get the job done."

Bowery Electric
18 | 13 | 16 | M

E Village | 327 Bowery (2nd St.) | B/D/F/M to B'way/Lafayette St. |
212-228-0228 | www.theboweryelectric.com

"Hipsters and bankers" get amped up by this "lively" Bowery double-decker whose alternating currents include live bands, "dance parties", "great" mix masters and even theater performances; fans plug it for "trying to keep the flame of CBGB's alive", but foes zap it as a "downtown bar chewed up, swallowed and regurgitated for a B&T crowd."

Bowery Hotel Bar
24 | 24 | 19 | VE

E Village | Bowery Hotel | 335 Bowery (bet. 2nd & 3rd Sts.) | F to Lower East Side/2nd Ave. | 212-505-1300 | www.theboweryhotel.com

An opulent "oasis of calm" on the Bowery, this "luxe" lobby bar bedecked with "old Persian rugs, dark-wood paneling and a stone fireplace" is "oh-so-worth" the expense – and the hassle of its "priority-seating-for-hotel-guests" policy – to sample the ultra-"cool vibe" with "high-end cocktail" accompaniment; P.S. it may "take some work", but try "talking your way" onto the "amazing" outdoor patio.

Bowery Poetry Club
18 | 15 | 15 | M

NoHo | 308 Bowery (bet. Bleecker & Houston Sts.) | F to Lower East Side/2nd Ave. | 212-614-0505 | www.bowerypoetry.com
Not just for connoisseurs of the spoken word, this "funky" NoHo performance space offers an "intimate setting" for all kinds of "poetry in motion", from music shows to "drag bingo"; there's booze for sale too, which can help arouse your inner "Kerouac" on "open-mike night."

Bowery Wine Company
19 | 18 | 20 | E

E Village | 13 E. First St. (bet. Bowery & 2nd Ave.) | F to Lower East Side/2nd Ave. | 212-614-0800 | www.bowerywineco.com
Another "clean" corrective to the Bowery's derelict image, this "friendly" East Village wine bar wields a modest, well-parsed list of vintages that can be paired with panini, pizza and the like; if it "lacks character" overall, at least occasional "live jazz" and "outdoor seating in warmer months" make for a "fun but calm night out."

Bowlmor
20 | 18 | 16 | M

G Village | 110 University Pl., 3rd fl. (bet. 12th & 13th Sts.) | 4/5/6/L/N/Q/R to 14th St./Union Sq. | 212-255-8188
NEW W 40s | 222 W. 44th St., 3rd fl. (bet. 7th & 8th Aves.) | 1/2/3/7/N/Q/R/S to 42nd St./Times Sq. | 212-680-0012
www.bowlmor.com
"Not your father's bowling alley", this "glammed up" Village roll-o-rama is a "clubby", "neon"-lit affair populated by pinheads willing to "spend an arm and a leg" to drink and play ball; too bad "slow service" and "long lines on weekends" roll gutter balls; P.S. the double-decker, 45-lane Times Square spin-off opened post-Survey.

Box, The
24 | 22 | 18 | VE

LES | 189 Chrystie St. (bet. Rivington & Stanton Sts.) | F to Lower East Side/2nd Ave. | 212-982-9301 | www.theboxnyc.com
"Be ready for the unexpected" at this LES take on a "Weimar-era cabaret", where "tawdry", "over-the-top" vaudeville acts supply X-rated amusement for "fashion-forward" folk and "random celebs lurking in corners"; brace yourself for "very expensive" tabs and - without "some serious name-dropping" - a "doorman who won't let you in."

Boxcar Lounge
▽ 18 | 17 | 20 | M

E Village | 168 Ave. B (bet. 10th & 11th Sts.) | L to 1st Ave. | 212-473-2830 | www.boxcarlounge.com
Should you choo-choose to come aboard this "reliable", rail-themed East Villager, don't mind the "tiny" digs - in a squeeze, just move your caboose to the heated patio; the real challenge is surviving its legendary two-for-one "happy hour", which seems to last "all the livelong day."

Boxers
- | - | - | M

Flatiron | 37 W. 20th St. (bet. 5th & 6th Aves.) | F to 23rd St. | 212-255-5082 | www.boxersnyc.com
The Flatiron is home to this gay sports bar, a big boxy thing stocked with flat-screens, pool tables and a pizza oven; though the warehousey

interior has a chainlike, suburban vibe, the outdoor rear smoking lounge draws the cooler cats in the crowd.

NEW Branded Saloon

| - | - | - | M |

Prospect Heights | 603 Vanderbilt Ave. (Bergen St.) | Brooklyn | 2/3 to Grand Army Plaza | 718-484-8704 | www.brandedsaloon.com

The Old West gallops into Prospect Heights via this new cowboy-themed honky-tonk tricked up with swinging doors and a player piano; the long, meandering space includes a DJ lounge in the rear and a billiards-equipped basement.

☒ Brandy Library

| 27 | 26 | 25 | VE |

TriBeCa | 25 N. Moore St. (bet. Hudson & Varick Sts.) | 1 to Franklin St. | 212-226-5545 | www.brandylibrary.com

When in the mood for "something warm and brown", this *Mad Men*-esque TriBeCa lounge boasts a "you-name-it-they-got-it" selection of booze served in a faux "library" setting by a "knowledgeable" crew; it's both "date heaven" and the ultimate "gentlemen's night out", but it's "probably unaffordable" if you're not a "bailed-out banker."

Brandy's Piano Bar

| 24 | 16 | 21 | M |

E 80s | 235 E. 84th St. (bet. 2nd & 3rd Aves.) | 4/5/6 to 86th St. | 212-744-4949 | www.brandysnyc.com

Have a "gay old time" regardless of your sexual orientation at this "guilty-pleasure" UES piano bar renowned for booze-infused "sing-alongs" led by "entertaining" staffers who really "get the crowd going"; just be aware that this "small joint" is perpetually "packed."

Brass Monkey

| 20 | 16 | 17 | M |

Meatpacking | 55 Little W. 12th St. (bet. 10th Ave. & Washington St.) | A/C/E/L to 14th St./8th Ave. | 212-675-6686 | www.brassmonkeynyc.com

A "bastion of normalcy" in the "glitzy" Meatpacking, this "solid" triplex offers "unpretentious" drinking at "affordable" rates and includes a tiny bonus roof deck; granted, it's "packed on weekends", so make the most of that "long wait to get a drink" by studying the "extensive beer list."

Brazen Head

| 20 | 14 | 20 | M |

Boerum Hill | 228 Atlantic Ave. (bet. Boerum Pl. & Court St.) | Brooklyn | F/G to Bergen St. | 718-488-0430 | www.brazenheadbrooklyn.com

Craft drafts are the name of the game at this "friendly" Boerum Hill suds specialist luring "beer lovers", "first-year law students" and "neighborhood regulars" with a "nice assortment" of brews including growlers and "cask-conditioned ales"; sure, it's a "simple" scene, but with "lots of daily promotions", supporters say it "feels like a find every time."

Broadway Dive

| 18 | 12 | 21 | M |

W 100s | 2662 Broadway (bet. 101st & 102nd Sts.) | 1 to 103rd St. | 212-865-2662 | www.divebarnyc.com

Upper Broadway "locals" who "run the gamut of the social scene" assemble at this "unpretentious" "hole-in-the-wall" to "exercise their livers", root for the Mets and feed the "good juke"; it's a "great place for anonymity", with "friendly" service and reasonable tabs to boot.

| | APPEAL | DECOR | SERVICE | COST |

Brooklyn Ale House
23 | 17 | 20 | M

Williamsburg | 103 Berry St. (N. 8th St.) | Brooklyn | L to Bedford Ave. |
718-302-9811 | www.brooklynalehouse.com
"Everyone gets along great – even the dogs" – at this "pooch-friendly"
Williamsburg suds "sanctuary" dubbed "one of the least pretentious
bars" in the nabe; an "attentive" staff oversees the "great selection" of
mostly "local" brews and tends to a mixed crowd that ranges from
"hipsters to old souls."

☒ Brooklyn Bowl
27 | 26 | 23 | M

Williamsburg | 61 Wythe Ave. (bet. N. 11th & N. 12th Sts.) | Brooklyn | L to
Bedford Ave. | 718-963-3369 | www.brooklynbowl.com
"So much more than a bowling alley", this "unique", "warehouse-size"
Williamsburg multitasker incorporates 16 state-of-the-art lanes with
a 600-capacity performance space and tops it off with "spot-on" food
courtesy of Blue Ribbon; quite simply, it's a "blast" and one of the
"best" in the city – fans think "this must be what heaven looks like."

Brooklyn Brewery
23 | 15 | 19 | M

Williamsburg | 79 N. 11th St. (bet. Berry St. & Wythe Ave.) | Brooklyn | L to
Bedford Ave. | 718-486-7422 | www.brooklynbrewery.com
Only open on Friday nights plus Saturday and Sunday afternoons, this
"stellar" Williamsburg microbrewery offers hopsheads the chance to
go "straight to the source" and sample "cheap", "none-fresher" frost-
ies; even though lines to the tap "can be long" and the "only food available is via delivery", it's still a "great all-around" experience.

ᴺᴱᵂ Brooklyneer, The
- | - | - | M

W Village | 220 W. Houston St. (bet. 6th Ave. & Varick St.) | A/B/C/
D/E/F/M to W. 4th St. | 646-692-4911 | www.brooklyneer.com
An untraveled part of the West Village near the Holland Tunnel is
home to this new gastropub celebrating all things Brooklyn, with craft
suds and locavore eats imported from across the river (even the bar is
made from wood salvaged from the Coney Island boardwalk); mellow
atmospherics and close proximity to the Film Forum guarantee a
crowd at all hours.

Brooklyn Inn ⊅
25 | 23 | 20 | M

Boerum Hill | 148 Hoyt St. (Bergen St.) | Brooklyn | F/G to Bergen St. |
718-522-2525
Locals hoping to "hide from the Smith Street scene" head for this "totally old-school" Boerum Hill taproom best known for its "gorgeous"
19th-century bar and "pool table in back" ("good luck getting in on a
game"); a real "taste of Brooklyn", it's the ultimate "low-key" setting
for "simple drinks" and "quiet" conversation.

Brooklyn Public House
▽ 17 | 17 | 14 | M

Fort Greene | 247 Dekalb Ave. (Vanderbilt Ave.) | Brooklyn | G to
Clinton/Washington Aves. | 347-227-8976 |
www.brooklynpublichouse.com
A robust beer selection and "not-for-dieters" pub grub are the house
specialties at this "unpretentious" Fort Greene spot, a "comfy" Irish
pub with a Victorian look that's agreeable to lone "blokes" and "snog-
ging" couples alike; still, a few fault the "pedestrian" scene, saying it's
more "rest home than public house."

	APPEAL	DECOR	SERVICE	COST

Brooklyn Social ⊄

22 | 19 | 19 | M

Carroll Gardens | 335 Smith St. (bet. Carroll & President Sts.) | Brooklyn | F/G to Carroll St. | 718-858-7758

One of the first "speakeasy-inspired" places in Carroll Gardens, this erstwhile Italian social club now serves "well-made" cocktails in a "chill", "old-timey-but-not-really" setting; regulars avoid it on weekends, when the "crazy busy" scene (replete with too many guys in "Buddy Holly glasses") "feels like Williamsburg."

NEW Brooklyn Winery

- | - | - | M

Williamsburg | 213 N. Eighth St. (bet. Driggs Ave. & Roebling St.) | Brooklyn | L to Bedford Ave. | 347-763-1506 | www.bkwinery.com

The rare wine bar that actually makes wine on-site, this Williamsburg newcomer also draws in oenophiles with knowledgeable staffers and mellow atmospherics; set off the beaten path in the old Supreme Trading digs, it's furnished in old-timey-Brooklyn style, with carefully distressed furnishings that give the room a Dickensian feel.

Brookvin

▽ 23 | 21 | 19 | E

Park Slope | 381 Seventh Ave. (bet. 11th & 12th Sts.) | Brooklyn | F/G to 7th Ave. | 718-768-9463 | www.brookvin.com

"Excellent" vinos and "yummy snacks" conveyed by "smart staffers" sum up the "sweet little" scene at this Park Slope wine bar where an "outdoor garden" adds floral notes in warm weather; oenophiles inspired to take the tasting party home can stock up at Big Nose Full Body, its sister shop across the street.

Broome Street Bar

17 | 12 | 17 | M

SoHo | 363 W. Broadway (Broome St.) | C/E to Spring St. | 212-925-2086

Imagine "Berkeley in the late '60s" to get the gist of this proudly "unpretentious" SoHo "staple" that skips all that "mixology nonsense" in favor of "cheap drinks" and "friendly" attitude; the grub's "decent" too ("love that burger"), sealing the deal for "locals and tourists" alike.

⚡ Brother Jimmy's BBQ

17 | 14 | 17 | M

E 70s | 1485 Second Ave. (bet. 77th & 78th Sts.) | 6 to 77th St. | 212-288-0099
E 90s | 1644 Third Ave. (92nd St.) | 6 to 96th St. | 212-426-2020
Garment District | 416 Eighth Ave. (31st St.) | A/C/E to 34th St./Penn Station | 212-967-7603
Gramercy | 116 E. 16th St. (bet. Irving Pl. & Union Sq. E.) | 4/5/6/L/N/Q/R to 14th St./Union Sq. | 212-673-6465
Murray Hill | 181 Lexington Ave. (31st St.) | 6 to 33rd St. | 212-779-7427
W 80s | 428 Amsterdam Ave. (bet. 80th & 81st Sts.) | 1 to 79th St. | 212-501-7515
www.brotherjimmys.com

"Welcome back to college!" could be the motto of these "always rowdy" Southern-style "frat-holes" where "fishbowls" and "cheap tall boys" ferried by waitresses in "denim shorts" fuel the "*Animal House*"-like shenanigans; regular airings of "ACC" game action ensure that "Chapel Hill" never feels too far away.

B-Side

▽ 22 | 17 | 19 | M

E Village | 204 Ave. B (bet. 12th & 13th Sts.) | L to 1st Ave. | 212-475-4600

Cheap PBR-and-whiskey pairings and an "eclectic" jukebox make hipsters happy at this "chill" Alphabet City dive; other attractions include foosball and "weeknight movies" screened by "friendly" staffers who "know almost everyone by name."

B61 ⊅

-	-	-	M

Carroll Gardens | 187 Columbia St. (Degraw St.) | Brooklyn | F/G to Carroll St. | 718-643-5400 | www.almarestaurant.com

"Regular" types like the "low-key" mood at this Carroll Gardens "gem" that's "named after the bus route" and offers a pretty awesome "view" of the Manhattan skyline across the East River; it's a "fun place to end the night", and having Alma restaurant upstairs is a definite "bonus."

Bua

21	17	18	M

E Village | 122 St. Marks Pl. (bet. Ave. A & 1st Ave.) | 6 to Astor Pl. | 212-979-6276 | www.buabar.com

Candlelight and a "comfortable" setting (including a front "porch" that's "perfect in summer") add a dab of "class" to this "convivial" East Village Irish pub; the "tasty snacks" are a "nice touch" too, but be prepared to be "packed in like a sardine" – it's usually "too crowded."

☒ Bubble Lounge

21	21	19	VE

TriBeCa | 228 W. Broadway (bet. Franklin & White Sts.) | 1 to Franklin St. | 212-431-3433 | www.bubblelounge.com

Lower Manhattan's "high temple of champagne", this "change-of-pace" TriBeCa lounge uncorking 300 varieties of bubbly is an "intimate" venue for indulging in flutes of fancy with that "special someone" ("don't trip over all the guys proposing"); but the brut reality includes "break-the-bank" tabs and a growing consensus that it "feels a little run-down."

Buceo 95

24	19	23	E

W 90s | 201 W. 95th St. (bet. Amsterdam Ave. & B'way) | 1/2/3 to 96th St. | 212-662-7010 | www.buceo95.com

A "varied wine selection" stressing Spanish labels teams up with "delicious" tapas to render a "nice treat" for the locals, romancers and "pre–Symphony Space" set at this "grown-up" Upper West Side nook; granted, the real estate may be a "little tight", but "attentive" staffers help to distract.

Building on Bond

▽ 24	27	24	M

Boerum Hill | 112 Bond St. (Pacific St.) | Brooklyn | A/C/G to Hoyt/Schermerhorn Sts. | 347-853-8687 | www.buildingonbond.com

Thanks to this "quirky" multitasker, "arty" Boerum Hill types now have a "hip" one-stop shop for WiFi-enhanced "coffee in the morning" and a "good selection" of cocktails at night; its "good-humored" staff, "very social" mood and "cozy", "hand-hewn" digs lead fans to call it "exactly what the neighborhood needed."

Bull's Head Tavern

16	13	17	M

Gramercy | 295 Third Ave. (bet. 22nd & 23rd Sts.) | 6 to 23rd St. | 212-685-2589 | www.bullsheadtavern.com

"Divey" Gramercy joint with a heavy-duty frat-boy following thanks to pool, darts and "beautiful women behind the bar"; it's most "happening" (i.e. "crowded") on Thursday nights when Jim Roberti's "fun cover band" performs.

Z NEW Bunker, The

	-	-	-	E

Meatpacking | 24 Ninth Ave. (bet. 13th & 14th Sts.) | A/C/E/L to 14th St./
8th Ave. | 212-837-4700 | www.bunkerclubnyc.com

Hidden underground near Dos Caminos' Meatpacking branch, this hot
new cellar lives up to its name with bomb shelter–chic decor that incorporates living-room atmospherics with a disco-balled dance floor;
brought to you by Matt Abramcyk (Beatrice Inn, Employees Only), it's
hooking some of the hippest cats in town, so brace yourself for a much
rougher door than 675 Bar, buried in the same hole.

Burp Castle

21	17	18	M

E Village | 41 E. Seventh St. (bet. 2nd & 3rd Aves.) | 6 to Astor Pl. |
212-982-4576 | www.burpcastlenyc.wordpress.com

'Tis true, the "monks behind the bar" at this "candlelit" East Village
suds sanctuary have "hung up their robes", but they still tap an "extensive selection" of "unusual" brews; the fabled "peace-and-quiet" policy also remains in effect, with rowdy types silenced with a "shush."

Bushwick Country Club

∇ 17	12	19	M

Williamsburg | 618 Grand St. (Leonard St.) | Brooklyn | L to Grand St. |
718-388-2114 | www.bushwickcountryclub.com

"PBR tall boys" and "mini-golf" collide at this "laid-back" Williamsburg
watering hole boasting a funky six-hole putt-putt course out back and
a photo booth within; one look at its "covered-in-tattoos" crowd and
you'll know that it's "definitely a hipster bar."

NEW Buskers

-	-	-	M

G Village | 92 W. Houston St., downstairs (W. B'way) | B/D/F/M to
B'way/Lafayette St. | 212-381-4911 | www.buskersnyc.com

New subterranean bar/lounge on the SoHo/Greenwich Village border
in the former Yama digs; the long, narrow setting includes a pool table
and a petite loft area, and there's an outdoor patio for nature lovers.

Buttermilk Bar

21	16	16	M

Park Slope | 577 Fifth Ave. (16th St.) | Brooklyn | R to Prospect Ave. |
718-788-6297

"Cheap" brews, "buxom, tattooed" barmaids and a "classic rock"–
stocked jukebox make this Park Sloper a "no-frills" refuge from the
area's accelerating gentrification; pinball and arcade games take a
night of "kicking back" in a more competitive direction.

Cabanas

22	22	17	E

Chelsea | Maritime Hotel | 88 Ninth Ave., rooftop (enter at 16th or 17th Sts.) |
A/C/E/L to 14th St./8th Ave. | 212-835-5537 | www.themaritimehotel.com

It "feels like you're on vacation" at these tropical-themed rooftops in
the Maritime Hotel, both "excellent summer destinations" for scoping
out "beautiful peeps"; too bad about the "expensive" pops, "Ninth
Avenue" view and "B&T" crowd, but it's still "great for a girls' night out."

Cabaret
(fka Ten's)

-	-	-	VE

Flatiron | 35 E. 21st St. (bet. B'way & Park Ave. S.) | N/R to 23rd St. |
212-254-7777 | www.cabaretnewyork.com

The name has changed (fka Ten's), but the "thrill" of titillation remains
at this Flatiron "jugs joint" where "well-heeled" guys eyeball the

"well-endowed" dolls; don't forget to bring along the "Amex platinum card" – the "hefty door charge" is just the beginning.

Cabin Down Below
- | - | - | M

E Village | 132½ E. Seventh St., downstairs (bet. Aves. A & B) | L to 1st Ave. | 212-614-9798

"Kind of secret" even though it's been around for over a year, this cozy East Village basement is done up like someone's living room and draws "elite" rock 'n' roll types and the models they date; the former entrance through an Avenue A pizzeria is closed, so it's now accessed via a Seventh Street alleyway.

⊠ Cafe Carlyle
27 | 25 | 26 | VE

E 70s | Carlyle Hotel | 35 E. 76th St. (Madison Ave.) | 6 to 77th St. | 212-744-1600 | www.thecarlyle.com

See "how the other half" parties at this Carlyle Hotel "luxury cabaret", an "upscale" yet "intimate" venue frequented by "diamond-earringed" "old-money" types who appreciate "famous entertainers" (everyone still "misses Bobby Short"); sure, an evening here will give your credit card a "good workout", but it's "worth it" for a taste of the "good life."

Cafe Wha?
19 | 12 | 16 | E

G Village | 115 MacDougal St., downstairs (bet. Bleecker & W. 3rd Sts.) | A/B/C/D/E/F/M to W. 4th St. | 212-254-3706 | www.cafewha.com

"Still going after all these years", this "cramped", "kitschy" Village basement around since the '50s now features "talented" resident bands that keep its "energy" level high; just be prepared for "shoulder-to-shoulder tourists", "expensive" tabs and a "fun hangover in the morning."

Cake Shop
21 | 17 | 16 | M

LES | 152 Ludlow St. (bet. Rivington & Stanton Sts.) | F/J/M/Z to Delancey/Essex Sts. | 212-253-0036 | www.cake-shop.com

There's a "DIY aesthetic" in play at this Lower East Side "hipster haven", a combination coffeehouse/record store/rock venue where "music enthusiasts" can experience "cupcakes on the ground floor, PBRs downstairs" and the joys of an "experimental thrash band" in both live and vinyl formats; since it doesn't cost much dough, what more could you knead?

Calico Jack's Cantina
16 | 13 | 16 | M

E 40s | 800 Second Ave. (42nd St.) | 4/5/6/7/S to 42nd St./Grand Central | 212-557-4300 | www.calicojacksnyc.com

"After work", this U.N.-area cantina turns into a "meathead-filled" meat market drawing tipsy "twentysomethings" and the "spillover from McFadden's next door"; ultimately, its real appeal is the one-two combo of "great drink specials" and "proximity to Grand Central."

Camp
21 | 19 | 19 | M

Boerum Hill | 179 Smith St. (bet. Warren & Wyckoff Sts.) | Brooklyn | F/G to Bergen St. | 718-852-8086

"Sleeping bags" aren't required at this "lodge"-like Boerum Hill theme bar that re-creates the "summer-camp" experience with "deer heads and canoes on the wall" and "s'mores" for snacking; if you "like the idea of camping" but "don't like actually being outdoors", look no further.

| | | APPEAL | DECOR | SERVICE | COST |

☒ Campbell Apartment
25 26 20 VE

E 40s | Grand Central Terminal | 15 Vanderbilt Ave. (bet. 42nd & 43rd Sts.) | 4/5/6/7/S to 42nd St./Grand Central | 212-953-0409 | www.hospitalityholdings.com

The "Gilded Age" lives on at this "luxe" '20s-era lair hidden inside Grand Central, once the office of a railroad "robber baron" and now a "classy" "after-work" magnet for modern tycoons who like its "private-club" vibe and can afford the seriously "pricey" tabs; just remember there is a "dress code" – although if you're wearing a "black cocktail dress" you "may be mistaken for a server."

Canal Room
21 16 16 E

TriBeCa | 285 W. Broadway (Canal St.) | A/C/E to Canal St. | 212-941-8100 | www.canalroom.com

A "diverse" and "generally good" roster of performers keeps folks lining up at this "nicely set up" TriBeCa music venue; a popular draw is Rubix Kube, a "fab '80s cover band" that busts out the big-hair classics weekly.

Cargo
20 17 17 M

Staten Island | 120 Bay St. (Victory Blvd.) | 718-876-0539 | www.cargocafe.com

With its "eclectic" clientele and "arty" attitude, "you wouldn't know you're on Staten Island" at this "local" favorite that's a "blessing for the North Shore's lost souls"; from live bands to Twister tournaments, "every night brings something new" here, and it's "close to the ferry" to boot.

Carnegie Club
23 23 22 VE

W 50s | 156 W. 56th St. (bet. 6th & 7th Aves.) | N/Q/R to 57th St./7th Ave. | 212-957-9676 | www.hospitalityholdings.com

"Mature" clubbers unwind with "a cigar and a single malt" at this "superb" (and legal) smoking lounge near Carnegie Hall; it's "not the cheapest place around" – nor the liveliest – though the "somnolent" scene picks up on Saturdays with a Frank Sinatra cover band.

Carolines
21 16 15 E

W 40s | 1626 Broadway (bet. 49th & 50th Sts.) | N/R to 49th St. | 212-757-4100 | www.carolines.com

"Prime-time" laughs are a good bet when "big-name" comedians take the stage at this big-box Times Square house of mirth, though the "high prices" and "low-quality" food and drink aren't as amusing; hecklers wish that the service was "less of a joke" as well.

NEW Casa Mezcal
- - - M

LES | 86 Orchard St. (bet. Grand & Broome Sts.) | F/J/M/Z to Delancey/Essex Sts. | 212-777-2600

Ambitious is the word for this new LES triplex that aims to be a Oaxacan cultural center with a Mexican cantina on the ground floor, an art gallery above and a performance space/screening room in the basement; tipplers tout its esoteric array of mezcals and fiestalike mood.

Cask Bar
- - - M

Murray Hill | 167 E. 33rd St. (bet. Lexington & 3rd Aves.) | 6 to 33rd St. | 212-300-4924 | www.casknyc.com

A grown-up alternative to Murray Hill's typical frat offerings, this cozy tavern serves hand-pumped cask ales as well as craft brews and specialty cocktails; the warm, amber-lit digs employ reclaimed wood, weathered brick and plank floors to very mellow effect, though the bar in the cellar is an alternative for more festive merry-making.

Castello Plan
- - - M

Ditmas Park | 1213 Cortelyou Rd. (bet. Argyle & Westminster Rds.) | Brooklyn | B/Q to Cortelyou Rd. | 718-856-8888 | www.thecastelloplan.com
The latest along Ditmas Park's emerging Restaurant Row, this wine bar specializes in Belgian beers and esoteric wines, with cheeses, salumi and such to soak them up; its small corner space done up with reclaimed wood gains some airiness from its frontage of windows looking out onto busy Cortelyou, plus there's a postage-stamp deck for fair-weather imbibing; P.S. cartographer's fun fact: it takes its name from the first map of Manhattan.

☑ Cávo
26 26 21 E

Astoria | 42-18 31st Ave. (bet. 42nd & 43rd Sts.) | Queens | R/M to Steinway St. | 718-721-1001 | www.cavoastoria.com
Astoria's take on "Ibiza", this "sleek" Greek restaurant "turns clubby by night" when they "turn up the music" and let in a "hot crowd" ready to party till dawn; it's "best in warmer weather" when you can mingle in the "gorgeous courtyard" and marvel at its "cascading waterfalls."

NEW Cayenne Lounge
- - - E

G Village | 128 W. Houston St. (Sullivan St.) | A/C/E to Spring St. | 212-674-4080 | www.cayennelounge.com
Set on the border of SoHo and Greenwich Village, this new bar/lounge in the former XR digs aims to draw cool cats with brand-name DJs; the wide-open setting allows plenty of room to spread out.

Cellar Bar
21 23 18 E

W 40s | Bryant Park Hotel | 40 W. 40th St., downstairs (bet. 5th & 6th Aves.) | 7/B/D/F/M to 42nd St./Bryant Park | 212-642-2211 | www.bryantparkhotel.com
"Strong drinks", "low lights" and a "stunning" vaulted ceiling set the "atmospheric" mood at this "sexy" subterranean lounge in the Bryant Park Hotel that's either "overly crowded" or "just you and the bartenders"; its "too-cool" following reports the "attitude is poured on thick" here, reflecting a scene that's far from bargain basement costwise.

Central
22 23 19 M

Astoria | 20-30 Steinway St. (bet. 20th Ave. & 20th Rd.) | Queens | R/M to Steinway St. | 718-726-1600 | www.centrallounge.com
"Beautiful" Astorians hit this "classy" Queens club-a-lopolis on weekends to party hardy in a posh setting that includes an outdoor courtyard; it may be located in a ho-hum area (yo, "taxi!"), but look on the bright side: the same kind of fun "costs much more in Manhattan."

Central Bar
19 18 20 M

E Village | 109 E. Ninth St. (bet. 3rd & 4th Aves.) | 6 to Astor Pl. | 212-529-5333 | www.centralbarnyc.com
You get two venues in one at this "convenient" East Villager housing both a "typical" Irish pub with ample "sports-watching" opportunities plus an "upstairs lounge" on weekends for the "dance party" thang; as varied as the energy can be, however, "college kids" remain the target audience.

| | APPEAL | DECOR | SERVICE | COST |

Champagne Bar at the Plaza
24 | 25 | 23 | VE

W 50s | Plaza Hotel | 768 Fifth Ave. (59th St.) | N/R to 5th Ave./59th St. | 212-546-5309 | www.theplaza.com

The Plaza's "refined" lobby bar "captures the essence of NY" at its most "luxurious", offering opulence by the magnum-load to "locals and tourists" who've donned "their very best" duds – and refinanced their mortgages, in some cases – for the sparkling, "very expensive" experience.

Chelsea Brewing Co.
20 | 18 | 19 | M

Chelsea | Chelsea Piers | Pier 59 (Hudson River & W. 18th St.) | A/C/E/L to 14th St./8th Ave. | 212-336-6440 | www.chelseabrewingco.com

Ok, it's "way out of the way" in Chelsea Piers, but this mammoth microbrewery is worth the trek thanks to its "excellent" beer list and "one of the best views of the Hudson River" from its alfresco terrace; for best results, go in "summer, when you can sit by the water" and "watch the sunset."

NEW Chelsea Room
- | - | - | E

Chelsea | Chelsea Hotel | 222 W. 23rd St., downstairs (bet. 7th & 8th Aves.) | C/E to 23rd St. | 212-675-3600 | www.thechelseanyc.com

The Chelsea Hotel is home to this appropriately named underground venue, once a warren of smaller rooms when it was Star Lounge, now revamped into a single swank space; while its exposed-brick walls and salvaged barn-wood floors conjure up the past, its bottle service-ready banquettes are all about the present.

Cherry Tavern
17 | 8 | 15 | I

E Village | 441 E. Sixth St. (bet. Ave. A & 1st Ave.) | F to Lower East Side/2nd Ave. | 212-777-1448

A jukebox, a purple-felt pool table and a "sticky" glaze on everything else sum up the decor at this East Village "total dive" where "trust-fund hipsters" abound; but even though there's "nothing fancy going on" here, six bucks gets you a beer and a shot – enough said.

Cherry Tree
- | - | - | M

Park Slope | 65 Fourth Ave. (bet. Bergen St. & St. Marks Pl.) | Brooklyn | 2/3/4/5/B/D/N/Q/R to Atlantic Ave. | 718-399-1353

Park Slope saplings sprout up at this "standard" pub with more beer varieties than you can shake a branch at; a fireplace heats up the scene indoors, while in the summer, a "large back patio" helps folks cool down.

Chloe
23 | 20 | 18 | VE

LES | 81 Ludlow St., downstairs (bet. Broome & Delancey Sts.) | F/J/M/Z to Delancey/Essex Sts. | 212-677-0067 | www.chloe81.com

An "impossible door" signals the "hot-spot" reputation of this "very small", "very hip" LES basement lounge, a white-tiled playground located down an "extremely steep staircase"; expect to mingle with "models", ex-Beatrice Inn regulars and random folk who "know the bouncers."

Church Lounge
22 | 23 | 19 | VE

TriBeCa | Tribeca Grand Hotel | 2 Sixth Ave. (White St.) | A/C/E to Canal St. | 212-519-6600 | www.tribecagrand.com

"Film industry" types, the "financial crowd" and "out-of-towners" cross paths at this "lofty lounge" in the Tribeca Grand Hotel best

	APPEAL	DECOR	SERVICE	COST

known for its "spacious", "gorgeous" atrium setting; trendsters yawn this 10-year-old is "past its prime", but others say it's "still a decent standby" for "sophisticated", "Black Amex–priced" cocktails.

Cibar

22	21	18	E

Gramercy | Inn at Irving Pl. | 56 Irving Pl. (bet. 17th & 18th Sts.) | 4/5/6/L/N/Q/R to 14th St./Union Sq. | 212-460-5656 | www.cibarlounge.com

Whether you "score a seat by the fireplace" or "abscond to the garden", it's easy to get "cozy" at this "intimate", "adult" lounge set in a Gramercy townhouse; even though its "fantastic" martinis "don't come cheap", few fuss when a "great date" is the potential payoff.

Cielo

23	20	18	E

Meatpacking | 18 Little W. 12th St. (bet. 9th Ave. & Washington St.) | A/C/E/L to 14th St./8th Ave. | 212-645-5700 | www.cieloclub.com

"Powerhouse DJs" draw "people from all over the world" to this "too cool" Meatpacking danceteria, a "timeless" destination for "real house-music lovers"; ok, the "sunken dance floor" (and the club itself) is on the "small" side, but "potent drinks", an "unrivaled sound system" and that "outdoor smoking lounge" more than compensate.

Cienfuegos

-	-	-	E

E Village | 95 Ave. A, 2nd fl. (bet. 6th & 7th Sts.) | F to Lower East Side/ 2nd Ave. | 212-614-6818 | www.cienfuegosny.com

Hidden above a nondescript East Village corner, this rum bar specializes in punches and fizzes that can be ordered by the glass or the bowl; the shabby-chic pink-and-green interior suggests Havana before Castro, though the pricing is decidedly more up to date.

Circa Tabac

24	17	20	E

SoHo | 32 Watts St. (bet. 6th Ave. & Thompson St.) | A/C/E to Canal St. | 212-941-1781 | www.circatabac.com

One of the few places in town where it's legal to smoke indoors, this "civilized" SoHo lounge is a puffer's "delight", vending 150-plus cigar and cigarette varietals as well as cocktails and snacks; its vaguely deco decor "harkens back to the '20s", adding a whiff of "nostalgia" to the proceedings.

City Winery

25	23	20	E

Hudson Square | 155 Varick St. (Vandam St.) | C/E to Spring St. | 212-608-0555 | www.citywinery.com

"Vast" Hudson Square complex (the "snazzy" brainchild of Knitting Factory founder Michael Dorf) that's a combination wine bar, music venue and working winery, all rolled up into one "highly recommended" package; fans tout its "diverse", "baby-boomer's-dream" talent roster, and add that even though the place can be "overwhelming", it's a "young vintage that promises to mature wonderfully."

Cleopatra's Needle

19	14	17	E

W 90s | 2485 Broadway (bet. 92nd & 93rd Sts.) | 1/2/3 to 96th St. | 212-769-6969 | www.cleopatrasneedleny.com

"Spontaneous entertainment" erupts on the UWS at this "straight-ahead" venue that presents live jazz for "no cover" every night of the week; a few needle the "lax" service and "noisy" acoustics, but most of its "older" following report coming away "satisfied."

	APPEAL	DECOR	SERVICE	COST

Clover Club

25 | 23 | 23 | E

Cobble Hill | 210 Smith St. (bet. Baltic & Butler Sts.) | Brooklyn | F/G to Bergen St. | 718-855-7939 | www.cloverclubny.com

"Equal parts bar and time machine", this "swanky" Cobble Hill "classic" from über-mixologist Julie Reiner dials drinkers back to the age of "Gatsby" with "carefully crafted" cocktails served in "serene", "bespoke" digs; the need for "wads o' cash" when the check arrives may "seem more fitting in Manhattan", but ultimately this "adult" place fits right in on "gentrified Smith Street."

Club Macanudo

24 | 25 | 22 | VE

E 60s | 26 E. 63rd St. (bet. Madison & Park Aves.) | 4/5/6/F/N/R/Q to 59th St./Lexington Ave. | 212-752-8200 | www.clubmacanudo.com

"Well-heeled gents" toss back drinks and indulge in the "pleasures of tobacco" at this "upscale" UES cigar bar, "one of the few places left" where you can legally smoke indoors; be prepared for an older, "manly"-men crowd and very "pricey" tipples, though younger sorts wish they'd "lighten up with the dress code" already.

NEW Coal Yard

- | - | - | I

E Village | 102 First Ave. (bet. 6th & 7th Sts.) | 6 to Astor Pl. | 212-677-4595 | www.coalyardbar.com

The East Village spot once home to squeaky clean Lilly Coogan's has dropped the Irish pub trappings and been reinvented as a dark, down-to-earth joint (no surprise, it comes from the owners of the divey International Bar); an attitude-free vibe and cheap pops keep its local crowd content.

Cock, The ⌀

17 | 7 | 13 | M

E Village | 29 Second Ave. (bet. 1st & 2nd Sts.) | F to Lower East Side/2nd Ave. | no phone

"Unspeakably horny" dudes creep into this "dank" East Village gay roost for "sure hookups" with like-minded "meat-market" shoppers; greenhorns gasp it's "not for the faint of heart", but old-timers report its "appeal lies more in the memories" of its earlier, raunchier Avenue A incarnation.

Coliseum Bar

15 | 12 | 21 | M

W 50s | 312 W. 58th St. (bet. 8th & 9th Aves.) | 1/A/B/C/D to 59th St./Columbus Circle | 212-977-3523 | www.thecoliseumpub.com

With few convenient options at their disposal, "Fordham students" and "CNN staffers" favor this Irish pub off Columbus Circle for its "laid-back" vibe and "friendly" barkeeps; like the former convention center that it's named after, it's both spacious and "standard."

Columbus 72

17 | 17 | 16 | E

W 70s | 246A Columbus Ave. (bet. 71st & 72nd Sts.) | 1 to 79th St. | 212-769-1492 | www.columbus72.com

"Shake your booty without schlepping downtown" at this "spacious" Upper West Side club featuring two dance floors, two lounges and "all kinds of music" to groove to, but opinion splits on the net result: supporters say it's "great for serious dancers", but opponents shrug as "average as they come."

	APPEAL	DECOR	SERVICE	COST

Comedy Cellar
22 11 16 E

G Village | 117 MacDougal St., downstairs (bet. Bleecker & W. 3rd Sts.) | A/B/C/D/E/F/M to W. 4th St. | 212-254-3480 | www.comedycellar.com

It's funny, you'd think being "packed" into a "dingy basement" is an awful idea for a "hysterical night out", yet this "brick-wall Village comedy club" is *the* place to go" to catch "famous" comics "trying out new material" and "making fun of your date"; tipsters note that "midweek is your best chance to see the brand names" perform.

Comic Strip
20 13 15 E

E 80s | 1568 Second Ave. (bet. 81st & 82nd Sts.) | 6 to 77th St. | 212-861-9386 | www.comicstriplive.com

"On a good night", it's "LOL" all the way at this UES comedy club that showcases performances from legends like "Eddie Murphy"; but critics say the "claustrophobic need not apply", citing a setting so "tightly packed" that "your neighbor's drink could spill into your own."

Common Ground
18 17 18 M

E Village | 206 Ave. A (bet. 12th & 13th Sts.) | L to 1st Ave. | 212-228-6231 | www.commongroundnyc.com

A "breath of fresh air" in the otherwise "über-cool" East Village, this "local" barroom offers "board games galore" in a "low-key" setting with a "library-ish feel"; although critics find "nothing special" going on, at least there are "no hassles to get in."

Commonwealth
20 16 20 M

Park Slope | 497 Fifth Ave. (12th St.) | Brooklyn | D/F/G/N/R to 4th Ave./9th St. | 718-768-2040 | www.commonwealthbar.com

"True Park Slope neighborhood bar" where a "smart local crowd" digs its "laid-back" vibe; it earns bonus points for its "awesome" indie-rock jukebox, "ample" patio and "brutally honest personal ads on the wall."

Connolly's Pub
17 15 19 M

E 40s | 14 E. 47th St. (bet. 5th & Madison Aves.) | E/M to 5th Ave./53rd St. | 212-867-3767

E 40s | 150 E. 47th St. (bet. Lexington & 3rd Aves.) | 6 to 51st St. | 212-692-9342

W 40s | 121 W. 45th St. (bet. B'way & 6th Ave.) | 1/2/3/7/N/Q/R/S to 42nd St./Times Sq. | 212-597-5126

W 50s | 43 W. 54th St. (bet. 5th & 6th Aves.) | E/M to 5th Ave./53rd St. | 212-489-0271

www.connollyspubandrestaurant.com

"Convenience" is the calling card of this Midtown quartet of "textbook" Irish pubs whose "borderline Bennigan's" style is forgiven in light of "dependable" service and easy access to "commuter" hubs; "if you wear a suit and need a drink", you'll fit in with its "standard after-work crowd."

Continental ⇗
17 8 14 I

E Village | 25 Third Ave. (bet. 9th St. & St. Marks Pl.) | 6 to Astor Pl. | 212-529-6924 | www.continentalnyc.com

Getting "sloppy drunk" for "cheap" has never been easier than at this "seedy" East Village booze bin renowned for its brain cell–busting "five-shots-for-$10" deal; it "doesn't draw a classy crowd" and its "historic" days as a "rock 'n' roll temple" are long gone, yet fans of "skank" still think it's "fabulous."

	APPEAL	DECOR	SERVICE	COST

NEW Copia

- | - | - | M

E 50s | 307 E. 53rd St. (bet. 1st & 2nd Aves.) | 6/E to 51st-53rd Sts./ Lexington Ave. | 212-838-0007 | www.copianyc.com

Midtown after-work magnet Metro 53 has morphed into this new bar/ eatery that's retained its predecessor's main asset, a great big wide-open layout; look for corporate types early on, yielding to a more party-hearty scene as the night wears on.

Cornerstone Tavern

19 | 17 | 21 | M

E 50s | 961 Second Ave. (51st St.) | 6 to 51st St. | 212-888-7403 | www.cornerstonetavern.com

"Typical"-for-the-genre East Midtown sports bar featuring the usual flat-screens and tap brews, jazzed up with a split-level layout and an unusually long happy hour (starting at 11 AM); it's "always busy", but there's an inner passageway leading to its more sedate next-door sibling, the Stag's Head.

Counting Room

- | - | - | E

Williamsburg | 44 Berry St. (N. 11th St.) | Brooklyn | G to Nassau Ave. | 718-599-1860 | www.thecountingroombk.com

Sprawling Williamsburg duplex with a split personality: upstairs, it's a wine-and-tapas dispenser, below, a fancy-schmancy cocktail lounge, but either way it's pretty pricey; refashioned from a former quinine factory, the à la mode design mixes distressed concrete and reclaimed wood with weathered brick and Edison light bulbs.

Coyote Ugly

15 | 12 | 14 | M

E Village | 153 First Ave. (9th St.) | L to 1st Ave. | 212-477-4431 | www.coyoteuglysaloon.com

Sassy barmaids in "half shirts" and "short shorts" "dance on the bar" and do "belly shots" at this "tacky" East Village "dump" that's become a "tourist beacon" thanks to its infamous "movie namesake"; but since it's "nothing like" the flick, most yawn the "novelty wears off" quickly.

Crash Mansion

15 | 14 | 13 | M

LES | 199 Bowery (Spring St.) | J/Z to Bowery | 212-982-0740 | www.crashmansion.com

Like many of the onstage "garage bands" hoping "to be discovered", this "underground cave" on the Bowery supplies "decent" amusement but is "nothing stellar" overall; despite "clueless" service and a "spotty drink selection", at least there's "plenty of room" to spread out here.

Creek and the Cave

- | - | - | M

LIC | 10-93 Jackson Ave. (bet. 11th St. & 49th Ave.) | Queens | 7 to Vernon Blvd./Jackson Ave. | 718-706-8783 | www.creeklic.com

Comedy shows, live music, movie screenings and even "Wii meet-ups" are on the docket at this "casual" LIC event specialist near PS 1; other notable features include an outdoor patio and well-priced Mexican munchies for the "starving artists" in the crowd.

Crocodile Lounge

19 | 11 | 17 | M

E Village | 325 E. 14th St. (bet. 1st & 2nd Aves.) | L to 1st Ave. | 212-477-7747

The "perfect recession bar" due to its "buy-a-drink-get-a-free-pizza" gimmick, this "laid-back" East Village dive is targeted to folks on a "strict budget"; Skee-Ball and a photo booth "add to the appeal", though some say those "low ceilings" make the digs feel like a "dungeon."

Crosby Bar   24 | 26 | 20 | VE

SoHo | Crosby Street Hotel | 79 Crosby St. (bet. Prince & Spring Sts.) | 6 to Spring St. | 212-226-6400 | www.crosbystreethotel.com

An import from Britain's Firmdale group, this SoHo boutique hotel is home to this "upscale" barroom, a high-ceilinged, forest-green affair most notable for its "witty" collection of modern art; the fashionably low-key mood is only jolted by the jaw-dropping cocktail prices, but otherwise it's a "perfect fit" for the neighborhood.

Croton Reservoir Tavern   17 | 16 | 17 | M

W 40s | 108 W. 40th St. (bet. B'way & 6th Ave.) | 1/2/3/7/N/Q/R/S to 42nd St./Times Sq. | 212-997-6835 | www.crotonnyc.com

"Named after the former reservoir" that's now Bryant Park, this "reliable" if "generic" Midtown duplex has two bars, so there's plenty of room for the "after-work" masses; convenience to both Grand Central and Port Authority keeps it "loud" at rush hour.

Croxley Ales   19 | 14 | 18 | M

E Village | 28 Ave. B (bet. 2nd & 3rd Sts.) | F to Lower East Side/2nd Ave. | 212-253-6140 | www.croxley.com

A "solid selection" of brews, "great wing specials" and multiple flat-screens keep jocks jumpin' at this Alphabet City suds specialist; drawing both the "scruffy" and the "fratty", it gets "cramped" on "NFL Sundays", though spoilsports say it's "not the same since the garden closed."

Cubby Hole ⌀   19 | 17 | 17 | M

W Village | 281 W. 12th St. (W. 4th St.) | A/C/E/L to 14th St./8th Ave. | 212-243-9041 | www.cubbyholebar.com

Luring both the "stylish" and the "flannel"-clad, this Village lesbian lair exudes a "down-to-earth" air, partly because of the "kitschy" memorabilia dangling from its ceiling; still, the "colossal crowds" jamming in on weekends feel this "aptly named" joint is way "too small."

🆕 Culturefix   - | - | - | M

LES | 9 Clinton St. (bet. Houston & Stanton Sts.) | F/J/M/Z to Delancey/Essex Sts. | 646-863-7171 | www.culturefixny.com

A bar, art gallery and performance space combine at this new LES multitasker that's atmospherically gritty in the upfront barroom and a bit more refined in the back gallery space; wine, beer and Basque nibbles slake appetites, backed up by an ever-changing events roster.

Daddy-O   21 | 15 | 22 | M

W Village | 44 Bedford St. (Leroy St.) | 1 to Houston St. | 212-414-8884

"Pocket-size but rarely overcrowded", this "old-school" haunt housed on a "quiet" West Village corner offers a well-curated brew list ferried by a "super-friendly" crew; the scene is typically "low-key", except when it yields to "Pittsburgh Steelers fans" who "rule the roost on NFL Sundays."

Daddy's   - | - | - | M

Williamsburg | 437 Graham Ave. (bet. Frost & Richardson Sts.) | Brooklyn | L to Graham Ave. | 718-609-6388

For "cheap" pops off Williamsburg's beaten path, this "average" "neighborhood" hang is known for its house specialty drink, the

Margaveza, whipped up behind a horseshoe-shaped bar; it also offers an "excellent juke", makeshift outdoor patio and, for hungry hipsters, tofu hot dogs.

Danny and Eddie's

| - | - | - | M |

E 80s | 1643 First Ave. (bet. 85th & 86th Sts.) | 4/5/6 to 86th St. | 212-396-2090 | www.dannyandeddies.com

Yorkville's lean nightlife pickings include this straightforward tavern where fairly priced drinking occurs amid pool, darts and karaoke; an outdoor patio that's "awesome in warm weather" is its ace in the hole.

Dark Room

| ▽ 15 | 13 | 14 | M |

LES | 165 Ludlow St., downstairs (bet. Houston & Stanton Sts.) | F to Lower East Side/2nd Ave. | 212-353-0536

The "light levels match the name" of this "ridiculously dark" LES basement "dive" where most "can't comment on the decor" because they "can't see it"; it's "usually packed" with "free-spirited" folk "talking up strangers" – and "feeling like giants" given the "low ceilings."

Dave & Buster's

| 17 | 14 | 13 | M |

W 40s | 234 W. 42nd St., 3rd fl. (bet. 7th & 8th Aves.) | A/C/E to 42nd St./Port Authority | 646-495-2015 | www.daveandbusters.com

Adults "can be kids" again at this "upbeat" playland in the "middle of Times Square", a "guilty pleasure" where those who "don't want to grow up" "blow off steam" via cocktails and arcade games; but party-poopers say this "dose of strip-mall culture" draws "droves of tourists" and is priced accordingly.

David Copperfield's

| 20 | 16 | 19 | M |

E 70s | 1394 York Ave. (74th St.) | 6 to 77th St. | 212-734-6152 | www.davidcopperfields.com

Even if the excitement level "tends to stay low" at this "neighborhood" Yorkville pub, its "stellar" craft suds selection is "extensive" enough to entice "beer snobs" from all over town; regulars say the "friendly" barkeeps really "know how to pour" one here.

⚡ D.B.A.

| 22 | 15 | 18 | M |

E Village | 41 First Ave. (bet. 2nd & 3rd Sts.) | F to Lower East Side/2nd Ave. | 212-475-5097

⚡ D.B.A. Brooklyn

Williamsburg | 113 N. Seventh St. (bet. Berry St. & Wythe Ave.) | Brooklyn | L to Bedford Ave. | 718-218-6006 www.drinkgoodstuff.com

Both "the connoisseur and the casual drinker" are drawn to this "homey" twosome known for their "Darn Big Assortment" of "smartly curated" hooch ranging from beer to bourbon and beyond; though the decor is strictly "bare-bones", the "eclectic crowd" is too busy "discussing the world's problems" to notice.

NEW Dbar

| - | - | - | M |

Chelsea | 263 W. 19th St. (bet. 7th & 8th Aves.) | 1 to 18th St. | 212-493-5150

Restaurateuse Donatella Arpaia's first barroom, this Chelsea newcomer has a long, narrow layout, dim lighting and serious mixology going on behind the bar; a rear door connects the saloon to her eponymous new pizzeria, and the entire menu is available in both establishments.

	APPEAL	DECOR	SERVICE	COST

Dead Poet
20 | **16** | **20** | **M**

W 80s | 450 Amsterdam Ave. (bet. 81st & 82nd Sts.) | B/C to 81st St. | 212-595-5670 | www.thedeadpoet.com

A "small bar with a big fan club", this "narrow" literary-themed Irish pub on the Upper West Side is staffed by a "nice" crew that whips up cocktails named after dead poets; "free popcorn" causes some to re-Joyce.

⊠ Death & Co
26 | **24** | **23** | **E**

E Village | 433 E. Sixth St. (bet. Ave. A & 1st Ave.) | 6 to Astor Pl. | 212-388-0882 | www.deathandcompany.com

"Expertly crafted", "out-of-this-universe" cocktails are concocted at this "moody" East Village vault where "bow-tied, suspendered" bartenders reenact the "speakeasy" era in a "Goth"-tinged setting; a no-standing policy makes "waiting in line" part of the package, and "mind-blowing" prices also come with the territory.

Decibel
24 | **16** | **19** | **E**

E Village | 240 E. Ninth St., downstairs (bet. 2nd & 3rd Aves.) | 6 to Astor Pl. | 212-979-2733 | www.sakebardecibel.com

"Charmingly run-down" East Village sake/soju den that delights rice wine aficionados with an "impressive list" of varietals paired with "interesting" snacks; set in a "cool underground" space with enough graffiti on the walls to suggest a "Tokyo dive bar", it draws an "eclectic" mix of "hipsters" and Japanese expats.

Delancey, The
19 | **19** | **17** | **M**

LES | 168 Delancey St. (bet. Attorney & Clinton Sts.) | F/J/M/Z to Delancey/Essex Sts. | 212-254-9920 | www.thedelancey.com

Like "three different bars in one", this LES triplex includes a "classy" ground-floor lounge, an "awesome", "canopied" roof deck and a "divey" basement performance space; parked opposite the Williamsburg Bridge off-ramp, it's "not the most convenient spot" around, so when the "cooler-than-thou" crowd shows up on weekends, they stay awhile.

Delia's Lounge
24 | **22** | **22** | **E**

Bay Ridge | 9224 Third Ave. (93rd St.) | Brooklyn | R to 95th St. | 718-745-7999 | www.deliaslounge.com

For a candlelit "touch of Manhattan" minus the train ride, Bay Ridge locals sink into comfy couches and sip "tasty" martinis at this "friendly" "neighborhood" lounge; "romantic" touches like "chocolate-dipped strawberries" make this one very "nice" for a date.

ᴺᴱᵂ Delta House
- | **-** | **-** | **I**

E 80s | 1683 First Ave. (87th St.) | 4/5/6 to 86th St. | 212-860-4020 | www.deltahousenyc.com

The former Aces & Eights has (lightly) morphed into this UES frat bar where recent grads reenact their college days in a sprawling, sticky setting; tube sports, beer pong and Jell-O shots make for a sloppy, no-surprises scene.

Der Schwarze Kölner ⊘
- | **-** | **-** | **M**

Fort Greene | 710 Fulton St. (S. Oxford St.) | Brooklyn | 2/3/4/5/B/D/N/Q/R to Atlantic Ave. | 347-841-4495 | www.ex49.com

This Fort Greene beer garden vends an affordable flow of German brews that can be gulped in its roomy if "loud" black-and-white tiled interior or its leafy outdoor garden; theme-appropriate noshes (like pretzels and wursts) help soak up the suds.

Desnuda
∇ 21 | 23 | 23 | E

E Village | 122 E. Seventh St. (bet. Ave. A & 1st Ave.) | 6 to Astor Pl. | 212-254-3515 | www.desnudany.com

Wines from South America are well represented – and fittingly matched with creative ceviche – at this "cute" but "tiny" vino venue from the Bourgeois Pig team; despite upmarket pricing, the decor is artfully stripped down in keeping with the name, which translates as 'naked.'

Destination
- | - | - | M

E Village | 211 Ave. A (13th St.) | L to 1st Ave. | 212-388-9844 | www.destinationbarnyc.com

The name may be wishful thinking, but this travel-themed East Villager strives to live up to it with a classy reworking of the former Boysroom digs, incorporating damask wallpaper, a curvy bartop and French doors that open up to the street; still, they haven't lost sight of their client base: both fancy cocktails and Jell-O shots are available.

Dewey's Flatiron
14 | 14 | 16 | M

Flatiron | 210 Fifth Ave. (bet. 25th & 26th Sts.) | N/R to 23rd St. | 212-696-2337 | www.deweysflatiron.com

Flatiron pub-zilla that peaks after work when "nearby workers" jostle for space during happy hour; though flat-screens galore encourage longer-term occupation, most report there's "nothing memorable about it."

Diamond, The
- | - | - | M

Greenpoint | 43 Franklin St. (bet. Calyer & Quay Sts.) | Brooklyn | G to Greenpoint Ave. | 718-383-5030 | www.thediamondbrooklyn.com

Frisky competition around the shuffleboard table and backyard quoits (a bar-safe version of horseshoes) lends some sparkle to this "chill" Greenpoint spot; a lengthy beer list spelled out on two chalkboards and a small selection of wines and cheeses served by personable bartenders help compensate for its "out-of-the-way" location.

Ding Dong Lounge
18 | 13 | 17 | I

W 100s | 929 Columbus Ave. (bet. 105th & 106th Sts.) | 1 to 103rd St. | 212-663-2600 | www.dingdonglounge.com

"Punk is alive and well" at this "grungy" den in Morningside Heights that's "dimly lit for a reason"; "stiff, straightforward" drinks and "cool bathroom artwork" make up for the "odd location" and "wack" patrons.

'Disiac
23 | 21 | 21 | M

W 50s | 402 W. 54th St. (bet. 9th & 10th Aves.) | C/E to 50th St. | 212-586-9880 | www.disiacloungenyc.com

"Getting in the mood" is a snap at this mod nod to Morocco, a "tiny" Hell's Kitchen "oasis" with a sweet little back patio and "friendly" staffers vending "well-made, worth-the-price" nips; regulars regret that it's not as "undiscovered" as it used to be.

NEW District 36
- | - | - | E

Garment District | 29 W. 36th St. (bet. 5th & 6th Aves.) | B/D/F/M/N/Q/R to 34th St./Herald Sq. | 212-244-3636 | www.d36nyc.com

NYC's sluggish dance club scene gets a boost via this airy new triplex, spinning house and techno in a former Garment District warehouse; a killer sound system and 14,800 sq. ft. to thrash around in separates it from the pack.

Dive Bar

`18` `13` `18` `M`

W 90s | 732 Amsterdam Ave. (bet. 95th & 96th Sts.) | 1/2/3 to 96th St. | 212-749-4358 | www.divebarnyc.com

"Congenial" UWS watering hole that can get "seriously crowded" with "locals and Columbia students"; despite having one of the "worst names" in town, it's "better than it looks from the outside" and "good for a last drink" before going home or a first drink on the way out.

Dive 75

`19` `13` `19` `M`

W 70s | 101 W. 75th St. (bet. Amsterdam & Columbus Aves.) | 1/2/3 to 72nd St. | 212-362-7518 | www.divebarnyc.com

"Perks" are plentiful at this "laid-back", "not-so-divey" UWS venue, ranging from "tons of board games" to "free candy" and even a "big fish tank"; what's more, drinking's no trivial pursuit here, thanks to an "impressive selection" of beer and whiskey.

ⓩ Dizzy's Club Coca-Cola

`27` `26` `23` `VE`

W 60s | Time Warner Ctr. | 10 Columbus Circle, 5th fl. (60th St.) | 1/A/B/C/D to 59th St./Columbus Circle | 212-258-9595 | www.jalc.org

"Named for Dizzy Gillespie", this "Cadillac of jazz clubs" in the Time Warner Center "lives up to his standards" with "soulful" performers, "flawless acoustics" and the clincher, an "exceptional view" of Columbus Circle and Central Park; fans say there's "not a bad seat in the house" – nor a cheap one, except during select late-night sets.

Doc Holliday's

`18` `13` `16` `I`

E Village | 141 Ave. A (9th St.) | L to 1st Ave. | 212-979-0312

"Texas" turns up in the East Village at this "grungy" roadhouse with "cheap" pops, a squawkin' country juke and "outgoing biker chicks" behind the bar who are "quick with a beer and quicker with a jibe"; even though Alphabet City may be "gentrifying", "no one told this place."

Doc Watson's

`17` `13` `19` `M`

E 70s | 1490 Second Ave. (bet. 77th & 78th Sts.) | 6 to 77th St. | 212-988-5300 | www.docwatsons.com

This "unpretentious" UES pub "catering to the neighborhood" is commended as a good "standby" in a "sea of heartless area alternatives"; "friendly" staffers, "live" traditional Irish music and "yummy grub" lend some elementary appeal.

D.O.C. Wine Bar

`24` `22` `21` `E`

Williamsburg | 83 N. Seventh St. (Wythe Ave.) | Brooklyn | L to Bedford Ave. | 718-963-1925 | www.docwinebar.com

"As if you took the subway to Italy", this "mom-and-pop" Williamsburg enoteca is a "homey" hangout where "informed servers" pour "excellent" Italian vintages paired with "tasty" antipasti; as a bonus, the "small outdoor seating area" is "especially nice in warm weather."

Donnybrook

`-` `-` `-` `M`

LES | 35 Clinton St. (Stanton St.) | F/J/M/Z to Delancey/Essex Sts. | 212-228-7733 | www.donnybrooknyc.com

Exposed-brick walls, barn-wood tables and a long marble bartop take this "friendly" LES pub into vintage territory, positioning it as a toned-down "neighborhood standby" in an increasingly juiced-up area; a mini-menu of Irish-focused grub was recently added to the mix.

Don't Tell Mama

| 20 | 13 | 19 | E |

W 40s | 343 W. 46th St. (bet. 8th & 9th Aves.) | A/C/E to 42nd St./ Port Authority | 212-757-0788 | www.donttellmamanyc.com

Cabaret/piano bar/sing-along joint on Restaurant Row that will put you in a "NY state of mind" when its "flamboyant" performers and "talented" staffers grab the mike and belt out vintage "show tunes"; it's ever a "good old standby", especially when you have to "support a friend's delusional dream of singing on Broadway."

Dorrian's Red Hand

| 17 | 12 | 16 | M |

E 80s | 1616 Second Ave. (84th St.) | 4/5/6 to 86th St. | 212-772-6660 | www.dorrians.com

"Around since your parents were your age", this "infamous" UES bar with a "checkered history" draws "privileged Ivy Leaguers" and *Gossip Girl* wannabes" who feel like they've "died and gone to Ralph Lauren heaven"; it's "perfectly acceptable to show up here in a tux after a benefit", but to really fit in, make sure to "have at least one trust fund."

Double Down Saloon

| - | - | - | M |

E Village | 14 Ave. A (bet. Houston & 2nd Sts.) | F to Lower East Side/ 2nd Ave. | 212-982-0543 | www.doubledownsaloon.com

Las Vegas' underbelly rears its head at this East Village spin-off, a graffiti-tagged "punk bar" where low-rollers order bacon martinis and try to avoid using the "disgusting bathrooms"; "porn playing on the TV" adds a final "dirty" touch.

Double Windsor ⊄

| - | - | - | M |

Park Slope | 210 Prospect Pk. W. (16th St.) | Brooklyn | F to 15th St./ Prospect Park | 347-725-3479

This laid-back spot courtesy of the Cake Shop team sits on a hangout-deprived patch of Park Slope "right off Prospect Park" and lures locals into its horseshoe-shaped bar with a welcoming, window-wrapped setting; an "interesting" selection of microbrews, cocktails and snacks keeps them there.

Dove, The

| 21 | 23 | 19 | M |

G Village | 228 Thompson St., downstairs (bet. Bleecker & W. 3rd Sts.) | A/B/C/D/E/F/M to W. 4th St. | 212-254-1435 | www.thedoveparlour.com

Providing some "needed class to the NYU scene" in the Village, this "sophisticated" underground lounge is done up in "Victorian" parlor-style with "damask wallpaper", "comfortable couches" and "creative drinks" served on doilies; it's a "welcome respite" from rowdy Bleecker Street that "transports you to another era."

Down the Hatch

| 16 | 12 | 16 | M |

W Village | 179 W. Fourth St., downstairs (bet. 6th Ave. & 7th Ave. S.) | A/B/C/D/E/F/M to W. 4th St. | 212-627-9747 | www.nycbestbars.com

It "feels like college never ended" at this "nonstop" West Village "party" where frat boys get "blind drunk" and sorority girls "prepare for the walk of shame" the following morning; sure, it's "dank" and "cramped" with "blasting music" and a "loud crowd", but word is "if you can't have fun here, you can't have fun anywhere."

NEW Draft, The

– | – | – | M

LES | 157 Ludlow St. (bet. Rivington & Stanton Sts.) | F/J/M/Z to Delancey/Essex Sts. | 212-777-7708 | www.thedraftbarnyc.com

Set in the former Blue Seats digs, this new Lower Eastsider retains its sports bar roots, but is now more populist than its swanky predecessor, having removed the semi-private booths (but it still retains the fancy rear screening room); the result is roomier and less pretentious, boasting a sea of widescreens along with the usual suds and noshes.

Draft Barn

– | – | – | M

Gowanus | 530 Third Ave. (bet. 12th & 13th Sts.) | Brooklyn | D/F/G/N/R to 4th Ave./9th St. | 718-768-0515
Gravesend | 317 Ave. X (W. 1st St.) | Brooklyn | F to Ave. X | 718-285-2356
www.draftbarnny.com

That "obscure" brew you've "always wanted to try" but couldn't find is probably among the 200-plus varieties on hand at these "cavernous" Brooklyn beer stables; in keeping with the beer list's Eastern European slant, there's "greasy" grub available to soak up the suds.

Dram

– | – | – | M

Williamsburg | 177 S. Fourth St. (bet. Driggs Ave. & Roebling St.) | Brooklyn | J/M/Z to Marcy Ave. | 718-486-3726 | www.drambar.com

Williamsburg's former Chickenbone Cafe is now a bar with a speakeasy feel thanks to dim lighting and warm wood (even on the ceiling); a short, snappy cocktail list and a rotating beer-and-wine menu is complemented by such esoteric items as housemade ginger beer and Mexican Coca-Cola.

Dram Shop

18 | 14 | 18 | M

Park Slope | 339 Ninth St. (bet. 5th & 6th Aves.) | Brooklyn | D/F/G/N/R to 4th Ave./9th St. | 718-788-1444 | www.dramshopbrooklyn.com

A kinda-sorta "sports bar" where the "crowd leaves its testosterone at home", this "grown-up" Park Slope playroom offers darts, billiards, shuffleboard and board games as well as action on the tube; for sedentary sorts, "comfy banquettes" make swell staging grounds for sampling the "great tap selection."

Drop Off Service

21 | 14 | 20 | M

E Village | 211 Ave. A (bet. 13th & 14th Sts.) | L to 1st Ave. | 212-260-2914

In an area awash with rowdy watering holes, this East Village former Laundromat turned "upscale dive" offers a "mellow", "dog-friendly" vibe matched by an "excellent" suds selection dispensed by "nice folks"; "unbeatable happy-hour deals" are another reason to "include it in your next bar crawl."

Druids

21 | 17 | 21 | M

W 50s | 736 10th Ave. (bet. 50th & 51st Sts.) | C/E to 50th St. | 212-307-6410

A "wonderful back garden" made for drinking "under the stars" is the secret weapon of this "otherwise run-of-the-mill" Irish pub in Way West Hell's Kitchen; crime buffs cite "Westies lore" as an additional hook, given its '70s rep as a gang hangout back in the day when it was called Sunbrite Bar.

| | APPEAL | DECOR | SERVICE | COST |

Drunken Horse
— | — | — | M

Chelsea | 225 10th Ave. (bet. 23rd & 24th Sts.) | C/E to 23rd St. | 212-604-0505 | www.drunkenhorse.net

Chelsea wine bar from a Turks & Frogs alum that trots out a list of Euro-centric vinos and small plates; the modest, wood and brick-lined setting emits a rustic glow, while the subdued atmosphere is a sharp contrast to the hectic goings-on at its next-door neighbor, the Red Cat.

Dublin House
17 | 10 | 19 | M

W 70s | 225 W. 79th St. (bet. Amsterdam Ave. & B'way) | 1 to 79th St. | 212-874-9528 | www.dublinhousenyc.com

Take a cue from the "linoleum and tacky wood paneling" – this circa-1933 UWS Irish pub is a "real-deal" joint catering to "old-school" sorts that's as far "away from hip" as you get; a "dump in the best sense of the word", it also sports one of the coolest neon signs in town.

Dublin 6
21 | 18 | 21 | M

W Village | 575 Hudson St. (bet. Bank & W. 11th Sts.) | A/C/E/L to 14th St./8th Ave. | 646-638-2900 | www.dublin6nyc.com

A wee bit "nicer" than the average Irish pub, this "homey" Villager attracts a "diverse crowd" ("it's nice to interact with people over 25!") that digs its "down-to-earth" hospitality and "reasonable" tabs; in the summer, fans catch some fresh Eire on the "great outdoor" sidewalk seats.

Duff's
— | — | — | I

Williamsburg | 168 Marcy Ave. (bet. Broadway & S. 5th St.) | Brooklyn | J/M/Z to Marcy Ave. | 718-599-2092 | www.duffsbrooklyn.com

It's not a bar, "it's a lifestyle" say fans of this hard-core salute to "heavy metal" now in South Williamsburg; owned by the "legendary Jimmy Duff" (of Bellevue Bar fame), it's known for its horror/biker memorabilia, "one-of-a-kind jukebox" and "excellent" staff.

Duplex, The
20 | 14 | 19 | M

W Village | 61 Christopher St. (7th Ave. S.) | 1 to Christopher St. | 212-255-5438 | www.theduplex.com

"Gay and straight alike" get liquored up and "sing along" with the "excellent pianists" at this longtime West Village piano bar-cum-cabaret; true, the "dilapidated" decor is "not much to speak of" (ditto the "touristy" crowd), but ultimately this one's an "only-in-NY" experience.

⌷ Dutch Kills
26 | 20 | 21 | E

LIC | 27-24 Jackson Ave. (Dutch Kills St.) | Queens | E/M/R to Queens Plaza | 718-383-2724 | www.dutchkillsbar.com

"Trendy" proof that Long Island City can do "more than the local-bar" thing, this "dark, moody" saloon from mixologist Sasha Petraske lures hip boozers with an "inventive" lineup of "really strong" cocktails served in high-ceilinged, "speakeasy"-ish digs lined with mahogany wainscoting; other "throwback" touches include "hand-chopped ice" and occasional live jazz.

Eagle, The ⌷
21 | 15 | 16 | M

Chelsea | 554 W. 28th St. (bet. 10th & 11th Aves.) | C/E to 23rd St. | 646-473-1866 | www.eaglenyc.com

If you like your men "furry and musky", "adjust your harness" and check out this "leather-oriented" West Chelsea gay bar that draws more daddies than twinks; inside, it's "purposely dim and dingy" but the "fantastic roof deck" works for fresh-air fetishism during Sunday's "very cruisy" beer blasts.

Eamonn's

17 | 15 | 19 | E

TriBeCa | 41 Murray St. (Church St.) | 1/2/3 to Chambers St. | 212-962-7300 | www.eamonns.com
Brooklyn Heights | 174 Montague St. (Clinton St.) | Brooklyn | 2/3/4/5/N/R to Borough Hall | 718-596-4969 | www.eamonns.net

"Standard" Irish pubs on opposite ends of the Brooklyn Bridge that are "conveniently located" if you're a "lawyer, judge, juror or bail bondsman"; since they "clear out" on the early side, the late-night scene is "not rollicking."

Ear Inn

23 | 15 | 19 | M

Hudson Square | 326 Spring St. (bet. Greenwich & Washington Sts.) | 1 to Houston St. | 212-226-9060 | www.earinn.com

"One of NY's oldest bars", this Hudson Square "classic" erected in 1817 has "lots of history behind it", but today it's a charmingly "shabby" joint furnished with a mix of "antiques and found objects"; frequented by everyone from "bikers to bohemians", it's a "place for a PBR, not a Pinot Noir" (though it does sell wine), and has been around so long "because it knows how to make people happy."

East End Tavern

▽ 17 | 15 | 18 | M

E 80s | 1589 First Ave. (bet. 82nd & 83rd Sts.) | 4/5/6 to 86th St. | 212-249-5960 | www.eastendtavernnyc.com

It's a bit "out of the way" on First Avenue, so naturally this "decent neighborhood" sports bar is a "quiet place to grab a drink"; 12 tap brews, "happy-hour specials" and mini-TVs in each booth make "game days fun" here.

Easternbloc ⌀

18 | 17 | 17 | M

E Village | 505 E. Sixth St. (bet. Aves. A & B) | 6 to Astor Pl. | 212-777-2555 | www.easternblocnyc.com

There's plenty of "East Village energy" to be had at this "Soviet"-themed gay bar, populated by "skinny, unshaven" party members flaunting "anti-workout bodies"; some say it's "not particularly friendly", but admit it's usually "packed" thanks to the "cute bartenders", "good music" and "go-go boys in the middle of it all."

East Village Tavern

19 | 15 | 20 | M

E Village | 158 Ave. C (10th St.) | L to 1st Ave. | 212-253-8400 | www.evtnyc.com

A "knowledgeable staff" and "fantastic rotating beer selection" (including microbrews and hand-drawn cask ales) keep East Villagers pumped about this funky Avenue C tavern; but the "loud", "newly 21" crowd yelling "who dat?" can be admittedly "annoying."

EastVille Comedy Club

- | - | - | E

E Village | 85 E. Fourth St. (2nd Ave.) | F to Lower East Side/2nd Ave. | 212-260-2445 | www.eastvillecomedy.com

"Amateur comedians" – along with seasoned stand-ups like Damon Wayans, Sarah Silverman and Judah Friedlander – crack wise at this "divey" East Village laugheteria; the prices for the "limited drinks and food" on offer, however, are "no laughing matter."

	APPEAL	DECOR	SERVICE	COST

1849
17 | 15 | 15 | M

G Village | 183 Bleecker St. (bet. MacDougal & Sullivan Sts.) | A/B/C/D/E/F/M to W. 4th St. | 212-505-3200 | www.1849nyc.com

"Hokey" but "ever popular", this Gold Rush–themed Villager is where "NYU" goldbricks pitch camp to "watch sports" on rations of "laid-back beers" and "hot wings"; picky prospectors pan the "mediocre" milieu, but "reasonable" rates keep it boomtown "busy during term time."

8th St. Winecellar
23 | 20 | 22 | E

G Village | 28 W. Eighth St., downstairs (bet. 5th & 6th Aves.) | A/B/C/D/E/F/M to W. 4th St. | 212-260-9463 | www.8thstwinecellar.com

It's "easy to walk right by" this Village wine cellar hidden below Eighth Street's shopping strip, but it's a particularly "welcome respite" featuring a "varied", "well-priced" vino list poured by a "convivial" crew; "cozy" atmospherics and "delicious nibbles" make it an "excellent date spot."

11th St. Bar
20 | 16 | 20 | M

E Village | 510 E. 11th St. (bet. Aves. A & B) | L to 1st Ave. | 212-982-3929 | www.11thstbar.com

"Local" loyalists and "Liverpool supporters" make up the fan base of this "mellow" East Villager, an "exposed-brick" Irish pub home to occasional poetry showcases and "live music" in a Gaelic vein; tack on a "nice back room" and it's an "all-around comfortable hang."

Ella
20 | 22 | 19 | E

E Village | 9 Ave. A (bet. 1st & 2nd Sts.) | F to Lower East Side/2nd Ave. | 212-777-2230 | www.ellalounge.com

"Still a little under the radar", this "upscale" East Village duplex named after Ella Fitzgerald features "throwback"-to-the-'40s decor with its "stylish", Dorothy Draper–esque cocktail lounge and "retro" downstairs piano bar; a soundtrack ranging from live jazz to DJ-spun "old-school hip-hop" mixes well with its "inventive takes on classic cocktails."

El Morocco
20 | 19 | 17 | E

Harlem | 3534 Broadway (145th St.) | 1 to 145th St. | 212-939-0909 | www.elmorocconyc.com

"Spacious" Harlem nightclub, name-checking the legendary supper club of old, where a "zebra-meets-leopard"-meets-palm-trees design harkens "back to the '50s"; today, the music is "hard-core Latin", the preferred footwear "salsa shoes" and the time to arrive "after 1 AM."

Emmett O'Lunney's
21 | 19 | 23 | M

W 50s | 210 W. 50th St. (B'way) | 1 to 50th St. | 212-957-5100 | www.emmettolunneys.com

A "convenient" Theater District location draws a "mix of tourists and after-workers" to this double-decker Irish tavern where a "friendly" atmosphere and flat-screen sports add up to one heck of a "good time."

Empire Hotel Lobby Bar
22 | 22 | 19 | E

W 60s | Empire Hotel | 44 W. 63rd St. (bet. B'way & Columbus Ave.) | 1 to 66th St. | 212-265-7400 | www.empirehotelnyc.com

"Pricey but classy", this hotel lobby lounge near Lincoln Center is an "exercise in sophistication", with "genteel" barmen shaking cocktails in an "elegant", high-ceilinged setting done up in "chocolate and caramel" hues; decidedly more "quiet than the rooftop melee" 12 floors above, it's just the ticket for those in the mood for a "romantic" moment.

❷ Empire Hotel Rooftop

| 24 | 22 | 17 | E |

W 60s | Empire Hotel | 44 W. 63rd St., 12th fl. (bet. B'way & Columbus Ave.) | 1 to 66th St. | 212-956-3313 | www.empirehotelnyc.com

"Beneath that huge Hotel Empire sign" lies this "really cool" rooftop bar boasting "gorgeous" views of Lincoln Center and the "bright lights of Broadway"; a "retractable roof" makes it an "inside/outside" option year-round, but a recent appearance on *Gossip Girl* means you better "be ready to wait in line" to get in – and to "drop some serious coin" for the privilege.

Empire Room

| - | - | - | E |

Garment District | Empire State Bldg. | 350 Fifth Ave. (enter on 33rd St., bet. 5th & 6th Aves.) | 6 to 33rd St. | 212-643-5400 | www.hospitalityholdings.com

Easily the Garment District's swankiest option, this luxe bar/lounge on the ground floor of the Empire State Building comes from the owner of Campbell Apartment and Carnegie Club; the '70s deco decor includes a subtly swooping bar and plenty of cozy seating arrangements, the better to soothe you before the spendy check arrives. P.S. forget the official address – it's parked on 33rd between Fifth and Sixth.

❷ Employees Only

| 23 | 20 | 20 | E |

W Village | 510 Hudson St. (bet. Christopher & W. 10th Sts.) | 1 to Christopher St. | 212-242-3021 | www.employeesonlynyc.com

"Irreplaceable" West Village watering hole where the "hardest-working bartenders in NY" whip up "mean cocktails" in "mellow" digs exuding an "old-school" "'20s ambiance"; too bad the "masses have found out about it", "filling it to the brim" on weekends, so regulars sidestep the crowds by showing up "super-late."

Enid's

| ▽ 22 | 18 | 19 | I |

Greenpoint | 560 Manhattan Ave. (Driggs Ave.) | Brooklyn | L to Bedford Ave. | 718-349-3859 | www.enids.net

Greenpoint's "cool kids" dig this spacious barroom with "lots of seats", a "relaxed" mood and a menu of "delish comfort-food" items; regulars tout the Harrison, the "potent" signature cocktail that amps up the "loud and lively" weekend scene.

Entwine

| ▽ 23 | 24 | 22 | E |

W Village | 765 Washington St. (bet. Bethune & W. 12th Sts.) | A/C/ E/L to 14th St./8th Ave. | 212-727-8765 | www.entwinenyc.com

This West Village wine bar manages to cram a lot into its "little" duplex setting, i.e. a fireplace, two bars and a variety of "quaint" mismatched furniture, plus an "appealing" garden; while the vino and small-plates offerings don't deviate from the norm, the "charming", labor-of-love vibe separates this one from the pack.

Epistrophy ⊄

| ▽ 23 | 21 | 21 | M |

NoLita | 200 Mott St. (bet. Kenmare & Spring Sts.) | 6 to Spring St. | 212-966-0904 | www.epistrophycafe.com

Modeled after a Roman cafe, this "relaxed" NoLita wine bar draws a crowd of "newly arrived Europeans" with its rustic decor, international labels and "perfect music" (it's named for a Thelonious Monk modern jazz composition); fans say the transporting ambiance makes it easy to "forget where you are."

Epstein's Bar ⊭ | 16 | 11 | 18 | M |

LES | 82 Stanton St. (Allen St.) | F to Lower East Side/2nd Ave. | 212-477-2232 | www.epsteinsbarnyc.com

There's "no pretense" at this "loud" Lower Eastsider with an "ingenious" moniker (it's named in honor of Juan Epstein, a character on *Welcome Back, Kotter*); "cheap drinks" keep "locals" and "freshly minted undergrads" happy, though critics complain the place is "not sure what it is."

Escuelita | ∇ 21 | 14 | 18 | M |

Garment District | 301 W. 39th St., downstairs (bet. 8th & 9th Aves.) | A/C/E to 42nd St./Port Authority | 212-631-0588 | www.enyclub.com

"Get ready to salsa" at this skeevy gay Latino dance club hidden in a Garment District basement where a "diverse" crowd of "urban types", go-go boys and sassy drag queens collides; while the "drinks are standard" and the room's nothing to look at, the raunchy mood keeps it "crowded."

Europa | ∇ 19 | 17 | 21 | E |

Greenpoint | 98 Meserole Ave. (bet. Lorimer St. & Manhattan Ave.) | Brooklyn | G to Greenpoint Ave. | 718-383-2322 | www.europaclub.com

A plus-size Polish nightspot in Greenpoint that does double duty as a both a dance hall and a performance space showcasing everything from "punk to metal bands" and beyond; still, there's grumbling about the "crap sound system" and "overpriced drinks."

Excelsior ⊭ | ∇ 19 | 16 | 18 | M |

Park Slope | 390 Fifth Ave. (bet. 6th & 7th Sts.) | Brooklyn | D/F/G/N/R to 4th Ave./9th St. | 718-832-1599 | www.excelsiorbrooklyn.com

Park Slope's "only gay bar" is a "neighborhoody" thing with a "relaxed, noncruisy" air, "affable" service and a "nice outdoor patio"; alright, it doesn't attract a "Manhattan-class" crowd, but at least the local "Brooklyn boys have a place to go."

Exchange Bar & Grill | - | - | - | M |

Gramercy | 256 Third Ave. (21st St.) | 6 to 23rd St. | 646-596-9039 | www.exchangebarandgrill.com

Supply and demand is the gimmick at this stock market–themed Gramercy tavern where drink prices fluctuate on a scrolling digital ticker over the bar: the more popular the beverage, the higher the tab, while the cost of the same kind of tipples drops accordingly; otherwise, it's a standard-issue joint with flat-screens, mix-and-match decor and an aging frat-cat crowd.

Faces & Names | 18 | 17 | 19 | M |

W 50s | 159 W. 54th St. (bet. 6th & 7th Aves.) | C/E to 50th St. | 212-586-9311 | www.facesandnames.com

"Typical" Midtown saloon with a "loyal" following that resembles an "overcrowded kegger" after work but settles down into a "pleasant" enough "comfort zone" as the night wears on; though some yawn "average", it's convenient when you need a "quick drink before City Center."

Failte ▽ 17 | 13 | 16 | M

Murray Hill | 531 Second Ave. (bet. 29th & 30th Sts.) | 6 to 28th St. | 212-725-9440 | www.failtenyc.com
Indulge your inner Celt at this "cool Kips Bay pub" offering a variety of Irish whiskeys in a rustic, fireplace-equipped setting that's a halfway decent approximation of the Auld Sod; "not too packed, but not too empty", it's always "fun" with a group.

Fanelli's Cafe 20 | 16 | 17 | M

SoHo | 94 Prince St. (Mercer St.) | N/R to Prince St. | 212-226-9412
This "classic old SoHo" bar – "one of the oldest in town", dating back to 1847 – draws nostalgic types with its "old-school" looks, "awesomely cranky bartenders" and "good stiff drinks"; maybe there are "no surprises" in store, but it sure comes in handy "when your imagination is on strike."

Fashion 40 ▽ 18 | 15 | 15 | E

Garment District | 202 W. 40th St. (7th Ave.) | A/C/E to 42nd St./ Port Authority | 212-221-3628 | www.fashion40lounge.com
Locationwise it may be "lost among the fabric stores" on the fringes of the Garment District, but this upscale bar/lounge comes in handy for "cool" cocktails after work or on the way to Port Authority; modellike staffers and a slick-for-the-area setting make the "overpriced" drinks easier to swallow.

Fat Baby 17 | 15 | 15 | M

LES | 112 Rivington St. (bet. Essex & Ludlow Sts.) | F to Lower East Side/ 2nd Ave. | 212-533-1888 | www.fatbabynyc.com
"Hipsters" and music lovers turn up at this LES multitasker, furnished with a semi-swank upstairs bar (complete with a chandelier) backed up by a "hole-in-the-wall basement" where "live bands" perform; the "obnoxious bouncers" are a bummer, but overall it's generally "fun" for late-night "sloppiness."

Fat Black Pussycat 17 | 15 | 15 | M

G Village | 130 W. Third St. (bet. MacDougal St. & 6th Ave.) | A/B/C/D/ E/F/M to W. 4th St. | 212-533-4790 | www.thefatblackpussycat.com
"Something for everybody" could be the motto of this multilevel "NYU" magnet made up of a "pub-style" front bar, "sexy" side lounge and downstairs dance club (the Village Underground) where DJs alternate with live bands; some hiss about "stinky service" and a "young, loud, loser" crowd, but more purr it's a "good place to do bad things."

Fat Cat 21 | 13 | 16 | M

W Village | 75 Christopher St. (bet. Bleecker St. & 7th Ave. S.) | 1 to Christopher St. | 212-675-6056 | www.fatcatmusic.org
A "treasure trove of distractions" awaits at this West Village den of "nerdy fun", where the activities roster includes pool, shuffleboard, Ping-Pong, "every board game imaginable" and, oh yeah, "live jazz"; despite the "grungy" basement setting and the fact that it only serves beer and wine, it's "great entertainment for the ordinary man" – and for "people who can't dance."

	APPEAL	DECOR	SERVICE	COST

☑ Feinstein's at Loews Regency
26 | 25 | 24 | VE

E 60s | Loews Regency Hotel | 540 Park Ave. (61st St.) | 4/5/6/F/N/R/Q to 59th St./Lexington Ave. | 212-339-4095 | www.feinsteinsattheregency.com

They "know how to put on a show" at this "deluxe" Regency Hotel cabaret where co-owner/performer Michael Feinstein presents "outstanding crooners" in a "sophisticated" milieu; alright, the cover and minimums can be "brutal" (hence the predominantly "moneyed senior crowd"), but for "special occasions", it's "worth dressing up" and ponying up for.

Fiddlesticks
16 | 13 | 17 | M

W Village | 56 Greenwich Ave. (bet. 6th Ave. & 7th Ave. S.) | 1/2/F/L to 14th St./7th Ave. | 212-463-0516 | www.fiddlesticksnyc.com

Brace yourself for "post-college rewind" at this "popular" West Village Irish pub that may be "huge" but somehow "always gets packed" on the weekends; it skews toward "rowdy" – "lots of birthdays" are celebrated here – and certainly "smells like a bar", but most of the crowd is having too much "fun" to notice.

55 Bar ♉
25 | 15 | 21 | M

W Village | 55 Christopher St. (bet. 6th Ave. & 7th Ave. S.) | 1 to Christopher St. | 212-929-9883 | www.55bar.com

Get "maximum character" for "moderate" dough at this "classic" West Village "dive" (since 1919) that showcases live jazz and blues for a cut-rate cover; like its longtime patrons, the "cozy" underground space is "old and feels it", but it's "vital" to beboppers who brand it the "last of a breed."

Finnegans Wake
19 | 14 | 22 | M

E 70s | 1361 First Ave. (73rd St.) | 6 to 77th St. | 212-737-3664

Upper Eastsiders like the "cozy pub feel" of this long-standing Irish joint where "friendly service" and "surprisingly good food" keep the trade brisk; though usually "filled with old people", young people pop in occasionally since it's so "reasonably priced."

Finnerty's
∇ 20 | 18 | 23 | I

E Village | 221 Second Ave. (bet. 13th & 14th Sts.) | L to 1st Ave. | 212-677-2655 | www.finnertysnyc.com

"Standard" East Village Irish pub that got a new lease on life after a move from Third Avenue to bigger digs on Second; fans say "we need more cheap bars like this one", citing its variety of tap brews and allegiance to the San Francisco Giants.

Fitzgerald's Pub
– | – | – | M

Murray Hill | 336 Third Ave. (bet. 24th & 25th Sts.) | 6 to 23rd St. | 212-679-6931 | www.fitzgeraldspubnyc.net

There's "plenty of room to bring a party" to this family-owned Irish pub in Murray Hill featuring a bright blue facade without and stained-glass light fixtures within; "prompt" service pleases its "agreeable crowd", heavy with "Baruch College kids."

Flashdancers
21 | 16 | 17 | VE

W 50s | 1674 Broadway, downstairs (bet. 52nd & 53rd Sts.) | 1 to 50th St. | 212-315-5107 | www.flashdancersnyc.com

Midtown's "top spot for girls with no tops", this veteran stripteaser rolls out lots of "Eastern European" chicks who "look better from afar than close up"; foes report "overpriced" hooch and an overall "overdone" scene, but "action" lovers leer "they've been there forever" for a reason.

Flatiron Lounge

| 22 | 21 | 20 | E |

Flatiron | 37 W. 19th St. (bet. 5th & 6th Aves.) | 1 to 18th St. | 212-727-7741 | www.flatironlounge.com

"One of the first places to take cocktails seriously", this "classy" Flatiron watering hole serves "work-of-art" drinks concocted from "Prohibition-era" recipes in a "Jazz Age"–inspired setting; sure, the crowd's a bit "vanilla" and the pricing "expensive", but this "you-get-what-you-pay-for" joint is still an "ideal date spot."

Flight 151

| 16 | 15 | 17 | M |

Chelsea | 151 Eighth Ave. (bet. 17th & 18th Sts.) | A/C/E/L to 14th St./ 8th Ave. | 212-229-1868

Those who "love to fly" tout this "aviation-themed" Chelsea bar, a "no-frills" affair save for some random memorabilia and the famed "faux cockpit recordings in the bathrooms"; even though there's "nothing special" about it, "reasonable prices" and Tuesday flip nights ("flip a coin, call it right and your drink is free") make for a smooth flight.

Floyd, NY

| 20 | 16 | 17 | M |

Brooklyn Heights | 131 Atlantic Ave. (bet. Clinton & Henry Sts.) | Brooklyn | 2/3/4/5/N/R to Borough Hall | 718-858-5810 | www.floydny.com

"Pabst Blue Ribbon and bocce ball" are quite the "combination" at this Brooklyn Heights taproom, a "spacious" thing furnished in "grandma-Gothic style" with lots of "distressed furniture" and a much-loved in-door clay court; "affordable drinks" paired with Kentucky beer cheese snacks pull in a "smart" local crowd that's "ready to mingle."

⚡ Flûte

| 23 | 22 | 21 | VE |

Flatiron | 40 E. 20th St. (bet. B'way & Park Ave. S.) | N/R to 23rd St. | 212-529-7870

W 50s | 205 W. 54th St., downstairs (bet. B'way & 7th Ave.) | N/Q/R to 57th St./7th Ave. | 212-265-5169
www.flutebar.com

"Champagne lovers" pop their corks over this "romantic" twosome specializing in "high-quality" bubbly including many vintages that you "usually can't get by the glass"; the larger Flatiron outpost can be "packed or empty" depending on the night, while the Midtown original (a real-deal former speakeasy) is "dark enough to canoodle with your mistress while sitting next to your wife"; either way, "bring the gold card."

Fontana's

| 21 | 16 | 19 | M |

LES | 105 Eldridge St. (bet. Broome & Grand Sts.) | B/D to Grand St. | 212-334-6740 | www.fontanasnyc.com

"Undiscovered", "down-home" LES joint with a something-for-everyone philosophy set in a "huge" tri-level space equipped with three bars, a pool table, a movie screen and a downstairs performance area; the crowd may be "hit-or-miss" but regulars say it's a "hidden treasure."

Fort Defiance

| - | - | - | M |

Red Hook | 365 Van Brunt St. (bet. Coffey & Dikeman Sts.) | Brooklyn | F/ G to Smith-9th Sts. | 347-453-6672 | www.fortdefiancebrooklyn.com

Named for a Revolutionary War fort that once stood nearby, this re-mote Red Hook joint has a pleasing been-there-forever feel enhanced by old-school checkerboard floors, wainscoting and artwork; with carefully crafted cocktails priced under $10 and interesting pub grub, it has quickly gained a local following; P.S. by day, it dispenses Counter Culture coffee and pastries from Colson.

48 Lounge
▽ 26 | 25 | 26 | E

W 40s | 1221 Sixth Ave. (enter on 48th St., bet. 6th & 7th Aves.) | B/D/F/M to 47-50th Sts./Rockefeller Ctr. | 212-554-4848 | www.48nyc.com
Equal parts Rande Gerber bar and Las Vegas ultra-lounge, this swanky spot near Rock Center offers "pricey" potables, "stylish" staffers and a high-ceilinged, leather-banquetted room that's as "plush" as it gets in Midtown; expect a full house after work, more breathing room mid-evening and some late-night high jinks when off-the-clock local restaurant workers roll in.

☒ 40/40
19 | 19 | 17 | VE

Flatiron | 6 W. 25th St. (bet. B'way & 6th Ave.) | N/R to 23rd St. | 212-832-4040 | www.the4040club.com
"Your average sports bar looks like a rookie" beside this "alpha" Flatiron spot, where "big spenders" unwind and "people-watch" in a "swanky" lounge setting with big-league cred courtesy of co-owner Jay-Z; jumbo plasma screens, an "awesome" hip-hop soundtrack and memorabilia-studded VIP rooms boost its standing, though some oddsmakers wonder if it's "lost a step or two."

Forty Four
22 | 24 | 19 | VE

W 40s | Royalton Hotel | 44 W. 44th St. (bet. 5th & 6th Aves.) | 7/B/D/F/M to 42nd St./Bryant Park | 212-944-8844 | www.royaltonhotel.com
"Swanky" is the word on the Royalton Hotel's "beautifully decorated" lobby lounge, a "pricey" Midtown landing spot for "civil conversation" or "unwinding after a hard day"; though its "double-sided fireplace" provides a "warm feeling", "great martinis" also leave guests feeling nice and toasty.

49 Grove
18 | 16 | 16 | E

W Village | 49 Grove St., downstairs (Bleecker St.) | 1 to Christopher St. | 212-727-1100 | www.49grovenyc.com
West Village basement club that's a "safe choice" for grooving to "up-beat" sounds in a "low-ceilinged" setting; its "fun-time atmosphere" is "not as pretentious as some", though party-poopers dismiss the "overcrowded" "wannabe" scene as "no big deal."

Forum
18 | 19 | 18 | M

E Village | 127 Fourth Ave. (bet. 12th & 13th Sts.) | 4/5/6/L/N/Q/R to 14th St./Union Sq. | 212-505-0360 | www.theforumnyc.com
"Dark" and "lovely", this slick duplex near Union Square comes equipped with a long bar, illuminated white stone walls and lots of leather banquettes; but even though it "looks cute", some say it "should be elsewhere" – its *Sex and the City* crowd is "misplaced in this nabe."

☒ Four Seasons Hotel Bar
26 | 26 | 25 | VE

E 50s | Four Seasons Hotel | 57 E. 57th St. (bet. Madison & Park Aves.) | 4/5/6/F/N/R/Q to 59th St./Lexington Ave. | 212-758-5700 | www.fourseasons.com
"Watch rich older people drink" at this "recession-free" barroom in the Four Seasons Hotel where the "power cocktails" are poured "with

a heavy hand" and served with much "pomp and circumstance"; it's a "total scene" after work what with all the "bankers" and "cougars" in attendance, so forget the "outrageous" price tags: you almost "feel good about spending the money" here.

Fourth Avenue Pub

| - | - | - | M |

Park Slope | 76 Fourth Ave. (Bergen St.) | Brooklyn | 2/3/4/5/B/D/N/Q/R to Atlantic Ave. | 718-643-2273

"Knowledgeable owners" have assembled a "superb selection" of craft beers at this "honest-to-goodness neighborhood bar" in Park Slope; "free popcorn" and "friendly service" are additional pluses, but some warn "if you're hipster-intolerant, this isn't the place for you."

4₂0

| 18 | 16 | 17 | M |

W 80s | 420 Amsterdam Ave. (80th St.) | 1 to 79th St. | 212-579-8450

"Neighborhood" chemistry comes to Amsterdam Avenue's "strip of pubs and frat joints" at this UWS watering hole, where "young" singletons connect in the "laid-back" upstairs bar or on the basement dance floor; altogether it's a "decent" enough "hangout", though "so-so" scenery may put a damper on things.

Frames

| 23 | 20 | 19 | M |

W 40s | 625 Eighth Ave., 2nd fl. (42nd St.) | A/C/E to 42nd St./Port Authority | 212-268-6909 | www.framesnyc.com

"Surprisingly cool for Port Authority", this "fun" pin palace off Times Square features à la mode touches like "club music" and "bowling in the dark" – "they love to turn the lights off here"; even better, keglers report that despite a recent remodel (and name change from Leisure Time Bowl), it's still "competitively priced."

NEW Freddy's Bar ⊄

| - | - | - | I |

Park Slope | 627 Fifth Ave. (bet. 17th & 18th Sts.) | Brooklyn | R to Prospect Ave. | 718-768-0131 | www.freddysbar.com

After being forced out of its longtime Prospect Heights home by the Atlantic Yards project, this much-beloved dive has been reborn in the South Slope, with the original bar, booths and 'Chains of Justice' making the trip; a back patio and side performance space allow for lots of wiggle room here.

☒ Frying Pan

| 26 | 19 | 15 | M |

Chelsea | Pier 66 Maritime (26th St. & West Side Hwy.) | C/E to 23rd St. | 212-989-6363 | www.pier66maritime.com

"Jersey never looked better" than it does from the deck of this literally "rockin'" outdoor bar scene set on a "really big" floating barge alongside a "rusty" salvaged lightship; sure, it "closes early" (1 AM) and it's usually so "insanely crowded" that getting a drink can be "chaotic", but most agree it's "impossible not to be happy" at this piece of "heaven on the Hudson"; P.S. open May–October.

Full Circle Bar

| - | - | - | M |

Williamsburg | 318 Grand St. (bet. Havemeyer St. & Marcy Ave.) | Brooklyn | L to Grand St. | 347-725-4588 | www.fullcirclebar.com

Skee-Ball is the name of the game at this single-minded South Williamsburg joint that not only hosts the sport's first local league but also lets the good times roll on four lanes (with a televised feed over the bar of the back-room action); at a buck a game, tabs can add up quickly but cheap canned brew compensates.

Full Cup ⊅

- | - | - | M

Staten Island | 388 Van Duzer St. (Beach St.) | 718-442-4224 | www.fullcupsi.com

Though spiffed up and rechristened since breaking from the Muddy Cup chain, this Staten Island coffeehouse remains a brick-lined boho "hangout" strewn with thrift-shop bric-a-brac; indie-rock bookings make it a place to "listen to new bands", so regulars say the clientele skews "much younger now."

Full Shilling

16 | 14 | 19 | M

Financial District | 160 Pearl St. (bet. Pine & Wall Sts.) | 2/3 to Wall St. | 212-422-3855 | www.thefullshilling.com

"Delightfully Irish" barkeeps dispense a "properly poured Guinness" (plus "nice, strong" drinks) at this "cozy", wood-paneled Financial District pub that's a "drunken-banker" magnet at happy hour; a 105-year-old bar "imported from Ireland" adds to the "authenticity."

g ⊅

21 | 22 | 18 | M

Chelsea | 225 W. 19th St. (bet. 7th & 8th Aves.) | 1 to 18th St. | 212-929-1085 | www.glounge.com

For best results, be "young and good-looking" at this Chelsea gay bar that may be "getting older" but remains a "zoo" at prime times; the "oval bar" still causes traffic jams and the frozen Cosmos are as "fabulous" as ever – even the bartenders' "attitude" is "still going strong."

Gaf Bar

16 | 13 | 19 | M

E 80s | 1715 First Ave. (89th St.) | 4/5/6 to 86th St. | 212-996-3278
W 40s | 401 W. 48th St. (bet. 9th & 10th Aves.) | C/E to 50th St. | 212-307-7536

"Blue-collar" Irish bars in Yorkville and Hell's Kitchen that are virtually "interchangeable" with others in the genre; despite darts, billiards and "great jukeboxes", they're "never crowded."

Galapagos

21 | 21 | 18 | M

Dumbo | 16 Main St. (Water St.) | Brooklyn | F to York St. | 718-222-8500 | www.galapagosartspace.com

Now in an "incredible" setting in Dumbo – with banquette seating floating above a pool of water – this "sophisticated" performance venue offers "different forms of entertainment", from concerts to comedy to more avant-garde fare; it's always "interesting", though some say the "concrete"-heavy digs feel too "cold."

GalleryBar

19 | 23 | 15 | M

LES | 120 Orchard St. (bet. Delancey & Rivington Sts.) | F/J/M/Z to Delancey/Essex Sts. | 212-529-2266 | www.gallerybarnyc.com

"Art gallery by day, lounge by night" is the "simple premise" behind this LES double-decker that also hosts "progressive DJs" in the basement; it's a "unique idea" and a definite "getaway from all the Midtown bankers", yet some sense a "bare-bones" scene.

Galway Hooker

18 | 16 | 18 | M

Murray Hill | 7 E. 36th St. (bet. 5th & Madison Aves.) | 6 to 33rd St. | 212-725-2353

(continued)

Galway Hooker

W Village | 133 Seventh Ave. S. (bet. Charles & 10th Sts.) | 1 to Christopher St. | 212-675-6220
www.galwayhookernyc.com

The "name's enough to draw interest" (it references an Irish sailboat), but these "casual" Celtic pubs draw "massive crowds" after work thanks to "many beer choices" and "convivial" atmospheres; the "gigantic" Murray Hill original is just as "popular" as the "Ginger Man next door", while the newer West Village satellite has a "more intimate" vibe.

Gansevoort Park Rooftop

| - | - | - | VE |

NEW Murray Hill | Gansevoort Park Hotel | 420 Park Ave. S. (29th St.) | 6 to 28th St. | 646-380-5391 | www.gansevoortpark.com

Perched atop Murray Hill's Gansevoort Park Avenue Hotel, this new rooftop features a duplex setting equipped with lounges, wraparound terraces, indoor/outdoor fireplaces and a (guest-only) swimming pool; like Plunge, its Meatpacking sibling, it draws a see-and-be-seen crowd with deep pockets.

Garage

| 19 | 17 | 18 | E |

W Village | 99 Seventh Ave. S. (bet. Barrow & Grove Sts.) | 1 to Christopher St. | 212-645-0600 | www.garagerest.com

"No-cover" nightly jazz is the hook at this "spacious" West Villager, a 1920s automobile garage transformed into a club/eatery with bonus summertime "sidewalk seating"; though it skews "expensive", the "free music" makes the "overpriced drinks" more tolerable.

Gaslight

| 18 | 16 | 17 | M |

Meatpacking | 400 W. 14th St. (9th Ave.) | A/C/E/L to 14th St./8th Ave. | 212-807-8444

G2

Meatpacking | 39 Ninth Ave. (bet. 13th & 14th Sts.) | A/C/E/L to 14th St./8th Ave. | 212-807-8444
www.gaslightnyc.com

Folks looking for "low-key fun" in the Meatpacking recommend this "friendly" bar that's "not as hard to get into" as its neighbors and more "affordable" to boot; it's a good "staging" place at the beginning of the night, and if it gets too "crowded" there's always its loungier sibling, G2.

Gate, The

| 20 | 16 | 17 | M |

Park Slope | 321 Fifth Ave. (3rd St.) | Brooklyn | R to Union St. | 718-768-4329 | www.thegatebrooklyn.blogspot.com

It's the "carefully chosen beer selection" that keeps this Park Slope suds specialist "packed", though its "dog-friendly" policy and moderate prices also help; in warm weather, the "hard-to-nab" outdoor tables are a "perfect place" to have a brew and watch the world go by.

Genesis

| 19 | 16 | 21 | M |

E 80s | 1708 Second Ave. (bet. 88th & 89th Sts.) | 4/5/6 to 86th St. | 212-348-5500 | www.genesisbar.com

Yes, "it's a sports bar" with "TVs everywhere", but this Upper Eastsider distinguishes itself from the pack with "surprisingly good" food, including a much vaunted hamburger; especially "friendly" service seals the deal for its "local crowd."

George Keeley

	APPEAL	DECOR	SERVICE	COST
	21	15	21	M

W 80s | 485 Amsterdam Ave. (bet. 83rd & 84th Sts.) | 1 to 86th St. | 212-873-0251 | www.georgekeeley.com

A "change of pace amid the sameness" of the Amsterdam Avenue bar scene, this "basic" Irish pub boasts a "hands-down, bottoms-up" selection of "fantastic" craft brews along with some cask ales; hard-core hopsheads "taste 100 beers and get their name on the wall."

Gibson, The

	-	-	-	M

Williamsburg | 108 Bedford Ave. (N. 11th St.) | Brooklyn | L to Bedford Ave. | 718-387-6296 | www.thegibsonnyc.com

Bourbon and scotch is the focus of this low-lit Williamsburg venue near McCarren Park that's pretty subdued compared to its earlier incarnation as the rowdy Triple Crown; Wii bowling and pitcher specials draw mellow crowds.

Gift

	▽ 28	26	22	E

W 40s | Room Mate Grace Hotel | 125 W. 45th St. (bet. 6th & 7th Aves.) | 1/2/3/7/N/Q/R/S to 42nd St./Times Sq. | 212-354-2323 | www.room-matehotels.com

Hidden from the "hustle and bustle" of Times Square is this "chic hotel bar" with an in-house swimming pool, which you can dive into for a $35 fee plus a two-drink minimum (bathing suits not included); "good DJs" and a particularly witty loo are available at no additional charge.

☑ Ginger Man

	21	17	18	M

Murray Hill | 11 E. 36th St. (bet. 5th & Madison Aves.) | 6 to 33rd St. | 212-532-3740 | www.gingerman-ny.com

"Embrace your inner beer snob" at this Murray Hill "temple" of suds where "suits", "frat boys" and "girls looking for bankers" cram in to sample its "seemingly infinite" choices; after work, it's an "absolute mob scene" since "everyone and their mother knows about it", so insiders go off-peak to take advantage of that "nice lounge in the back."

Ginger's ☞

	▽ 18	17	16	M

Park Slope | 363 Fifth Ave. (bet. 5th & 6th Sts.) | Brooklyn | D/F/G/N/R to 4th Ave./9th St. | 718-788-0924

The "best lesbian bar in Brooklyn" – ok, just about the *only* lesbian bar in Brooklyn" – this 11-year-old Park Sloper may be "not exceptional", but is certainly "nice" enough on the "patio in good weather"; "lots of ladies meet their online dates here."

Gin Mill

	17	13	17	M

W 80s | 442 Amsterdam Ave. (bet. 81st & 82nd Sts.) | 1 to 79th St. | 212-580-9080 | www.nycbestbar.com

"Down-to-earth" sports bar "staple on the Amsterdam Avenue circuit" frequented by "young professionals", "post-softball" teams and "Florida Gators" fans; supporters "nostalgic for college days of yore" call it "dependable", but skeptics shrug "run-of-the-mill."

Glass Bar

	-	-	-	E

Chelsea | Indigo Hotel | 127 W. 28th St., 20th fl. (bet. 6th & 7th Aves.) | 1 to 28th St. | 212-973-9000 | www.indigochelsea.com

Chelsea's Indigo Hotel is home to this off-the-beaten-path rooftop nest with duel decks offering both northern and southern exposures;

while the views themselves aren't particularly newsworthy, the mid-size setting lends a more casual air compared to the frenetic scenes at some of its larger competitors.

Globe, The ▽ 20 | 21 | 21 | M

Gramercy | 158 E. 23rd St. (bet. Lexington & 3rd Aves.) | 6 to 23rd St. | 212-477-6161

"Old-school" is putting it mildly at this "low-key" Gramercy Irish pub, in business (under various names) since 1880; "surprisingly large" with a "standard bar" up front and a "fireplace"-equipped back lounge, it's "comfortable", "super-friendly" and its bartenders "take pouring a Guinness seriously."

NEW GMT Tavern - | - | - | E

G Village | 142 Bleecker St. (La Guardia Pl.) | A/B/C/D/E/F/M to W. 4th St. | 646-863-3776 | www.gmtny.com

Big is the word on this new British-inspired Villager in the former Senor Swanky's digs, where tall windows and leather-and-mahogany decor lend a tavern-esque vibe; the name's short for 'Greenwich Mean Time', the mood nominally British and the crowd primarily from NYU.

Z GoldBar 25 | 27 | 20 | VE

Little Italy | 389 Broome St. (bet. Centre Market Pl. & Mulberry St.) | 6 to Spring St. | 212-274-1568 | www.goldbarnewyork.com

There's a "hot, very LA scene" in progress at this "petite" but "ornate" Little Italy lounge drawing "beautiful people" and "music industry insiders" who shrug off the "high prices" and "pretentious" mood; its "awesome" design elements include "gold skull–lined walls" in the back lounge and an iron "velvet rope" out front.

NEW Good Co. - | - | - | M

Williamsburg | 10 Hope St. (bet. Havemeyer & Roebling Sts.) | Brooklyn | L to Bedford Ave. | 718-218-7191 | www.goodcobk.com

It's all about the cool alfresco patio at this new Williamsburg saloon set in the former Hope Lounge digs; inside, there's lots of salvaged wood as well as suds-and-shots deals, but in warmer months, the action moves outdoors where picnic tables, darts and Ping-Pong keep the crowds entertained.

Gossip ▽ 22 | 22 | 22 | M

W 40s | 733 Ninth Ave. (bet. 49th & 50th Sts.) | C/E to 50th St. | 212-265-2720 | www.gossipbarnyc.com

This Hell's Kitchen double-decker brings some class to the "modern Irish pub" genre with a sprawling, spic-and-span setting that includes a working "fireplace" and an upstairs party room that helps "keep the traffic flowing"; decent pricing and a variety of bar bites keep regulars regular.

Gotham Comedy Club 20 | 14 | 15 | E

Chelsea | 208 W. 23rd St. (bet. 7th & 8th Aves.) | 1 to 23rd St. | 212-367-9000 | www.gothamcomedyclub.com

"Top-notch talent" takes the stage at this "classy" Chelsea comedy club that's "not as cramped" as some of the competition, but just as "expensive" when the "drink minimums" are factored in; although "no one is safe from the comics' sharp tongues", "if you sit in the front row, you'll get picked on."

Gowanus Yacht Club ⊅

22 | 13 | 18 | I

Carroll Gardens | 323 Smith St. (President St.) | Brooklyn | F/G to Carroll St. | 718-246-1321

"Ironic name" aside, this seasonal Carroll Gardens beer garden supplies "skuzzy" thrills to "rowdy" hipsters drawn by its "cheap beer and good eats" – not the "gross bathroom", "uncomfortable seats" and "questionable grilling skills"; word is out, so expect it to be "at capacity with the slightest ray of sunshine."

☑ NEW Gramercy Terrace

– | – | – | VE

Gramercy | Gramercy Park Hotel | 2 Lexington Ave., 16th fl. (21st St.) | 6 to 23rd St. | 212-201-2171 | www.gramercyparkhotel.com

Once a private space, this verdant aerie atop the Gramercy Park Hotel is now open to all comers yet remains something of a best-kept secret, despite being one of the lushest rooftops in town; wicker furniture, vine-laced trellises and art-lined indoor salons make for ultracivilized imbibing, while a retractable glass roof allows all-seasons access; P.S. advance reservations required.

Grand Bar

23 | 24 | 21 | VE

SoHo | SoHo Grand Hotel | 310 W. Broadway, 2nd fl. (bet. Canal & Grand Sts.) | A/C/E to Canal St. | 212-965-3000 | www.sohogrand.com

Life remains grand at this bar in the SoHo Grand Hotel that's "not so much a place to be seen any longer", yet still manages to draw an "attractive" crowd of free-spending "European tourists"; no surprise, all this "style" comes at a high price.

Grand Café

20 | 21 | 19 | M

Astoria | 37-01 30th Ave. (37th St.) | Queens | N/Q to 30th Ave. | 718-545-1494 | www.grandcafelounge.com

"Thirtieth Avenue's 'it' place", this Greek cafe by day morphs into a "happening" Astoria scene after dark, with palm trees, bamboo chairs and a fish tank lending a "great" Miami-meets-Athens ambiance; high-def TVs satisfy athletic supporters who show up to "watch the Greek national team."

Grape and Grain

23 | 19 | 22 | E

E Village | 620 E. Sixth St. (bet. Aves. B & C) | F to Lower East Side/2nd Ave. | 212-420-0002 | www.grapeandgrain.net

Even though it's "a bit out of the way" in the far East Village, this "cozy" little wine bar still boasts an enthusiastic fan base that praises its "unpretentious atmosphere", "gracious" service and more than "decent" vino selection (including 25 by the glass); however, a minority finds it "overpriced" and "overhyped."

Grassroots Tavern ⊅

19 | 10 | 16 | I

E Village | 20 St. Marks Pl. (bet. 2nd & 3rd Aves.) | 6 to Astor Pl. | 212-475-9443

"Dirty and sticky", this "old-time" St. Marks Place "dive" has been home to the "same local customers" occupying the same "well-worn barstools" for over 35 years; besides the "free popcorn", "wonderful jukebox" and "cheap (but flat) beer", fans say there's a certain "je ne sais quoi" about it.

Great Lakes

▽ 18 | 12 | 21 | I

Park Slope | 284 Fifth Ave. (1st St.) | Brooklyn | R to Union St. | 718-499-3710
When in the mood for an "old-school dive", Park Slopers "grab a brew" at this "serviceable" neighborhood joint fitted out with thrift-shop furniture; it's best known for its "indie music"–heavy jukebox.

Greenhouse

21 | 23 | 18 | VE

Hudson Square | 150 Varick St. (Vandam St.) | 1 to Houston St. | 212-807-7000 | www.greenhouseusa.com
"Eco-friendly" Hudson Square club, a "fun", bi-level affair drawing an "anything-goes" crowd with "lush" decor that includes everything from "crystals" to "plants on the ceiling"; cynics nix the "rude" doormen, "debatable clientele" and "hastily prepared drinks", but fans say this "sexy" spot is "hard to get into" for a reason.

Griffin, The

21 | 22 | 20 | VE

Meatpacking | 50 Gansevoort St. (bet. Greenwich & Washington Sts.) | A/C/E/L to 14th St./8th Ave. | 212-255-6676 | www.thegriffinny.com
"Party like a rock star" – and spend like one too – at this swanky Meatpacking club where you'll be "coddled till there is no more money in your pocket"; its chandeliers, velvet couches and parquet floors are a fitting backdrop for the "good-looking", "dressed-up" crowd, though some sense a "pretentious" scene.

Gstaad

19 | 19 | 19 | M

Chelsea | 43 W. 26th St. (bet. B'way & 6th Ave.) | F to 23rd St. | 212-683-1440 | www.gstaadnyc.com
Channeling a "relaxed" "ski chalet" where you can "almost smell the pine trees", this "lodge"-like Chelsea lounge flaunts a coolly minimal aesthetic with "skiing videos projected on the walls"; since it's "never too crowded", the "lift lines are usually quite short."

Gutter, The

▽ 19 | 17 | 15 | M

Greenpoint | 200 N. 14th St. (bet. Berry St. & Wythe Ave.) | Brooklyn | G to Nassau Ave. | 718-387-3585 | www.thegutterbrooklyn.com
The name may be "too descriptive" for some, but this "step back in time" brings "vintage bowling" to Greenpoint via funky, "not-state-of-the-art" lanes, "ratty shoes" and an adjacent "grungy" barroom; still, the atmosphere's "hip", the beer selection "good" and you can "bring in your own food."

GYM Sportsbar

20 | 15 | 19 | M

Chelsea | 167 Eighth Ave. (bet. 18th & 19th Sts.) | A/C/E/L to 14th St./8th Ave. | 212-337-2439 | www.gymsportsbar.com
"Less showy and pretentious" than the typical "Chelsea boy" scene, this sorta-"butch" gay sports bar is the "opposite of g", with a crowd of "regular guys" guzzling "cheap strong drinks" and feigning interest in the televised action; no surprise, there are more dudes "looking for jocks than actual jocks" in attendance.

Hairy Monk

15 | 11 | 17 | M

Murray Hill | 337 Third Ave. (25th St.) | 6 to 23rd St. | 212-532-2929 | www.thehairymonknyc.com
"If you love anything Boston", you'll dig this "solid", "un-Murray Hill" sports bar that's usually "bursting at the seams during Sox and

Patriots games"; otherwise, it's an "unassuming" joint "without many distinguishing characteristics."

Half King
20 | 15 | 19 | M

Chelsea | 505 W. 23rd St. (10th Ave.) | C/E to 23rd St. | 212-462-4300 | www.thehalfking.com

Everyone from "literary wonks" to "hockey boys" from nearby Chelsea Piers likes this "manly" Irish pub that offers a "cool" intellectual vibe; it's a good "alternative" to the trendier 10th Avenue watering holes, and also "nice after walking the High Line."

Half Pint
21 | 19 | 20 | M

G Village | 76 W. Third St. (Thompson St.) | A/B/C/D/E/F/M to W. 4th St. | 212-260-1088 | www.thehalfpintnyc.com

This "solid Village hangout" gets full support for its "extensive", "ever-changing" beer list (25 on tap and over 100 by the bottle) served in "cozy", "low-lit" digs; despite its heart-of-NYU address, it seems "less fratty" than the norm and is "rarely mobbed – save for Saturday night."

Hammerstein Ballroom
19 | 15 | 13 | E

Garment District | 311 W. 34th St. (bet. 8th & 9th Aves.) | A/C/E to 34th St./Penn Station | 212-279-7740 | www.mcstudios.com

Over a century old, this midsize Garment District music hall (originally built as an opera house) is a "classic venue for the right performer" with "standing room" only downstairs and "scattered seating" in the balcony; "overpriced" drinks and underwhelming service are the downsides.

Happy Ending
18 | 15 | 15 | M

LES | 302 Broome St. (bet. Eldridge & Forsyth Sts.) | J/Z to Bowery | 212-334-9676 | www.happyendinglounge.com

Its "titillating past" as a "massage parlor" provides a cheap thrill at this "provocatively named" LES "hideaway" that's a "safe bet" for "good times"; it "still has its original fixtures" from yesteryear (think waist-high showerheads), provoking responses ranging from "cheesy" to "creepy."

Harefield Road ⊅
▽ 25 | 21 | 23 | M

Williamsburg | 769 Metropolitan Ave. (bet. Graham Ave. & Humboldt St.) | Brooklyn |'L to Graham Ave. | 718-388-6870

"Lots of wood" and "exposed brick" gives this Williamsburg saloon a "lodgey" feel, while its far-flung address makes it "less crowded and noisy" than others in these parts; a "sweet" selection of microbrews and a "backyard patio" are catnip to its "hipster" following.

Harlem Lanes
20 | 17 | 18 | E

Harlem | 2116 Adam Clayton Powell Jr. Blvd., 3rd fl. (126th St.) | A/B/C/D to 125th St. | 212-678-2695 | www.harlemlanes.com

Rolling out 24 state-of-the-art lanes, 24 plasma screens and two bars, this Harlem bowling alley is both "cool" and "never crowded"; there seems to be but one strike against it: numerous kids' parties can lead to "stray children running into your frame."

NEW Hash Fifty Five
- | - | - | E

W 50s | 47 W. 55th St. (bet. 5th & 6th Aves.) | F to 57th St. | 212-957-1899 | www.hash55.com

This new hookah lounge above sibling eatery Fifty Five brings Meatpacking swank to Midtown via a slick mix of mirrors, gauzy curtains and white leather banquettes; though the cocktails aren't quite as pricey as the $30 water pipes, a black Amex will come in handy here.

Haven

| | | | E |

E 50s | 244 E. 51st St. (bet. 2nd & 3rd Aves.) | 6/E to 51st-53rd Sts./ Lexington Ave. | 212-906-9066 | www.havennewyork.com

Swanky Turtle Bay duplex where the top-shelf pours arrive in private club-like digs recalling a posh European villa furnished with *objets d'art*; a few still pine for the days "when it was Divine Bar", but overall its young professional clientele call it a safe haven.

Heathers

| | | | M |

E Village | 506 E. 13th St. (bet. Aves. A & B) | L to 1st Ave. | 212-254-0979 | www.heathersbar.com

"Small" but "interesting" East Villager with a "hipster" following thanks to "different DJs" every night, random listening parties and an overall artistic sensibility; its no-frills look includes metal stools, cafeteria-style tables and blackboards in the bathrooms.

Heights Bar & Grill

| 17 | 13 | 15 | M |

W 100s | 2867 Broadway, 2nd fl. (bet. 111th & 112th Sts.) | 1 to Cathedral Pkwy./110th St. | 212-866-7035 | www.theheightsnyc.com

Though it doesn't quite live up to its name, this Morningside Heights venue "gets the bar-and-grill concept right", with a "chill" setting that's usually "overrun by Columbia students"; its rooftop bar is "perfect for hot summer nights", though it's enclosed for year-round "fun."

Hell Gate Social

| | | | M |

Astoria | 12-21 Astoria Blvd. (bet. 12th & 14th Sts.) | Queens | N/Q to 30th Ave. | 718-204-8313 | www.hellgatesocial.com

"Unexpected" for Astoria, this "plenty hip" but "not overly hipster" barroom schedules everything from "live music" and "indie flicks" to "amazing" art exhibits; owners who "go all out to please" and an "outdoor garden space" add to the "fun experience."

Henrietta Hudson

| 20 | 15 | 19 | M |

W Village | 438 Hudson St. (Morton St.) | 1 to Christopher St. | 212-924-3347 | www.henriettahudson.com

A "classic in the lesbian world", this West Village vet lures a "mixed crowd" of "young 'uns, prime-timers and oldies", though it tends to skew "butch"; look for a particularly "great pickup" scene on weekends when the girls pile in to "get on the dance floor."

Hideaway, The

| 18 | 15 | 20 | E |

TriBeCa | 185 Duane St. (Greenwich St.) | 1/2/3 to Chambers St. | 212-334-5775 | www.thehideawaynyc.com

"Walk too fast and you'll miss the entrance" to this "mellow" TriBeCan, a "tiny but appealing" thing that's "more down-to-earth" than the norm in these parts (but just as "pricey"); its "old-school Wall Street crowd" reports that it "usually doesn't get too packed, which is nice."

Hi-Fi

| 20 | 13 | 18 | M |

E Village | 169 Ave. A (bet. 10th & 11th Sts.) | L to 1st Ave. | 212-420-8392 | www.thehifibar.com

One of the "best damn jukeboxes in NYC" is the attraction at this "atypical" East Villager that was formerly the "legendary club Brownies";

although on the "divey" side, there's "plenty of room to roam around" here, and the drinks are "strong" and fairly "cheap."

High Dive

| - | - | - | M |

Park Slope | 243 Fifth Ave. (Carroll St.) | Brooklyn | R to Union St. | 718-788-0401 | www.highdivebrooklyn.com

Anything but a dive, this instantly popular Park Sloper from the Commonwealth team goes for a random look, with '70s wallpaper, '90s rock posters and light fixtures from whenever, all topped by a lacquered tin ceiling; boozewise, think suds, with a variety of well-priced craft taps best savored in its sweet backyard patio.

Highlands

| ∇ 24 | 25 | 22 | M |

W Village | 150 W. 10th St (bet. Greenwich Ave. & Waverly Pl.) | 1 to Christopher St. | 212-229-2670 | www.highlands-nyc.com

"Scotland" alights in the West Village via this "sophisticated" gastropub that specializes in single malts accompanied by "tasty" eats; even though the food "looks amazing", the "young party" set that shows up to drink is so "loud" that you won't be able to "have a dinner conversation."

Highline Ballroom

| 21 | 16 | 16 | E |

Chelsea | 431 W. 16th St. (bet. 9th & 10th Aves.) | A/C/E/L to 14th St./8th Ave. | 212-414-5994 | www.highlineballroom.com

"State-of-the-art" music hall in Chelsea booking "awesome bands" and known for its "high-quality acoustics", "good sightlines" and "decently intimate" room (capacity 700); though the "bland" space may suffer from "lack of character", it's definitely a "great alternative to big stadiums."

Hill, The

| 16 | 17 | 16 | M |

Murray Hill | 416 Third Ave. (bet. 29th & 30th Sts.) | 6 to 28th St. | 212-481-1712 | www.thehillny.com

A Murray Hill "scene right out of *Gossip Girl*", this "sleek" lounge/sports bar combo is a "classy" enough hang where the "guy-watching" is almost as good as the game-watching; but foes citing "choppy" service and a "noisy, just-out-of-college" crowd sigh it's almost "as painful as the TV show with the similar name."

Hiro

| 20 | 22 | 14 | E |

Chelsea | Maritime Hotel | 371 W. 16th St. (9th Ave.) | A/C/E/L to 14th St./8th Ave. | 212-727-0212 | www.hiroballroom.com

This "Asian-themed" bi-level Chelsea lounge in the Maritime Hotel can be "quite the spectacle" with its "acrobatic performers", "trippy" music and "young, party-hardy" crowd; but despite the "pretentious doormen" and "excessive price tags", hip folks report it's "not very hip anymore."

HK Lounge

| 19 | 20 | 20 | E |

Garment District | 405 W. 39th St. (9th Ave.) | A/C/E to 42nd St./Port Authority | 212-947-4208 | www.hkhellskitchen.com

Given the "few choices in the area" around Port Authority, this "chic" double-decker lounge is a no-brainer for those "working their way back to the bus terminal"; the scene may have "died down" a bit from its heyday, but a "generally good-looking" crowd, "commendable service" and a "nice rooftop" keep it keeping on.

Hog Pit

APPEAL	DECOR	SERVICE	COST
14	11	15	M

Chelsea | 37B W. 26th St. (bet. B'way & 6th Ave.) | N/R to 28th St. | 212-213-4871 | www.hogpit.com

Compared to its original Meatpacking location, this relocated Chelsea roadhouse is "a little too clean and nice", though diehards say just "give it time"; though it's trying to hold onto its "niche", even the food is "overshadowed by the BBQ at Hill Country across the street."

Hogs & Heifers ⊄

18	12	13	M

Meatpacking | 859 Washington St. (13th St.) | A/C/E/L to 14th St./8th Ave. | 212-929-0655 | www.hogsandheifers.com

"Good old-fashioned sloppy debauchery" lives on at this "blue-collar" Meatpacking saloon, a "bucket-list" kind of joint known for its *Animal House* decor and "trash-talking", "Coyote Ugly–style" barmaids; surveyors say it "gets old extremely quickly", particularly since the crowd consists of "more tourists than you'll find at the Empire State Building."

Holiday Cocktail Lounge ⊄

∇ 18	9	15	M

E Village | 75 St. Marks Pl. (bet. 1st & 2nd Aves.) | 6 to Astor Pl. | 212-777-9637

What could be the "best daytime drinking bar in the East Village", this circa-1945 "genius dive" is a "cheap", "old-school" joint where "your business is welcomed"; since it's "only open when the owner feels like opening it", insiders always have a Plan B ready.

Home Sweet Home

∇ 18	16	15	M

LES | 131 Chrystie St., downstairs (bet. Broome & Delancey Sts.) | J/Z to Bowery | 212-226-5708 | www.homesweethomebar.com

"Hidden" in a "slightly out-of-the-way" LES basement, this "low-key" joint employs "funky" knickknacks and random taxidermy in an attempt to live up to its name; a "cool" following and "easygoing" staffers make up for not much air-conditioning and a "terrible sound system."

Honey

19	17	17	M

Chelsea | 243 W. 14th St. (bet. 7th & 8th Aves.) | A/C/E/L to 14th St./8th Ave. | 212-620-0222 | www.honeyny.com

Although now under "new ownership", this "narrow" Chelsea watering hole has retained its "loungey vibe" thanks to the ample use of "exposed brick and candlelight"; but given the off-the-beaten-path 14th Street address, it's a "bring-your-own-crowd" kind of place.

Hooters

15	12	17	M

W 50s | 211 W. 56th St. (bet. B'way & 8th Ave.) | N/Q/R to 57th St./7th Ave. | 212-581-5656 | www.originalhooters.com

"Girls and wings" are the formula at this West Midtown outlet of the national chain, where a "bunch of boobs" congregate to "gawk at" the shapely waitresses; for optimum results, it's best to have an "adolescent male mentality" – nobody here is "looking for culture or a fine sherry."

Hop Devil Grill

18	13	20	M

E Village | 129 St. Marks Pl. (bet. Ave. A & 1st Ave.) | L to 1st Ave. | 212-533-4468 | www.hopdevil.com

"Foreign" purveyors and "smaller U.S. breweries" make up the "outstanding" beer list of this St. Marks Place suds specialist, and there's "great service if you have trouble picking one out" to boot; but some call it a "great backup place" rather than a destination, citing "standard" chow and a "downhill" vibe.

NEW Hotel Chantelle
— | — | — | M

LES | 92 Ludlow St. (bet. Broome & Delancey Sts.) | F/J/M/Z to Delancey/Essex Sts. | 212-254-9100 | www.hotelchantelle.com
Circa-1940 Paris is the inspiration for this roomy new LES bar/lounge whose vintage charms include flowery wallpaper, tufted burgundy leather banquettes and wainscoting made from salvaged wood; another bar in the cellar and a rooftop deck are in the works.

Hotel Delmano
▽ 26 | 27 | 24 | E

Williamsburg | 82 Berry St. (9th St.) | Brooklyn | L to Bedford Ave. | 718-387-1945 | www.hoteldelmano.com
"Sophisticated and unassumingly cool", this "careful replica of an old New York bar" is one of "Williamsburg's best" for "expensive", "swanky cocktails" whipped up by "excellent mixologists"; too bad there's usually "waiting outside on the curb" prior to entry – this one is understandably "popular."

Houndstooth Pub
▽ 21 | 19 | 22 | M

Garment District | 520 Eighth Ave. (37th St.) | A/C/E to 34th St./Penn Station | 212-643-0034 | www.houndstoothpub.com
Since "there's nowhere else to go in the neighborhood", this Garment District watering hole from the owners of Stitch draws "after-work happy-hour" types to its "big, spacious" setting; otherwise, it's pretty "typical", save for vaguely "upscale" decor and "generous drinks."

House of Brews
19 | 15 | 19 | M

W 40s | 363 W. 46th St. (bet. 8th & 9th Aves.) | 1/2/3/7/N/Q/R/S to 42nd St./Times Sq. | 212-245-0551
W 50s | 302 W. 51st St. (bet. 8th & 9th Aves.) | C/E to 50th St. | 212-541-7080
www.houseofbrewsny.com
"Beer nerds rejoice" over this "bustling" twosome that live up to the name with a "wide assortment" of suds including a popular 96-oz. draft "brew funnel"; despite "mainstream" vibes and heart-of-the-Theater-District addresses, they're "surprisingly un-touristy."

Huckleberry Bar
▽ 24 | 25 | 25 | M

Williamsburg | 588 Grand St. (bet. Leonard & Lorimer Sts.) | Brooklyn | L to Lorimer St. | 718-218-8555 | www.huckleberrybar.com
"Posh" comes to East Williamsburg via this "awesome" joint vending "meticulously prepared cocktails" in a "speakeasy-ish" setting staffed by bartenders who "totally dress the part"; true, it's a bit "pricey for the neighborhood", but a "fun" crowd, "friendly" atmosphere and cool "outside patio" make up for it.

Hudson Bar and Books
23 | 24 | 21 | E

W Village | 636 Hudson St. (Horatio St.) | A/C/E/L to 14th St./8th Ave. | 212-229-2642 | www.barandbooks.cz
"Casually fashionable" types like the "cozy bookstore ambiance" at this longtime West Village cigar bar that's "hip in a retro way" and "one of the few smoking bars in the city"; it's a "great place for a scotch and a stogie" along with some "intellectual conversation."

| | APPEAL | DECOR | SERVICE | COST |

☑ Hudson Hotel Bar
24 | 25 | 18 | VE

W 50s | Hudson Hotel | 356 W. 58th St. (bet. 8th & 9th Aves.) | 1/A/ B/C/D to 59th St./Columbus Circle | 212-554-6000

☑ Hudson Hotel Library

W 50s | Hudson Hotel | 356 W. 58th St. (bet. 8th & 9th Aves.) | 1/A/ B/C/D to 59th St./Columbus Circle | 212-554-6000

☑ Hudson Hotel Sky Terrace

W 50s | Hudson Hotel | 356 W. 58th St., 15th fl. (bet. 8th & 9th Aves.) | 1/A/B/C/D to 59th St./Columbus Circle | 212-554-6000 www.hudsonhotel.com

Even though "not as 'in' as it used to be", this Hudson Hotel trio offers some "premium" nightlife options in "swank-to-the-max" settings: the "futuristic" bar features "log" seating and a "light-box floor", the more "civilized" library boasts "huge wing chairs" and a "purple felt pool table", while the "relaxing" rooftop rolls out "romantic" city views; no matter where you wind up, be prepared for "unbelievably expensive" pricing and "short-attention-span service."

Hudson Terrace
21 | 21 | 17 | VE

W 40s | 621 W. 46th St. (bet. 11th & 12th Aves.) | C/E to 50th St. | 212-315-9400 | www.hudsonterracenyc.com

"Loftlike" "upbeat" duplex in Way West Hell's Kitchen consisting of a chandeliered interior and walled garden terrace, though the real action lies on its year-round rooftop with "views of the Hudson and the Intrepid"; it's "not cheap" and can be "tough to get into", but fans say it's a natural for "group get-togethers."

☑NEW Hurricane Club
- | - | - | E

Flatiron | 360 Park Ave. S. (26th St.) | 6 to 28th St. | 212-951-7111 | www.thehurricaneclub.com

This new, over-the-top tiki bar/restaurant in the Flatiron gives the genre a swanky spin, with a flashy AvroKO design that includes barnacle-encrusted chandeliers and ceramic bone friezes in the bathrooms; the busy central bartop mixes predictably deadly cocktails, but insiders tout the basement shoe-shine stand equipped with its very own rum fountain.

Hustler Club
19 | 17 | 19 | VE

W 50s | 641 W. 51st St. (12th Ave.) | C/E to 50th St. | 212-247-2460 | www.hustlerny.com

"Not a place to bring a date", this West Hell's Kitchen strip club "pays homage to décolletage" via "hot dancers" who "can't speak English" (many are "from the Soviet bloc") but understand all about the "do-re-mi"; it's a "great place to spend other people's money" with an "awesome" rooftop perfect for a scotch and a stogie.

NEW Idle Hands
- | - | - | M

E Village | 25 Ave. B, downstairs (bet. 2nd & 3rd Sts.) | F to Lower East Side/ 2nd Ave. | 917-338-7090 | www.idlehandsbar.com

Hidden beneath the N'Awlins-themed roadhouse Billy Hurricane's, this East Village basement bar specializes in bourbon with over 80 varieties on hand (and 50 beers thrown in for good measure), all served in simple, no-frills digs signaling its unpretentious leanings; P.S. fun fact: in the '80s, it was the site of the after-hours scene Save the Robots.

Iggy's

APPEAL	DECOR	SERVICE	COST
15	10	18	M

E 70s | 1452 Second Ave. (bet. 75th & 76th Sts.) | 6 to 77th St. |
212-327-3043
LES | 132 Ludlow St. (Rivington St.) | F/J/M/Z to Delancey/Essex Sts. |
212-529-2731 | www.iggysnewyork.com
These "unpretentious" Irish bars share "dive" decor and "disgusting
bathrooms", though the UES original is also known for its "awesomely
fun" "loud karaoke" nights; downtown, there's a "rock 'n' roll" sensibility that's more in keeping with its LES address.

Iguana

20	19	18	E

W 50s | 240 W. 54th St. (bet. B'way & 8th Ave.) | C/E to 50th St. |
212-765-5454 | www.iguananyc.com
"Salsa nights are the best bet" at this Theater District Mexican bar/
eatery/dance club where the "downstairs is always jumpin'" with
chicks on an "impromptu girls' night out"; though they "make a mean
mojito" here, critics say the DJ is "as generic as the sofas."

NEW Immigrant, The

-	-	-	M

E Village | 341 E. Ninth St. (bet. 1st & 2nd Aves.) | L to 1st Ave. |
212-677-2545 | www.theimmigrantnyc.com
Unsung, unassuming East Villager that's flying under the radar despite
a vintage railroad-apartment layout (complete with an antique cash
register) and fairly priced wine and beer; it's the perfect Plan B when
you can't get into the more popular faux speakeasies nearby.

NEW Industry Bar ⊄

-	-	-	M

W 50s | 355 W. 52nd St. (bet. 8th & 9th Aves.) | C/E to 50th St. |
www.industry-bar.com
New Hell's Kitchen gay bar, set in a roomy former parking garage
that's been redone in industrial-chic style, with a flat-screen-
festooned front bar, semi-private lounge areas and a small rear stage;
brought to you by the daddies behind Barracuda and Elmo, it's already
an after-work scene, thanks to that nightly 4-to-9-PM happy hour.

International Bar

20	16	21	M

E Village | 120½ First Ave. (bet. 7th St. & St. Marks Pl.) | 6 to Astor Pl. |
212-777-1643
"East Village townie bar", a "tiny hole-in-the-wall dive" that's back following a hiatus; locals say the mood, the prices and the beer selection
are all "pretty decent" – "if you're looking to lay low, this is the place."

In Vino

24	20	24	E

E Village | 215 E. Fourth St. (bet. Aves. A & B) | F to Lower East Side/
2nd Ave. | 212-539-1011 | www.invino-ny.com
"Laid-back and unpretentious", this "lovely" East Village vino vendor
is set in a "wine cellar"–esque space that gives off a "warm" glow despite rather "small" dimensions; fans "can't get enough" of its "all-
Italian" list and "knowledgeable" service.

Iona ⊄

▽ 23	20	21	M

Williamsburg | 180 Grand St. (bet. Bedford & Driggs Aves.) | Brooklyn |
L to Bedford Ave. | 718-384-5008 | www.ionabrooklyn.com
One of the few Scottish bars in "scene-crazy Williamsburg", this
"neighborhood" pub "avoids cliché" with "homemade hot toddies"

and "Premier League" soccer games on the tube; regulars tout its rear garden "escape", equipped with a "Ping-Pong table" and a "fair amount of seating."

Iridium
21 | 17 | 17 | VE

W 50s | 1650 Broadway, downstairs (bet. 50th & 51st Sts.) | 1 to 50th St. | 212-582-2121 | www.iridiumjazzclub.com

"Convenient for a last-minute jazz attack", this long-"established" Theater District club set in a "cramped" subterranean space draws "serious listeners" willing to spend "lots of money"; maybe it "won't be the same without the late Les Paul" on Monday nights, but it still books "interesting" acts.

NEW Irish Exit
- | - | - | M

E 50s | 978 Second Ave. (bet. 51st & 52nd Sts.) | 6 to 51st St. | 212-755-8383 | www.irishexitnyc.com

This new East Side Irish pub is brought to you by seasoned vets of the Second Avenue singles scene (they also own Calico Jack's, McFadden's and Turtle Bay); expect a big, by-the-numbers kind of joint that's so squeaky clean it still has that new bar smell.

Irish Rogue
18 | 15 | 20 | M

W 40s | 356 W. 44th St. (bet. 8th & 9th Aves.) | A/C/E to 42nd St./ Port Authority | 212-445-0131 | www.theirishrogue.com

Ok, there's "nothing rogue" about this Theater District Irish pub, though it works well for "groups" since it's got plenty of room, including a "pool table"–equipped mezzanine; otherwise, "it is what it is" – "nothing spectacular, nothing terrible."

Irving Plaza
▽ 19 | 11 | 14 | E

Gramercy | 17 Irving Pl. (15th St.) | 4/5/6/L/N/Q/R to 14th St./ Union Sq. | 212-777-6817 | www.irvingplaza.com

Known again by its original moniker after a "dumb name change" to the Fillmore a few years back, this longtime Gramercy venue is renowned for its "good sound" system and "semi-established" acts; since it remains a "top" choice for "intimate performances", be prepared for "big lines" out front.

Jack Russell's
17 | 16 | 18 | M

E 80s | 1591 Second Ave. (bet. 82nd & 83rd Sts.) | 4/5/6 to 86th St. | 212-472-2800 | www.jackrussellsnyc.com

"Tons of TVs" broadcasting a "variety of games" (including "individual" ones in each booth) draw "good crowds" to this Upper East Side sports bar, a wide-"open" joint also stocked with pool tables and video games; while "a little sterile" to some, at least it's "friendly and laid-back."

Jade Bar
▽ 22 | 21 | 18 | VE

Gramercy | Gramercy Park Hotel | 2 Lexington Ave. (21st St.) | 6 to 23rd St. | 212-920-3300 | www.gramercyparkhotel.com

Something of an also-ran compared to Rose Bar, its scenier next-door neighbor, this just-as-"hip" Gramercy Park Hotel venue has its own "celeb" sightings and equally "expensive" pricing; the "beautiful" decor comes via painter Julian Schnabel, whose haute bohemian design is a cool mix of red velvet, reclaimed wood and serious works of art.

	APPEAL	DECOR	SERVICE	COST

Jadis
22 | 23 | 23 | E

LES | 42 Rivington St. (bet. Eldridge & Forsyth Sts.) | F to Lower East Side/
2nd Ave. | 212-254-1675 | www.jadisnyc.com

Bringing a "much-needed grown-up" vibe to the LES, this "nice 'n'
cozy" wine bar "hidden" on a nonsceney stretch of Rivington Street
proffers a "great variety" of vinos in a "down-to-earth" brick-walled
setting; "generous seating" in the rear lounge area lends a "romantic"
note to the proceedings.

Jake's Dilemma
17 | 14 | 17 | M

W 80s | 430 Amsterdam Ave. (bet. 80th & 81st Sts.) | 1 to 79th St. |
212-580-0556 | www.nycbestbar.com

"Local misfits" and "regular guys and gals" party hardy at this "fratty"
UWS "dive" on Amsterdam Avenue's "gold coast of bars"; though fans
like its "upbeat", "energetic" mood, sinkers see too much "amateur
drinking" going on; P.S. "if you're over 30, be prepared to feel old" here.

Jake's Saloon
15 | 14 | 18 | M

Chelsea | 202 Ninth Ave. (bet. 22nd & 23rd Sts.) | C/E to 23rd St. |
212-366-5110
Chelsea | 206 W. 23rd St. (bet. 7th & 8th Aves.) | 1 to 23rd St. |
212-337-3100
W 50s | 875 10th Ave. (57th St.) | 1/A/B/C/D to 59th St./Columbus Circle |
212-333-3100
www.jakessaloon-nyc.com

"Low-key" Irish pub trio that "doesn't pretend to be anything else" than
what they are: "typical" spots that are "relatively affordable" and
"friendly"; at the Hell's Kitchen original, you'll be drinking alongside lots
of Fordham "law students" and revelers at "Katie Couric's holiday party."

JakeWalk, The
24 | 23 | 21 | M

Carroll Gardens | 282 Smith St. (Sackett St.) | Brooklyn | F/G to Carroll St. |
347-599-0294 | www.thejakewalk.com

Named after the jerky stride caused by "Prohibition"-era bootleg
booze, this "dimly lit", speakeasy-ish Carroll Gardens saloon rolls out
a "wonderful selection" of wine and whiskey accompanied by "generous cheese plates"; it's hip but "unpretentious", and thankfully the
moms and dads at the bar "leave the strollers at home."

Jameson's Pub
18 | 14 | 19 | M

E 50s | 975 Second Ave. (bet. 51st & 52nd Sts.) | 6 to 51st St. | 212-980-4465
"Basic" East Midtown "workingman's pub" where the bartenders are
"Irish, charming and great conversationalists" and the atmosphere is
"classic" (think dark woods, brick walls, stained glass); although
"worth a drink if you're in the neighborhood", it's "not exactly a night-
out kind of place."

☒ Jane Hotel Lobby Bar
26 | 26 | 19 | VE

W Village | Jane Hotel | 113 Jane St. (bet. Washington & West Sts.) |
A/C/E/L to 14th St./8th Ave. | 212-924-6700 | www.thejanenyc.com

Atmosphere is king at this transporting West Village bar/lounge, set
in a longtime, seen-it-all waterfront hotel that sheltered Titanic survi-
vors in 1912 and more recently housed an avant-garde theater; the
"perfectly detailed" design is a riff on fading grandeur with soaring
ceilings, an airy mezzanine and kooky *objets d'art* (a "glass-encased

stuffed monkey", a dilapidated disco ball, refrigerator-size urinals); neighbor troubles shuttered the main ballroom for a time, but it's back now, and the door's as "tough" as ever.

⛿ Jazz Standard
25 | 19 | 21 | E

Murray Hill | 116 E. 27th St., downstairs (bet. Lexington Ave. & Park Ave. S.) | 6 to 28th St. | 212-576-2232 | www.jazzstandard.net

"Great jazz" + "unusually good" BBQ from Blue Smoke upstairs" = "heaven" at this Murray Hill underground club that's "much more comfortable" than the norm owing to a semi-"swanky" setting with "lots of room"; throw in "top-name" acts, "good sightlines" and "fine acoustics", and you're in for a "very smoooth night" indeed.

Jekyll & Hyde
18 | 20 | 15 | E

W Village | 91 Seventh Ave. S. (bet. Barrow & W. 4th Sts.) | 1 to Christopher St. | 212-989-7701 | www.jekyllpub.com

There's nothing "haunting" about this "gimmicky" West Village "tourist trap", whose mad-scientist theme includes "shots served in test tubes" and "restrooms behind secret doors"; its "extensive beer list" draws huzzahs, but most say the "only scary thing here is the size of the bill."

Jeremy's Ale House
17 | 11 | 17 | I

Financial District | 228 Front St. (bet. Beekman St. & Peck Slip) | 2/3/4/5/A/C/J/Z to Fulton St./B'way/Nassau | 212-964-3537 | www.jeremysalehouse.com

"Cheap" "huge beers" served in Styrofoam cups are the hook at this FiDi veteran near the Seaport with a "fascinating mix of customers" – everyone from "lower Manhattan scum" to "young professionals"; there's "not a lot to look at" in the "grungy" setting, save for "NYC's best bra collection", dangling from the rafters.

⛿NEW Jimmy
- | - | - | E

SoHo | James Hotel | 15 Thompson St. (bet. Canal & Grand Sts.) | 1/2 to Canal St. | 212-201-9118 | www.jameshotels.com

SoHo's latest rooftop aerie is this classy little nest perched atop the James Hotel that's focused around a (hotel guests–only) swimming pool; inside, a midsize, all-seasons cocktail lounge wows with a leather-trimmed bar and a gas fireplace, not to mention sweeping views of Downtown; fans call it the Mini-Me version of the Boom Boom Room.

Jimmy's Corner
21 | 16 | 19 | M

W 40s | 140 W. 44th St. (bet. B'way & 6th Ave.) | 1/2/3/7/N/Q/R/S to 42nd St./Times Sq. | 212-221-9510

A "shrine to boxing" and "throwback to the seedier days of Times Square", this "narrow hole-in-the-wall" owned by former trainer Jimmy Glenn has been around "long before Disney" arrived; "sexy" barmaids, "argumentative" barflies and pugilist memorabilia on the walls supply the appropriate "punch."

Joe's Pub
24 | 20 | 18 | E

E Village | Public Theater | 425 Lafayette St. (bet. Astor Pl. & E. 4th St.) | 6 to Astor Pl. | 212-539-8778 | www.joespub.com

Offering an "up-close-and-personal" view of "your favorite performers", this "intimate" music hall in the Public Theater complex draws an "arty older crowd", maybe because of its "steep" tabs; despite "perfunctory" service and "cramped" conditions, it's a "real NY" experience with "no fuss and no pretense"; P.S. to "ensure seating, make dinner reservations."

Johnny Foxes

| 15 | 14 | 21 | M |

E 80s | 1546 Second Ave. (bet. 80th & 81st Sts.) | 6 to 77th St. | 212-472-9193 | www.johnnyfoxesnyc.com

"Large", "nondescript" UES Irish pub that's a "casual" option for drinks in the glow of "tons of TVs" broadcasting "your favorite game"; locals report it's "usually quiet", despite an "all-day happy hour."

Johnny's Bar

| - | - | - | I |

W Village | 90 Greenwich Ave. (bet. Jane & W. 12th Sts.) | A/C/E/L to 14th St./8th Ave. | 212-741-5279 | www.johnnysbarnyc.com

"Filling the West Village dive-bar void", this "awesome hole-in-the-wall" is a "real drinking establishment" for folks bent on getting blitzed for cheap; there's "no cheery bartender or friendly patrons", and the decor consists of a bumper-stickered bartop with a "Megatouch in back."

Johnny Utah's

| 20 | 19 | 16 | E |

W 50s | 25 W. 51st St., downstairs (bet. 5th & 6th Aves.) | B/D/F/M to 47-50th Sts./Rockefeller Ctr. | 212-265-8824 | www.johnnyutahs.com

For a "little bit of Texas" in Rock Center, check out this subterranean "rodeo"-themed joint best known for its "mechanical bull" near the entrance, a "great way to embarrass yourself and your friends"; it's usually "rowdy and boisterous", but regulars find it "better on a weekday when you aren't dodging the bachelorette parties."

Joshua Tree

| 15 | 13 | 15 | M |

Murray Hill | 513 Third Ave. (bet. 34th & 35th Sts.) | 6 to 33rd St. | 212-689-0058 | www.joshuatreebar.com

This "fraternity heaven" bar on the Murray Hill runway gets "inexplicably crowded", despite "nondescript" looks and "'80s music videos" played "ad nauseum" on the flat-screens; on the weekends, "willing and able B&T singles" throw some "fist-pumping" into the mix.

Josie Wood's

| ∇ 17 | 12 | 20 | I |

G Village | 11 Waverly Pl., downstairs (bet. Greene & Mercer Sts.) | N/R to 8th St. | 212-228-9909 | www.josiewoods.com

There's "lots of college students" on the prowl at this Village saloon, where the basement setting means "no cell-phone service" and "no windows"; still, it's "cheap" enough to "shoot some pool and watch a game."

Juliet Supperclub

| 23 | 24 | 21 | VE |

Chelsea | 539 W. 21st St. (bet. 10th & 11th Aves.) | C/E to 23rd St. | 212-929-2400 | www.julietsupperclub.com

Sparkly is the word for this "classy" club in Way West Chelsea lined with so much mirrored tile it feels like being inside a giant disco ball; though there's some interest in its small plates–centric Med menu, the grub plays second fiddle to all those "models and finance guys" and thumping bass lines.

Julius ⊅

| 16 | 9 | 17 | M |

W Village | 159 W. 10th St. (Waverly Pl.) | 1 to Christopher St. | 212-243-1928 | www.juliusbarnyc.com

Purportedly the "oldest gay bar" in town, this West Village vet is known for its "cheap" pops and "surprisingly tasty" burgers; even if the "regulars' joints are stiffer than the drinks", it remains a "welcoming" site "for older gentlemen who like older gentlemen."

K & M Bar ⊄

| | – | – | – | M |

Williamsburg | 225 N. Eighth St. (Roebling St.) | Brooklyn | L to Bedford Ave. | 718-388-3088

Set in a former Williamsburg pierogi shop, this old-school bar features a "great beer list" and "surprisingly good DJs"; its "classic" decor includes a tin ceiling, tile flooring and tufted leather booths.

Karaoke One 7

| | – | – | – | M |

Flatiron | 29 W. 17th St. (bet. 5th & 6th Aves.) | 4/5/6/L/N/Q/R to 14th St./Union Sq. | 212-675-3527 | www.karaoke17.com

Croon your "favorite tunes" at this Flatiron karaoke joint where warblers can "sing in public at the bar" or retreat to a "rented room" in back; drinks are "well priced", and though there's a "great song selection" (80,000-plus choices), there's "no food selection", save for random bar snacks.

Karma

| | 23 | 20 | 18 | M |

E Village | 51 First Ave. (bet. 3rd & 4th Sts.) | F to Lower East Side/ 2nd Ave. | 212-677-3160 | www.karmanyc.com

It's legal to "smoke cigarettes" inside this "mellow" East Village "hookah joint" where flavored tobaccos and Marlboro Lights scent the air; the "dimly lit", Moroccan-themed premises consist of a "low-key" bar and lounge on the main floor, plus a "decent party room" in the basement.

Kastel

| | – | – | – | VE |

Hudson Square | Trump Soho Hotel | 246 Spring St. (Varick St.) | C/E to Spring St. | 212-842-5500 | www.trumpsohohotel.com

Ultraexpensive ultra-lounge set on the ground floor of Hudson Square's Trump Soho Hotel, chicly outfitted in leather, chain mail and reclaimed wood; it's open to ordinary folk in the afternoon and early evening, but becomes guest-list-only after 10 PM.

Katra

| | 16 | 19 | 16 | E |

LES | 217 Bowery (bet. Prince & Rivington Sts.) | B/D to Grand St. | 212-473-3113 | www.katranyc.com

"Sexy" and "dark", this Bowery duplex channels "sensual" Morocco with hookahs, pillow-strewn banquettes and occasional "belly dancers"; though party-poopers find "nothing special" going on (outside of the "expensive" pricing), its basement level is a "good place for special events."

Katwalk

| | 16 | 16 | 15 | M |

Garment District | 2 W. 35th St. (bet. 5th & 6th Aves.) | B/D/F/M/N/ Q/R to 34th St./Herald Sq. | 212-594-9343 | www.katwalknyc.com

Even though it "tries to be trendy", this Garment District lounge is borderline "unimpressive", except "after work" when local desk jockeys pile in for happy hour; "don't expect to see any runway models", but you might catch *The Making of the Sports Illustrated Swimsuit Edition* unreeling on one of its flat-screens.

🆕 Keg No. 229

| | – | – | – | M |

Seaport | 229 Front St. (bet. Beekman St. & Peck Slip) | 2/3/4/5 to Fulton St. | 212-566-2337 | www.keg229.com

Tap it yourself is the gimmick at this new Seaport beer specialist where four self-service, pay-by-the-ounce spigots turn patrons into bartenders; a spin-off of the wine-centric Bin No. 220 across the street, it features a warm, brick-lined space with plenty of old-NY appeal.

Z NEW Kenmare
`-` | `-` | `-` | VE

Little Italy | 98 Kenmare St., downstairs (bet. Lafayette & Mulberry Sts.) | 6 to Spring St. | 212-274-9898

The nightlife adjunct to the same-named Little Italy eatery, this subterranean lounge draws fashionable late-nighters mainly because of its charismatic owners, Paul Sevigny (Beatrice Inn) and Nur Khan (ex Rose Bar); though the restaurant's not as hot as it initially was, it's still a scene downstairs, so be prepared for a tough door.

Kenny's Castaways
19 | 14 | 15 | M

G Village | 157 Bleecker St. (bet. Sullivan & Thompson Sts.) | A/B/C/D/E/F/M to W. 4th St. | 917-475-1323 | www.kennyscastaways.net

It was a "decent place back when" it opened in 1967, but now this "college hangout" on Bleecker Street's "live music row" books less-renowned acts, a mix of "up-and-comers" plus "never-will-bes"; the drinks are "reasonably priced", and as for the decor, "picture your dad's basement."

Kettle of Fish
19 | 14 | 18 | M

W Village | 59 Christopher St. (bet. 7th Ave. S. & Waverly Pl.) | 1 to Christopher St. | 212-414-2278 | www.kettleoffishnyc.com

"Literary" West Village bar on the scene (in different locations) since 1950 that's famed for entertaining everyone from Jack Kerouac to Bob Dylan; today, it's a "laid-back" joint with pinball and video games that draws a "huge following" when the Packers are playing.

Keybar
19 | 14 | 21 | M

E Village | 432 E. 13th St. (bet. Ave. A & 1st Ave.) | L to 1st Ave. | 212-478-3021 | www.keybar.com

"Tiny" but "friendly", this "fun" East Village bar is best known for its "killer happy hour" (offering "two-for-one drinks till 10 PM") as well as "hot bartenders" and a toasty fireplace; insiders tout its signature Rolo shots, but warn that "they creep up on you."

KGB Bar
20 | 17 | 16 | M

E Village | 85 E. Fourth St., 2nd fl. (bet. Bowery & 2nd Ave.) | F to Lower East Side/2nd Ave. | 212-505-3360 | www.kgbbar.com

"Columbia MFA grads" and "Russian expats" coexist peacefully at this "clandestine" East Village "literary haven" where "nightly readings" and "other nerdy events" are staged in "small" digs decorated with "Soviet propaganda" and "spy paraphernalia"; comrades commend the "old-school Commie feel" of this "nice safe house."

Z King Cole Bar
27 | 27 | 25 | VE

E 50s | St. Regis Hotel | 2 E. 55th St. (5th Ave.) | E/M to 5th Ave./53rd St. | 212-339-6721 | www.kingcolebar.com

A "bucket-list requirement for any serious drinker", this "absolutely first-class" barroom in the St. Regis Hotel reeks of "gravitas" thanks to a "magical" Maxfield Parrish mural and staffers well versed in "old-world panache"; sure, the "classic" cocktails come at "prices only a king could afford" and seats are often "impossible to score", but ultimately it's one of the most "civilized" places in town; P.S. for best results, "dress up."

	APPEAL	DECOR	SERVICE	COST

King's Head Tavern

| | 16 | 13 | 17 | M |

E Village | 222 E. 14th St. (bet. 2nd & 3rd Aves.) | L to 3rd Ave. | 212-473-6590

"Hole meets wall" at this "roomy" but "divey" East Village tavern that draws a "young" following mainly due to its "convenient" 14th Street address; despite "beer pong" and "reasonably priced drinks", unloyal subjects call it "run-of-the-mill."

Kinsale Tavern

| | 21 | 17 | 22 | M |

E 90s | 1672 Third Ave. (bet. 93rd & 94th Sts.) | 6 to 96th St. | 212-348-4370 | www.kinsale.com

In the Upper-Upper East Side "nightlife wasteland", this "old reliable" stands out as a "truly Irish" pub where a "courteous" staff "pours the Guinness right"; it can be a "madhouse" when "international soccer" matches are televised, but even during off hours it's a "solid" option.

Kiss & Fly

| | 20 | 20 | 14 | VE |

Meatpacking | 409 W. 13th St. (bet. 9th Ave. & Washington St.) | A/C/E/L to 14th St./8th Ave. | 212-255-1933 | www.kissandflyclub.com

It's "impossible not to party" at this "pretty cool" Meatpacking club where "over-the-top effects" like "lasers and fog machines" are unleashed in a classical Roman setting (think arches and a Michelangelo-like ceiling); the "Euro"-heavy crowd doesn't mind the "slow service" and "zillion-dollar drinks", too distracted by all the "craziness" to notice.

Klimat

| | - | - | - | M |

E Village | 77 E. Seventh St. (1st Ave.) | 6 to Astor Pl. | 212-777-1112 | www.klimatlounge.com

It's always fair weather at this beer-and-wine specialist where the potables are imported from Eastern Europe but the mood is strictly East Village; while the funky first floor is convivial enough, insiders say the partying is best in the "fun cellar."

Knitting Factory

| | 21 | 14 | 15 | M |

Williamsburg | 361 Metropolitan Ave. (Havemeyer St.) | Brooklyn | L to Lorimer St. | 347-529-6696 | www.knittingfactory.com

Third time's a charm for this "unique" long-running music venue that originated on the LES, relocated to TriBeCa and is now settled into the former Luna Lounge digs in Williamsburg; look for the same eclectic roster of "up-and-coming indie artists" and quirky niche acts, but this time around, there's but a single "intimate" stage – along with a no-cover-charge front bar that overlooks it, skybox-style.

Kush

| | 19 | 21 | 15 | E |

LES | 191 Chrystie St. (bet. Rivington & Stanton Sts.) | F to Lower East Side/2nd Ave. | 212-677-7328 | www.thekushnyc.com

There's plenty of "Kasbah flair" at this "cool" LES lounge next door to The Box, where "fun hookahs" and "Moroccan-themed" decor make for a transporting experience; it's still a bit "under the radar", maybe because of the "inattentive" service and "overpriced" drinks.

NEW Lair

| | - | - | - | M |

Little Italy | 201 Lafayette St. (Kenmare St.) | 6 to Spring St. | 212-334-5247

The former Little Italy lounge Obivia – whose primary claim to fame was its proximity to La Esquina – returns to the scene and lives up to its new moniker with a dark lighting scheme involving lots of candles and black chandeliers; doors on both Lafayette and Mulberry Streets facilitate quick getaways.

Lakeside Lounge

21 | 15 | 20 | M

E Village | 162 Ave. B (bet. 10th & 11th Sts.) | L to 1st Ave. | 212-529-8463 | www.lakesidelounge.com

"East Village diviness" is alive and well at this "friendly neighborhood" bar best known for its "cool photo booth" and "live bands" thrashing away in its back performance space; it's "dark", "crowded" and priced with "thrifty" wallets in mind.

La Lanterna Next Door

24 | 23 | 18 | E

G Village | 131 MacDougal St. (bet. W. 3rd & 4th Sts.) | A/B/C/D/E/ F/M to W. 4th St. | 212-529-5945 | www.lalanternacaffe.com

"Perfect for dates", this ultra-"romantic" Village nook next to the restaurant La Lanterna di Vittorio comes equipped with a "fire-place", "good" wines and "light" Italian nibbles; a cozily "rustic" setting and nightly "live jazz" help distract from service that "could be a little bit better."

NEW Lani Kai

- | - | - | E

SoHo | 525 Broome St. (bet. Sullivan & Thompson Sts.) | C/E to Spring St. | 646-596-8778 | www.lanikainy.com

Mixology queen Julie Reiner (Flatiron Lounge, Clover Club) goes Hawaiian at this new lounge/eatery set in the SoHo space last home to Tailor; look for a list of Hawaiian/Polynesian libations – don't call it tiki – served in a stripped-down space with little reference to South Seas culture other than its bamboo wallpaper and seashell chandelier.

Lansdowne Road

22 | 19 | 22 | M

W 40s | 599 10th Ave. (bet. 43rd & 44th Sts.) | A/C/E to 42nd St./ Port Authority | 212-239-8020 | www.lansdowneroadnyc.com

Named after a Dublin rugby stadium, this Irish sports bar in West Hell's Kitchen is a "comfortable" place with a conversation-starting "ice strip on the bar to keep your drinks cool"; "attentive" service, "abundant beers" and "delicious wings" are your "reward for making it to 10th Avenue."

NEW Lantern's Keep

- | - | - | E

W 40s | Iroquois Hotel | 49 W. 44th St. (bet. 5th & 6th Aves.) | B/D/F/ M to 42nd St./Bryant Park | 212-453-4233 | www.lanternskeepny.com

Swanky mixology comes to the Theater District's Iroquois Hotel via this grown-up newcomer specializing in Prohibition-era cocktails; the petite, 25-seat space channels a Parisian salon thanks to a judicious blend of dark-wood paneling, marble-topped tables and prints of De-gas ballerinas on the walls.

La Pomme

▽ 19 | 20 | 20 | VE

Chelsea | 37 W. 26th St. (bet. B'way & 6th Ave.) | N/R to 28th St. | 212-725-3860 | www.lapommenyc.com

High-style, boutique-size Chelsea club, a reworking of the former Ultra, where the hyper-designed setting flaunts a video wall, photo murals of fashion models and "cool" Victorian wallpaper with a sub-liminal razor-blades-and-brass-knuckles pattern; the crowd's the "usual B&T" peeps, the pops pricey and bottle service its raison d'être.

	APPEAL	DECOR	SERVICE	COST

Larry Lawrence
24 | 25 | 22 | M

Williamsburg | 295 Grand St. (bet. Havemeyer & Roebling Sts.) | Brooklyn |
L to Bedford Ave. | 718-218-7866 | www.larrylawrencebar.com
"Williamsburg's answer to Manhattan's secret bars", this "barely
marked" boîte is a "simply perfect" rendezvous for cool cats trying
to escape the maddening crowds; a "spacious" affair made of brick
and wood, its "high-design" details include a glass-enclosed
mezzanine for smokers.

Last Exit
18 | 14 | 19 | M

Cobble Hill | 136 Atlantic Ave. (bet. Clinton & Henry Sts.) | Brooklyn |
2/3/4/5/N/R to Borough Hall | 718-222-9198 | www.lastexitbar.com
"Home away from home" on Atlantic Avenue, this Cobble Hill "neighborhood joint" has a "generic hipster" vibe and draws "slightly older"
types who "don't know where else to go"; regulars say the bi-monthly
trivia contests are the "best thing" about it.

Latitude
15 | 15 | 16 | M

W 40s | 783 Eighth Ave. (bet. 47th & 48th Sts.) | C/E to 50th St. |
212-245-3034 | www.latitudebarnyc.com
"Young professionals" looking to unwind "after work" stop by this
"huge" Theater District triplex, an "open, airy" nexus for "happy-hour"
cocktails; though there's "nothing original" about it, surveyors give it
latitude for its upstairs "party balconies" and "friendly bartenders who
will buy you rounds."

Ⓩ NEW Lavo
- | - | - | VE

E 50s | 39 E. 58th St., downstairs (bet. Madison & Park Aves.) | 4/
5/6/F/N/R/Q to 59th St./Lexington Ave. | 212-750-5588 |
www.lavony.com
Migrating the Meatpacking mood to Midtown, this new underground
club transplanted from Vegas has annexed the old Au Bar digs and is
drawing the same kind of bottle service–friendly mix of older, moneyed types and blasé young Euros who want something local; above
the club, a same-named restaurant serves Italian food in a Keith
McNally–esque space.

Lea
▽ 25 | 22 | 18 | E

E 40s | Helmsley Bldg. | 230 Park Ave., East Walkway (bet. 45th & 46th
Sts.) | 4/5/6/7/S to 42nd St./Grand Central | 212-922-1546 |
www.leanyc.com
Gilt-framed paintings and "bordello-red walls" set the swanky tone at
this "Midtown hideaway" parked on the east walkway of the Helmsley
Building; given its proximity to Grand Central, it's usually standing
room only with "suburban commuters" after work, but more cozy later
on – and not open at all on weekends.

Ⓩ NEW Le Bain
- | - | - | VE

Meatpacking | Standard Hotel | 848 Washington St., 18th fl. (13th St.) |
A/C/E/L to 14th St./8th Ave. | 212-645-4646
The latest impenetrable citadel in the Standard Hotel, this 18th-floor
roofdeck has the same impossible door as its swish neighbor, the
Boom Boom Room; if you can wiggle in, you'll find a poolside bar,
bathing-suit vending machines, fake green grass, pink waterbeds and,
of course, drop-dead views of Gotham.

| | APPEAL | DECOR | SERVICE | COST |

Le Bateau Ivre
E 50s | The Pod Hotel | 230 E. 51st St. (bet. 2nd & 3rd Aves.) | 6/E to 51st-53rd Sts./Lexington Ave. | 212-583-0579 | www.lebateauivrenyc.com

21 | 20 | 18 | E

"Well-known" East Side wine bar with a "great selection" of French labels that complement the "transported-to-Paris" atmospherics; though "snooty waiters" are also part of the package, it still works for a "casual drink and a catch-up with a close friend."

LelaBar
W Village | 422 Hudson St. (Leroy St.) | 1 to Houston St. | 212-206-0594 | www.lelabar.com

22 | 21 | 23 | E

The "oval bar" lends itself to "optimal people-watching" at this "cute" West Village vino vendor, a "small place with so much charm"; its globe-trotting wine list can be paired with "unique" charcuterie, and "smart service" makes the overall experience all the more "delightful."

Lenox Lounge
Harlem | 288 Lenox Ave. (125th St.) | 2/3 to 125th St. | 212-427-0253 | www.lenoxlounge.com

23 | 19 | 21 | E

Take "a trip back in time" to this "old Harlem haunt", a vintage-1939 jazz club where legends like Billie Holiday and Miles Davis once performed; nowadays, it draws an "interesting crowd" with its "nice looks" and "smooth performances" in its "historic Zebra Room."

Le Poisson Rouge
G Village | 158 Bleecker St., downstairs (bet. Sullivan & Thompson Sts.) | A/B/C/D/E/F/M to W. 4th St. | 212-505-3474 | www.lepoissonrouge.com

20 | 17 | 17 | E

There's "something for everyone" on the "eclectic" roster at this "hip" Village music venue; the "barnlike" space includes a stage with "excellent sound" as well as a "cramped" lounge area featuring "cool art exhibits", but wherever you wind up, it's "totally fun."

Le Souk Harem
G Village | 510 La Guardia Pl. (bet. Bleecker & Houston Sts.) | A/B/C/D/E/F/M to W. 4th St. | 212-777-5454 | www.lesoukny.com

22 | 21 | 17 | E

Spun off from the notorious East Village original, this "sexy" bar/lounge/hookah den brings the same decadence to NYU-land, this time in a triplex space tarted up with Moroccan lanterns, atmospheric arches and jiggling "belly dancers"; outdoor seating and a North African small-plates menu make the "snotty" service easier to endure.

Levee, The
Williamsburg | 212 Berry St. (N. 3rd St.) | Brooklyn | L to Bedford Ave. | 718-218-8787 | www.theleveenyc.com

- | - | - | I

"Homesick Texpats" like the "Texas beers and Frito pies" served at this Williamsburg bar that's admittedly a "dive, but a fun one"; "Connect Four" and a pool table satisfy competitive types, but ultimately it's the "cheap drink specials" that bring in the "hipsters" and "frat boys."

NEW Lex Bar
Murray Hill | St. Giles Hotel, The Court | 130 E. 39th St. (Lexington Ave.) | 4/5/6/7/S to 42nd St./Grand Central | 212-592-8844 | www.gerberbars.com

- | - | - | E

Murray Hill's former Wet Bar gets a light reworking at this slinky lounge in the new St. Giles Court Hotel (formerly the W Court); still run by Rande Gerber, it flaunts all of his trademark touches: dim lights, pricey pops, foxy waitresses, little black dresses.

NEW Lexicon

–	–	–	E

E 50s | 226 E. 54th St. (bet. 2nd & 3rd Aves.) | 6/E/M to Lexington Ave./ 53rd St. | 212-688-5577 | www.lexiconclub.com

One of the few UES dance halls, this reworked/renamed club (fka Branch) is best known for its *picante* Latin nights; only open to the public Friday and Saturday, it's a private-event space the rest of the week.

Lexington Bar and Books

22	20	21	E

E 70s | 1020 Lexington Ave. (73rd St.) | 6 to 77th St. | 212-717-3902 | www.barandbooks.cz

"Older sophisticated types" convene at this "classy" UES cigar bar, perfect for a "proper drink" in a "proverbial smoke-filled room"; sure, the prices are "over the top" and there's a "dress code" (jackets suggested), but fans say this "gem" is great for "good, old-fashioned" cocktailing.

Libation

16	16	16	E

LES | 137 Ludlow St. (bet. Rivington & Stanton Sts.) | F to Lower East Side/ 2nd Ave. | 212-529-2153 | www.libationnyc.com

Surveyors split on this "large" LES triplex with an "upscale" "clublike" feel: admirers say it stays "crowded" thanks to "hot bartenders" and "great mixes" from the DJs, but critics retort that this "B&T go-to" is all "hype", with "long lines for no reason"; your call.

Library

21	19	18	M

E Village | 7 Ave. A (bet. Houston & 2nd Sts.) | F to Lower East Side/ 2nd Ave. | 212-375-1352

Despite the brainy-sounding name, this East Villager is "one of the best dives in Lower Manhattan" with "cheap drinks", a "hipster" following and a particularly "terrific" punk rock jukebox; bookshelf decor and B movies projected on the walls add to its "interesting" vibe.

L.I.C. Bar

∇ 22	19	16	M

LIC | 45-58 Vernon Blvd. (46th Ave.) | Queens | 7 to Vernon Blvd./ Jackson Ave. | 718-786-5400 | www.licbar.com

Those seeking TLC in LIC tout this "great neighborhood spot", a "cozy" saloon with a tin ceiling, brick walls and a "wonderful back patio"; its "friendly bartenders" remember both "the locals *and* their dogs."

Lillie's

23	23	19	M

Flatiron | 13 E. 17th St. (bet. B'way & 5th Ave.) | 4/5/6/L/N/Q/R to 14th St./Union Sq. | 212-337-1970 | www.lilliesnyc.com

Named after 19th-century actress Lillie Langtry, this "fun" Flatiron Irish pub is a hit with 21st-century "yuppies" and "arty" types who are thrilled that its "friendly" bartenders have "resurrected the forgotten art of the buy-back"; the "huge" space has a "true Victorian feel" with chandeliers and gold-leafed columns aplenty and is "usually packed."

Lion's Head Tavern

19	15	20	M

W 100s | 995 Amsterdam Ave. (109th St.) | 1 to Cathedral Pkwy./ 110th St. | 212-866-1030 | www.lionsheadnyc.com

Morningside Heights is home to this "neighborhood" sports bar that compensates for "not much decor" with "cheap drinks"; no surprise, it's "often filled with Columbia students", especially for "NFL games."

| | APPEAL | DECOR | SERVICE | COST |

Lips

E 50s | 227 E. 56th St. (bet. 2nd & 3rd Aves.) | 4/5/6/F/N/R/Q to 59th St./Lexington Ave. | 212-675-7710 | www.lipsnyc.com

20 | 20 | 18 | E

Watch "drag performers" onstage while being served by a "drag waiter" at this swanky supper club that's perfect for a "night out with the girls or the gays" (especially if someone's celebrating a "birthday"); though a few find the show "cheesy" and the food "so-so", most say the "talented" crossdressers are a "hoot"; P.S. a move from the West Village to fancier digs in Midtown puts its Decor Score in question.

Lit

E Village | 93 Second Ave. (bet. 5th & 6th Sts.) | 6 to Astor Pl. | 212-777-7987 | www.litloungenyc.com

18 | 16 | 17 | M

The "seedy East Village of the '80s lives on" at this murky music joint comprised of a "divey" street-level "bar-cum–art gallery" and a "dingy basement" where live "urban rock" bands perform; though a "mixed bag" at best, it's like a "worn black leather jacket" – "always cool."

Little Branch ⊘

W Village | 20 Seventh Ave. S., downstairs (Leroy St.) | 1 to Christopher St. | 212-929-4360

24 | 20 | 23 | E

"Sophisticated drinkers" bough to this "perfect little" Village speakeasy via mixology whiz Sasha Petraske, a "cavelike" underground den where "talented bartenders" whip up "insanely good throwback" cocktails; true, the '20s "time-warp" setting gets "cramped" and your cash "disappears quickly", but big "crowds waiting outside" suggest a "winning formula"; P.S. "getting up the stairs at the end of the night is a de facto sobriety test."

Littlefield

Gowanus | 622 Degraw St. (bet. 3rd & 4th Aves.) | Brooklyn | R to Union St. | 718-855-3388 | www.littlefieldnyc.com

- | - | - | M

Big performance venue in Gowanus that combines state-of-the-art acoustics with an eco-friendly philosophy (i.e. recycled tires for the sound walls, a bar built from salvaged bowling alley lanes); its diverse programming includes everything from jazz and hip-hop to art exhibits and film screenings.

Living Room ⊘

LES | 154 Ludlow St. (bet. Rivington & Stanton Sts.) | F to Lower East Side/ 2nd Ave. | 212-533-7235 | www.livingroomny.com

23 | 18 | 19 | M

"Intimate concerts" are the forte of this "mellow" LES music venue where acoustically inclined "emerging talents" do their thing in a basic "sit-and-listen" setting where "you'll practically be onstage"; its "come-as-you-are" crowd reports that the living is "down-to-earth" and "decently priced" here.

Local

Garment District | 1 Penn Plaza (33rd St., bet. 7th & 8th Aves.) | A/C/ E to 34th St./Penn Station | 212-629-7070 | www.localcafenyc.com

▽ 19 | 16 | 16 | M

Whether "you're throwing back a couple before a game" or "waiting for the train", this Garment District dispensary is a "decent alternative" to the typical MSG-area gin mills, mostly due to its "sweet" roof deck; while a bit "pricey" given the basic decor, it's always "crowded" come rush hour.

Local 138

| - | - | - | M |

LES | 138 Ludlow St. (bet. Rivington & Stanton Sts.) | F/J/M/Z to Delancey/Essex Sts. | 212-477-0280

"Grungy but so right", this "minimally decorated" Irish pub unites locals thanks to its "friendly" tapsters, "great draft beer selection" and "snug" window booths; regulars "stake out a good spot" for one of the "best happy hours on the LES."

Local 269

| - | - | - | M |

LES | 269 E. Houston St. (Suffolk St.) | F to Lower East Side/2nd Ave. | 212-228-9874 | www.thelocal269.com

Everything a "dive bar" should be, this LES joint pours "reliable if unimaginative drinks" in grungy digs adorned with mismatched chandeliers and non-flat-screen TVs; still, it's the "interesting" nightly live music performed on a makeshift stage that makes it worth a visit.

Loki Lounge

| 19 | 18 | 19 | M |

Park Slope | 304 Fifth Ave. (2nd St.) | Brooklyn | R to Union St. | 718-965-9600 | www.lokilounge.com

Park Slopers are partial to this roomy hybrid for its "inviting" front bar, rear patio and "comfortable" lounge area furnished with thrift-shop settees; diversions include darts, pool and weekend DJs, and its low-key clientele is grateful it's "never overly crowded."

Lolita

| 20 | 17 | 18 | M |

LES | 266 Broome St. (bet. Allen & Orchard Sts.) | F/J/M/Z to Delancey/Essex Sts. | 212-966-7223 | www.lolitabar.net

"No-fuss" LES "neighborhood" joint that's a longtime hipster "standby", comprised of a ground-floor bar and a "laid-back" basement lounge; outsider art on the walls, "cheap happy hours" and a spacious, "easy-to-navigate" layout are additional pluses.

Loreley

| 22 | 17 | 19 | M |

LES | 7 Rivington St. (bet. Bowery & Chrystie St.) | J/Z to Bowery | 212-253-7077

Williamsburg | 64 Frost St. (Meeker Ave.) | Brooklyn | G/L to Metropolitan Ave./Lorimer St. | 718-599-0025
www.loreleynyc.com

"Bigger-than-your-head" steins of "outstanding" Rhineland regional brews keep this rough-hewn, Cologne-style brauhaus "rollicking" with LES suds buffs and "German expats"; Teutonic comfort food and a tented back garden enhance the "beer cheer"; P.S. a Williamsburg branch opened post-Survey.

Lott, The

| - | - | - | M |

Flatiron | 55 W. 21st St. (bet. 5th & 6th Aves.) | F to 23rd St. | 212-675-8007 | www.thelottnyc.com

Aping Porky's, its predecessor, this Flatiron roadhouse doles out fishbowls and kegs while encouraging dancing on the bar; there's not much decor, but the idea is to be too hammered to notice.

Z Louis 649

| 27 | 26 | 26 | M |

E Village | 649 E. Ninth St. (bet. Aves. B & C) | L to 1st Ave. | 212-673-1190 | www.louis649.com

Even though they're "no longer doing live jazz", this compact East Villager remains a "trusty" haven for cocktail connoisseurs seeking "cool drinks" made with "high-quality ingredients"; the "romantic" setting is as soothing as a "friend's living room."

Lovers of Today

| - | - | - | M |

E Village | 132½ E. Seventh St., downstairs (bet. Aves. A & B) | L to 1st Ave. | 212-420-9517

The former Lei Bar beneath East Village stalwart Niagara has been refitted into this nifty lair, its tacky tiki knickknacks banished in favor of a speakeasy-in-a-cave look; it's a good Plan B when you can't wiggle into its more exclusive next-door neighbor, Cabin Down Below.

LQ

| 18 | 18 | 15 | E |

(aka Latin Quarter)

E 40s | Radisson Lexington Hotel | 511 Lexington Ave. (bet. 47th & 48th Sts.) | 6 to 51st St. | 212-593-7575

"Hips sway and toes tap" at this East Midtown reincarnation of the Latin Quarter, a "spacious" club where an "upbeat" mix of merengue, salsa and hip-hop "gets everyone moving" on the "good-sized dance floor"; even if "hoochie mama outfits" are turning up on the "used-to-be-trendy" crowd, it's still a "fun" cha-cha-"change of pace."

Luca Bar ⊅

| ∇ 17 | 15 | 16 | M |

E Village | 119 St. Marks Pl. (bet. Ave. A & 1st Ave.) | L to 1st Ave. | 212-254-1511 | www.lucaloungenyc.com

Luca Lounge ⊅

E Village | 222 Ave. B (bet. 13th & 14th Sts.) | L to 1st Ave. | 212-254-1511 | www.lucaloungenyc.com

"Neighborhood" types roll in to these rustic East Villagers, favoring the "smaller" Luca Bar for its homey style and the roomier Lounge for its "beautiful" back patio; either way, they're an accessible "escape", but "don't go looking for a crazy time."

Lucky Jack's

| - | - | - | M |

LES | 129 Orchard St. (bet. Delancey & Rivington Sts.) | F/J/M/Z to Delancey/Essex Sts. | 212-477-6555 | www.luckyjacksnyc.com

A 60-ft. bar stretches through the railroad layout of this "low-key" LES Irish pub, providing ample elbow room for the "casual" customers stepping in for a pint or a game of pool; even if you opt for the downstairs lounge, it won't set you back much jack.

Lucky Strike Lanes

| 22 | 22 | 19 | E |

W 40s | 624-660 W. 42nd St. (bet. 11th & 12th Aves.) | A/C/E to 42nd St./Port Authority | 646-829-0170 | www.bowlluckystrike.com

It's life in the "fast lanes" at this "fancy" bowl-a-rama in Way West Hell's Kitchen, a "massive party place" where the "dazzling" alleys are augmented with loungey seating, "cool music" and potent martinis to "distract from your gutter balls"; sure, it'll put a "serious dent in the wallet", but "if you want to take a date bowling", this place "rocks."

Lucky 13 Saloon ⊅

| - | - | - | I |

Park Slope | 273 13th St. (bet. 5th & 6th Aves.) | Brooklyn | D/F/G/N/R to 4th Ave./9th St. | 718-499-7553

"If you like heavy metal", you're in luck at this Park Slope mosh pit where "raucous" rock 'n' roll rebels bang their heads to an "awesome" parental-advisory jukebox, with band art wallpaper and "pole dancing" for distraction; it's "not exactly a date spot", but nonconformists are in for "a ton of fun."

Lucy's ⊄ | ▽ 20 | 11 | 21 | I |

E Village | 135 Ave. A (bet. 9th St. & St. Marks Pl.) | 6 to Astor Pl. | 212-673-3824

Regulars "love Lucy" at this "old-time" East Village "standby", a "favorite dive" among "salt-of-the-earth" sorts who "drink away" as "stoic but friendly" barkeeps (including the eponymous owner) keep the low-cost sauce coming; video games and "serious pool" round out its "straightforward" charms.

Lunasa | 21 | 16 | 22 | M |

E Village | 126 First Ave. (bet. 7th St. & St. Marks Pl.) | L to 1st Ave. | 212-228-8580 | www.lunasabar.com

"Casual" Gaelic "neighborhood haunt" that's "much appreciated" by "loyal" East Villagers who monitor sports on "multiple TVs" or play "board games" while "attentive" tapsters pull the "well-priced" pints; come summer, the "great backyard" is the place to "get soused in the sun."

MacDougal Street Ale House | 18 | 12 | 16 | M |

G Village | 122 MacDougal St., downstairs (bet. Bleecker & W. 3rd Sts.) | A/B/C/D/E/F/M to W. 4th St. | 212-254-0006

An "easily accessible" Village barhop stop, this underground collegiate taproom awaits with budget brews, satellite sports and "pool and darts in the back"; even though it's strictly "run-of-the-mill", claustrophobes are relieved that "it's generally not very crowded."

Madame X | 17 | 16 | 16 | M |

G Village | 94 W. Houston St. (bet. La Guardia Pl. & Thompson St.) | A/B/C/D/E/F/M to W. 4th St. | 212-539-0808 | www.madamex.com

Channeling the "waiting room of a bordello", this Village bar/lounge features "dim red" lights, crimson velvet couches, a heated patio and "arty nudie pics" to stoke the libidos of "mid-twenties" libertines; but even though it's "desperately trying to be sexy", skeptics assess the scene as "a little worn out."

☑ Madam Geneva | 28 | 25 | 22 | E |

NoHo | 4 Bleecker St. (Bowery) | 6 to Bleecker St. | 212-254-0350 | www.madamgeneva-nyc.com

"Gin is their expertise" at this NoHo back-room bar that salutes its signature tipple with both its name (Victorian jargon for 'gin') and its "pricey" specialty drinks, finished with the "old-school English twist" of a spoonful of jam; a "chic" but "subdued" clientele makes the AvroKO-designed space an "elegant" retreat, and despite the "hidden aspect", it's "always crowded."

Mad46 | 24 | 20 | 19 | E |

E 40s | Roosevelt Hotel | 45 E. 45th St., 19th fl. (enter on 46th St., bet. Madison & Vanderbilt Aves.) | 4/5/6/7/S to 42nd St./Grand Central | 221-885-6095 | www.mad46.com

Parked "in the shadow of Grand Central", this seasonal rooftop "escape" atop the Roosevelt Hotel offers Midtown desk jockeys the "chance to be outdoors" in a "not overly packed" environment; ok, it's "pricey" and "a bit of a wannabe" viewwise – "there really isn't much to see" – but overall it's one of the few "decent places" in this nightlife-starved neighborhood.

Mad River

13 | 10 | 14 | M

E 80s | 1442 Third Ave. (bet. 81st & 82nd Sts.) | 4/5/6 to 86th St. | 212-988-1832 | www.madrivergrille.com

"Home away from home for U of Wisconsin grads", this Yorkville "staple of the Upper East Side bar scene" draws a sea of "frat boys" with rivers of "cheap" hooch and DJs to help "get your grind on"; while it "doesn't look like much", it can be a "packed" madhouse – albeit in a majorly "cheesy" way.

Maggie's Place

18 | 17 | 22 | M

E 40s | 21 E. 47th St. (bet. 5th & Madison Aves.) | B/D/F/M to 47-50th Sts./ Rockefeller Ctr. | 212-753-5757 | www.maggiesnyc.com

Commuters who "need a cold one near Grand Central" slip into this pubby Midtowner, a "typical" way station with "lots of beer on tap" and "quality service" from "real Irish" staffers; while "crowded" after work, it "dies out pretty quickly" and becomes "more relaxed" as the evening progresses.

Magician, The ⌀

21 | 12 | 21 | I

LES | 118 Rivington St. (Essex St.) | F/J/M/Z to Delancey/Essex Sts. | 212-673-7851

A Lower East Side "locals' hideout", this "quiet joint" conjures up something of a crowd with "low prices", "plentiful seating" and film-noir atmospherics; while there's not "much going for it on the surface", it does the trick for "casual" quaffing with "no weekenders screaming in your ear."

Z NEW Maison Premiere

– | – | – | E

Williamsburg | 298 Bedford Ave. (bet. Grand & S. 1st Sts.) | Brooklyn | L to Bedford Ave. | 347-335-0446 | www.maisonpremiere.com

The Big Easy gets the Williamsburg treatment at this atmospheric new cocktail-and-oyster specialist, an homage to New Orleans' Olde Absinthe House featuring fleur de lis–patterned tin wainscoting and a horseshoe-shaped bar replete with an absinthe tower; plans are in the works to open a large rear garden.

Mama's Bar

– | – | – | I

E Village | 34 Ave. B (3rd St.) | F to Lower East Side/2nd Ave. | 212-777-5729 | www.mamasbarnyc.com

This "endearingly quirky" East Villager nurtures a "colorful mix of hipsters and professionals" with "stiff" house-infused vodkas and a "fab" jukebox; a "no-frills" space done up in Salvation Army Modern, it's equally "chill" whether starting off the evening or ending it with a "late, late" nightcap.

Manhattan Inn

– | – | – | M

Greenpoint | 632 Manhattan Ave. (Nassau Ave.) | Brooklyn | G to Nassau Ave. | 718-383-0885 | www.themanhattaninn.com

Greenpoint takes a crack at Manhattan cool by way of this vintagey bar/eatery near McCarren Park, where the speakeasy-ish setting includes a white baby grand and a pianist pounding out jazzy ragtime rhythms; the decor philosophy is all about repurposing, with school-desk dining tables, doorknob tap handles and seats reclaimed from a movie theater.

Manitoba's

25 | 20 | 25 | I

E Village | 99 Ave. B (bet. 6th & 7th Sts.) | F to Lower East Side/2nd Ave. | 212-982-2511 | www.manitobas.com

"Real live" '70s rocker 'Handsome Dick' Manitoba (of Dictators fame) owns and sometimes operates this "down-to-earth" East Village dive bar, a "tribute to punk history" sporting "iconic" photos and a "solid jukebox", along with "bartenders who know as much about the songs as the suds"; "tasty pints" and "cheap" tabs to the contrary, it "deserves bigger crowds."

Manny's on Second

∇ 19 | 13 | 19 | M

E 90s | 1770 Second Ave. (bet. 92nd & 93rd Sts.) | 6 to 96th St. | 212-410-3300 | www.mannysonsecond.com

Notwithstanding a name change and a light "face-lift", this Upper Eastsider (fka Blondies) remains a "raucous sports bar" frequented by "frat" folk; an upstairs addition features pool and live music.

Marie's Crisis ⊅

24 | 13 | 20 | M

W Village | 59 Grove St. (bet. Bleecker St. & 7th Ave. S.) | 1 to Christopher St. | 212-243-9323

"Belt out" Broadway classics with a "heavily gay crowd" at this West Village piano-bar "warhorse", a "must-be-seen-to-be-believed" dump that's catnip for amateur warblers and "show-tune queens" who "miss Ethel Merman"; even though it's rumored to be where retired "chorus boys go to die", you "don't need talent" here – you just need to "know all the words."

Marquee

21 | 21 | 17 | VE

Chelsea | 289 10th Ave. (bet. 26th & 27th Sts.) | C/E to 23rd St. | 646-473-0202 | www.marqueeny.com

"Once hot, now not", this West Chelsea club is still a "decent time out" for "flashy" folk who like a semi-"selective" door, "stylish" environs and the opportunity to "drop serious cash"; since it peaked "five years ago", now there's a better chance of experiencing the "thrill of being let in."

Mars Bar ⊅

19 | 14 | 19 | I

E Village | 25 E. First St. (2nd Ave.) | F to Lower East Side/2nd Ave. | 212-473-9842

This ultraskuzzy East Villager is a "real-deal" dive providing haven for a "plain crazy" assortment of die-hard punks and *Barfly*-caliber boozehounds; there's "no food here – the roaches ate it all" – and beveragewise it's probably best to stick to drinks served in a bottle; catch it while you can – word is it's about to close.

Marshall Stack ⊅

∇ 24 | 18 | 24 | M

LES | 66 Rivington St. (Allen St.) | F to Lower East Side/2nd Ave. | 212-228-4667

Refreshingly "unpretentious" for a self-styled rock bar, this "laid-back" Lower Eastsider serves "quality" suds and worthy wines to an "over-25" cohort that applauds the "kick-ass" retro jukebox; despite being named for an arena-ready wall of amps, it stacks up as a low-fi scene "that the neighborhood needs."

| | APPEAL | DECOR | SERVICE | COST |

Matchless ⌖
▽ 21 | 19 | 20 | I

Greenpoint | 557 Manhattan Ave. (Driggs Ave.) | Brooklyn | G to
Nassau Ave. | 718-383-5333 | www.barmatchless.com

A "sleeper hit" that's now a match for "Enid's across the street", this
Greenpoint joint in a former auto-parts shop has "everything you
could ask for", namely "friendly bartenders", "skilled DJs", a "fun
crowd" and bands in the back room; it's "another hipster hive" that's
"continuing to evolve."

Matt Torrey's ⌖
– | – | – | M

Williamsburg | 46 Bushwick Ave. (bet. Bushwick & Humboldt Aves.) |
Brooklyn | L to Grand St. | 718-218-7646

Pretty slick for East Williamsburg, this roomy taproom from some
Harefield Road vets rolls out a very long bar, hardwood floors and a
stool-lined expanse of floor-to-ceiling windows; the idiosyncratic beer
list comes from New York State, and there are plenty of schmoozey
booths in the back.

Max Fish ⌖
19 | 17 | 17 | M

LES | 178 Ludlow St. (bet. Houston & Stanton Sts.) | F to Lower East Side/
2nd Ave. | 212-529-3959 | www.maxfish.com

A "neighborhood standby for decades", this "brightly lit" bar is a
"true Lower East Side classic" with "twentysomething boozers" swimming by to blithely sip "stiff drinks" against a backdrop of "eccentric
art"; it's a "dependably good time" – assuming you're "cool enough
to be there"; P.S. die-hards should stop by soon – lease issues put its
future in question.

☑ Mayahuel
26 | 24 | 23 | E

E Village | 304 E. Sixth St. (bet. 1st & 2nd Aves.) | 6 to Astor Pl. |
212-253-5888 | www.mayahuelny.com

"Taking tequila to a more refined level", this East Village double-
decker offers "much more than your basic margarita" thanks to "expert"
mixologists concocting "amazing" top-shelf cocktails; downstairs, the
"Mexican Gothic" decor channels a "speakeasy", while the crimson-lit
lounge above is "fantastic for dates."

M Bar
24 | 25 | 22 | E

W 40s | Mansfield Hotel | 12 W. 44th St. (bet. 5th & 6th Aves.) | 7/B/
D/F/M to 42nd St./Bryant Park | 212-277-8888 |
www.mansfieldhotel.com

M-inently urbane, this subdued Midtown hotel bar boasts a "classic"
interior (think lofty bookshelves and a beaux arts skylight) that's "extremely comfortable" for an illicit "tryst" or "conversation" over properly prepared cocktails; the tabs are steep, but worth it "if you're
celebrating something special."

McAleer's Pub
15 | 11 | 19 | M

W 80s | 425 Amsterdam Ave. (bet. 80th & 81st Sts.) | 1 to 79th St. |
212-362-7867 | www.mcaleerspub.com

"Downscale" but "welcoming", this "simple" Irish tavern is a longtime
Upper West Side area fixture (around since 1953) with a "solid"
following that is partial to "Mets games" and "laid-back" brews;
"if you don't mind the smell of stale beer", it's an affordable neighborhood "respite" for parched locals.

	APPEAL	DECOR	SERVICE	COST

McCormack's
`- | - | - | M`

Murray Hill | 365 Third Ave. (26th St.) | 6 to 28th St. | 212-683-0911 | www.mccormacks.net

Murray Hill footy fans rely on this Irish sports pub to air European soccer in "cookie-cutter" surroundings that don't distract from the action; beyond the plasma screens, it's a handy "after-work" site for those who prefer "nothing over the top."

McFadden's
`15 | 13 | 15 | M`

E 40s | 800 Second Ave. (42nd St.) | 4/5/6/7/S to 42nd St./Grand Central | 212-986-1515 | www.mcfaddens42.com

Aka "McFratten's", this Irish pub near the U.N. entertains hordes of "fresh-out-of-college" kids in search of "sports action", "drunken hookups" and "girls dancing on the bar"; it gets "very busy after work", though insiders say "all of the action is on the sidewalk."

❷ McSorley's ∅
`23 | 17 | 18 | M`

E Village | 15 E. Seventh St. (bet. 2nd & 3rd Aves.) | 6 to Astor Pl. | 212-254-2570 | www.mcsorleysnewyork.com

The "sawdust on the floors" hasn't changed since this "must-visit" East Village "landmark" opened in 1854, and today "merry throngs" still show up to drink "nothing but beer" and "soak up the history"; expect "blunt bartenders", a limited suds selection – "either light or dark" – and "epic numbers of tourists" and "frat boys"; P.S. "they adhere to the motto 'Drink or be Gone.'"

Mehanata
`- | - | - | M`

LES | 113 Ludlow St. (bet. Delancey & Rivington Sts.) | F/J/M/Z to Delancey/Essex Sts. | 212-625-0981 | www.mehanata.com

A "dive through and through", this "fun" LES Bulgarian bar is truly "something different" with vodka "flowing freely" and live bands bringing "Balkan" boogie fever to the dance floor; the duplex setup is "just seedy enough" to make the "totally random" crowd go totally "bonkers."

Merc Bar
`22 | 21 | 17 | E`

SoHo | 151 Mercer St. (bet. Houston & Prince Sts.) | N/R to Prince St. | 212-966-2727 | www.mercbar.com

The "ski lodge comes to SoHo" at this longtime "class" act, a "chic place to get a well-mixed drink" in a "soothing" setting equipped with "wood paneling" and a "canoe on the ceiling"; "around too long to be trendy", it's "lost the 'it' crowd, which is actually a good thing."

Mercer Bar
`22 | 21 | 20 | VE`

SoHo | Mercer Hotel | 99 Prince St. (Mercer St.) | N/R to Prince St. | 212-966-5454

Once a magnet for "movie-biz big shots", this "fancy" SoHo hotel bar is still "appealing" as a "sophisticated" stop for "expensive" cocktailing injected with a dose of "NY chic"; however, cynics say "it might as well be LA" what with the "staff attitude" and all the "poseurs" in the crowd.

Mercury Bar
`15 | 13 | 15 | M`

Murray Hill | 493 Third Ave. (bet. 33rd & 34th Sts.) | 6 to 33rd St. | 212-683-2645 | www.mercurybareast.com

(continued)

(continued)

Mercury Bar

W 40s | 659 Ninth Ave. (46th St.) | C/E to 50th St. | 212-262-7755 | www.mercurybarnyc.com

With its "overplayed set list" and "collegians" on the prowl, the Murray Hill outlet of this sports bar duo is a "clone" of every pickup hub on the Third Avenue strip; conversely, the Hell's Kitchen outlet has "lots of TVs" on the walls and the scent of "testosterone in the air."

Mercury Lounge
21 | 13 | 17 | M

LES | 217 E. Houston St. (bet. Essex & Ludlow Sts.) | F to Lower East Side/ 2nd Ave. | 212-260-4700 | www.mercuryloungenyc.com

"Quasi-discovered acts" are the draw at this "essential" LES music venue split into two parts: a front bar vending "fairly priced" drinks and a "small" stage in the rear; even though there's "zero atmosphere" and the "limited seating" means you'll probably be "standing all night", it's still "one of the best places to see new bands" in Manhattan.

Metro Grill Roof Garden
23 | 21 | 19 | E

Garment District | Metro Hotel | 45 W. 35th St. (bet. 5th & 6th Aves.) | B/D/F/M/N/Q/R to 34th St./Herald Sq. | 212-279-3535 | www.hotelmetronyc.com

After a "major face-lift", this seasonal "rooftop oasis" capping a Garment District hotel went from a "quiet" scene to "quite a scene" with a smart setting to match its drop-dead view of the Empire State Building; fans say the upgrade makes it "worth the money."

Metropolitan ∌
∇ 18 | 17 | 20 | M

Williamsburg | 559 Lorimer St. (bet. Devoe St. & Metropolitan Ave.) | Brooklyn | G/L to Metropolitan Ave./Lorimer St. | 718-599-4444

Ok, "it's a gay bar, but a pretty mixed-demographic one" given the random breeders in the crowd at this "unassuming" Williamsburg joint; "cheap drinks", dual fireplaces, a pool table and a "lush patio" are among its virtues – indeed, fans say that "even the hipsters are hip here."

☑ Metropolitan Room
25 | 22 | 24 | E

Flatiron | 34 W. 22nd St. (bet. 5th & 6th Aves.) | F to 23rd St. | 212-206-0440 | www.metropolitanroom.com

"Consistently excellent" acts have fans jazzed on this Flatiron cabaret where both "known names" and "local talent" perform in a "swanky" setting "small enough" to afford most comers a "good seat"; true, it's "pricey", but then again it's "one of the last remaining cabarets" in town.

Mickey Mantle's
18 | 19 | 16 | E

W 50s | 42 Central Park S. (bet. 5th & 6th Aves.) | N/R to 5th Ave./ 59th St. | 212-688-7777 | www.mickeymantles.com

Baseball goes "Planet Hollywood" at this Central Park South sports bar celebrating the Mick with wall-to-wall "Yankees" memorabilia; "throngs of tourists", "production-line food" and "high-priced" pours lead some to say "it would work better in Times Square."

Milady's
15 | 11 | 19 | I

SoHo | 160 Prince St. (Thompson St.) | N/R to Prince St. | 212-226-9340

Like the "middle of Pittsburgh" plopped down into SoHo, this 81-year-old "dive" is a magnet for "rent-stabilized" locals; sure, it's "affordable", but given the "posh" neighborhood, some wonder "how it survives."

◪ Milk and Honey ⇗   25 | 22 | 25 | VE

LES | 134 Eldridge St. (bet. Broome & Delancey Sts.) | J/Z to Bowery | no phone | www.mlkhny.com

A "bastion of trendy mixology" with a "twist of mystery", this "dark", secretive LES den, now in its 10th year, "takes making drinks to an art form" as "serious" barkeeps create "spectacular" cocktails from the "freshest ingredients"; reservations can now be made two or three days in advance via e-mail: milkandhoneyreservations@gmail.com; P.S. five people is the largest party it can accommodate.

◪ Mission Dolores   - | - | - | M

Park Slope | 249 Fourth Ave. (bet. Carroll & President Sts.) | Brooklyn | R to Union St. | 718-399-0099 | www.missiondoloresbar.com

Parked on the Slope's more industrial Fourth Avenue, this former tire shop has been converted into a serious beer bar; pinball, board games and a spacious outdoor patio fuel the lively vibe, while 20 rotating craft ales (no bottles) appease the pickiest hopsheads.

🆕 Mister H   - | - | - | VE

SoHo | Mondrian Soho Hotel | 150 Lafayette St. (bet. Grand & Howard Sts.) | 6/J/N/Q/Z to Canal St. | 212-389-1000

Nightlife player Armin Amiri (Bungalow 8, Socialista) is the mind behind this atmospheric newcomer in the Mondrian Soho that channels a 1930s Shanghai opium den with crimson lighting and Chinese lanterns; behind a beaded curtain lies a VIP nook already famed for its neon sign proclaiming 'this is not a brothel, there are no prostitutes at this address.'

◪ MO Bar   24 | 26 | 25 | VE

W 60s | Mandarin Oriental Hotel | 80 Columbus Circle, 35th fl. (60th St.) | 1/A/B/C/D to 59th St./Columbus Circle | 212-805-8800 | www.mandarinoriental.com

High above Columbus Circle, this "refined" enclave in the Mandarin Oriental plies "pricey" "Asian-inspired" specialty cocktails in elegantly "minimal" environs; there's "no view" since its windows face a neighboring tower, so insiders slip into the adjacent lobby lounge where seating is limited but the Central Park vistas are "breathtaking."

Moda Outdoors   - | - | - | E

W 50s | Flatotel | 135 W. 52nd St. (bet. 6th & 7th Aves.) | B/D/F/M to 47-50th Sts./Rockefeller Ctr. | 212-887-9880 | www.flatotel.com

One of Midtown's "few outdoor" drinking options, this seasonal hotel bar is set in a "covered" breezeway that's packed after work and deserted once the commuters head home; high tabs are "typical" for the area, but the chance to drink alfresco "even in the rain" compensates.

Molly Pitcher's Ale House   16 | 13 | 19 | M

E 80s | 1641 Second Ave. (85th St.) | 4/5/6 to 86th St. | 212-249-3068 | www.mollypitchersnyc.com

It's "not a standout", but this UES Irish sports bar is a "decent" enough supplier of "standard" brews and nibbles to scarf down while cheering the team on; when it's overrun by the "inevitable" frat cats, insiders head for the "attached snug" for "somewhat of a respite."

	APPEAL	DECOR	SERVICE	COST

Molly's
23 | 18 | 21 | M

Gramercy | 287 Third Ave. (bet. 22nd & 23rd Sts.) | 6 to 23rd St. |
212-889-3361 | www.mollysshebeen.com

The authenticity "never fails to charm" at this long-standing Gramercy Irish pub, a "cozy retreat" where the "Guinness just tastes better" maybe because of its "roaring fireplace", "sawdust"-strewn floor and "traditional" Gaelic barkeeps (straight out of "Central Casting"); quite simply, it's "in a class by itself."

Monday Room
▽ 25 | 25 | 25 | E

NoLita | 210 Elizabeth St. (bet. Prince & Spring Sts.) | 6 to Spring St. |
212-343-7011 | www.themondayroom.com

There's "never a dud glass" to be found among the "excellent" vintages at this "quiet little" wine-sipping nook inside NoLita's Public restaurant that forgoes the usual bar setup in favor of table service; stylish retro looks, "top-notch" service and "tasty small bites" help justify the "too-high" tabs.

M1-5 Bar
17 | 12 | 15 | M

TriBeCa | 52 Walker St. (bet. B'way & Church St.) | 1/2 to Canal St. |
212-965-1701 | www.m1-5.com

"Space isn't an issue" at this "massive" watering hole, a "sparsely decorated airplane hangar" of a place that offers "decent music", billiards and "moderately priced" booze in an admittedly "isolated" part of TriBeCa; it's a no-brainer for a "nothing-fancy" night out, though it may seem "too big for the amount of people" who show up.

☒ Monkey Bar
23 | 22 | 21 | VE

E 50s | Elysée Hotel | 60 E. 54th St. (bet. Madison & Park Aves.) |
6/E to 51st-53rd Sts./Lexington Ave. | 212-308-2950 |
www.monkeybarnewyork.com

A "famous" "oldie but goodie" that's been revived by owner (and *Vanity Fair* helmer) Graydon Carter, this "classy" Midtown hotel bar is a "hopping" joint where "well-dressed and well-moneyed" types monkey around; from the "expertly made" cocktails to the "whimsical" chimp murals, it's "worth a visit" – if you can swing the "staggering cost."

Monster, The ⌷
21 | 17 | 19 | M

W Village | 80 Grove St. (Sheridan Sq.) | 1 to Christopher St. |
212-924-3558 | www.manhattan-monster.com

When you "want to feel young again", this venerable gay "crossroads" in the West Village merges a ground-floor piano bar recalling "Liberace's living room" with a basement danceland thumping out "Lady Gaga" and "old-time disco"; "stiff drinks" keep the "mixed crowd" of locals and yokels in "super-friendly" spirits.

Morrell Wine Bar
23 | 18 | 21 | E

W 40s | 1 Rockefeller Plaza (49th St., bet. 5th & 6th Aves.) | B/D/F/M to 47-50th Sts./Rockefeller Ctr. | 212-262-7700 |
www.morrellwinebar.com

Both the "real estate" and the vino selection are "better than most" at this "upscale" Rock Center wine bar where oenophiles sample an "extensive" by-the-glass list while vying for a "seat at the bar" (there's also "outdoor" seating in clement weather); yes, it's rell-atively "expensive" and "overrun by tourists", but at least the bottles are cheaper at its adjacent retail shop.

Motor City ⌐

16	15	16	I

LES | 127 Ludlow St. (bet. Delancey & Rivington Sts.) | F/J/M/Z to Delancey/Essex Sts. | 212-358-1595 | www.motorcitybar.com

"Strap on your seat belt" and get ready to rock 'n' roll at this "gritty" dive that proudly "pays homage" to Rust Belt excess with "dirt-cheap" hooch, "auto-industry" decor and a DJ partial to metal played "way too loud"; a relic of the Lower East Side's "edgy" past, it "gets it just right."

Mr. Dennehy's

▽ 20	17	23	M

W Village | 63 Carmine St. (bet. Bedford St. & 7th Ave. S.) | A/B/C/D/E/F/M to W. 4th St. | 212-414-1223 | www.mrdennehys.com

There's nary a cardboard shamrock in sight at this West Village Irish pub, whose unadorned quarters have a "local feel" courtesy of the "friendly" barkeeps and sports fans monitoring the flat-screens; it's a stress-free standby for an "after-work" pick-me-up, even if purists shrug it's "as vanilla as it gets."

Mug's Ale House

20	13	20	I

Williamsburg | 125 Bedford Ave. (N. 10th St.) | Brooklyn | L to Bedford Ave. | 718-486-8232 | www.mugsalehouse.com

"Beer is the reason you're here" say the mugs who frequent this "friendly" Williamsburg suds specialist that's "justifiably known" for tapping an "amazing" lineup of "hard-to-find" brews for "decent" dough; otherwise, there's "not much else going for it" besides the "neighborhood" tavern vibe.

❷NEW Mulberry Project

-	-	-	E

Little Italy | 149 Mulberry St., downstairs (bet. Grand & Hester Sts.) | B/D to Grand St. | 646-448-4536 | www.mulberryproject.com

The crowd's the thing at this instant scene in Little Italy, formerly the short-lived My Little Secret, now reinvented as a select speakeasy that packs fashionable folks into its tight, underground setting; expert mixology, tasty small plates and a tough door divert attention away from the low-ceilinged, nothing-special room.

Music Hall of Williamsburg

23	15	15	M

Williamsburg | 66 N. Sixth St. (bet. Kent & Wythe Aves.) | Brooklyn | L to Bedford Ave. | 718-486-5400 | www.musichallofwilliamsburg.com

Brooklyn's "version of Bowery Ballroom", this Williamsburg music club provides "exceptional" sound in a triple-tiered space with "great sightlines" that make it seem "you're never far from the stage"; while the name's "stupid" and its three bars "nothing to speak of", it's still "100 times better" than predecessor Northsix.

Naked Lunch

18	13	16	M

SoHo | 17 Thompson St. (bet. Canal & Grand Sts.) | A/C/E to Canal St. | 212-343-0828 | www.nakedlunchnyc.com

"Major crowds" of millennials make this longtime SoHo barroom perpetually "loud" and "crazy", even though it's a "fight for your life" to reach "the bar or the *one* restroom"; "fun" DJs with set lists incorporating "a little bit for everyone" add to the party-hearty goings-on.

	APPEAL	DECOR	SERVICE	COST

Nancy Whiskey Pub
16 | 6 | 14 | I

TriBeCa | 1 Lispenard St. (W. B'way) | 1/2 to Canal St. | 212-226-9943 | www.nancywhiskeypub.com

"Locals dominate" this "down-and-dirty" TriBeCa staple, an aging "dive" that's frill-free save for the shuffleboard table and a jukebox turned "just under 'too loud'"; while there's "no reason to travel there", it is a bona fide "bargain for this neighborhood."

National Underground
– | – | – | M

LES | 159 E. Houston St. (bet. Allen & Eldridge Sts.) | F to Lower East Side/2nd Ave. | 212-475-0611 | www.thenationalunderground.com

A low-hassle means to hear "halfway decent music", this bi-level LES performance venue (part-owned by songster Gavin DeGraw) is split into an Austin-ish upstairs bar hosting "intimate" unplugged acts and an underground den reserved for electric jams; when there's no music, it works as a good old "cheap place to drink."

Nectar
– | – | – | E

Harlem | 2235 Frederick Douglass Blvd. (bet. 120th & 121st Sts.) | A/B/C/D to 125th St. | 212-961-9622 | www.nectarwinenyc.com

Right "next to its sister wine store", this "small", "sleek" Harlem vino bar is a "real gem" with a "well-priced" lineup by the glass accompanied by "excellent" nibbles and "extroverted" service; the look may be "futuristic", but the "unpretentious" vibe keeps things down to earth.

Nevada Smith's
16 | 10 | 14 | M

E Village | 74 Third Ave. (bet. 11th & 12th Sts.) | L to 3rd Ave. | 212-982-2591 | www.nevadasmiths.net

"Simply *the* place to watch soccer" with other "extreme fans", this "no-frills" East Villager broadcasts virtually "all the European matches" with attendance peaking "during the World Cup" (the "doors open at 7 AM" on game days); come nightfall, it reverts to "just another sports bar" for the "NYU grunge crowd."

New York Comedy Club
18 | 13 | 15 | E

Murray Hill | 241 E. 24th St. (bet. 2nd & 3rd Aves.) | 6 to 23rd St. | 212-696-5233 | www.newyorkcomedyclub.com

The stand-up is always good for "some laughs" at this Murray Hill jest-fest, a forum for junior jokesmiths "trying their lot" along with intermittent sets from pros; a few "boo" the dubious decor, but fans argue you're "there for the entertainment" and "nothing else."

Niagara
19 | 15 | 18 | M

E Village | 112 Ave. A (7th St.) | L to 1st Ave. | 212-420-9517 | www.niagarabar.com

East Village "mainstay" that's "not really classy" but "kind of cool" when you feel like Avenue A "people-watching" through its "big beautiful windows" – or just "making out in the photo booth"; following a redo, the basement tiki bar is no more, remade into a sexy nexus, Lovers of Today.

NEW Night of Joy
– | – | – | M

Williamsburg | 667 Lorimer St. (Brooklyn Queens Expwy.) | Brooklyn | G/L to Metropolitan Ave./Lorimer St. | 718-388-8693

Grandma never downed drinks like the rosemary-infused bourbon or muddled-basil gimlets concocted at this Williamsburg cocktail bar hugging the BQE, but its kitschy sconces, vintage birdcage and patterned seat cushions might have come straight from her sitting room; with a pool table, Grand Central–style ceiling and French pop–heavy soundtrack, it manages to feel leisurely and current rather than contrived, and the upstairs deck is happening too.

Nikki Midtown

20 | 23 | 17 | VE

E 50s | 151 E. 50th St. (bet. Lexington & 3rd Aves.) | 6/E to 51st-53rd Sts./ Lexington Ave. | 212-753-1144 | www.nikkimidtown.net

"Champagne popping and tabletop stomping" provide the sound effects at this "swank" Midtown outpost, a "kicking" duplex outfitted with "stylish" white-on-white furnishings and "indoor cabanas"; hopefully the ultra-"expensive" elixirs will "transport you to St. Tropez" – and make all the "Eurotrash bankers" in the crowd more attractive.

925 Café & Cocktails

▽ 22 | 20 | 21 | E

E 40s | 800 Second Ave. (42nd St.) | 4/5/6/7/S to 42nd St./Grand Central | 646-360-3998 | www.925loungenyc.com

Nine-to-fivers seeking a comparatively "classy place to unwind" near Tudor City slip into this ultranarrow bar for "social drinks" served by a "cool" crew who make it "easy to become a regular"; it's a "much needed" option in comparison to the area's frattier options.

NEW Ninth Ward

- | - | - | M

E Village | 180 Second Ave. (bet. 11th & 12th Sts.) | L to 1st Ave. | 212-979-9273 | www.ninthwardnyc.com

From the Shoolbred's team across the street comes this new East Village homage to New Orleans, where Abitas and Sazeracs are the thing to order; the dark, atmospheric setting is very *Streetcar Named Desire*, with hurricane shutters, curtained private booths and a fountain-equipped back garden.

No Idea

15 | 11 | 17 | M

Flatiron | 30 E. 20th St. (bet. B'way & Park Ave. S.) | 4/5/6/L/N/Q/R to 14th St./Union Sq. | 212-777-0100 | www.noideabar.com

"No frills" is more like it at this "divey" Flatiron saloon where "NYU students", "professionals who still want to be frat kids" and the "unemployed" throw back "cheap" hooch served in pint glasses; "you drink for free" if your name matches the name of the day posted on its website.

No Malice Palace

21 | 13 | 17 | M

E Village | 197 E. Third St. (bet. Aves. A & B) | F to Lower East Side/2nd Ave. | 212-254-9184 | www.nomalice.com

"Young" things populate this unfancy East Villager, a dimly lit refuge known for its "fantastic DJs", "concrete patio" and "pickup" potential; it's an easy "landing spot on a weekday", but on weekends you'll have to "squeeze through the crowd."

Nowhere ⊅

▽ 21 | 15 | 22 | M

E Village | 322 E. 14th St. (bet. 1st & 2nd Aves.) | L to 1st Ave. | 212-477-4744

Gay ladies and gents populate this "diverse" East Village "hole-in-the-wall", where "stiff drinks", "mellow" atmospherics and "reasonable" prices add up to a "great time"; it's nowhere near the familiar haunts, though, so turnout varies: "sometimes packed, sometimes empty."

| | APPEAL | DECOR | SERVICE | COST |

Nublu ⌂
22 | 17 | 18 | M

E Village | 62 Ave. C (bet. 4th & 5th Sts.) | F to Lower East Side/2nd Ave. |
212-533-4080 | www.nublu.net
New sounds surface at this Alphabet City enclave of "cool", where
"laid-back" hipsters relax in the "jazzy" lounge or rear garden as DJs
and live musicians entertain; there's always a "variety" of "intriguing
performances", some hyping the house's "own record label."

Nurse Bettie
▽ 20 | 20 | 22 | M

LES | 106 Norfolk St. (bet. Delancey & Rivington Sts.) | F/J/M/Z to
Delancey/Essex Sts. | 917-434-9072 | www.nursebettieles.com
Fifties cheesecake model Bettie Page is the muse of this under-the-
radar LES bar where classy cocktails arrive in a "small", "sexy" space
hung with "pinup" posters; despite the "fun ambiance", some say
"boring" and "overpriced."

Nuyorican Poets Cafe
23 | 15 | 19 | M

E Village | 236 E. Third St. (bet. Aves. B & C) | F to Lower East Side/
2nd Ave. | 212-505-8183 | www.nuyorican.org
"Poetry slam" enthusiasts catch the "real thing" at this landmark East
Village cafe, famed for its Friday-night face-offs and "eclectic" live entertainment the rest of the week encompassing jazz, comedy and theater; it "continues to shine" as a "change of pace", so "arrive early" or
be prepared for "standing room only."

☑ Oak Bar
25 | 25 | 22 | VE

W 50s | Plaza Hotel | 10 Central Park S. (bet. 5th & 6th Aves.) | N/R to
5th Ave./59th St. | 212-758-7777 | www.oakroomny.com
The Plaza's "venerable" sanctum of "civilization", this "wonderfully
preserved" vintage-1945 watering hole boasts a "distinguished" setting replete with "warm woodwork", "windows overlooking Central
Park" and museum-quality Everett Shinn murals; true, "there's no
such thing as happy hour here", but the "sticker-shock" tabs are worth
it just to "feel the history."

☑ Oak Room
25 | 25 | 23 | VE

W 40s | Algonquin Hotel | 59 W. 44th St. (bet. 5th & 6th Aves.) | 7/B/
D/F/M to 42nd St./Bryant Park | 212-840-6800 |
www.algonquinhotel.com
"Hear your favorite singers or discover new ones" at this "enduring" cabaret in Midtown's Algonquin Hotel, a bastion of "total
class" where "top-drawer" vocalists warble standards for a tony
audience; ok, it's "pricey" and the "long, narrow room" can be "un-
comfortably crowded", but this "special-occasion" place is worth it
"for the talent" alone.

Off the Wagon
17 | 13 | 18 | I

G Village | 109 MacDougal St. (bet. Bleecker & W. 3rd Sts.) |
A/B/C/D/E/F/M to W. 4th St. | 212-533-4487 |
www.nycbestbar.com
"Woo-hoo!", this "heart-of-NYU" Village sports bar is a "super-cheap,
super-smelly" magnet for the "just-got-out-of-college-and-wish-I-
was-still-there" set ("bring on the beer pong"); the "down-and-dirty"
antics ensure there's "never a dull moment", but noncollegians might
want to "think twice."

| | APPEAL | DECOR | SERVICE | COST |

O'Flaherty's Ale House
19 | **15** | **19** | **M**

W 40s | 334 W. 46th St. (bet. 8th & 9th Aves.) | A/C/E to 42nd St./ Port Authority | 212-581-9366 | www.oflahertysnyc.com

"Enjoy a black and tan by the fireplace" at this Restaurant Row Irish pub, an "inviting" patch o' the Auld Sod that supplies "Guinness drafts" and nightly "live music" to a mix of locals and out-of-towners; nitpickers quibble that the interior's due for a "spruce-up", but there's always that "hidden" garden.

O'Flanagan's
20 | **16** | **20** | **M**

E 60s | 1215 First Ave. (bet. 65th & 66th Sts.) | 6 to 68th St. | 212-439-0660 | www.oflanagans.com

While easily mistaken for a "frat bar plunked down on the UES", this "longtime" Irish hang is "frequented by all types" who share a taste for suds, sports and "pool tables"; when rotating cover bands take the back stage, it's "always a good time."

Old Town Bar
21 | **17** | **17** | **M**

Flatiron | 45 E. 18th St. (bet. B'way & Park Ave. S.) | 4/5/6/L/N/Q/R to 14th St./Union Sq. | 212-529-6732 | www.oldtownbar.com

"Just as crusty as ever", this circa-1892 Flatiron tavern is a "tin-ceilinged" "step back in time" that's managed to "retain its charm" in an otherwise "fancy-pants neighborhood"; as a "relic" of "old-school Gotham", it "doesn't get much more authentic", but "don't wear your best" attire – it's decidedly "run-down."

O'Lunney's
17 | **16** | **20** | **M**

W 40s | 145 W. 45th St. (bet. B'way & 6th Ave.) | 1/2/3/7/N/Q/R/S to 42nd St./Times Sq. | 212-840-6688 | www.olunneys.com

With its "roomy" layout and "convenient" Times Square address, this "huge" Irish pub is a natural "meeting point" after work or pre-theater; but critics say its "glitzy, Disneyfied" atmosphere makes for one "boring tourist trap."

One & One
16 | **13** | **15** | **M**

E Village | 76 E. First St. (1st Ave.) | F to Lower East Side/2nd Ave. | 212-598-9126 | www.oneandoneny.com

Thanks to its "roomy" interior and "neat-and-clean" mien, this East Village Irish pub is a "neighborhood" nexus for tap beer, sports galore and alfresco drinking on sidewalk seats; otherwise, it's "pretty run-of-the-mill" – save for the "surprisingly decent" lounge in the basement.

151
19 | **15** | **15** | **M**

LES | 151 Rivington St., downstairs (bet. Clinton & Suffolk Sts.) | F/J/M/Z to Delancey/Essex Sts. | 212-228-4139

"Less crazed" than the LES norm, this "black-hole-dark" subterranean lounge features DJs cueing up "non-cheesy rock" in a "low-key" setting channeling a "'70s rec room"; "good prices" make it a "safe bet" for "down-to-earth" types.

☑ 1 Oak
24 | **22** | **18** | **VE**

Chelsea | 453 W. 17th St. (bet. 9th & 10th Aves.) | A/C/E/L to 14th St./ 8th Ave. | 212-242-1111 | www.1oaknyc.com

Near the "top of the nightlife eco-system", this "hip" but "elitist" Chelsea lounge is a magnet for "Victoria's Secret" models, "A-list" celebs ("Leo", "Giselle", "A-Rod") and "Euro playboys" "spewing cash like an ATM"; no surprise, "bottle service is king", the doormen are "pompous" and the velvet rope is so "tight" that "even Ben Franklin can't get in"; P.S. the "later it gets, the better it is."

NEW 1 Republik Lounge

| | - | - | - | I |

Murray Hill | 613 Second Ave. (bet. 33rd & 34th Sts.) | 6 to 33rd St. | 646-455-0813 | www.1republiklounge.com

Annexing the former Underground space, this big, brick-walled Murray Hill newcomer offers three rooms plus a back patio to get your drink on; though the different areas have theme-park names (the Rat Pack Lounge, the Wizard of Oz Room), the decor throughout is strictly dive bar.

169 Bar

| | 18 | 14 | 20 | M |

LES | 169 E. Broadway (Rutgers St.) | F to E. B'way | 212-473-8866 | www.169barnyc.com

"Funky characters" populate this "divey" Lower Eastsider, a "no-pretension" zone that's notable for hosting "decent live music" from bayou-belt bands; while there's "not much decor" – "leopard-print pool table" excepted – overall it's "ok for the money."

124 Rabbit Club ⊄

| | 22 | 19 | 22 | E |

G Village | 124 MacDougal St., downstairs (bet. Bleecker & W. 3rd Sts.) | A/B/C/D/E/F/M to W. 4th St. | 212-254-0575

"Bohemian" Village suds specialist set in a "long, skinny" underground space that's a "welcome" refuge from MacDougal Street's "drunken masses" (it's accessed via a "speakeasy-type" buzzer); inside, "affable" staffers "steer you toward beer enlightenment" via a "superb" lineup of "international" bottles that will make you forget the "cramped" surroundings.

123 Burger Shot Beer

| | 19 | 13 | 17 | M |

W 50s | 738 10th Ave. (bet. 50th & 51st Sts.) | C/E to 50th St. | 212-315-0123 | www.123burgershotbeer.com

Folks on a "restricted budget" "relive their fraternity years" at this "rowdy" Hell's Kitchen sports bar where the namesake "deal" – $1 sliders, $2 shots, $3 beers – is almost "impossible to beat"; after work, it's usually "packed" with "blitzed" collegians who've figured out there's no more economical way to "get fed and drunk."

Onieal's Grand Street

| | ▽ 24 | 22 | 22 | M |

Little Italy | 174 Grand St. (bet. Baxter & Mulberry Sts.) | B/D to Grand St. | 212-941-9119 | www.onieals.com

Once a real-deal speakeasy, this longtime Little Italy bar/lounge has preserved the space's "old-school architecture" to complement its "elegant service" and "special cocktails"; a destination for "preppies" and "women drinking pink somethings" (its "part of the *Sex and the City* tour"), it's normally "calm" but can get mighty "crowded" on the weekends.

NEW On the Rocks

| | - | - | - | M |

W 40s | 696 10th Ave. (bet. 48th & 49th Sts.) | C/E to 50th St. | 212-247-2055

Way West Hell's Kitchen has a new watering hole, this itty-bitty pub specializing in whiskey and bottled beer; the brown spirits on offer match the room's brown color scheme, while a sea of votive candles provide the mood lighting; P.S. there are no TVs, so have some conversational gambits ready.

Opal

APPEAL	DECOR	SERVICE	COST
16	14	14	M

E 50s | 251 E. 52nd St. (2nd Ave.) | 6/E to 51st-53rd Sts./Lexington Ave. | 212-593-4321 | www.opalbar.com

"Young white-collar" folks fuel the "after-work scene" at this "crowded" Midtown watering hole known for its "happy-hour deals" and "major meat market" vibe; though some detect a whiff of *"Jersey Shore*-ness" in the air, it can be "really fun" – so long as "you're drinking a lot."

NEW Orient Express

APPEAL	DECOR	SERVICE	COST
-	-	-	E

W Village | 325 W. 11th St. (bet. Greenwich & Washington Sts.) | 1/2 to Christopher St./Sheridan Sq. | 212-691-8845 | www.orientexpressnyc.com

Brought to you by the owner of Turks & Frogs, this new West Villager lives up to its name by channeling a first-class railroad car from the bygone era when traveling was considered glamorous; vintage suitcases, long-expired passports and built-in overhead luggage racks make for a trains-porting mood, helped along by fancy pricey cocktails.

Otheroom

APPEAL	DECOR	SERVICE	COST
24	21	20	M

W Village | 143 Perry St. (bet. Greenwich & Washington Sts.) | 1 to Christopher St. | 212-645-9758 | www.theroomsbeerandwine.com

"Largely undiscovered", this "dark and cozy" West Villager "feels local" (at least during the week) and "should be everyone's favorite bar – but you're glad it's not"; regulars report it's beer-and-wine only, with "something akin to a make-out room in back."

Otto's Shrunken Head ⌀

APPEAL	DECOR	SERVICE	COST
18	18	16	M

E Village | 538 E. 14th St. (bet. Aves. A & B) | L to 1st Ave. | 212-228-2240 | www.ottosshrunkenhead.com

Something completely "different", this "divey" East Village "punk tiki bar" splices "kitschy" Polynesian decor with a "rock 'n' roll" sensibility; whether listening to headbanging DJs up front or catching "live acts in the back", the "weird voodoo" vibe has yokels wondering "is this for real?"

Overlook Lounge

APPEAL	DECOR	SERVICE	COST
18	14	18	M

E 40s | 225 E. 44th St. (bet. 2nd & 3rd Aves.) | 4/5/6/7/S to 42nd St./Grand Central | 212-682-7266 | www.overlooknyc.com

"Serviceable if you work in the area", this "no-attitude" boozer near Grand Central is "dependable" for "sports-watching" with the "rambunctious" regulars or hanging out on the makeshift "upstairs deck"; circa-1976 cartoon art on the walls makes it easier to overlook the otherwise "average" atmospherics.

Pacha

APPEAL	DECOR	SERVICE	COST
17	16	15	E

W 40s | 618 W. 46th St. (bet. 11th & 12th Aves.) | A/C/E to 42nd St./Port Authority | 212-209-7500 | www.pachanyc.com

"Megaclub" culture raves on at this Hell's Kitchen "slice of Ibiza", a "humongous", multilevel thing where "off-the-hook" international DJs rally a "fist-pumping", "glow stick"–waving cast of thousands itching to "get their groove on"; but cynics report too many "fake tans", "hair extensions" and "meatheads with no shirt on", dubbing it "*Jersey Shore on 46th Street.*"

Pacific Standard

22 | 20 | 21 | M

Boerum Hill | 82 Fourth Ave. (bet. Bergen St. & St. Marks Pl.) | Brooklyn | 2/3/4/5/B/D/N/Q/R to Atlantic Ave. | 718-858-1951 | www.pacificstandardbrooklyn.com

The Left Coast lands in Boerum Hill via this "welcoming" barroom and its "wonderful" rotating lineup of "NoCal"-centric microbrews on tap, served in an appropriately "laid-back" style; "quiz nights, board games", literary readings and a frequent-drinker program give it "favored local" cred for "thirtysomething hipsters."

Paddy Reilly's Music Bar

- | - | - | M

Murray Hill | 519 Second Ave. (bet. 28th & 29th Sts.) | 6 to 28th St. | 212-686-1210

"If you don't like Guinness, you'd better like the music" at this veteran Murray Hill Irish bar, where Vitamin G is "all they serve" on draft and traditional Celtic bands rule the stage in back; smiling service and a simple, cottagelike setting pad out the picture.

Painkiller

- | - | - | E

LES | 49 Essex St. (bet. Grand & Hester Sts.) | F/J/M/Z to Delancey/ Essex Sts. | 212-777-8454 | www.painkillernyc.com

The Dutch Kills team alights on the LES via this urban tiki bar in the former East Side Company Bar digs, where the rum-heavy drink menu includes traditional offerings like Zombies, Scorpions and mai tais; the long, narrow space mixes bamboo with graffiti art for an island-of-Oahu-meets-island-of-Manhattan vibe.

Palio Bar

∇ 23 | 26 | 23 | VE

W 50s | Equitable Center Arcade | 151 W. 51st St. (bet. 6th & 7th Aves.) | B/D/F/M to 47-50th Sts./Rockefeller Ctr. | 212-399-9400 | www.pianoduenyc.net

A Midtown "oasis" for "mature audiences", this "beautiful" watering hole features an oval bar surrounded by a "gorgeous" wraparound mural by Sandro Chia; stiff pricing and a hidden entrance off a midblock breezeway keep the crowd thin at this "low-key" spot.

Panda

- | - | - | M

LES | 139 Chrystie St. (bet. Broome & Delancey Sts.) | F/J/M/Z to Delancey/Essex Sts. | 212-334-6770 | www.thepandanyc.com

By day, this Lower Eastsider operates as a coffee shop/gallery space, but after dark it morphs into a club-ish nexus for arty types; the narrow space is outfitted with rudimentary furniture (it used to be a woodworking shop) and brought to you by alums of the much-missed Passerby.

P&G Cafe

21 | 16 | 21 | M

W 70s | 380 Columbus Ave., downstairs (78th St.) | B/C to 81st St. | 212-787-5150 | www.pandgbar.com

Those who miss this "classic" Upper West Side "neighborhood dive" report it's relocated from Amsterdam and 73rd to "nicer, larger" digs nearby with "two pool tables" and a "stage for live music"; the regulars "still stop in", the barkeeps "always have a story" and everyone's "glad they're back."

	APPEAL	DECOR	SERVICE	COST

Paramount Bar
| | - | - | - | VE |

W 40s | Paramount Hotel | 235 W. 46th St. (bet. 7th & 8th Aves.) | A/C/E to 42nd St./Port Authority | 212-413-1010 | www.nycparamount.com

The oft-interpreted ground-floor barroom in the Paramount Hotel gets an upscale spin at this newcomer whose no-nonsense name mirrors its stylized setting; velvety banquettes and vintage photo blowups on the walls provide the backdrop for swanky, albeit pricey, imbibing.

Paris, The
| | 20 | 17 | 21 | M |

Seaport | 119 South St. (Peck Slip) | 2/3/4/5/A/C/J/Z to Fulton St./B'way/Nassau | 212-240-9797 | www.theparistavern.com

Despite a touristy Seaport address, this long-standing remnant of "historic NY" (since 1873) has "retained its character" as an Irish "old faithful"; the graying regulars are "still greeted by name", though a few say it has a "glorious past, but not much of a present."

NEW Park Avenue Tavern
| | - | - | - | M |

Murray Hill | 99 Park Ave. (39th St.) | 4/5/6/7/S to 42nd St./Grand Central | 212-867-4484 | www.parkavenuetavernnyc.com

Once known as Bogart's, this virtually identical new tavern near Grand Central draws after-work crowds with basic hooch and pub grub; in short, it's as comfortable as an old shoe, with one twist: the downstairs Barrel Room has beer taps built into the booths.

Park Bar
| | 23 | 20 | 19 | M |

Flatiron | 15 E. 15th St. (bet. 5th Ave. & Union Sq. W.) | 4/5/6/L/N/Q/R to 14th St./Union Sq. | 212-367-9085

One of the "coziest" retreats near Union Square, this petite 10-year-old with a been-there-forever feel draws crowds with "crisp cocktails" served "without pretense"; indeed, the "warm", tin-ceilinged space has only "one drawback: too many people know about it."

Parkside Lounge
| | - | - | - | I |

LES | 317 E. Houston St. (Attorney St.) | F to Lower East Side/2nd Ave. | 212-673-6270 | www.parksidelounge.net

Parked on the LES since 1955, this "standard" saloon is now a "go-to" for hip types out to do the "dive-bar thing" in a "cleaner" environment, with a "not so skeezy" crowd; no surprise, the draws include "cheap beer" and live local bands in back.

Park Slope Ale House
| | 19 | 17 | 20 | M |

Park Slope | 356 Sixth Ave. (5th St.) | Brooklyn | F/G to 7th Ave. | 718-788-1756

"What a neighborhood joint should be" – in a "nice neighborhood" – this "pubby" Park Sloper is "convivial" enough for socializing but "quiet enough for good conversation"; it's equipped with a pool table and an "outside sitting area", and there's "always a seat available."

Parlour, The
| | 16 | 14 | 18 | M |

Garment District | 247 W. 30th St. (bet. 7th & 8th Aves.) | A/C/E to 34th St./Penn Station | 212-967-1070
W 80s | 250 W. 86th St. (bet. B'way & West End Ave.) | 1 to 86th St. | 212-580-8923
www.theparlour.com

Beyond its super-sized dimensions, this "down-to-earth" UWS Irish pub is a "friendly" spot for locals to "unwind" and "watch soccer";

overall it may be "nothing spectacular", but the downstairs party space is "fun when in the mood for beer pong"; P.S. the Penn Station-area spin-off opened post-Survey.

Patrick Kavanagh's

			M
-	-	-	M

Murray Hill | 497 Third Ave. (bet. 33rd & 34th Sts.) | 6 to 33rd St. | 212-889-4304

"Straightforward" Murray Hill Irish watering hole offering the "typical" matchup of tap beer and televised sports (soccer and rugby included) minus the usual fratmosphere; although "nothing special", it's a "better choice" for mellow elbow-bending than the "loud" meet markets nearby.

Patriot Saloon ⊅

16	8	21	I

TriBeCa | 110 Chambers St. (Church St.) | 1/2/3 to Chambers St. | 212-748-1162

"Don't bring a date" to this TriBeCa honky-tonk, "one of the skeeziest bars imaginable", where the "drinks are cheap", the "waitresses are cheaper" and the "bathrooms look like a *CSI* crime scene"; the jukebox plays "two types of music: country and western", but you'll probably be too "blind drunk" to notice.

☑ PDT

27	23	23	E

E Village | 113 St. Marks Pl. (bet. Ave. A & 1st Ave.) | 6 to Astor Pl. | 212-614-0386 | www.pdtnyc.com

Exuding a "clandestine feel" from the "secret entryway through a phone booth" in Crif Dogs to its "dark interior", this East Village "pseudo speakeasy" serves "incredible potions" made by "bartenders who know their stuff"; the name stands for 'Please Don't Tell', but since "everybody knows", reservations are "recommended" – and "so worth the trouble."

Peculier Pub ⊅

20	15	18	M

G Village | 145 Bleecker St. (bet. La Guardia Pl. & Thompson St.) | 1 to Houston St. | 212-353-1327 | www.peculierpub.com

Hopsheads are "never at a loss for exotic choices" at this 30-year-old Village stalwart where the "world-class beer selection" runs to 300-plus international brands; "cheap" prices and "stained wooden pews" please its "loud" college crowd, the "jammed" room and "cash-only" rule not so much.

Peggy O'Neill's

▽ 20	21	19	E

Coney Island | KeySpan Park | 1904 Surf Ave. (19th St.) | Brooklyn | D/F/N/Q to Coney Island/Stillwell Ave. | 718-449-3200

"Always a fun time during the Cyclones' season", this Coney Island Irish bar "near KeySpan Park" is a handy place to meet pals and throw back a couple "before or after a ball game"; plenty of "summertime outdoor seating" means you may never miss the beach.

☑ Pegu Club

25	24	22	E

SoHo | 77 W. Houston St., 2nd fl. (bet. W. B'way & Wooster St.) | B/D/F/M to B'way/Lafayette St. | 212-473-7348 | www.peguclub.com

"Long Island Iced Tea drinkers need not apply" to Audrey Saunders' very "upscale" SoHo "gin joint" where "magicianlike" bar chefs "shake their stuff" with the kind of "attention to detail" reserved for "bomb-defusing specialists"; the "seating is limited", the Burmese Colonial decor "seductive" and the tabs "pricey", befitting a place that celebrates "drinking as an art form."

Pencil Factory ⊘

▽ 24 | 22 | 21 | M

Greenpoint | 142 Franklin St. (Greenpoint Ave.) | Brooklyn | G to Greenpoint Ave. | 718-609-5858 | www.pencilfactorybar.com

With a rough-hewn interior recalling its days as a dockworkers' haunt, this "inviting" Greenpoint pub is now a "solid" bet for beer buffs seeking a "carefully chosen" tap selection for "low" dough; pretty "perfect" for an unpretentious pop, it's a "big neighborhood fave."

Penthouse 808

- | - | - | E

LIC | Ravel Hotel | 8-08 Queens Plaza S. (Vernon Blvd.) | Queens | 7/N to Queensboro Plaza | 718-289-6101 | www.ravelhotel.com

High-end in every respect, this rooftop lounge crowning a LIC boutique hotel affords a "spectacular" skyline view of Manhattan from a tony glassed-in space topped by a retractable roof; alright, it's "out of the way" and the signature swizzles are "a bit expensive for Queens", but ultimately fans say it's "worth it."

Penthouse Executive Club

23 | 20 | 20 | VE

W 40s | 603 W. 45th St. (11th Ave.) | A/C/E to 42nd St./Port Authority | 212-245-0002 | www.penthouseexecutiveclub.com

As strip clubs go, this Hell's Kitchen "den of iniquity" is a "cut above" the rest with "hot girls" undressing for success in "swanky" surroundings; of course, the come-ons can get "aggressive" and you'll say ta-ta to "large coin", but most boobs agree the other "flesh markets" "should live up to this standard."

Perdition

▽ 19 | 20 | 24 | M

W 40s | 692 10th Ave. (bet. 48th & 49th Sts.) | C/E to 50th St. | 212-582-5660 | www.perditionnyc.com

Despite the "dark" setting, a "friendly neighborhood vibe" prevails at this West Hell's Kitchen Irish pub, owing to its "very chill" tapmeisters; denizens report bargain drink deals and "no-frills fun" that can get a little "crazy" on "random late nights."

Perfect Pint

20 | 19 | 22 | M

E 40s | 203 E. 45th St. (bet. 2nd & 3rd Aves.) | 4/5/6/7/S to 42nd St./Grand Central | 212-867-8159
W 40s | 123 W. 45th St. (bet. B'way & 6th Ave.) | B/D/F/M to 47-50th Sts./Rockefeller Ctr. | 212-354-1099
www.theperfectpintnyc.com

Crosstown Irish "suit traps", perfectly serviceable for sampling a "decent beer selection" in "multilevel" digs with "plenty of room" to circulate (check out that "great rooftop" on the East Side); perfectionists yawn "pretty standard", yet they're pretty "popular" after work.

Peter McManus Cafe

21 | 16 | 21 | M

Chelsea | 152 Seventh Ave. (19th St.) | 1 to 18th St. | 212-929-9691

Since 1936, this Chelsea pub has been supplying economical quaffs to a "mix of regulars" running the gamut from FIT, the NYFD, local "comedy troupes" and beyond; even if it's "showing signs of age", it's "routinely hopping."

Pete's Candy Store

25 | 21 | 21 | M

Williamsburg | 709 Lorimer St. (bet. Frost & Richardson Sts.) | Brooklyn | G/L to Metropolitan Ave./Lorimer St. | 718-302-3770 | www.petescandystore.com

"Williamsburg's thinking man's bar", this sweetly scruffy former candy store draws in patrons with "affordable alcohol", "trivia nights", spelling bees and "off-the-radar" bands performing on the "coolest little" rear stage; it's "usually crowded but not overly so", while a "great back garden" appeals to nature lovers.

Pete's Tavern

21 | 18 | 19 | M

Gramercy | 129 E. 18th St. (Irving Pl.) | 4/5/6/L/N/Q/R to 14th St./Union Sq. | 212-473-7676 | www.petestavern.com

There's "lots of history" ingrained in this "Civil War"–era Gramercy "landmark", "one of the oldest" watering holes in town, as well as the site where O. Henry's *Gift of the Magi* was written"; "ancient" and "decorated accordingly", it's undeniably "touristy" yet "everyone ends up here at some time."

Phoenix

21 | 12 | 20 | M

E Village | 447 E. 13th St. (bet. Ave. A & 1st Ave.) | L to 1st Ave. | 212-477-9979

"Normal working" stiffs frequent this "no-frills" East Village gay bar, a "neighborhoody" place with "cool, friendly" service and no "over-pumped, overwaxed" patrons; most of its "arty" customer base is long "past their twenties" and looking for a spot that's "not too cruisy."

Pianos

18 | 13 | 14 | M

LES | 158 Ludlow St. (bet. Rivington & Stanton Sts.) | F to Lower East Side/2nd Ave. | 212-505-3733 | www.pianosnyc.com

"New bands shine" at this LES performance venue known for "indie"-oriented live shows in the "cramped", "sweaty" back room; upstairs, a DJ lounge draws a "mixed crowd" of "hipsters", "punks" and "office-cubicle" refugees, who keep the place "jammed on the weekends."

Pieces ⊅

17 | 14 | 18 | M

W Village | 8 Christopher St. (bet. Gay St. & Greenwich Ave.) | 1 to Christopher St. | 212-929-9291 | www.piecesbar.com

Some gay bars "opt for glitz", but this long-standing West Village "hole-in-the-wall" thrives on "easy laughs and cheap booze" as "locals" ogle "vicious drag queens" putting on campy shows like Tuesday's "wonderfully obnoxious" karaoke; sure, it's the "diviest", but if you "don't go expecting to see preening Chelsea boys" it can be a "great time."

Pierre Loti

23 | 22 | 22 | E

Chelsea | 258 W. 15th St. (bet. 7th & 8th Sts.) | A/C/E/L to 14th St./8th Ave. | 212-645-5684

Gramercy | 53 Irving Pl. (bet. 17th & 18th Sts.) | 4/5/6/L/N/Q/R to 14th St./Union Sq. | 212-777-5684

www.pierrelotiwinebar.com

A "European vibe" pervades this "cute" Gramercy wine bar, a "wonderful little find" for sampling an "excellent" – albeit "pricey" – label lineup; an "appealing outdoor seating" heightens the charm, and the Chelsea spin-off is an equally "intimate" option for a "quiet evening."

	APPEAL	DECOR	SERVICE	COST

Pig N Whistle
18 | 15 | 20 | M

E 50s | 922 Third Ave. (bet. 55th & 56th Sts.) | 4/5/6/F/N/R/Q to 59th St./Lexington Ave. | 212-688-4646

E 50s | 951 Second Ave. (bet. 50th & 51st Sts.) | 6 to 51st St. | 212-832-2021 | www.pignwhistleon2.com

W 40s | 165 W. 47th St. (bet. 6th & 7th Aves.) | N/R to 49th St. | 212-302-0112 | www.pignwhistlets.com

NEW **W 40s** | 58 W. 48th St. (bet. 6th & 7th Aves.) | B/D/F/M to 47-50th Sts./Rockefeller Ctr. | 212-819-0095

An "easy in-and-out" for a "pre-theater or after-work" jolt, these "casual", separately owned Irish pubs are "reasonably priced" standbys that are usually "lively" if "average"; the "serviceable" setups include occasional Celtic "live music" to wet your whistle.

Pine Tree Lodge
21 | 18 | 18 | M
(aka Cabin Club)

Murray Hill | 326 E. 35th St. (bet. 1st & 2nd Aves.) | 6 to 33rd St. | 212-481-5490

Lodged "off the beaten path" of Murray Hill's "rowdy frat row", this rustic barroom owes its "odd charm" to a "kitschy" setting knotted with "lots of nooks" to camp out in, including an outdoor patio; it may "fly under the radar", but it's "gaining a following" among "local characters" pining to "change up the scenery."

Pinkerton Wine Bar
- | - | - | M

Williamsburg | 263 N. Sixth St. (Havemeyer St.) | Brooklyn | L to Bedford Ave. | 718-782-7171 | www.pinkertonwinebarnyc.com

Williamsburg wine bar offering affordable New World vinos in a moody, film-noir setting (think ancient tile floors, interrogation-worthy furniture, windows galore); the name references the *Madame Butterfly* character, not so much the Weezer album or the detective agency.

Pink Pony
▽ 17 | 20 | 18 | M

LES | 176 Ludlow St. (bet. Houston & Stanton Sts.) | F to Lower East Side/2nd Ave. | 212-253-1922 | www.pinkponynyc.com

With its poetry readings, shelves of books and occasional film screenings, this "faux French" LES cafe exudes literati-lair cachet; it's also a "solid" bet for socializing over beer and wine, and fans are pleased that it now accepts plastic when it's time to pony up.

P.J. Carney's
20 | 16 | 22 | M

W 50s | 906 Seventh Ave. (bet. 57th & 58th Sts.) | N/Q/R to 57th St./7th Ave. | 212-664-0056 | www.pjcarneys.com

A "pub right out of the old world", this "homey" Irish joint hard by Carnegie Hall is an "easygoing" pit stop for chatting with "friendly bartenders" who keep the suds "continuously flowing"; "convenient" enough to attract "tourists and locals" alike, it's typically "busy."

☑ P.J. Clarke's
21 | 18 | 20 | E

E 50s | 915 Third Ave. (55th St.) | 6/E to 51st-53rd Sts./Lexington Ave. | 212-317-1616

P.J. Clarke's at Lincoln Square

W 60s | 44 W. 63rd St. (bet. B'way & Columbus Ave.) | 1 to 66th St. | 212-957-9700

(continued)

(continued)

P.J. Clarke's on the Hudson

Financial District | 4 World Financial Ctr. (Vesey St.) | 1/R to Rector St. | 212-285-1500
www.pjclarkes.com

"Your grandfather probably spent time" at this Midtown "landmark boozer", an "age-old", circa-1884 Irish pub that's still "jammed" with everyone from executives "waiting to catch the 7:05 to Mineola" to out-of-towners awed by its industrial-size urinals; meanwhile, the "more corporate" WFC knockoff offers "mostly suits" an alfresco scene "on the water" while the Lincoln Center site is a "bustling" nexus for a "pre- or post-show quickie."

P.J. Hanley's

− | − | − | M

Carroll Gardens | 449 Court St. (4th Pl.) | Brooklyn | F/G to Carroll St. | 718-834-8223 | www.pjhanleysnyc.com

Although heavily "renovated", this 1874-vintage Carroll Gardens pub stands as one of the "oldest" taprooms in the borough; it caters to "neighborhood" locals with few strangers included, but if you turn up alone, there are "always friendly people there."

ⓩ Plaza Athénée Bar Seine

27 | 27 | 24 | VE

E 60s | Plaza Athénée Hotel | 37 E. 64th St. (bet. Madison & Park Aves.) | 6 to 68th St. | 212-606-4647 | www.plaza-athenee.com

Ultra-"upscale" yet "comfortable", this UES hotel bar in the Plaza Athénée is a "warm" Moroccan retreat with "lovely" burgundy-lacquered walls and a leather floor; "older business" types nursing "crisp" cocktails tout its "traditional" charms but acknowledge "it doesn't come cheap."

Plug Uglies

15 | 8 | 19 | I

Gramercy | 257 Third Ave. (bet. 20th & 21st Sts.) | 6 to 23rd St. | 212-780-1944 | www.plugugliesnyc.com

The "signature shuffleboard table" is free of charge at this Gramercy Irish "dive", but hustlers beware: it's a well-known "cop bar"; while there's "no scene" ("I wouldn't go there for chicks"), law-abiding types plug it as a good place "to start the night."

ⓩ Plunge

26 | 25 | 17 | VE

Meatpacking | Gansevoort Hotel | 18 Ninth Ave. (bet. Little W. 12th & 13th Sts.) | A/C/E/L to 14th St./8th Ave. | 212-206-6700 | www.chinagrillmgt.com

Known as the "place that *made* the Meatpacking", this indoor/outdoor rooftop lounge atop the Gansevoort Hotel should be "way past its prime", but remains perennially "cool" thanks to its "sweeping views of the city and the Hudson" and "gorgeous", swimming pool–equipped interior; so even though the throngs can be as "aggravating" as the drink prices, it's still a destination for "trendy" things "trolling" for company.

Polar

− | − | − | VE

Murray Hill | Marcel at Gramercy Hotel | 201 E. 24th St., downstairs (3rd Ave.) | 6 to 23rd St. | 212-696-3800 | www.nycpolar.com

Compact, Antarctica-themed lounge beneath the Murray Hill hit restaurant 'inoteca, done up in North-Pole-bachelor-pad style with silvered brick walls, snowy white sofas and three private 'caves' for group get-togethers or serious canoodling; even if you don't spring for bottle service, $17 cocktails give big spenders the thrill of dropping some serious cash.

Pony Bar
23 | 17 | 21 | I

W 40s | 637 10th Ave. (45th St.) | A/C/E to 42nd St./Port Authority | 212-586-2707 | www.theponybar.com

"If you're into draft beer", the "impressive tap list" at this Hell's Kitchen suds specialist "stands out" with a "dizzying" rotating selection featuring "American craft brews only" at $5 a pop; "informative" staffers oversee the "small", "rustic" digs, and those who "try 100" varieties get a T-shirt and a place on the plaque of honor.

Posh
18 | 13 | 17 | M

W 50s | 405 W. 51st St. (bet. 9th & 10th Aves.) | C/E to 50th St. | 212-957-2222 | www.poshbarnyc.com

Even if it doesn't live up to its name, this "down-to-earth" Hell's Kitchen gay bar is a serviceable "local" that may be "dilapidated" but is "comfortable" enough to lure grown-ups with "no attitude"; though "not the ultimate place to be", it works as a "last-stop-of-the-night kind of place."

NEW Post Office
- | - | - | M

Williamsburg | 188 Havemeyer St. (bet. S. 3rd & 4th Sts.) | Brooklyn | J/M/Z to Marcy Ave. | 718-963-2574 | www.postofficebk.com

Whiskey – small-batch bourbons in particular – is the specialty of this new South Williamsburg saloon near the BQE, where the compact space is done up with vintage wallpaper and light fixtures made from whiskey bottles; the crowd's a mix of neighborhood types and Charles Bukowski fans – it's named after the booze connoisseur's first novel.

☑ Pravda
22 | 21 | 19 | E

NoLita | 281 Lafayette St., downstairs (bet. Houston & Prince Sts.) | 6 to Bleecker St. | 212-226-4944 | www.pravdany.com

"Relive the Communist era" at this "underground" NoLita "staple" where the "sophisticated" Soviet-style surroundings and "delicious infused vodkas" draw "good-looking" comrades running up tabs too "pricey" for the proles; da, the scene's "lost steam over the years", but many say "this place never gets old" – and is now more "accessible" than ever.

☑ Press Lounge
- | - | - | VE

W 40s | Ink48 Hotel | 653 11th Ave., 16th fl. (48th St.) | C/E to 50th St. | 212-757-2224 | www.ink48.com

The latest in swanky rooftop lounges, this sprawling Hell's Kitchen aerie atop the Ink48 Hotel features drop-dead, 360-degree views of Midtown and the Hudson from its 16th-floor perch; a far-flung address on an avenue better known for car dealerships than lounges may help keep crowding to a minimum.

Professor Thom's
19 | 14 | 19 | M

E Village | 219 Second Ave. (bet. 13th & 14th Sts.) | L to 3rd Ave. | 212-260-9480 | www.professorthoms.com

"Red Sox fans watch games unmolested" at this "spacious" East Village sports bar that adds a professed "Boston" bias to "standard" items like multiple flat-screens, low-cost sauce and that "frat row" feel; meanwhile, the upstairs lounge is a "completely different" story with its antiquey decor and weekend DJ sets.

Prohibition

19	16	17	M

W 80s | 503 Columbus Ave. (bet. 84th & 85th Sts.) | 1 to 86th St. | 212-579-3100 | www.prohibition.net

Renowned for hosting free "live music every night", this UWS "local" is also "one of the few adult bars in the area" – and thus more "accommodating" to "mature" merrymakers than its "collegiate neighbors"; otherwise, it's a "strictly functional" scene.

⚡ Provocateur

-	-	-	VE

Meatpacking | Gansevoort Hotel | 18 Ninth Ave. (bet. Little W. 12th & 13th Sts.) | A/C/E/L to 14th St./8th Ave. | 212-206-6700 | www.provocateurny.com

The Meatpacking keeps on keeping on with this Gansevoort Hotel venue divided into two parts: a hiply mellow lounge with a fur swing, live trees, trompe l'oeil drapery and a retractable roof, and a dark, state-of-the-art nightclub with black chandeliers and giant angel wings; the target audience is Euro playboys, the door's tight as can be and though the pricing is wildly expensive, the attitude's free.

PS 450

20	19	17	M

Murray Hill | 450 Park Ave. S. (bet. 30th & 31st Sts.) | 6 to 28th St. | 212-532-7474 | www.ps450.com

As a somewhat "classy alternative to the Third Avenue" playpens, this massive Murray Hill bar enrolls lots of "young professionals" who make it a "mecca" for "after-work happy hour" and an "unpretentious" DJ scene into the night; upfront, it "can get pretty packed", but the rear lounge is more "stress free."

Public Assembly

-	-	-	M

Williamsburg | 70 N. Sixth St. (bet. Kent & Wythe Aves.) | Brooklyn | L to Bedford Ave. | 718-384-4586 | www.publicassemblynyc.com

"Handily filling" the cultured shoes of "former occupant Galapagos", this "spacious" Williamsburg bar/performance venue assembles a "wonderful" lineup of live bands, burlesque shows and art installations in a setting that retains the "killer" bridge-over-water entrance of old; for an "interesting night out", the prices are thankfully "reasonable."

NEW Pub One

-	-	-	M

Dumbo | 5 Front St. (Old Fulton St.) | Brooklyn | A/C to High St. | 347-844-9149 | www.puboneny.com

From the Ainsworth team comes this new Dumbo gastropub set in the former Five Front digs; look for exposed brick, wood paneling and an expansive outdoor patio – plus an equally expansive burger menu.

Puck Fair

20	17	19	M

SoHo | 298 Lafayette St. (bet. Houston & Prince Sts.) | 6 to Bleecker St. | 212-431-1200 | www.puckfairbarnyc.com

With its "respectable" "old-world" look and "solid" draft selection, this "higher-end" SoHo Irish pub is a "second home" to "early-thirties" professionals; the "narrow" main floor can be "a hassle when crowded", so to hoist your pint "without getting bumped", try the balcony or more "intimate" basement bar.

	APPEAL	DECOR	SERVICE	COST

Puffy's Tavern
14 | 12 | 15 | M

TriBeCa | 81 Hudson St. (Harrison St.) | 1 to Franklin St. | 212-227-3912 | www.puffystavernnyc.com

Ok, admirers say it's "not what it once was" since the "remodel", but this 1945-vintage "neighborhood pub" remains a "laid-back alternative" with simple surroundings and fair prices for TriBeCa; still, the "too-mainstream" mood has partisans pleading "please bring back the old Puffy's."

Pyramid Club ⊄
18 | 11 | 17 | M

E Village | 101 Ave. A (bet. 6th & 7th Sts.) | L to 1st Ave. | 212-228-4888 | www.thepyramidclub.com

The "'80s stay alive" at this "old East Village legend" where many "relive their youth" grinding to a "danceable" playlist featuring "early Madonna and Pet Shop Boys" tracks; varying theme nights cater to "all kinds" of tastes, but be prepared for "seedy" digs oozing the "cumulative sweat from three decades"; P.S. the long-running weekly 1984 party is no more.

Quarter
- | - | - | M

Greenwood Heights | 676 Fifth Ave. (bet. 20th & 21st Sts.) | Brooklyn | R to Prospect Ave. | 718-788-0989 | www.quarterbarbrooklyn.com

Sandwiched between a bodega and Laundromat, this unassuming Greenwood Heights bar purveys swanky seasonal cocktails for reasonable Brooklyn rates; candlelight and dark wood lend a moody glow, while outside there's a patio where you can wash down your muddled mix around a freestanding bathtub.

NEW Queen Vic
- | - | - | M

E Village | 68 Second Ave. (4th St.) | F to Lower East Side/2nd Ave. | 917-262-0512 | www.queenvicnyc.com

The East Village revolving-door space last known as 2 by 4 has been reinvented as a British pub, with plenty of brew to wash down the bangers and mash on the menu; cheeky Victorian parlor decor (i.e. damask wallpaper, Beatles photos) and newly uncovered windows enhance its quaint vibe.

Raccoon Lodge
18 | 10 | 19 | I

TriBeCa | 59 Warren St. (bet. Church St. & W. B'way) | 1/2/3 to Chambers St. | 212-227-9894

"Construction workers", "politicians", "hipsters" and "everyone in between" turn up at this "blue-collar" TriBeCa "dive", a long-standing nexus for "flirty" barmaids, "cheap beer" and cutthroat pool; it's usually "not insanely crowded", especially once happy hour ends and "everyone stumbles home."

☒ Radegast Hall
26 | 23 | 17 | M

Williamsburg | 113 N. Third St. (Berry St.) | Brooklyn | L to Bedford Ave. | 718-963-3973 | www.radegasthall.com

"Munich comes to Billyburg" via this "totally rad" German beer hall vending "amazing European" brews in "old-fashioned" brauhaus digs with an adjacent biergarten outfitted with "communal" picnic tables and a retractable roof; if nothing else, it's "seriously fun" to see all those "hipsters pretending to be frat boys."

	APPEAL	DECOR	SERVICE	COST

☑ Raines Law Room
27 | 26 | 26 | E

Flatiron | 48 W. 17th St., downstairs (bet. 5th & 6th Aves.) | 4/5/6/L/N/Q/R to 14th St./Union Sq. | no phone | www.raineslawroom.com

"Intimate and civilized", this "lesser known" Flatiron "speakeasy" is a "class act all the way" with a semi-"secret" entrance, "plush" "Orient-Express" decor, "chains on the wall" to summon the staff and "masterful cocktails" concocted by "true mixologists"; maybe the "prices aren't for the faint of heart", but it "doesn't disappoint" for a "sexy date."

Randolph, The
- | - | - | E

Little Italy | 349 Broome St. (bet. Bowery & Elizabeth St.) | 6 to Spring St. | 212-274-0667 | www.randolphnyc.com

Covert Little Italy bar that's "a little off the typical path", equipped with wooden booths, an old-school piano and a random motorcycle; the cocktails are "unique" if "pricey", and plans are underway to expand its hours and launch a coffee program during the day.

Rare View
24 | 21 | 19 | E

Chelsea | Fashion 26 Hotel | 152 W. 26th St. (bet. 6th & 7th Aves.) | 1 to 28th St. | 212-807-7273

Murray Hill | Shelburne Murray Hill Hotel | 303 Lexington Ave. (37th St.) | 4/5/6/7/S to 42nd St./Grand Central | 212-481-8439 www.rarebarandgrill.com

The "glamorous" NYC skyline is the draw at this seasonal Murray Hill rooftop, an "after-work" favorite for corporate sorts "willing to pay high prices" for a bird's-eye perch that's "cozier than 230 Fifth" though "not as high as some of the others"; since "everyone gets in", "come early to avoid the line"; P.S. its new Chelsea sibling features more spectacular views than the original.

Rathbones Pub
16 | 13 | 19 | M

E 80s | 1702 Second Ave. (88th St.) | 4/5/6 to 86th St. | 212-369-7361 | www.rathbonesnyc.com

"Frat boys, sports and brewskis" sum up the scene at this UES "pub-crawl" stronghold where there's "always a happy bunch" thanks to the "warm" service and "friendly" vibe; the bonehead "crowd can get annoying", but "when not packed" it works for "cheap eats and a pint."

Rattle N Hum
- | - | - | M

Murray Hill | 14 E. 33rd St. (bet. 5th & Madison Aves.) | 6 to 33rd St. | 212-481-1586 | www.rattlenhumbarnyc.com

Craft beers – and lots of 'em – are the draws at this Murray Hill pub where 40 taps and over 100 bottled brews keep hopsheads happy; otherwise, it's typical for the genre with tube sports, pub grub munchies and communal tables for making new friends.

Rawhide ⊅
16 | 12 | 21 | M

Chelsea | 212 Eighth Ave. (21st St.) | C/E to 23rd St. | 212-242-9332

"Newbies beware", this "cowboy gay bar" in Chelsea is "light years away from 'starter bar' status" with its "down-and-dirty" mood and "lost-in-the-'70s" decor; "cheap drinks" and "beefy" go-go boys rope in an "older" crowd that's "more rugged" than the norm.

	APPEAL	DECOR	SERVICE	COST

R Bar
18 | 16 | 14 | M

NoLita | 218 Bowery (bet. Prince & Spring Sts.) | 6 to Spring St. |
212-334-0484 | www.rbarnyc.com

"Young" carousers like this crimson-lit Bowery mega-bar, citing its "vibrant" mood, "really good tunes" and "stripper pole"-equipped back room that's a magnet for "show-offs"; given its "popularity" with "birthday" celebrants, be ready for "a line down the block" on weekends and not much service.

RDV
∇ 22 | 24 | 17 | VE

Meatpacking | 409 W. 13th St., downstairs (bet. 9th Ave. &
Washington St.) | A/C/E/L to 14th St./8th Ave. | 212-255-1933

The initials are short for 'rendezvous', and this petite Meatpacking District "secret" kicks it up old-school style with a vaguely Victorian vibe, heavy on the velvet and the chandeliers, with some modern art thrown in for good measure; a super-tough door, ultrapricey pops and a "snobby", Eurocentric crowd come with the territory.

Rebar
24 | 22 | 21 | M

Dumbo | 147 Front St. (bet. Jay & Pearl Sts.) | Brooklyn | F to York St. |
718-766-9110 | www.rebarnyc.com

Set "in the wilds of Dumbo", this "one-of-a-kind" multilevel venue in a "converted" factory boasts "tons of space" but "somehow seems cozy" with its "raw" brick and "cool" vintage touches; "unique beers", an "all-green" wine list and "art shows" have admirers vowing to "re-turn often."

Rebel
- | - | - | M

Garment District | 251 W. 30th St. (bet. 7th & 8th Aves.) | A/C/E to
34th St./Penn Station | 212-695-2747 | www.rebelnyc.com

With "three floors to choose from", this Garment District club-cum-music venue has "more than enough space" for rockers in "skinny jeans and Chucks" to dig live bands on the ground level while others head upstairs for dancing and lounging; nonetheless, some rebel against the "missed opportunities" of a second-rate scene.

Red Bench
- | - | - | M

SoHo | 107 Sullivan St. (bet. Prince & Spring Sts.) | C/E to Spring St. |
212-274-9120

Petite SoHo boîte that's a "dark", "cozy" hideaway with an ultradiscreet vibe and eponymous canoodling pew in back; slip in "before or after dinner" and try to guess which of your fellow couples are there "for affairs."

Redemption
21 | 16 | 20 | M

E 50s | 1003 Second Ave. (53rd St.) | 6/E to 51st-53rd Sts./Lexington Ave. |
212-319-4545 | www.redemptionnyc.com

A "little bit more than a regular pub" on the Second Avenue runway, this semi-stylish UES bar/lounge attracts a "really loud" crowd but is redeemed by its "good-looking" staff; still, some say the scenery "isn't all that appealing" unless you're "way B&T" or "just turned 21."

Red Lion
20 | 14 | 18 | M

G Village | 151 Bleecker St. (Thompson St.) | 6 to Bleecker St. |
212-260-9797 | www.redlionnyc.com

Nightly bands bring this Village "rock hangout" a "student"-heavy following, but it doubles as a "centrally located destination" for expats to catch "Euro soccer" on the tube; the price of admission "usually gets you a good time", even though it can be "busy, busy, busy."

Red Sky

| 17 | 14 | 17 | M |

Murray Hill | 47 E. 29th St. (bet. Madison & Park Aves.) | 6 to 28th St. | 212-447-1820 | www.redskynyc.com

Giving "Murray Hill drinkers" plenty of room to "spread out", this tri-level venue includes a first-floor bar, upstairs "Top-40" lounge and a tiki-fied "roof deck" for partying "under the stars"; though "out of the way" and "not overly impressive", it "draws a fair crowd."

Regency Hotel Library Bar

| 23 | 22 | 22 | VE |

(aka Loews Regency Hotel Library Bar)

E 60s | Loews Regency Hotel | 540 Park Ave. (61st St.) | 4/5/6/F/N/Q/R to 59th St./Lexington Ave. | 212-339-4050 | www.loewshotels.com

It's "not a hot spot", but "formality" fans say this Regency Hotel lobby bar is a "classy", book-lined retreat where the well-to-do can "sink into an armchair" with a top-shelf tipple; "priced for Park Avenue", it's "perfect for consummating a business deal" but "a bit stiff for a date."

Reservoir Bar

| 15 | 12 | 18 | M |

G Village | 70 University Pl. (bet. 10th & 11th Sts.) | N/R to 8th St. | 212-475-0770

Tanked-up "NYU students" settle in for some "straightforward drinking" at this "local" taproom, "University Place's very own dive bar"; if it seems like just another "relaxed", "reasonably priced" haunt, "that's what it is."

NEW Réunion Surf Bar

| - | - | - | M |

W 40s | Film Center Bldg. | 357 W. 44th St., downstairs (9th Ave.) | A/C/E to 42nd St./Port Authority | 212-582-3200 | www.reunionbar.com

Replacing Kemia Bar beneath the restaurant Marseille, this Hell's Kitchen newcomer serves island-themed cocktails and eats in a casual setting decorated with vintage surfboards and lots of weathered wood; it's named after the French-owned Indian Ocean island where surfing rules, and since it was the first place to adopt euros, they're also accepted as payment here.

Revival

| 19 | 17 | 21 | M |

Gramercy | 129 E. 15th St. (bet. Irving Pl. & 3rd Ave.) | 4/5/6/L/N/Q/R to 14th St./Union Sq. | 212-253-8061

This "fun" Gramercy "meeting spot" consists of a "dim" downstairs bar, a "larger" second-floor lounge and a "pleasant garden" out back; its "mixed-age" adherents turn up for the "cheap drinks" and "no-drama" setting.

RF Lounge

| - | - | - | M |

W Village | 531 Hudson St. (bet. Charles & 10th Sts.) | 1 to Christopher St. | 917-262-0836 | www.rflounge.com

An underserved nightlife contingent – gay gals – get together at this upscale West Villager set in the former Rubyfruit digs; this time out, the initials stand for 'real friends' and the loungey duplex setting aims to be hipper and sleeker than before.

	APPEAL	DECOR	SERVICE	COST

Richardson, The — | — | — | M

Williamsburg | 451 Graham Ave. (Richardson St.) | Brooklyn | L to Graham Ave. | 718-389-0839 | www.therichardsonnyc.com

"Speakeasy"-esque East Williamsburg bar, a sizable but "lovely" thing whose "delicious" specialty drinks are "made by experts" in a "dark", deftly retro setting (now with "outside seating"); its far-out locale helps it maintain a "quiet atmosphere" for "romantic" rendezvousing.

Rick's Cabaret 23 | 19 | 19 | E

Garment District | 50 W. 33rd St. (bet. B'way & 5th Ave.) | B/D/F/M/ N/Q/R to 34th St./Herald Sq. | 212-372-0850 | www.ricks.com

"Classing up" the strip-club sector, this Garment District chapter of the Texas chain is a tri-level jiggle joint that's fit to bust with "decently attractive" entertainers; though fans praise its "comparatively less expensive" tabs and "good food and drink", pragmatists retort "no one goes there for the food"; P.S. there's no cover if you show up before 7 PM.

NEW Riff Raff's — | — | — | E

Flatiron | 360 Park Ave. S. (enter on 26th St., bet. Madison Ave. & Park Ave. S.) | 6 to 28th St. | www.riffraffsnyc.com

A 'round-the-corner adjunct to the Hurricane Club, this new Flatiron tiki bar/lounge offers the usual deadly rum cocktails (as well as communal punch bowls and late-night conga lines) in a compact, Balinese-esque setting designed by AvroKO; steep tabs and overzealous bouncers are the downsides.

Rink Bar ▽ 21 | 16 | 14 | E

W 50s | Rockefeller Plaza | 20 W. 50th St. (bet. 5th & 6th Aves.) | B/D/F/M to 47-50th Sts./Rockefeller Ctr. | 212-332-7620 | www.patinagroup.com

You "can't beat the location" of this seasonal (May–September) Rock Center bar set in an "outdoor" plaza that's the site of the ice-skating rink in winter; while admittedly a "tourist trap" with "awkward" service, it still can be "much fun" for a little "after-work" 'rinking.

Riposo 46 21 | 20 | 23 | E

W 40s | 667 Ninth Ave. (bet. 46th & 47th Sts.) | C/E to 50th St. | 212-247-8018

Riposo 72

W 70s | 50 W. 72nd St. (bet. Columbus Ave. & CPW) | 1/2/3 to 72nd St. | 212-799-4140

www.riposonyc.com

Locals rely on this "warm" wine bar duo for "worthwhile" vinos and "yummy" snacks, with the Upper Westsider providing significantly more selection – and space – than the "tiny" Hell's Kitchen original; while quarters are "close" at either location, they're just right for an "intimate date."

Ritz, The 23 | 19 | 21 | E

W 40s | 369 W. 46th St. (bet. 8th & 9th Aves.) | C/E to 50th St. | 212-333-4171

Ritzier following "renovations", this double-decker gay bar/lounge on Restaurant Row combines upper and lower "mingle" areas with a small outdoor terrace; the crowd gets "younger and hotter as the evening wears on", but beware the "sweaty boys looking for their next kill."

| | APPEAL | DECOR | SERVICE | COST |

Ritz-Carlton Star Lounge
26 | 26 | 25 | VE

W 50s | Ritz-Carlton Central Park | 50 Central Park S. (bet. 5th & 6th Aves.) | N/R to 5th Ave./59th St. | 212-521-6125 | www.ritzcarlton.com

"They just do it right" at this "subdued" watering hole in the Ritz-Carlton Hotel – "your very own Central Park South living room" – where the "pro" staff "remembers your drink even when you don't"; no kidding, it's "expensive", but that doesn't seem to faze all the "Gordon Gekkos" and "well-heeled tourists" in attendance.

Riviera Cafe
19 | 16 | 20 | M

W Village | 225 W. Fourth St. (7th Ave. S.) | 1 to Christopher St. | 212-929-3250

"Boston sports fans unite" at this been-there-forever Villager, a "home away from home" for "jocks" cheering on the Pats and the Red Sox; it "leaves something to be desired" if you're not there to "catch a game", as it's "super-quiet in the off-season."

Rockbar
- | - | - | I

W Village | 185 Christopher St. (bet. Washington & West Sts.) | 1 to Christopher St. | 212-675-1864 | www.rockbarnyc.com

After stints as the Dugout and Ramrod, this longtime gay trough at the tail end of Christopher Street has a new moniker, though it's retained the same beat-up roadhouse decor and what-the-hell mood from days gone by; its Sunday afternoon beer blast draws bears from all over town.

Rock Shop
- | - | - | M

Park Slope | 249 Fourth Ave. (bet. Carroll & President Sts.) | Brooklyn | R to Union St. | 718-230-5740 | www.therockshopny.com

Situated in the former Cattyshack digs, this bi-level saloon features a sizable street-level bar with a stage area topped by a second floor equipped with flat-screens, a pool table and a roof deck; late-night hours have Park Slope night owls hooting about the increasingly bustling scene on Fourth Avenue.

☑ Rockwood Music Hall
26 | 19 | 21 | M

LES | 196 Allen St. (bet. Houston & Stanton Sts.) | F to Lower East Side/2nd Ave. | 212-477-4155 | www.rockwoodmusichall.com

Music venues don't get much more "intimate" than this "tiny" Lower Eastsider where "solid" singer-songwriters "cut their teeth" nightly; "excellent sound", an "efficient bar" and "no cover" add to its allure, but "get there early" or "you'll be standing the whole time."

Rodeo Bar
19 | 18 | 17 | M

Murray Hill | 375 Third Ave. (27th St.) | 6 to 28th St. | 212-683-6500 | www.rodeobar.com

This "true honky-tonk" in Murray Hill is a "jumpin'" "total Texas" joint featuring a "horse trailer used as a bar", "peanut shells on the floor" and live bands with an "authentic Southern accent", all for "no cover"; one of the "few places in town" that "glorifies cowboy culture", it's "tons of fun."

Rogue
17 | 15 | 20 | M

Chelsea | 757 Sixth Ave. (25th St.) | F to 23rd St. | 212-242-6434 | www.roguenyc.com

A "big" sports bar in an "area that lacks them", this "low-key" Chelsea "alternative" fields a wall full of flat-screens broadcasting the "most

popular games" for rogues "ranging from their twenties to their for-
ties"; while "nothing special", it "isn't expensive or crowded" and
sometimes that's "appealing enough."

Room, The
25 | 18 | 21 | M

SoHo | 144 Sullivan St. (bet. Houston & Prince Sts.) | C/E to Spring St. |
212-477-2102 | www.theroomsbeerandwine.com

It's a "tight squeeze", but when there's room this "tiny" SoHo "gem" is
a "charming", candlelit nook for sampling a "wonderful selection" of
wine and beer (with a suds list emphasizing Belgian brews); the "dark,
cozy" digs are made for "making out", though the "narrow" confines
can get too "crowded on the weekends."

🛂 Rose Bar
25 | 27 | 19 | VE

Gramercy | Gramercy Park Hotel | 2 Lexington Ave. (21st St.) | 6 to
23rd St. | 212-920-3300 | www.gramercyparkhotel.com

There's a "top-of-the-line" scene in full bloom at this "exclusive" re-
doubt in the Gramercy Park Hotel, a "swanky" magnet for the "who's
who of the entertainment world", equipped with a "blazing" fireplace,
red-felt billiards table and "million-dollar art on the walls"; predictably, prices are "from another world" and "getting in can be quite
thorny" ("you need a reservation after 9 PM"), but regulars say all the
"hassle" is "seriously worth it."

Rose Club
∇ 22 | 24 | 21 | VE

W 50s | Plaza Hotel | 768 Fifth Ave. (59th St.) | N/R to 5th Ave./59th St. |
212-759-3000 | www.theplaza.com

From the parquet floors to the lavender lighting, the Plaza Hotel's
walnut-paneled mezzanine lounge exudes "classic" traditional "appeal" from a balcony perch above the lobby; with "friendly" mixologists stirring high-priced pops, it's an "enjoyable" place to "not be
seen", though sometimes it gets "more lively than you'd expect."

Roseland
20 | 14 | 13 | E

W 50s | 239 W. 52nd St. (bet. B'way & 8th Ave.) | C/E to 50th St. |
212-247-0200 | www.roselandballroom.com

Some "mighty fine acts" land at this "famous" Theater District ballroom, a "large concert space" with "warehouse"-size dimensions and
"grungy dump" looks; alright, you can "wait forever" to get an "expensive" drink and there's "no place to sit" ("wear comfy shoes"), but fans
say you're "there for the entertainment – the rest is extraneous."

Royale
∇ 21 | 13 | 19 | M

E Village | 157 Ave. C (bet. 9th & 10th Sts.) | L to 1st Ave. | 212-254-6600 |
www.royalenyc.com

Although "out of the way" on Avenue C and "generally pretty ordinary", this East Village saloon is "worth stopping by" for its "awesome" eponymous burgers washed down with "low-key" quaffs;
commoners note the prices are a "relative bargain", and that year-
round "garden seating" a "nice touch."

Royal Oak ⌀
18 | 18 | 15 | M

Williamsburg | 594 Union Ave. (N. 11th St.) | Brooklyn | L to Bedford Ave. |
718-388-3884

"Just far enough" away from Williamsburg's main drag to cultivate a
"genuinely cool" scene, this "sprawling" barroom features chocolate-

colored booths and a "cozy side room" for more "intimate conversation"; it's ordinarily "laid-back", but "good weekend DJs" can shake things up.

Rudy's Bar ⊘

APPEAL	DECOR	SERVICE	COST
20	7	17	I

W 40s | 627 Ninth Ave. (bet. 44th & 45th Sts.) | A/C/E to 42nd St./Port Authority | 212-974-9169 | www.rudysbarnyc.com

"Taking 'dive' to an art form", this "raunchy" Hell's Kitchen joint dates back to the Depression and still features "older broads" dispensing "dirt-cheap" hooch to a clientele ranging from "local alcoholics" to "hipsters that aren't hip"; it's best known for its gratis, "eat-at-your-own-risk" hot dogs, served in a "dank" room that's "scary" yet "strangely appealing."

Rue B

APPEAL	DECOR	SERVICE	COST
22	17	21	M

E Village | 188 Ave. B (bet. 11th & 12th Sts.) | L to 1st Ave. | 212-358-1700 | www.ruebnyc.com

Per its Parisian leanings, this East Village boîte plays it "unpretentious but cool" with "mellow sepia lighting", "terrific" specialty cocktails and "live jazz" that "keeps you entertained", but stays "low-key" in case "you want to talk"; its hep partisans sum it up in a word: "cozy."

Rum House

APPEAL	DECOR	SERVICE	COST
-	-	-	M

W 40s | Edison Hotel | 228 W. 47th St. (bet. B'way & 8th Ave.) | 1 to 50th St. | 646-490-6924 | www.edisonrumhouse.com

Folks "nostalgic" for an "old-school experience" tout this age-old Theater District piano bar that's been taken over by the owners of TriBeCa's Ward III; look for a cooler crowd, significantly upgraded mixology and a keyboardist playing everything from Billie Holiday to Nirvana.

Russian Vodka Room

APPEAL	DECOR	SERVICE	COST
23	18	20	E

W 50s | 265 W. 52nd St. (bet. B'way & 8th Ave.) | C/E to 50th St. | 212-307-5835 | www.russianvodkaroom.com

"*Eastern Promises*" comes to the Theater District via this "boozy" Russian "martini heaven" that carries every "flavored vodka you can possibly think of – and many that you can't"; granted, the "masculine" setting "isn't very sexy", but don't worry – "you won't remember" it anyway.

☑ Rusty Knot

APPEAL	DECOR	SERVICE	COST
20	18	18	M

W Village | 425 West St. (W. 11th St.) | A/C/E/L to 14th St./8th Ave. | 212-645-5668

"Scruffy arty types drink Red Stripe" at this Way West Village "yuppie dive" parked on the West Side Highway that's done up like a "nautically themed" beach house decked out with an "aquarium", tacky paneling and random "bamboo furniture"; after a couple of "affordable" Dark 'n' Stormys, it's "like visiting Tahiti" with a bonus "view of Jersey."

Ryan's Daughter

APPEAL	DECOR	SERVICE	COST
18	13	20	M

E 80s | 350 E. 85th St. (bet. 1st & 2nd Aves.) | 4/5/6 to 86th St. | 212-628-2613

"Hidden" on a side street, this UES Irish pub "feels like home" to its loyal "neighborhood" following thanks to "hospitable" barkeeps and complimentary potato chips ("BBQ or original"); sure, it's a little "dingy" and the crowd skews "older", but there's a reason why it's "been there forever."

Ryan's Irish Pub

▽ 17 | 15 | 18 | M

E Village | 151 Second Ave. (bet. 9th & 10th Sts.) | 6 to Astor Pl. |
212-979-9511 | www.ryansnyc.com

"If you're on Second Avenue" craving a "low-key" pint, this compact
East Village Irish pub is well kept enough to gratify anyone "expecting
more of a dive" inside; otherwise, it's strictly "typical."

Rye House

▽ 24 | 24 | 24 | E

Flatiron | 11 W. 17th St. (bet. 5th & 6th Aves.) | 4/5/6/L/N/Q/R to
14th St./Union Sq. | 212-255-7260 | www.ryehousenyc.com

"Rye-sing star" in the Flatiron serving eclectic draft beers, "crafty
cocktails" and a highfalutin selection of bourbon and rye that really
"steals the show"; manned by barkeeps with a "genuine interest" in
"brands and distilleries", it exudes a "vintage feel" thanks to "solid"
woodwork and a marble countertop.

Sackett, The

- | - | - | M

Park Slope | 661 Sackett St. (bet. 4th & 5th Aves.) | Brooklyn | R to
Union St. | 718-622-0437 | www.thesackett.com

Off Park Slope's beaten path near Fourth Avenue comes this quirky
boîte, a compact, brick-walled thing jazzed up with vintage notes like
gold wallpaper and French doors; the pricing's fair, ladies seem to like
it and it might even work for a romantic rendezvous.

☑ Salon de Ning

25 | 25 | 20 | VE

W 50s | Peninsula Hotel | 700 Fifth Ave., 23rd fl. (55th St.) | E/M to 5th Ave./
53rd St. | 212-903-3097 | www.salondening.com

Boasting a "gorgeous" view from its "prime Midtown" address "high
above Fifth Avenue", this fancy-schmancy Peninsula Hotel rooftop is
done up in '30s Shanghai style, with a "lovely" indoor bar and daybed-
equipped deck; some call it a "gold-diggers' gold mine" given its
"wealthy", "well-dressed" following unfazed by the "insane" pricing.

NEW Salon Millesime

- | - | - | E

Murray Hill | Carlton Hotel | 92 Madison Ave. (29th St.) | N/R to 28th St. |
212-889-7100 | www.millesimerestaurant.com

Annexing the former Café at Country digs in the Carlton Hotel, this
new Murray Hill lounge exudes retro vibes with dark-wood paneling,
animal-print upholstery and old-school cocktails (for ultracontempo-
rary dough); after work, the mood's mellow as a pianist tickles the ivo-
ries, but it shifts into party mode after 9 PM when DJs hit the decks.

Saloon

18 | 16 | 19 | M

E 80s | 1584 York Ave. (bet. 83rd & 84th Sts.) | 4/5/6 to 86th St. |
212-570-5454 | www.saloonnyc.com

Hailed as the UES fratfest that "tries the hardest", this sprawling
dance club has post-grads whooping it up with so many "strong
drinks" that they "don't remember making it home"; but party-poopers
say the mob can be "overwhelming" at this "average" place.

Sample

- | - | - | M

Cobble Hill | 152 Smith St. (Bergen St.) | Brooklyn | F/G to Bergen St. |
718-643-6622

Just a simple spot, this "small" Smith Street wine bar has a "certain
allure" for "slightly older (read: not collegiate)" sorts who praise

its "extensive" vino list, creative cocktails and modest munchables; though service is "down-to-earth", a few fret over "long waits between rounds."

🅩 Santos Party House

25 | 15 | 20 | M

Chinatown | 96 Lafayette St. (bet. Walker & White Sts.) | 6/J/N/Q/Z to Canal St. | 212-584-5492 | www.santospartyhouse.com

You'll "party hard" at this bi-level Chinatown "dance den", the kind of place that "welcomes everybody" whether you're "fresh off the turnip truck" or a "seasoned" nightlife vet; true, the setup is spartan, but for an "incredible" sound system, "appropriate prices" and absolutely "no attitude", this is "where you need to be."

Sapphire Lounge

18 | 15 | 15 | M

LES | 249 Eldridge St. (Houston St.) | F to Lower East Side/2nd Ave. | 212-777-5153 | www.sapphirenyc.com

"Great times" lie in store at this "shoebox-size" Lower East Side dance club featuring "incredible DJs" who get patrons out of their seats to "shake their rumps" on its "tiny" floor; though the "dark" digs are largely "no-frills", the "crowded" late-night scene is "well worth" the "cheap admission."

Satellite Lounge

- | - | - | I

Williamsburg | 143 Havemeyer St. (bet. S. 1st & 2nd Sts.) | Brooklyn | J/M/Z to Marcy Ave. | no phone | www.satellitelounge.net

The mod name to the contrary, this South Williamsburg joint is a dive through and through, with bare-bones decor that matches the bare-bones scene; still, pinball machines, a carefully loaded jukebox and a $5 beer-and-a-shot special provide some lift-off.

Scores

18 | 16 | 17 | VE

Chelsea | 536 W. 28th St. (bet. 10th & 11th Aves.) | C/E to 23rd St. | 212-868-4900 | www.scoresny.com

"Silicone" enthusiasts "love the decor" at this West Chelsea stripperama, a "real men's night out" where topless teasers jiggle their assets and unbalance your checkbook; but even with the quasi-"classy" remodeling job, knockers reckon it's "even more mercenary than its competitors."

Scratcher

▽ 21 | 15 | 19 | M

E Village | 209 E. Fifth St., downstairs (bet. 2nd & 3rd Aves.) | 6 to Astor Pl. | 212-477-0030

East Villagers itching for an "unpretentious" pint turn to this "standard" but "welcoming" Gaelic pub, home to a "mellow vibe" and a "twentysomething" clientele; its name is Irish slang for 'bed' and the atmosphere's appropriately sleepy, but at least there's "plenty of room" to stretch out.

Session 73

17 | 14 | 16 | M

E 70s | 1359 First Ave. (73rd St.) | 6 to 77th St. | 212-517-4445 | www.session73.com

"Partying" prevails at this "huge" UES music joint where a "young crowd" grooves to an "eclectic" lineup of live bands playing blues, jazz and funk, not to mention Monday night's "popular" salsa sessions; ok, it's a "completely typical college" milieu, but can be "fun regardless" so long as you "don't go sober."

	APPEAL	DECOR	SERVICE	COST

7B
(aka Vazac's Horseshoe Bar)   19 | 12 | 18 | I

E Village | 108 Ave. B (7th St.) | F to Lower East Side/2nd Ave. | 212-677-6742
A "lovable", longtime East Village "dive", this "grungy institution" is renowned for its "cheap" pours, "awesome curving bar" and punk-powered juke; though its "rough-and-tumble" "cast of characters" is now tempered with "frat" and "B&T" elements, all are "glad it's still around."

17 Murray
19 | 14 | 17 | M

Financial District | 17 Murray St. (bet. B'way & Church St.) | R to City Hall | 212-608-3900 | www.17murray.com
"Government types" from City Hall and Centre Street assemble at this "homey" Financial District watering hole to sling scuttlebutt over brew and burgers; though its "middle-ground" appeal helps its standing in the polls, non-regulars "wouldn't write home about it."

Shade
▽ 24 | 17 | 24 | M

G Village | 241 Sullivan St. (bet. Bleecker & W. 3rd Sts.) | A/B/C/D/E/F/M to W. 4th St. | 212-982-6275
Although "close to NYU", this "quaint little" Villager generally maintains its "low-key vibe" for "cool" customers looking to "nurse a glass" of vino, munch "tasty crêpes" and "just relax"; given the overall "comfort" level, this one's got "first date" written all over it.

Shalel Lounge
23 | 24 | 19 | M

W 70s | 65½ W. 70th St., downstairs (bet. Columbus Ave. & CPW) | B/C to 72nd St. | 212-873-2300
"Your next stop is back to her place" after a visit to this romantically "intimate" underground lounge "hidden" beneath an UWS taverna, a "slinky" den of "Middle Eastern mystique" replete with a waterfall and "dark" nooks that are perfect for "making out"; considering its "seal-the-deal" reputation, no one notices that the "service is spotty."

Ship of Fools
15 | 13 | 18 | M

E 80s | 1590 Second Ave. (bet. 82nd & 83rd Sts.) | 4/5/6 to 86th St. | 212-570-2651 | www.shipoffoolsnyc.com
UES jocks make fools of themselves at this "worthy sports bar" supplying "more TVs than you can look at" along with pitchers and wings served by an "accommodating staff"; on certain nights, it gets so "loud" that you'll "feel like you're at the game."

Shoolbred's
19 | 21 | 18 | M

E Village | 197 Second Ave. (bet. 12th & 13th Sts.) | L to 1st Ave. | 212-529-0340 | www.shoolbreds.com
One of the "pubbiest pubs" around, this "lovely" East Villager exudes an "authentic-as-heck" Scottish vibe in its "dark", burnished front bar and cozy back corner outfitted with armchairs and a fireplace; all that "warmth" makes it a "solid" spot for an "undercover" nip, but since the word's out it may be "crowded" on the weekends.

SideBar
18 | 16 | 18 | M

Gramercy | 120 E. 15th St. (Irving Pl.) | 4/5/6/L/N/Q/R to 14th St./Union Sq. | 212-677-2900 | www.sidebarny.com
Lounge meets sports bar at this "spacious" Gramercy hybrid that appeals to both "mid-twenties" professionals doing the "after-work"-

drinks thing and "post-frat types" there to eyeball the games "in style"; whoever you side with, it's "convenient" and "more upscale than others nearby", but beware of "loud" weekend mobs.

Sidecar
24 | 20 | 24 | M

Park Slope | 560 Fifth Ave. (bet. 15th & 16th Sts.) | Brooklyn | R to Prospect Ave. | 718-369-0077 | www.sidecarbrooklyn.com
Belying its "neighborhoody feel", this South Slope venue features a "carefully constructed cocktail menu" offering "seriously amazing" takes on tipples both classic and contempo; "good bartending", a traditional tin-ceilinged look and "upbeat" atmospherics add to the overall "excellent" experience.

Sing Sing Karaoke
19 | 11 | 15 | M

E Village | 81 Ave. A (bet. 5th & 6th Sts.) | L to 1st Ave. | 212-674-0700
E Village | 9 St. Marks Pl., 2nd fl. (bet. 2nd & 3rd Aves.) | 6 to Astor Pl. | 212-387-7800
www.karaokesingsing.com
They're "not the nicest karaoke" spots, but this East Village duo does offer an "unintimidating" chance to belt out an "unending list of songs" "without much investment"; still, regulars who want to "avoid the tone-deaf crowd by the bar" recommend "getting a private room."

Sip
- | - | - | M

W 100s | 998 Amsterdam Ave. (bet. 109th & 110th Sts.) | 1 to Cathedral Pkwy./110th St. | 212-316-2747 | www.sipbar.com
An "outpost of friendly cool" in Morningside Heights, this "tiny" coffeehouse/lounge skews soulful with "great" staffers mixing creative cocktails, "rotating" art exhibits and "no mind-numbing pop music" from the nightly DJs; indeed, "once you get settled in" it's a "top-notch" hang for an underserved area.

675 Bar
25 | 23 | 20 | M

Meatpacking | 675 Hudson St., downstairs (enter on 13th St., bet. Hudson St. & 9th Ave.) | A/C/E/L to 14th St./8th Ave. | 212-699-2410 | www.675bar.com
Rather "refreshing" and "accessible" for the Meatpacking District, this "no-frills" subterranean "hideaway" is furnished like "your parents' basement" and divided into raw-brick "alcoves" equipped with "foosball, board games and a pool table"; "fun drinks" and a "no-hassle" door boost its "popularity" among "younger" types, but "bring your elbows – you'll need them."

Sixth Ward
20 | 15 | 23 | M

LES | 191 Orchard St. (bet. Houston & Stanton Sts.) | F to Lower East Side/2nd Ave. | 212-228-9888 | www.sixthwardnyc.com
"Not too hip but still cool", this "no-frills" LES Irish pub is just the ticket for relaxing in a "large booth" or shooting pool while "sweet-as-pie" barkeeps pull the Guinness; if the interior's too "dark", a "gorgeous courtyard" awaits for "pints in the summertime."

67 Orange Street
∇ 23 | 23 | 20 | E

Harlem | 2082 Frederick Douglass Blvd. (113th St.) | B/C to Cathedral Pkwy./110th St. | 212-662-2030 | www.67orangestreet.com
"SoHa seems like the new SoHo" at this "itty-bitty" Harlem cocktail lounge that matches a "speakeasy vibe" with "sublime" specialty

drinks from some of the "friendliest" mixologists around; the bi-level setup is "tight" but well-suited "for a date", though a few moan it's "overpriced" for the neighborhood.

Skinny, The

— | — | — | M

LES | 174 Orchard St. (Stanton St.) | F/J/M/Z to Delancey/Essex Sts. | 212-228-3668 | www.theskinnybarlounge.com

The "name says it all" about this seriously "tight" Lower Eastsider, a "dive but knowingly so" with its downscale decor, budget drinks and hip DJs; on weekends, the "small", art-lined space is jam-packed and "loud", while other nights the crowd's as thin as the name.

Sky Room

— | — | — | E

Garment District | Marriott Fairfield Inn | 330 W. 40th St., 33rd fl. (bet. 8th & 9th Aves.) | A/C/E to 42nd St./Port Authority | 212-380-1195 | www.skyroomnyc.com

The rooftop craze comes to an obscure address opposite Port Authority via this snazzy double-decker atop a Garment District hotel; the swish setting offers a variety of cozy seating options both indoors and out, but it's the year-round roof level (topped with a retractable cover and billed as the highest bar in town) that's causing the most chatter.

⊠ SL

23 | 23 | 22 | VE

Meatpacking | 409 W. 14th St., downstairs (bet. 9th Ave. & Washington St.) | A/C/E/L to 14th St./8th Ave. | 646-289-3940 | www.simyonelounge.com

One of the "hottest" Meatpacking scenes is this subterranean lounge beneath Abe & Arthur's, drawing "chic" peeps to an intimate setting festooned with beveled mirrors, a reflective ceiling and random "x-rays of bones"; beside being "ridiculously priced" and beyond "tough" at the door, it has a lot to live up to – it's set on the former dance floor of the "old Lotus space."

Sláinte

17 | 14 | 17 | M

NoHo | 304 Bowery (bet. Bleecker & Houston Sts.) | B/D/F/M to B'way/Lafayette St. | 212-253-7030 | www.slaintenyc.com

For a plain old "drinkin' bar", low maintenance types recommend this "reliable" Irish joint on the Bowery offering a variety of tap brews and "lots of soccer" on the tube in a sizable if "typical" setting; its "down-to-earth" patrons report it somehow manages to be "never too crowded, never too empty."

Slate

20 | 18 | 16 | E

Flatiron | 54 W. 21st St. (bet. 5th & 6th Aves.) | F to 23rd St. | 212-989-0096 | www.slate-ny.com

"Nicer than a regular sports bar", this "spacious" Flatiron billiards hall is a "fairly civilized" retreat with a "chill" bar/lounge on the ground floor and "lots of pool" and Ping-Pong downstairs; alright, it's "pricey" and rather "corporate", but overall it chalks up as "cool" for "twenty-somethings and those who wish they still were."

Slaughtered Lamb Pub

17 | 15 | 17 | M

W Village | 182 W. Fourth St. (Jones St.) | A/B/C/D/E/F/M to W. 4th St. | 212-627-5262 | www.slaughteredlambpub.com

"Bar-crawl" cohorts sheepishly raise a pint to this West Village pub best known for a "spooky" theme incorporating replicas of werewolves and skeletons, plus a "decent" list of brews "from all over the world"; though some yawn "mediocre", it's a haunt of choice for "NYU folks" and "many tourists."

☑ Smalls

26 | 15 | 19 | M

W Village | 183 W. 10th St. (7th Ave. S.) | 1 to Christopher St. | 212-252-5091 | www.smallsjazzclub.com

"Inveterate jazz aficionados" dig "serious sounds" for a "modest cost" at this "no-frills, no-hassles" West Village club where "top-notch" talents "riff till the wee hours"; the seating's "not comfortable" and you "risk being shushed if you get too noisy", but that's all "part of the experience", man.

Smith & Mills

21 | 20 | 18 | E

TriBeCa | 71 N. Moore St. (Greenwich St.) | 1 to Franklin St. | no phone | www.smithandmills.com

Set in a "teeny-tiny" converted carriage house, this signless TriBeCa barroom draws "arty" types with "fantastic cocktails", "vintage" decor, lighting that ensures "everyone looks good" and an antique elevator-cab bathroom that's "a sight to see"; alas, it's developed a "hip reputation" so "space constraints" make it "tough to get in."

Smith's Bar

▽ 17 | 15 | 16 | M

W 40s | 701 Eighth Ave. (44th St.) | A/C/E to 42nd St./Port Authority | 212-246-3268 | www.smithsbar.com

Although this '30s-era Times Square relic "underwent a refurbishment", it remains a haven for tosspots and "tourists" trying to "escape the Midtown bustle" at a "reasonable" price; even "classed up" with a craft beer menu and live bands cranking out "some good tunes", its real appeal lies in its "pure grit."

Smoke

24 | 20 | 21 | M

W 100s | 2751 Broadway (bet. 105th & 106th Sts.) | 1 to 103rd St. | 212-864-6662 | www.smokejazz.com

"Some of New York's finest" jamsters get the joint jumpin' at this Upper West Side "jazz haunt", an "intimate" but "not suffocating" bar/supper club offering "good" sound, "superb" sightlines and "unobtrusive" service; it's "populated by regulars who come to listen", but even they get "rushed out as soon as the set is finished to make room for others."

NEW Snap

- | - | - | M

W Village | 248 W. 14th St. (bet. 7th & 8th Aves.) | A/C/E/L to 14th St./8th Ave. | 646-350-0539 | www.snapsportsbar.com

The typical sports bar gets an upgrade at this revolving-door 14th Street space (fka Country Club, fka Dirty Disco, fka 2i's) now featuring vintage Ivy League decor (i.e. athletics-themed wallpaper, pigskin upholstery); high-def flat-screens and a LED sports ticker built into the bar bring things up to date.

S.O.B.'s

21 | 16 | 17 | E

Hudson Square | 204 Varick St. (Houston St.) | 1 to Houston St. | 212-243-4940 | www.sobs.com

"Progressive, yet accessible music" is the bait at this "funky" Hudson Square "party" club, a "widely recognized" veteran offering "excellent" live global sounds – "Latin, fusion, reggae, whatever" – with plenty of "energy"; helped along by "strong" caipirinhas, its "very diverse crowd" gets "wall-to-wall on the dance floor."

Social
16 | 14 | 16 | M

W 40s | 795 Eighth Ave. (bet. 48th & 49th Sts.) | C/E to 50th St. | 212-459-0643 | www.socialbarnyc.com

"Professionals" praise this Theater District Irish pub since it's "less crowded than most" thanks to a big, "three-level" layout (not to mention a "pretty cool roof deck"); all that room comes in handy for dodging the "fratty", "striped-shirt" guys after work and the "Jersey crowd on the weekend."

Soda Bar
▽ 16 | 12 | 16 | M

Prospect Heights | 629 Vanderbilt Ave. (bet. Prospect Pl. & St. Marks Ave.) | Brooklyn | 2/3 to Grand Army Plaza | 718-230-8393

Once a soda fountain, this Prospect Heights "hangout" now cools off locals with draft beer poured cheap in a "multiroom" space with "mingling" up front, DJ "parties" in back and a good-sized garden; despite "lackadaisical service", it's a "strong" draw that typically fizzes when the "hipsters" show up.

Soft Spot ⊄
- | - | - | M

Williamsburg | 128 Bedford Ave. (bet. N. 9th & 10th Sts.) | Brooklyn | L to Bedford Ave. | 718-384-7768

A "narrow" thing that opens onto a "great" back patio, this Williamsburg watering hole is the epitome of a neighborhood bar; though it flies below the Bedford Avenue radar, it musters something of a crowd when the "happy-hour specials" are available.

Soho Billiards
19 | 12 | 16 | M

NoHo | 56 E. Houston St. (Mott St.) | B/D/F/M to B'way/Lafayette St. | 212-925-3753 | www.sohobilliardsny.com

Rack up a "night of pool and pals" at this "old-school", "budget-friendly" NoHo felt forum, a grungy "alternative to the usual haunts" with a very basic setup of 28 tables in a run-down industrial space; the action's "consistent" if "uneventful", though more discerning sharks suggest "upgrading the facility."

Solas
20 | 17 | 19 | M

E Village | 232 E. Ninth St. (bet. 2nd & 3rd Aves.) | 6 to Astor Pl. | 212-375-0297

It's "always someone's 23rd birthday" at this "energy-filled" East Villager with a first-floor bar that's "nicer than a dive" and a "dark" DJ lounge upstairs; it gets "loud and rambunctious" on weekends, but "if you can handle sweaty strangers", it's "reasonably priced" and certainly "unpretentious."

Sophie's
▽ 19 | 12 | 16 | M

E Village | 507 E. Fifth St. (bet. Aves. A & B) | F to Lower East Side/ 2nd Ave. | 212-228-5680

Still the same "authentic dive" it's always been, this grubby East Village "classic" is a holdout against neighborhood "gentrification" with a "rockin' jukebox" and stiff pours at fair prices; "cool neighborhood" characters report it's "survived a surge in popularity" and is "back to its old self again."

Southpaw

APPEAL 20 | DECOR 12 | SERVICE 18 | COST M

Park Slope | 125 Fifth Ave. (bet. Sterling & St. Johns Pls.) | Brooklyn | B/Q to 7th Ave. | 718-230-0236 | www.spsounds.com

One of the first "Manhattan-quality" music venues to rock Brooklyn, this "grimy" Park Slope "game changer" presents some of the "best damn" indie bands around; P.S. the lower-level lounge Down South has an AV feed from the stage upstairs.

Southside

▽ 20 | 18 | 17 | E

(aka Brinkley's)

Little Italy | 1 Cleveland Pl., downstairs (bet. Broome & Kenmare Sts.) | 6 to Spring St. | 212-680-5601 | www.nycsouthside.com

Aka "Dorrian's South", this semi-"hidden" underground lounge in Little Italy draws in "young" prepsters ready to "dance on the ban-quettes" and swill "high-end" booze; just hope that you can "wiggle your way past" an especially "tough door."

NEW Spanky & Darla's ⊘

- | - | - | I

E Village | 140 First Ave. (bet. 9th St. & St. Marks Pl.) | L to 1st Ave. | 212-254-6631

Only the name has changed at the East Village dive formerly known as Cheap Shots, still a dark, grungy destination for ultra-low-budget hooch; although it's sweetly named after two of the *Little Rascals*, the mood (and bartending) is along the lines of Mars Bar.

Spike Hill

▽ 18 | 15 | 18 | M

Williamsburg | 184 Bedford Ave. (N. 7th St.) | Brooklyn | L to Bedford Ave. | 718-218-9737 | www.spikehill.com

It may be a ringer for "your basic neighborhood pub", but this Williamsburg saloon ups the ante with a "sublime" beer list, "knockout" single-malt selection and nightly live music; there's also a "down-home" vibe and prime people-watching potential from the "window seats."

Spin New York

- | - | - | M

Flatiron | 48 E. 23rd St. (bet. Madison & Park Aves.) | 6 to 23rd St. | 212-982-8802 | www.spinyc.com

Ping-Pong gets its own designated clubhouse at this Flatiron space, a squeaky clean affair equipped with 15 tables, a pro shop and a bar/lounge; initially for members only, it's now open to anyone who can ante up its $20-per-half-hour fee (lower rates apply before 6 PM).

Spirit Cruises

23 | 20 | 21 | VE

Chelsea | Chelsea Piers | Pier 62 (Hudson River & W. 23rd St.) | C/E to 23rd St. | 866-483-3866 | www.spiritcruises.com

"Salute the Statue of Liberty" while downing an "expensive" cocktail on this dinner cruise embarking from Chelsea Piers, a "way to celebrate special occasions on the water" for both "visitors" and "hardened New Yorkers"; the main cabin's been renovated, though given the "medio-cre" food and entertainment, most go mainly "for the view."

Splash ⊘

21 | 18 | 18 | M

Flatiron | 50 W. 17th St. (bet. 5th & 6th Aves.) | 1/2/F/L to 14th St./6th Ave. | 212-691-0073 | www.splashbar.com

Longtime Flatiron gay bar "fixture" (and "rite of passage" for younger types) with a "massive", double-decker setting rife with "hot" bartenders, "fun" go-go boys and lots of dancing queens; sure, it attracts "tourists" and the B&T brigades, but there's "pickup" potential galore provided you "hit the gym first."

Spring Lounge
19 | 12 | 18 | M

NoLita | 48 Spring St. (Mulberry St.) | 6 to Spring St. | 212-965-1774
Long a NoLita "go-to", this "cheering" dive is just right for a "casual drink or three" chosen from a rotating selection of "well-priced" tap brews; if the "frat-tastic" weekend nights don't appeal, check out its 'Early Morning Drinkers Society', which commences when it opens at 8 AM.

NEW Spritzenhaus
- | - | - | I

Greenpoint | 33 Nassau Ave. (bet. Dobbin & Guernsey Sts.) | Brooklyn | G to Nassau Ave. | 347-987-4632
Rob Shamlian (Spitzer's Corner, Fat Baby) heads across the river to Greenpoint for this latest entry in the beer hall/garden craze, a gargantuan factory-chic hang pouring roughly 25 brews from two winding marble bars; added hipster bait includes a menu of German-leaning snacks, garage-style windows that open to the street, a homey fireplace and pedal-powered bathroom sinks.

Spuyten Duyvil
25 | 19 | 21 | M

Williamsburg | 359 Metropolitan Ave. (Havemeyer St.) | Brooklyn | L to Bedford Ave. | 718-963-4140 | www.spuytenduyvilnyc.com
The "only place for that rare Lambic or Gueuze", this Williamsburg bar seduces suds snobs with an "impressive" chalkboard beer menu highlighting "all things Belgian", plus a "savvy" staff that "works with you" to find the "perfect brew"; an "appealing" if thrown-together space with a "relaxing garden", it's "on the pricey side" but majorly "hip."

Stag's Head
▽ 22 | 19 | 22 | M

E 50s | 252 E. 51st St. (bet. 2nd & 3rd Aves.) | 6 to 51st St. | 212-888-2453 | www.thestagsheadnyc.com
Serious "beer drinkers" tout this East Midtown duplex for its rotating roster of all-American craft brews served in "relaxing" "tavern"-like digs by barkeeps who "know their stuff"; the tabs can add up, but that keeps a "better-than-average" clientele staggering in.

⚄ Standard Biergarten
24 | 20 | 17 | E

Meatpacking | Standard Hotel | 848 Washington St. (bet. Little W. 12th & 13th Sts.) | A/C/E/L to 14th St./8th Ave. | 212-645-4646 | www.standardhotels.com
Credited with "bringing the Meatpacking back", this "happening" alfresco beer garden "under the High Line" lures "beautiful people aplenty" with "tasty" suds, "good-looking waitresses", "larger-than-life pretzels" and "Ping-Pong too"; expect "lots of folks" having "lots of fun", though some groan "all that's missing is a sardine-can opener."

St. Andrews
20 | 18 | 21 | M

W 40s | 140 W. 46th St. (bet. 6th & 7th Aves.) | 1/2/3/7/N/Q/R/S to 42nd St./Times Sq. | 212-840-8413 | www.standrewsnyc.com
Best known for its encyclopedic single-malt lineup, this "one-and-only Scottish bar" in the Theater District is a double-decker dose of tartan spirit, where the tapsters "wear kilts" and many regulars roll in for postwork pints; it's adjusting to newish quarters that are "larger than the original", though sentimentalists "miss the nuances" of the old site.

Stand-Up NY Comedy Club
20 | 14 | 16 | E

W 70s | 236 W. 78th St. (bet. Amsterdam Ave. & B'way) | 1 to 79th St. | 212-595-0850 | www.standupny.com

"Cocky humor" comes to the Upper West Side via this veteran house of mirth that hosts a "fairly decent sampling" of "better comedians" (including occasional big guns) in a venue that's "less flashy than the touristy spots"; sure, it can be "crowded" and "expensive", but don't worry – everything seems "so much funnier" after a few rounds.

Stan's
21 | 14 | 17 | M

Bronx | 836 River Ave. (158th St.) | 4/B/D to Yankee Stadium | 718-993-5548 | www.stanssportsbar.com

Even though the entrance to the new Yankee Stadium is further away from this Bronx sports bar than before, boosters still believe it's a "prime" place to throw back budget brews, talk "smack" and get "crazy"; maybe the ambiance is "no standout", but the faithful feel "it's sort of a tradition"; P.S. it's only open during home games.

Stanton Public
22 | 20 | 18 | M

LES | 17 Stanton St. (bet. Bowery & Chrystie St.) | F to Lower East Side/ 2nd Ave. | 212-677-5555 | www.stantonpublic.com

Keeping it "cool" on the LES, this pretension-free pub stands out for its "amazing", globe-trotting brew selection that includes cask ales hand-drawn with a beer engine; dartboards and a year-round "back porch" help pep up the otherwise dodgy digs.

Stay
- | - | - | E

E Village | 244 E. Houston St. (bet. Aves. A & B) | F to Lower East Side/ 2nd Ave. | 212-982-3532 | www.stay-nyc.com

Lounging stays on a modest scale at this "little" East Villager, a contempo-styled space that brings in fans of "loud" DJ sets; too bad the easy door encourages an iffy crowd that seasoned scenesters "have to be drunk to enjoy."

St. Dymphna's
22 | 16 | 21 | M

E Village | 118 St. Marks Pl. (bet. Ave. A & 1st Ave.) | L to 1st Ave. | 212-254-6636

"Cozy", "welcoming" East Village Irish pub that's a "pretty easy" option for pints o' stout at a "reasonable" cost drawn by "cutie pies" behind the bar; if the "bare-wood" interior seems too "minimal", there's also a "patio in the back."

Still
- | - | - | M

Gramercy | 192 Third Ave. (bet. 17th & 18th Sts.) | 4/5/6/L/N/Q/R to 14th St./Union Sq. | 212-471-9807 | www.stillnyc.com

A "twenties crowd" with "wild tendencies" encouraged by daily drink specials provide a "good time for the money" at this standard-issue Gramercy fratfest; if the "easy women" don't work out, you can always "watch a game" on one of the plentiful plasma screens.

Stillwater
- | - | - | M

E Village | 78-80 E. Fourth St. (bet. Bowery & 2nd Ave.) | F to Lower East Side/ 2nd Ave. | 212-253-2237 | www.stillwaternyc.com

"Basically unchanged" from its prior incarnation as East 4th Street Bar, this East Village watering hole provides darts, billiards and video games to offset a slow social scene; it's a handy spot to "grab a quick pint", but regulars recommend arriving "with a friend."

Stir   18 | 18 | 17 | E

E 70s | 1363 First Ave. (bet. 73rd & 74th Sts.) | 6 to 77th St. | 212-744-7190 | www.stirnyc.com

This "classy little" UES lounge supplies enough specialty martinis (plus a "cozy" vibe) to create a stir with "twenties" types; yet a few fret it's rather "expensive" for "hit-or-miss" scenery with "a bit too much B&T."

Stitch   19 | 17 | 18 | M

Garment District | 247 W. 37th St. (bet. 7th & 8th Aves.) | 1/2/3 to 34th St./Penn Station | 212-852-4826 | www.stitchnyc.com

Given the "limited choices" in the Garment District, this mega-bar sews up the "happy-hour" action with "affordable" libations served in an "open", split-level setting that can get "pretty loud" and "crowded"; though "nothing special", it's still "above-average" for a "drink after work" in an "obscure neighborhood."

St. Jerome's   - | - | - | M

LES | 155 Rivington St. (bet. Clinton & Suffolk Sts.) | F/J/M/Z to Delancey/Essex Sts. | 212-533-1810

This bare-bones LES rock 'n' roll bar is a what-you-see-is-what-you-get kind of joint with nightly DJs, a rather "dingy" atmosphere and no specialty cocktail list; its biggest selling point is next-door proximity to the popular eatery Bondi Road.

St. Marks Ale House   18 | 12 | 20 | I

E Village | 2 St. Marks Pl. (3rd Ave.) | 6 to Astor Pl. | 212-260-9762 | www.stmarksalehouse.com

With "so many TVs to watch", there's "no bad seat in the house" at this "big-ish" East Village sports bar where brewskis and "noisy" cheerleading are "de rigueur" on game nights; though a totally "non-distinctive" "frat-boy hangout", at least it's "priced right."

St. Nick's Jazz Pub ⌗   ▽ 23 | 16 | 23 | M

Harlem | 773 St. Nicholas Ave. (149th St.) | 1 to 145th St. | 212-283-9728 | www.stnicksjazzpub.net

"Seriously talented" jazz maestros jam nightly at this "music hang" in Harlem's Sugar Hill, a mecca for bebop enthusiasts and "bohemians" alike since its '40s incarnation as Luckey's Rendezvous; the quarters may be cramped and plain, but the swingin' patrons "don't go for the decor."

Stone Creek   21 | 17 | 23 | M

Murray Hill | 140 E. 27th St. (bet. Lexington & 3rd Aves.) | 6 to 28th St. | 212-532-1037 | www.stonecreeknyc.com

A "change of pace" from the "Third Avenue frat scene", this Murray Hill hideout comprises a ranch house–style front bar abutting a rear lounge; the "accommodating" staff "takes great care of customers", but it's on less-traveled turf and usually on the "quiet" side.

Stonehome Wine Bar   - | - | - | M

Fort Greene | 87 Lafayette Ave. (bet. Portland Ave. & S. Elliott Pl.) | Brooklyn | G to Fulton St. | 718-624-9443 | www.stonehomewinebar.com

For a "cozy neighborhood" outfit, this Fort Greene wine bar gets ambitious as it uncorks 200 "quality" labels (35 by the glass) paired with "great" eats in spiffy digs where you can actually "hear your conversation"; augmented by a back garden, it's "ideal for BAM" and apt to be "packed" after a show.

Stone Rose

| 23 | 24 | 21 | VE |

W 60s | Time Warner Ctr. | 10 Columbus Circle, 4th fl. (60th St.) | 1/A/B/C/D to 59th St./Columbus Circle | 212-823-9769 | www.gerberbars.com

"Classy to the max", this "upbeat, upscale" Time Warner Center bar/lounge draws "more corporate types than an MBA graduation" thanks to its "impressive views" of Central Park and Columbus Circle; sure, it's "friggin' expensive" and you "need to walk through the mall to get there", but "hawt waitresses" and "high-end allure" keep this one rock solid.

Stonewall Inn

| 16 | 9 | 16 | M |

W Village | 53 Christopher St. (bet. 7th Ave. S. & Waverly Pl.) | 1 to Christopher St. | 212-488-2705 | www.thestonewallinnnyc.com

"Historic importance" (it's the site of the "infamous" '69 riots that jump-started the "gay rights movement") is the reason for this West Villager's staying power, even if the crowd and setting are "not spectacular" nowadays; locals concede it's "pretty much coasting on" its "landmark" status, but hey, there are "always tourists" to impress.

Stout

| 20 | 18 | 19 | M |

Garment District | 133 W. 33rd St. (bet. 6th & 7th Aves.) | 1/2/3 to 34th St./Penn Station | 212-629-6191 | www.stoutnyc.com

"Easy access" to Penn Station and MSG is the calling card of this "Costco"-size Irish pub offering a "huge beer selection" in a "convenient" multilevel space; "willing" service and "lots of TVs" earn it stout support despite the "mob scenes" before a game or concert.

☑ Studio Square ⌀
(aka Garden at Studio Square)

| 25 | 22 | 18 | M |

Astoria | 35-33 36th St. (bet. 35th & 36th Aves.) | Queens | M/R to 36th St. | 718-383-1001 | www.studiosquarenyc.com

The absence of Teutonic trappings may "defy the traditional", but otherwise this "ginormous" Astoria beer garden is one of the "best bars in Queens", offering a "great assortment" of affordable tap brews served in a "warehouse"-like interior or on a vast patio festooned with picnic tables and a fire pit; it's a bona fide "hot spot" in the summer and is now presenting a concert series.

NEW Studio XXI

| - | - | - | E |

Flatiron | 59 W. 21st St., 2nd fl. (bet. 5th & 6th Aves.) | F to 23rd St. | 212-359-4200 | www.studioxxinyc.com

Meant to suggest a luxe recording studio, this swanky Chelsea lounge (in the former Snitch space) features speaker grills in the ceiling, a faux equalizer on the bar and an obscure, second-floor address; brick walls, tufted leather banquettes and pricey signature drinks come with the territory.

Stumble Inn

| 20 | 18 | 21 | M |

E 70s | 1454 Second Ave. (76th St.) | 6 to 77th St. | 212-650-0561 | www.nycbestbar.com

"Just like being in college again", this "big", "congenial" Upper Eastsider (once Mo's Caribbean) is the "ultimate frat party" complete with beer pong, "ludicrously reasonable" drink deals and TVs galore loaded with "all the sports packages"; "consistently busy", it's "perfect for what it is."

SubMercer
24 | 23 | 19 | VE

SoHo | Mercer Hotel | 147 Mercer St. (Prince St.) | N/R to Prince St. | 212-966-6060

An unmarked door, freight elevator ride and underground labyrinth lead to this "great little dungeon" below SoHo's Mercer Hotel, a sub rosa lounge for the smart set equipped with brick arches and a stripper pole; since it's becoming better known and less "exclusive", some trendsters snub it as "tediously" overhyped.

Subway Inn
18 | 8 | 15 | I

E 60s | 143 E. 60th St. (Lexington Ave.) | 4/5/6/F/N/Q/R to 59th St./ Lexington Ave. | 212-752-6500

A "classic dump" oozing "sheer sleaze", this circa-1934 Upper East Side "survivor" is "one of the last true shot-and-a-beer halls" in town, sporting "worn seats" and "neon signs" right out of a "detective movie"; the backdrop and regulars may be pretty "dingy", but it's just right for some "liquid courage before venturing into Bloomingdale's" across the street.

Sugarland ⌀
- | - | - | M

Williamsburg | 221 N. Ninth St. (bet. Driggs Ave. & Roebling St.) | Brooklyn | L to Bedford Ave. | 718-599-4044

Gay hipsters "shake their groove things" at this down 'n' dirty "dive" that's one of the few places to "dance in Williamsburg"; the deliberately distressed setting is equipped with a bonus "outdoor porch", and surveyors report the overall experience can "vary from sloppy to epic."

Suite
- | - | - | M

W 100s | 992 Amsterdam Ave. (109th St.) | 1 to Cathedral Pkwy./ 110th St. | 212-222-4600 | www.suitenyc.com

Take a "vacation from the Chelsea scene" at this "unpretentious" Upper West Side gay bar drawing a "demographically skewed" cast of characters; weekly events like "drag-queen karaoke" keep the mood "energetic" here.

Sullivan Hall
▽ 21 | 11 | 19 | M

G Village | 214 Sullivan St. (bet. Bleecker & W. 3rd Sts.) | A/B/C/D/E/ F/M to W. 4th St. | 212-477-2782 | www.sullivanhallnyc.com

"Up-and-coming" rockers and "good tribute bands" perform at this NYU-area music venue, home to an "intimate" stage and a following that "tends to be young"; maybe the interior "lacks character" (and seating), but for live tunes and beer it "doesn't disappoint."

Sullivan Room
18 | 15 | 17 | M

G Village | 218 Sullivan St., downstairs (bet. Bleecker & W. 3rd Sts.) | A/B/C/D/E/F/M to W. 4th St. | 212-252-2151 | www.sullivanroom.com

"Dance music" is the thing at this underground Village lounge that books "world-class DJs" able to keep the "small" floor "hot and crowded"; though the layout can be a "logistical nightmare" ("think sardine can"), all that "big-name talent on the decks" makes for "lots of fun."

	APPEAL	DECOR	SERVICE	COST

Summit Bar
- | - | - | M

E Village | 133 Ave. C (bet. 8th & 9th Sts.) | L to 1st Ave. | no phone | www.thesummitbar.net

Rather swank for "out-of-the-way" Avenue C, this cozy nook achieves its relaxed effect via the use of soft lights, crystal chandeliers and velvety banquettes; it's quite an upgrade to the former Baraza space, and the pricing's not bad either: well-mixed pops start at nine bucks.

Sutra
19 | 19 | 16 | M

E Village | 16 First Ave. (bet. 1st & 2nd Sts.) | F to Lower East Side/2nd Ave. | 212-677-9477 | www.sutranyc.com

Tricked out in crimson velvet, this India-themed East Villager "catches the eye" and ear, thanks to a downstairs lounge where "awesome DJs" spin hip-hop-heavy sets; it's also "not too bad pricewise", though it can get so "packed" that some wonder if it's "worth the elbows."

Sutton Place
17 | 15 | 16 | M

E 50s | 1015 Second Ave. (bet. 53rd & 54th Sts.) | 6/E to 51st-53rd Sts./Lexington Ave. | 212-207-3777 | www.suttonplacenyc.com

"After a grueling day pitching investment deals", "young suits" head for this "popular" Midtown triplex that allows "plenty of room" to sniff around; though there's uniform praise for the "fun rooftop", others find it a "run-of-the-mill" scene with too much fratmosphere.

Suzie Wong
∇ 23 | 22 | 23 | VE

Chelsea | 547 W. 27th St. (bet. 10th & 11th Aves.) | C/E to 23rd St. | 212-268-5105 | www.suziewongnyc.com

"Great Asian decor" lends this West Chelsea club the air of a Shanghai bordello as scarlet lights, lanterns and random calligraphy set the scene for bottle service heavy on the first-class sakes; it's liable to cost a bundle, though, and the crowd rubs some the wong way.

Sway
20 | 17 | 14 | E

Hudson Square | 305 Spring St. (bet. Greenwich & Hudson Sts.) | 1 to Houston St. | 212-620-5220 | www.swaylounge.com

"Dark", Moroccan-themed Hudson Square club/lounge, a longtime "late-night favorite" that still "holds sway over" people who "like to listen to Morrissey and the Smiths"; maybe its "hot-spot luster" is beginning to fade, but "when the DJ is on", the "cool" factor is too.

⧉ Sweet Afton
25 | 22 | 24 | M

Astoria | 30-09 34th St. (bet. 30th & 31st Aves.) | Queens | N/Q to 30th Ave. | 718-777-2570 | www.sweetaftonbar.com

A "big thing" for Astoria, this "hip" Irish pub projects "soul without pretension" in a traditional brick-and-beam space; "immediately popular" with locals sweet on its "very Manhattan" style and low Queens prices, it's bound to be busy and "loud."

Sweet & Vicious
17 | 14 | 14 | M

NoLita | 5 Spring St. (bet. Bowery & Elizabeth St.) | 6 to Spring St. | 212-334-7915 | www.sweetandviciousnyc.com

"It's still sweet" declare the "mostly Downtown" denizens of this "solid" NoLita bar vending "reasonably priced" pops in a "low-key" "grunge" setting; like everywhere else, it gets "overrun by non-Manhattanites" on weekends, but the "refreshing outdoor terrace" offers some relief.

	APPEAL	DECOR	SERVICE	COST

Swift
22 | 21 | 23 | M

NoHo | 34 E. Fourth St. (bet. Bowery & Lafayette St.) | 6 to Astor Pl. | 212-227-9438 | www.swiftnycbar.com

A "phenomenal choice of beers" impresses "picky drinkers" at this well-kept NoHo "Irish mainstay" where the booze is swiftly served by "warm" barkeeps who are "as much fun as their customers"; still, it's a "low-key local", drawing lots of "firemen" from Engine Company 33 around the corner.

Swing 46 Jazz Club
23 | 19 | 17 | E

W 40s | 349 W. 46th St. (bet. 8th & 9th Aves.) | 1/2/3/7/N/Q/R/S to 42nd St./Times Sq. | 212-262-9554 | www.swing46.com

"Come with a partner" to this Restaurant Row supper club, an ode to "swing dancing" where live "big bands" give footloose folk the opportunity to "tear up the floor" – or "sit back and watch"; it's "tolerant of novices" (even offering "free lessons"), though skeptics sense it's more of a "tourist" thing.

NEW System
- | - | - | E

LIC | 32-10 37th Ave. (bet. 32nd & 33rd Sts.) | Queens | M/R to 36th St. | www.systemny.com

Long Island City is home to this big new danceteria, an 8,000-sq.-ft. affair formerly known as Sarabanda that's been rebuilt from scratch with a state-of-the-art sound system; musical director Jellybean Benitez is in charge of bookings, so expect name-brand DJs on the decks.

Taj II
17 | 20 | 15 | E

Flatiron | 48 W. 21st St. (bet. 5th & 6th Aves.) | F to 23rd St. | 212-620-3033 | www.tajlounge.com

With its carved teak decor, this "dark" lounge brings tasteful "Indian style" to the Flatiron, along with DJs and various "drink specials"; though critics dis the random "hoochies in Forever 21 dresses" in the crowd, most acknowledge a "decent" scene "for the money."

NEW Tammany Hall
- | - | - | M

LES | 152 Orchard St. (bet. Rivington & Stanton Sts.) | F/J/M/Z to Delancey/Essex Sts. | 212-982-7767 | www.tammanyhallny.com

The former Annex digs get a semi-swanky upgrade via this new LES 'rock bar' from the Crash Mansion team; the tri-level setting includes a street-level live performance space, bottle service–friendly balcony and a banquette-lined basement.

Tapeo 29
▽ 25 | 21 | 21 | M

LES | 29 Clinton St. (Stanton St.) | F to Lower East Side/2nd Ave. | 212-979-0002 | www.tapeo29.com

"Excellent" LES wine bar proffering a "large selection" of Spanish vintages (plus "tasty" sangria and tapas), all served by a "cool", "accommodating" crew; it's always "easy to get a seat" here, and the rustically "romantic" room will duly "impress your date."

NEW Taproom No. 307
- | - | - | M

Murray Hill | 307 Third Ave. (bet. 23rd & 24th Sts.) | 6 to 23rd St. | 212-725-4766 | www.taproom307.com

Murray Hill's Third Avenue runway gets a craft beer specialist with the arrival of this new spot offering 42 tap lines and a variety of bottled bevies that span the globe; dark-wood paneling and upscale bar bites up the ante and help explain why this one's been a hit right out of the box.

T.B.D.
- | - | - | M

Greenpoint | 224 Franklin St. (Green St.) | Brooklyn | G to Greenpoint Ave. | 718-349-6727 | www.tbdbrooklyn.com

Converted "with austerity" from an old warehouse, this Greenpoint venue attracts creative types with art and video installed in a "wide-open", "concrete"-laden setting whose "starkness" belies a "handsomely stocked bar"; a good-sized rear beer garden ices the cake.

Tea Lounge
22 | 20 | 20 | M

Park Slope | 837 Union St. (bet. 6th & 7th Aves.) | Brooklyn | R to Union St. | 718-789-2762 | www.tealoungeny.com

It may be "stroller central" by day, but this "spacious" Park Slope coffeehouse morphs into a nighttime "scene" for "casual" slackers relaxing on "old couches" while enjoying "inventive cocktails" and "live folk-type music"; even though it's "usually crowded", it suits a funky "first date" to a tee.

Teddy's
▽ 24 | 21 | 21 | M

Williamsburg | 96 Berry St. (N. 8th St.) | Brooklyn | L to Bedford Ave. | 718-384-9787 | www.teddyswilliamsburg.com

"Old-fashioned" is the word on this circa-1887 Williamsburg saloon with endearing touches like a hammered tin ceiling, "beautiful" stained-glass frontage, a famed Bloody Mary and whiskey sold "by the inch"; its "easygoing" crowd admits that "service can be slow", but it's always "friendly."

Temple Bar
23 | 24 | 20 | E

NoHo | 332 Lafayette St. (bet. Bleecker & Houston Sts.) | 6 to Bleecker St. | 212-925-4242 | www.templebarnyc.com

"Sophisticated" yet "sultry", this "dark" NoHo lounge has "sexy assignation" written all over it, and offers "old-fashioned cocktails" in an atmosphere so "clandestine" you might think that "Sinatra and his pack could walk in at any second"; sure, it's "been around for a long time", but it still works for "sneaking away" with somebody special.

Ten Bells
24 | 22 | 21 | E

LES | 247 Broome St. (bet. Ludlow & Orchard Sts.) | F/J/M/Z to Delancey/Essex Sts. | 212-228-4450 | www.thetenbells.com

A "true LES gem", this "cozy", Euro-centric wine bar is a "charming den" with an "eclectic" fan base extolling its "fabulous" list of organic vinos and "knowledgeable" staffers; named for the London pub frequented by Jack the Ripper, it exudes an appropriate "film-noir vibe."

Tenjune
22 | 20 | 17 | VE

Meatpacking | 26 Little W. 12th St., downstairs (bet. 9th Ave. & Washington St.) | A/C/E/L to 14th St./8th Ave. | 646-624-2410 | www.tenjunenyc.com

Maybe it's "no longer at the top of the pile", but this "classy" Meatpacking club still manages to draw "dressed-to-impress" "eye candy" with its "upbeat" DJs and "good-guy owners"; but even though the door remains "hard for the average man", the "bridge-and-tunnel" brigades are beginning to squeeze through.

	APPEAL	DECOR	SERVICE	COST

1020 Bar
17 | 12 | 17 | M

W 100s | 1020 Amsterdam Ave. (110th St.) | 1 to 110th St. | 212-531-3468

"You're out of place without a Columbia ID" at this "easygoing" Morningside Heights "dive" where "boozy" grad students ditch their books in favor of darts, pool and "affordable potables"; although "borderline grimy", it's "popular" with folks "who aren't that picky."

Terminal 5
19 | 14 | 14 | E

W 50s | 610 W. 56th St. (bet. 11th & 12th Aves.) | 1/A/B/C/D to 59th St./Columbus Circle | 212-582-6600 | www.terminal5nyc.com

"Things are rockin'" at this Hell's Kitchen music venue hosting a "great lineup" of indie acts in a medium-capacity multilevel hall that "gets very crowded" in spite of the "out-of-the-way" address; while the "industrial" decor, "expensive" hooch and acoustics akin to a "terminal at JFK" strike flat notes, it's "still better than an arena."

Terra Blues
▽ 22 | 19 | 20 | M

G Village | 149 Bleecker St., 2nd fl. (bet. La Guardia Pl. & Thompson St.) | A/B/C/D/E/F/M to W. 4th St. | 212-777-7776 | www.terrablues.com

"One of the few venues" in town showcasing "live blues", this "popular" Villager presents "good acts" nightly in a warm, second-floor setting; with an assist from the top-shelf bourbon and scotch selection, it just might "make you forget what you were blue about in the first place."

Terroir
26 | 22 | 25 | E

E Village | 413 E. 12th St. (bet. Ave. A & 1st Ave.) | L to 1st Ave. | no phone
TriBeCa | 24 Harrison St. (bet. Greenwich & Hudson Sts.) | 1 to Franklin St. | 212-625-9463
www.wineisterroir.com

Oenophiles are all over this "fantastic" East Village wine bar (sibling of nearby Hearth) where an "extensive" list of "interesting" international vinos and "tasty" small bites are dispensed by an "eager", "personable" team; the "cozy" setting is "small, small, small", however, so regulars plead "don't tell"; P.S. a bigger TriBeCa spin-off opened post-Survey.

T.G. Whitney's
16 | 14 | 18 | M

E 50s | 244 E. 53rd St. (bet. 2nd & 3rd Aves.) | 6/E to 51st-53rd Sts./Lexington Ave. | 212-888-5772 | www.tgwhitneys.com

East Midtown's "suited-up" twentysomethings make this "typical" Irish bar a "happy-hour staple" in spite of its "chain"-like feel; a terrace and weekend karaoke add extra incentive, but most agree "cheap" drinking after work is the "best reason to come."

🗹NEW Theater Bar
- | - | - | E

TriBeCa | 114 Franklin St. (bet. Church St. & W. B'way) | A/C/E to Canal St. | 212-334-3733

Mixology maestro Albert Trummer lands in TriBeCa with this long-in-the-making bar/lounge done up in an opulent, Moulin Rouge–esque style complete with theatrical red velvet curtains and flair bartending; the bartop bisects the long, narrow space, with the back area serving as a stage/VIP pen accessed by an underground passageway.

		APPEAL	DECOR	SERVICE	COST

Therapy
`22` `23` `19` `M`

W 50s | 348 W. 52nd St. (bet. 8th & 9th Aves.) | C/E to 50th St. | 212-397-1700 | www.therapy-nyc.com

There's "therapy in so many forms" at this "sceney" Hell's Kitchen gay bar, an "ultracool" duplex rendered in "ski-lodge chic", where "well-groomed" "professional types" toy with designer drinks; the "nightly entertainment" runs from drag shows to DJs, and "recent renovations" have made it more "classy" than ever.

Third & Long
`13` `9` `17` `I`

Murray Hill | 523 Third Ave. (35th St.) | 6 to 33rd St. | 212-447-5711 | www.thirdandlongnyc.com

Cash-strapped kegheads say this Murray Hill "standby" is worth visiting for its "dollar beers on select nights", though otherwise it's "nothing special" with "what-you-see-is-what-you-get" decor; it's an "easy" pick for watching tube sports and "always packed" during big games.

Thirsty Scholar
`17` `13` `17` `M`

E Village | 155 Second Ave. (bet. 9th & 10th Sts.) | 6 to Astor Pl. | 212-777-6514 | www.ryansnyc.com

"Quench your thirst for knowledge of beer" at this East Village Irish pub where deep thinkers from NYU ruminate over rounds of Guinness while "good bartending" keeps the taps flowing; the narrow digs may seem a "little dive-ish", but at least the suds are "not overpriced."

13
`18` `14` `15` `E`

G Village | 35 E. 13th St. (University Pl.) | 4/5/6/L/N/Q/R to 14th St./Union Sq. | 212-979-6677 | www.bar13.com

An after-school playhouse for the "NYU crowd", this double-decker Villager provides "lots of space" for "unpretentious" drinking and dancing, or stargazing on the "chill" rooftop deck; unluckily, though, the "generic" interior is "nothing to write home about."

🆕 13th Step
`-` `-` `-` `M`

E Village | 149 Second Ave. (bet. 9th & 10th Sts.) | 6 to Astor Pl. | 212-228-8020 | www.nycbestbar.com

The former Telephone Bar digs have morphed into this ironically named East Villager, which retains the same sprawling setting and genial atmospherics, sans red phone booths; otherwise, it's pretty standard issue, with Applebee's decor and a crowd that skews more frat than hipster.

Thom Bar
`25` `23` `20` `VE`

SoHo | 60 Thompson Hotel | 60 Thompson St., 2nd fl. (bet. Broome & Spring Sts.) | C/E to Spring St. | 212-219-3200 | www.thompsonhotels.com

"Very adult" and "very classy", this "cool" SoHo hotel bar draws "beautiful" folk with its "tasty cocktails" and "light lounge" soundtrack; given the stiff pricing, it's best enjoyed "on an expense account" – and even better if you can sneak onto A60, its semi-private rooftop.

300 New York
`21` `17` `17` `E`

Chelsea | Chelsea Piers | Pier 60 (Hudson River & W. 18th St.) | A/C/E/L to 14th St./8th Ave. | 212-835-2695 | www.3hundred.com

Tenpins get "trendy" at this loungelike Chelsea Piers bowling alley that courts "young singles" with 40 lanes, "state-of-the-art" lighting, a

| | APPEAL | DECOR | SERVICE | COST |

clubtastic soundtrack and "comfortable" couches; though it strikes low rollers as "expensive", bowled-over types say "nicely done."

NEW Three Monkeys — | — | — | M

W 50s | 236 W. 54th St. (bet. B'way & 8th Ave.) | B/D/E to 53rd St./7th Ave. | 212-586-2080 | www.thethreemonkeysbar.com

Divine Bar West in the Theater District has morphed into this new sports bar, a double-decker, just-folks joint that looks pretty much the same as its predecessor, right down to the sweet outdoor deck on the second floor; 36 tap brews and lots of flat-screens are the notable changes here.

NEW 3 Sheets Saloon — | — | — | M

G Village | 134 W. Third St. (bet. MacDougal St. & 6th Ave.) | A/B/C/D/E/F/M to W. 4th St. | 212-777-1733 | www.nycbestbar.com

Formerly Town Tavern, this Village sports bar seems to have done little more than change its name, retaining its beer-soaked, double-decker setup; now owned by the crew behind Down the Hatch and Off the Wagon, it's a magnet for NYU types who like cheap pops and the Philadelphia Eagles.

3 Steps 22 | 16 | 23 | M

Gramercy | 322 Second Ave. (bet. 18th & 19th Sts.) | 6 to 23rd St. | 212-533-5336 | www.3stepsnyc.com

It's all about "charm" at this "cute little" Gramercy Park watering hole, a "low-key" hangout drawing an "eclectic" following thanks to "excellent bartenders" and "well-priced" cocktails; now that it's "becoming discovered", the "narrow" setting can get "crowded on the weekends."

3 Ten Lounge 15 | 14 | 13 | M
(aka Crime Scene)

NoHo | 310 Bowery (1st St.) | 6 to Bleecker St. | 212-477-1979 | www.3tenlounge.com

The former Mannahatta parties on under a different name at this Bowery funhouse where both the front bar and rear lounge are "crowded" with ex-collegians in all their "B&T glory"; "decent" DJs also hold court, but cynics warn it "gets pricey" and "you'll feel weird if you're over 24."

Tillman's 23 | 23 | 18 | E

Chelsea | 165 W. 26th St. (bet. 6th & 7th Aves.) | 1 to 28th St. | 212-627-8320 | www.tillmansnyc.com

"Where Shaft would hang out today", this "secluded" Chelsea bar/lounge is a "soulful" take on "'70s" Harlem with a vintage vibe and a "chill" crowd knocking back "strong" cocktails as DJs spin "classic R&B"; it's "a bit pricier" than some, but the "sexy" ambiance has "winner written all over it."

Tír na Nóg 18 | 17 | 18 | M

Garment District | 5 Penn Plaza (8th Ave., bet. 33rd & 34th Sts.) | A/C/E to 34th St./Penn Station | 212-630-0249 | www.tirnanognyc.com

"Irish pride is alive and well" at this "authentic" Gaelic pub with a "key location" in the "Penn Station wasteland"; it's the kind of "old-fashioned" outfit where the vibe's "inviting" and the "Guinness is always fresh", hence its "popularity at rush hour."

	APPEAL	DECOR	SERVICE	COST

Tom & Jerry's ∅
(aka 288)

| | 21 | 14 | 20 | M |

NoHo | 288 Elizabeth St. (bet. Bleecker & Houston Sts.) | 6 to Bleecker St. | 212-260-5045

"Casual" is the word on this "old-school" NoHo "local" that's usually "full of regulars" unwinding with cost-effective pops and "no-attitude" service from "some of the nicest bartenders" around; a display of Tom & Jerry crockery behind the bar signals its "friendly", "nonfancy" style.

Tonic

| | 16 | 15 | 17 | M |

W 40s | 727 Seventh Ave. (bet. 48th & 49th Sts.) | 1 to 50th St. | 212-382-1059 | www.tonicbarnyc.com

Tonic East

Murray Hill | 411 Third Ave. (29th St.) | 6 to 28th St. | 212-683-7090 | www.toniceast.com

Known for their "huge", "strategically placed" projection screens, these "massive", "multilevel" sports bars broadcast "all sorts of sporting events" in "faux upscale" settings that strike some as "glorified frat houses"; the Murray Hill outlet also features a "great roof deck" and draws Penn State alums who show up to "cheer on the Nittany Lions."

❖ Top of the Strand

| | – | – | – | E |

Garment District | Strand Hotel | 33 W. 37th St., 21st fl. (bet. 5th & 6th Aves.) | B/D/F/M/N/Q/R to 34th St./Herald Sq. | 212-448-1024 | www.thestrandnyc.com

The Garment District's Strand Hotel houses this striking rooftop bar/lounge, one of Midtown's best-kept secrets – for now; decidedly more intimate than nearby 230 Fifth, it boasts an equally drop-dead view of the Empire State Building, along with a glass roof that retracts in warm weather.

❖ Top of the Tower

| | 26 | 22 | 20 | E |

E 40s | Beekman Tower Hotel | 3 Mitchell Pl., 26th fl. (1st Ave. & 49th St.) | 6 to 51st St. | 212-980-4796 | www.thetopofthetower.com

"Stunning views on all four sides" draw "elegant" types to this enduring Midtown aerie with an "old-NY feel" that's "perfect for a romantic interlude"; being "off the beaten path" makes it "less touristy" than other well-known rooftops, but the "expensive drinks" mean it's best to go as "someone's guest."

🆕 Toro

| | – | – | – | E |

TriBeCa | Smyth Hotel | 85 W. Broadway, downstairs (bet. Chambers & Warren Sts.) | 1/2/3 to Chambers St. | 212-204-5555, x5557

TriBeCa's Smyth Hotel is the site of this underground lounge, a dark, moody affair that takes its name from the bullhorns and framed matador capes on the walls; an off-the-radar address on Chambers Street keeps the traffic low, so it's perfect for an illicit rendezvous.

Tortilla Flats

| | 21 | 17 | 18 | M |

W Village | 767 Washington St. (12th St.) | A/C/E/L to 14th St./8th Ave. | 212-243-1053 | www.tortillaflatsnyc.com

You'll "never leave close to sober" from this "raucous" Village cantina where a "rowdy" crowd gets "sloshed on margaritas" in "cramped", "gaudy" digs that recall the "inside of a piñata"; given all the "festive" activities (trivia, bingo, "hula-hoop contests"), it's a "perennial favorite" for birthdays and bachelorettes.

Townhouse

| 20 | 22 | 20 | E |

E 50s | 236 E. 58th St. (bet. 2nd & 3rd Aves.) | 4/5/6/F/N/Q/R to 59th St./Lexington Ave. | 212-754-4649 | www.townhouseny.com

"Silver-haired" gay gents and "gold diggers hoping to hit the jackpot" collide at this "been-around-forever" double-decker near the Queensboro Bridge; some gather around the "show-tunes"-only piano bar, but the scene here is really about "grandpas looking for one last fling with a young chippie."

Traffic

| ∇ 22 | 21 | 23 | M |

E 50s | 986 Second Ave. (52nd St.) | 6/E to 51st-53rd Sts./Lexington Ave. | 212-813-1595

NEW **W 40s** | 701 Ninth Ave. (48th St.) | C/E to 50th St./8th Ave. www.trafficbarnyc.com

"Up and coming" in East Midtown, this duplex in the former Mantra digs includes a stylish bar festooned with "endless flat-screens" and a "smooth" upstairs lounge equipped with a tiny balcony overlooking Second Avenue; it sees lots of traffic from twenties types seeking a more "upscale" meet market, and now there's a new Hell's Kitchen spin-off.

Trailer Park

| 19 | 20 | 18 | M |

Chelsea | 271 W. 23rd St. (bet. 7th & 8th Aves.) | C/E to 23rd St. | 212-463-8000 | www.trailerparklounge.com

"Hilariously un-NY", this "trashy" Chelsea tribute to all things "blue collar" is a "kitsch explosion" that trots out everything from black-velvet "Elvis" art to a "screen door" and a "real trailer"; if you like "tater tots", "paper-towel napkins" and "champagne in cans", look no further.

Trash

| ∇ 15 | 13 | 12 | I |

Williamsburg | 256 Grand St. (bet. Driggs Ave. & Roebling St.) | Brooklyn | L to Bedford Ave. | 718-599-1000 | www.thetrashbar.com

"Carrying the torch" for die-hard punks and rockers, this Williamsburg local combines loud live shows in the basement with drink deals that will make for a "memorable (or not) night"; rest assured that "it lives up to its name as far as aesthetics go."

Tribeca Tavern

| 17 | 14 | 19 | M |

TriBeCa | 247 W. Broadway (bet. Walker & White Sts.) | A/C/E to Canal St. | 212-941-7671

For an "honest beer" "without breaking the bank", try this "low-key" saloon that's a "welcome alternative" to the "sophistication sweeping TriBeCa"; expect "no-nonsense" service, an active pool table and "lots of '80s power ballads" on the juke.

NEW Trilby, The

| - | - | - | E |

E Village | Cooper Square Hotel | 25 Cooper Sq. (bet. 5th & 6th Sts.) | 6 to Astor Pl. | 212-475-3400 | www.thecoopersquarehotel.com

Merging the bar and dining areas of the Cooper Square Hotel into one meandering, L-shaped lounge, this new Bowery arrival is geared toward the party crowd with dim lighting and lots of couches and banquettes; a swell outdoor patio is part of the package in warm weather.

	APPEAL	DECOR	SERVICE	COST

Triona's
-	-	-	M

G Village | 237 Sullivan St. (W. 3rd St.) | A/B/C/D/E/F/M to W. 4th St. | 212-982-5222

Not much has changed at this Village sports bar formerly known as Pinch, save for the name and ownership; look for the same darts, billiards and NYU-heavy crowd cavorting in pleasantly rough-and-tumble digs.

Trophy
∇ 19	17	19	E

Williamsburg | 351 Broadway (bet. Keap & Rodney Sts.) | Brooklyn | J/M/Z to Marcy Ave. | 347-227-8515 | www.trophybar.com

The founders of Williamsburg's Stay Gold gallery put plenty of effort into this barroom parked under the J/M/Z line, with polished wood floors and subway tile-lined walls; a back garden, hot DJs and a vintage jukebox playing 45s are bonus draws for its young, style-conscious following.

Turkey's Nest ∌
∇ 19	11	18	M

Williamsburg | 94 Bedford Ave. (N. 12th St.) | Brooklyn | L to Bedford Ave. | 718-384-9774

"Not a faux dive", this "real-deal" Williamsburg dump opposite McCarren Park provides "giant Styrofoam cups" of "super-cheap" brew to everyone from "ball players" and "old fogies" to "would-be hipsters"; the "down 'n' dirty" digs are "nothing appealing", but at least the mood is "friendly."

Turtle Bay
14	12	14	M

E 50s | 987 Second Ave. (bet. 52nd & 53rd Sts.) | 6/E to 51st-53rd Sts./Lexington Ave. | 212-223-4224 | www.turtlebaynyc.com

The "just-graduated" set piles into this "popular" East Midtown double-decker for "cheapish drinks" and "rowdy frolicking"; downstairs, it's a "totally run-of-the-mill" scene while the "beer-soaked" upstairs lounge is "too loud", but wherever you wind up, "don't wear good shoes."

Twelve
(aka XII)
∇ 18	16	20	M

Murray Hill | 206 E. 34th St. (3rd Ave.) | 6 to 33rd St. | 212-545-9912 | www.bar12.com

Like "similar bars in the area", this Murray Hill big sports specialist seduces "young college" lads with its umpteen plasma screens (including mini-sets on the taps) and manageable tabs; but given weekend DJs and "fancier" looks than others in its league, some sense an "identity crisis."

12th Street Ale House
19	16	21	M

E Village | 192 Second Ave. (12th St.) | L to 1st Ave. | 212-253-2323

Being a "typical neighborhood" joint, this East Villager "caters to locals and regulars" with "reasonably priced" pours from "chatty" tapsters in a "not-too-crowded" setting; the "unassuming" style works for a "low-key" quickie, but don't plan to "spend the whole night."

2A
20	13	18	M

E Village | 25 Ave. A (2nd St.) | F to Lower East Side/2nd Ave. | 212-505-2466

Now in its 26th year, this East Village "standby" is "still fairly cool" given the "ratty charm" of its "old-school" ground-level bar and "relaxed" second floor with windows overlooking the "Avenue A freak parade"; devotees dig the "friendly staff" and non-touristy "NYC crowd."

Two E — | — | — | VE

E 60s | Pierre Hotel | 2 E. 61st St. (5th Ave.) | N/R to 5th Ave./59th St. | 212-838-8000 | www.tajhotels.com

Think gold leaf and crystal chandeliers galore to get the gist of this opulent Midtown bar/lounge off the Pierre Hotel lobby that also serves coffee in the AM and high tea in the afternoon; though there's no dress code, it feels like there should be given the stately atmosphere, hushed acoustics and eye-poppingly priced pops.

200 Fifth — 17 | 17 | 16 | E

Park Slope | 200 Fifth Ave. (bet. Sackett & Union Sts.) | Brooklyn | R to Union St. | 718-638-2925 | www.200-fifth.com

It's all "beer and games" at this "testosterone-fueled" Park Slope sports bar, a "neighborhood" stalwart where "plenty of TVs" and "ever-flowing" tap brews draw a crowd that's been "going there since the dawn of time"; just "don't expect anything too fancy" and "get there early" to beat the "madhouse" weekend crowds.

200 Orchard — | — | — | M

LES | 200 Orchard St. (bet. Houston & Stanton Sts.) | F to Lower East Side/ 2nd Ave. | 212-253-2235 | www.200orchard.com

Set in the Orchard Bar space, this refurbed spot from the Sixth Ward team flaunts a stripped-down aesthetic – starting with the name – that pairs reclaimed wood with distressed brick to rustic effect; the back room's airier now that the stage has been removed.

⊿ 230 Fifth — 23 | 22 | 15 | VE

Chelsea | 230 Fifth Ave., penthouse (bet. 26th & 27th Sts.) | N/R to 28th St. | 212-725-4300 | www.230-fifth.com

There's lots of "scene and scenery" to be had at this "commanding" duplex near Madison Square, voted Most Popular nightspot in NYC; its "giant", "greenery"-lined roof deck with "killer views" of the Empire State Building draws "throngs" of "flirty corporate" types who ignore the "sky-high" tabs and penthouse level that looks "like something out of *Scarface*"; even though some of the crowd seems to be "auditioning for *Jersey Shore*", this one's "magical" on a summer night, and it's even accessible in winter thanks to "robes and heat lamps."

NEW Tzigan — | — | — | E

Meatpacking | 55 Gansevoort St., downstairs (bet. Greenwich & Washington Sts.) | A/C/E/L to 14th St./8th Ave. | 212-924-5559 | www.villapacri.com

Sparkly is the word for this subterranean Meatpacking boîte below Villa Pacri, where the Midas-touched walls and furniture are rendered in gold and silver; given the neighborhood, bottle service is de rigueur, though the gimmick here is storage lockers where you can stockpile the hooch – for a $500 monthly fee.

⊿ Ulysses — 20 | 16 | 17 | M

Financial District | 95 Pearl St. (off Hanover Sq.) | 4/5 to Bowling Green | 212-482-0400 | www.ulyssesbarnyc.com

"Work-hard-play-hard" types are all over this "high-energy" FiDi Irish pub as an "after-work mainstay" for "finance professionals and the women hoping to snag them"; be prepared for "major crowds" in the summer, when rear "outdoor seating" on cobblestoned Stone Street turns it into a "mob scene"; P.S. go early – it "dies out after 8 PM."

Uncle Charlie's
∇ 21 | 19 | 22 | M

E 40s | 139 E. 45th St., 2nd fl. (bet. Lexington & 3rd Aves.) | 4/5/6/7/S to 42nd St./Grand Central | 212-661-9097

UC Lounge

LES | 67 Ludlow St. (bet. Broome & Grand Sts.) | F/J/M/Z to Delancey/Essex Sts. | 212-677-1110
www.unclecharliesnyc.com

Whether you're into the "silver daddy" scene or not, this mature gay bar near Grand Central is touted for its "friendly service", outdoor terrace and separate piano bar; its LES adjunct foregoes the ivory tickling for a more basic bar/lounge approach.

Underbar
21 | 20 | 18 | E

Union Sq | W Union Square Hotel | 201 Park Ave. S., downstairs (17th St.) | 4/5/6/L/N/Q/R to 14th St./Union Sq. | 212-358-1560 | www.gerberbars.com

"Designed for making out", this "dark", subterranean den below the W Union Square Hotel is "perfect for an adventurous date", offering curtained-off "semi-private" nooks and "discreet" service; you betcha, it's "expensive" and there's "no cell phone service", but at least the door's "fairly democratic."

Underground Lounge
∇ 15 | 11 | 16 | M

W 100s | 955 West End Ave., downstairs (107th St.) | 1 to Cathedral Pkwy./110th St. | 212-531-4759 | www.theundergroundnyc.com

It's "mostly a neighborhood" thing going on at this sunken Morningside Heights haunt where diversions include a pool table and a back room featuring "stand-up comedy" and "live music"; "heavy Columbia" traffic keeps it "fairly busy", but for non-locals the scene may be underwhelming.

Union Bar
17 | 16 | 18 | E

Union Sq | 204 Park Ave. S. (bet. 17th & 18th Sts.) | 4/5/6/L/N/Q/R to 14th St./Union Sq. | 212-674-2105 | www.union-bar.com

Long-running Union Square bar/lounge that's an "acceptable" after-work retreat for youngish singles, with "adequate space" and a "reasonable" happy hour; but even with "decent music" and "generous" drinks, rebels find it "unremarkable" – it "needs more of a crowd."

☑ Union Hall
24 | 25 | 18 | M

Park Slope | 702 Union St. (bet. 5th & 6th Aves.) | Brooklyn | R to Union St. | 718-638-4400 | www.unionhallny.com

One of Park Slope's "coolest cats", this "huge", "all-around pleaser" includes an "intellectual" front bar replete with "bookcases" and a "fireplace", two "über-competitive" indoor bocce courts and a basement performance space; no surprise, it's "undeniably hip", "incredibly popular" and way "too crowded" on weekends.

Union Pool
19 | 16 | 15 | M

Williamsburg | 484 Union Ave. (Meeker Ave.) | Brooklyn | G/L to Metropolitan Ave./Lorimer St. | 718-609-0484

"Quintessential Williamsburg", this "former pool supply store" draws "skinny jeans"-wearers "like moths to a flame" with its "lively" mood and "cheap cans of beer"; a backyard patio alternates a "murky fountain" in summer with a "live fire pit" in winter, while a "taco truck" dispenses chow year-round; although "thoroughly hipster, it's still worth visiting."

United Palace

| - | - | - | M |

Washington Heights | 4140 Broadway (175th St.) | A to 175th St. | 212-568-6700 | www.unitedpalaceconcerts.com

A vintage-1930s Washington Heights movie palace has been reworked into a "live music" hall à la the Beacon Theatre, where fans can catch big-name acts in a 3,300-seat space; although it's an undeniably "beautiful" setting, a "terrific sound system" keeps the focus on the stage.

Upholstery Store ⊅

| - | - | - | M |

W Village | 713 Washington St. (bet. Perry & W. 11th Sts.) | 1 Christopher St. | 212-352-2300

A former West Village furniture shop has been transformed – except for its name and sign – into this wine bar "hideaway" whose global selections have a pronounced Austrian accent (thanks to its owner, top toque Kurt Gutenbrunner); the narrow slip of a setting is decidedly unpretentious and fittingly accepts neither reservations nor credit cards.

NEW Upstairs

| - | - | - | E |

E 50s | Kimberly Hotel | 145 E. 50th St., 31st fl. (bet. 2nd & 3rd Aves.) | 6 to 51st St. | 212-702-1600 | www.upstairsnyc.com

Perched atop the Kimberly Hotel, this rooftop aerie boasts picture-perfect views of Midtown and the Chrysler Building, as well as its own dedicated elevator; retractable glass ceilings and heated floors make it an all-seasons affair, though it's hard to top its ivy-encrusted back patio in summer.

Uptown Lounge

| 22 | 20 | 20 | M |

E 80s | 1576 Third Ave. (bet. 88th & 89th Sts.) | 4/5/6 to 86th St. | 212-828-1388 | www.uptownloungenyc.com

"Something of a rarity" amid the UES "sea of frat bars", this "mellow" lounge caters to "more mature" locals with its low-lit polish, "accommodating" service and "excellent drinks (particularly the martinis)"; it's an acknowledged "standby" for some "decent" atmosphere in an otherwise "void-of-character" neighborhood.

Urge, The

| ▽ | 18 | 16 | 19 | M |

E Village | 33 Second Ave. (bet. 1st & 2nd Sts.) | F to Lower East Side/2nd Ave. | 212-533-5757 | www.theurge.xbuild.com

"You'll get the urge all right" at this "good-times" East Village gay bar, a "cruisy" joint known for its "sexy go-go boys" and generally "friendly" vibe; regulars say there's "no way you'll leave alone if you don't want to."

U2 Karaoke

| - | - | - | M |

E Village | 6 St. Marks Pl. (bet. 2nd & 3rd Aves.) | 6 to Astor Pl. | 212-228-6250 | www.wewantu2sing.com

The old Mondo Kim's space on St. Marks Place has morphed into this ritzy karaoke parlor, a slick, white-on-white triplex featuring private rooms outfitted with high-def flat-screens and pulsing light shows; there's no liquor license yet, so regulars arrive already blotto.

| | APPEAL | DECOR | SERVICE | COST |

Valhalla
22 | 16 | 21 | M

W 50s | 815 Ninth Ave. (54th St.) | C/E to 50th St. | 212-757-2747
"Far from touristy or corporate", this "low-key" Hell's Kitchen bar rewards "serious beer connoisseurs" with an "outstanding" rotating roster featuring "many hard-to-find" bottles, plus tap microbrews; the offhand decor seems to be "going for an urban rustic look", but literalists "would love to see more Viking" flourishes.

Vander Bar
- | - | - | M

E 40s | Roosevelt Hotel | 45 E. 45th St. (bet. Madison & Park Aves.) |
4/5/6/7/S to 42nd St./Grand Central | 212-661-9600 |
www.vanderbar.com
Buzzing Roosevelt Hotel barroom cattycorner from Grand Central that's always busy with after-work-before-the-train types, but otherwise, it's strictly by the numbers, without much decor or atmosphere; P.S. closed weekends.

Van Diemens
▽ 19 | 17 | 20 | M

Murray Hill | 383 Third Ave. (bet. 27th & 28th Sts.) | 6 to 28th St. |
212-532-1123 | www.vandiemensnyc.com
Another entrant in the "crowded field of Third Avenue bars" in "frat-leaning" Murray Hill, this "more upscale" spot supplies the usual "drink specials" and "sports TVs", abetted by "prompt" service; since its split-level setting usually "doesn't get overpopulated", it's a "refreshing change from the usual."

NEW Vault at Pfaff's
- | - | - | E

G Village | 643 Broadway, downstairs (Bleecker St.) | 6 to Bleecker St. |
212-253-5421 | www.vaultatpfaffs.com
Set in (and named after) a circa-1855 beer cellar patronized by Walt Whitman, this subterranean Village lounge has been reinvented for the 21st century with leather banquettes, high-end cocktails and duck-slider bar bites; formerly the home of private-party space Woodson and Ford, it's now open to all comers.

V Bar
22 | 22 | 22 | M

G Village | 225 Sullivan St. (bet. Bleecker & W. 3rd Sts.) | A/B/C/D/E/
F/M to W. 4th St. | 212-253-5740

V Bar St. Marks
E Village | 132 First Ave. (St. Marks Pl.) | 6 to Astor Pl. | 212-473-7200
www.vbar.net
With its "warm" atmosphere and "free WiFi", this "small", "Euro-styled" West Village wine bar is a "steady" local favorite with "no surprises" – and "that can be a good thing"; an East Village spin-off with a full liquor license opened post-Survey.

Velvet Cigar Lounge
21 | 20 | 19 | E

E Village | 80 E. Seventh St. (bet. 1st & 2nd Aves.) | 4/5/6/L/N/Q/R to
14th St./Union Sq. | 212-533-5582 | www.velvetcigars.com

Velvet Lounge
Williamsburg | 174 Broadway (bet. Bedford & Driggs Aves.) | Brooklyn |
J/M/Z to Marcy Ave. | 718-302-4427 | www.velvetbrooklyn.com
"For a stogie and conversation", this BYO East Village cigar lounge provides a place to puff (no cigarettes allowed) in a "microscopic" setting usually filled with "regulars"; the roomier, separately owned

Williamsburg outpost next door to Peter Luger's vends cocktails along with "excellent handmade cigars", though smoking's permitted only outside.

Verlaine

APPEAL	DECOR	SERVICE	COST
21	18	19	M

LES | 110 Rivington St. (bet. Essex & Ludlow Sts.) | F/J/M/Z to Delancey/Essex Sts. | 212-614-2494 | www.verlainenyc.com
"Sceney" and pretty "spiffy" for the LES, this "crowded" lounge is renowned for having one of the "best happy hours in town", serving signature "lychee martinis" for $5 every night until 10 PM; it's a magnet for "beautiful young ladies" who like the "long, slim" design and revolving art shows.

Vero

APPEAL	DECOR	SERVICE	COST
22	19	21	E

E 50s | 1004 Second Ave. (53rd St.) | 6/E to 51st-53rd Sts./Lexington Ave. | 212-935-3530
E 70s | 1483 Second Ave. (bet. 77th & 78th Sts.) | 6 to 77th St. | 212-452-3354
www.veronyc.com
"Grown-up" singles dote on this "cute little" Upper East Side enoteca and its more spacious Midtown sibling as "sociable" alternatives to the otherwise raucous Second Avenue shenanigans; "slightly more classy" (and "pricey") than the norm, they're good for "first dates", save for the "loud" acoustics.

Vertigo

APPEAL	DECOR	SERVICE	COST
20	18	19	M

Murray Hill | 354 Third Ave. (26th St.) | 6 to 23rd St. | 212-696-1011 | www.vertigobarnewyork.com
"Wraparound" windowed walls that "open up wonderfully on warm days" give an "added boost" to this Murray Hill bar that's otherwise an "average" hangout for "happy hour" and sports-watching; it's "nice" enough "if you live in the area", but "doesn't aspire to great heights", despite the name.

Vig Bar

APPEAL	DECOR	SERVICE	COST
23	16	20	M

NoLita | 12 Spring St. (Elizabeth St.) | 6 to Spring St. | 212-625-0011 | www.vigbar.com
"Small but awesome", this "cool" NoLita "hideaway" is a "laid-back" lounge that attracts "good-lookers" and "really gets going" when the "DJ starts spinning"; "large crowds" tend to descend on weekends, but the partying is groovier in the sexy back room.

Vig 27

APPEAL	DECOR	SERVICE	COST
17	17	17	M

Murray Hill | 119 E. 27th St. (bet. Lexington Ave. & Park Ave. S.) | 6 to 28th St. | 212-686-5500 | www.vig27.com
Reoriented into "Murray Hill's only gay bar", this used-to-be-straight lounge has retained its "simple" but "aesthetically pleasing" looks and "tasty drink menu"; it's "a bit off the beaten path for the HK/Chelsea boy" set, though, so "you may have the place all to yourself."

Village Lantern

APPEAL	DECOR	SERVICE	COST
17	15	19	M

G Village | 167 Bleecker St. (bet. Sullivan & Thompson Sts.) | A/B/C/D/E/F/M to W. 4th St. | 212-260-7993 | www.villagelantern.com
"NYU students, tourists" and "locals" alight at this Village bar/eatery, an "overall decent" pick on a "crowded" strip given its slate of live bands, weekend DJs and nightly comedy; with "reasonable" tabs

and an "open-front facade", it satisfies with "none of the pretense" of the trendier hangs.

Village Pourhouse

| 15 | 11 | 16 | M |

E Village | 64 Third Ave. (11th St.) | 4/5/6/L/N/Q/R to 14th St./ Union Sq. | 212-979-2337
NEW **W 40s** | 366 W. 46th St. (bet. 8th & 9th Aves.) | A/C/E to Port Authority/42nd St. | 212-979-2337
W 100s | 982 Amsterdam Ave. (bet. 108th & 109th Sts.) | 1 to Cathedral Pkwy./110th St. | 212-979-2337
www.villagepourhouse.com

A "major draw" for "recently graduated" sports fans and buds on a "bar crawl", this "lively" trio features a "pretty extensive" beer lineup poured for "cheap" plus "plenty of TVs" beaming college ball; they're "best to avoid at peak hours" when they morph into "loud, drunken messes."

Village Underground

| ▽ 20 | 16 | 20 | M |

G Village | 130 W. Third St., downstairs (bet. MacDougal St. & 6th Ave.) | A/B/C/D/E/F/M to W. 4th St. | 212-533-4790 | www.thevillageunderground.com

Sited "smack under the Fat Black Pussycat", this "simple" Village club/ performance space books "robust" bands "that will get you dancing in your seat" if you're in the "college"-to-"late-twenties" demo; underdecorated but "reasonably priced", its allure is all about the "talent."

☑ Village Vanguard

| 27 | 16 | 18 | E |

W Village | 178 Seventh Ave. S. (11th St.) | 1/2/F/L to 14th St./7th Ave. | 212-255-4037 | www.villagevanguard.com

"Nirvana for the jazz lover", this circa-1935 West Villager is a "mythic" venue known for its "immortal" past performers (like John Coltrane, Dizzy Gillespie and Miles Davis), but it "still swings" with "excellent" acts both "big-time" and small-time; despite "cramped" seating and "mediocre decor", beboppers believe it "deserves its fame" – "it's all about the music", daddy-o.

Vino

| ▽ 22 | 19 | 23 | E |

E 60s | 1268 Second Ave. (bet. 66th & 67th Sts.) | 6 to 68th St. | 212-744-5370

Upper Eastsiders toast this "gem" of an enoteca from the owners of neighboring Mediterraneo, citing a "wonderful" Italian wine list, decanted by a "knowledgeable" crew behind the marble bar; with rustic Tuscan looks and "friendly" atmospherics, it measures up as a vinner.

Vino 313

| 22 | 20 | 23 | E |

Murray Hill | 201 E. 31st St. (3rd Ave.) | 6 to 33rd St. | 212-725-8466 | www.vino313.com

An oenophile's "oasis in the heart of frat boy–driven Murray Hill", this "upscale-casual" wine bar pairs its "nice" vinos with "top-notch" small plates in a setting that's "more cafe than bar"; it's "a little expensive", but much "needed" for "civilized" sipping in these parts.

Vintage

| 21 | 20 | 19 | M |

W 50s | 753 Ninth Ave. (bet. 50th & 51st Sts.) | C/E to 50th St. | 212-581-4655

Famed for its "awesome martini list", this Hell's Kitchen veteran may require "30 minutes for perusing the cocktail menu", but the results are more than "yummy"; otherwise, it's "nothing to do cartwheels over", though it works for "low-key" imbibing "without all the typical b.s." at the "younger, hipper" joints.

Vintry Wine & Whiskey
	-	-	-	E

Financial District | 57 Stone St. (bet. Coenties Slip & Hanover Sq.) | 4/5 to Wall St. | 212-480-9800 | www.vintrynyc.com

Stone Street kingpin Peter Poulakakos (owner of Ulysses and Adrienne's Pizza Bar, among others) expands his portfolio with this dark little boîte offering a globe-trotting list of wines and whiskeys; the space is cozy yet manly, with a redwood bar and a handful of marble-topped tables, while the pricing varies from an $8 bottle of beer to a $23,000 Bordeaux.

VIP Club
∇	23	23	19	VE

Flatiron | 20 W. 20th St. (bet. 5th & 6th Aves.) | N/R to 23rd St. | 212-633-1199 | www.thevipclubnyc.com

One of the big-shot "jiggle joints", this Flatiron strip club boasts the "killer combination" of "good-looking" lasses and a comparatively classy backdrop; it comes with VIP pricing, but guys seeing "the sights" swear that's the "last thing" you'll be thinking about; P.S. it morphs into Club 20 on Sundays, a gay showcase with go-go boys.

Vlada
21	21	18	M

W 50s | 331 W. 51st St. (bet. 8th & 9th Aves.) | C/E to 50th St. | 212-974-8030

A "great infused-vodka selection" is the specialty of the house at this Hell's Kitchen gay lounge, a "stylish", bi-level thing also known for its "ice"-lined bar that's "not really functional" but still "looks cool" as hell; though the scene can be "hit-or-miss", a "pretty young crowd" of "poseurs" and "regular folks" is the norm here.

Vol de Nuit
22	17	16	M

G Village | 148 W. Fourth St. (bet. MacDougal St. & 6th Ave.) | A/B/C/D/E/F/M to W. 4th St. | 212-979-2616 | www.voldenuitbar.com

Hidden behind a "stealth entryway" and through an "appealing" courtyard, this "über-Euro" Villager vends a "fantastic list of Belgian beers" in "bohemian" digs bathed in the same kind of "dim red light" used for "developing pictures"; too bad it's "tragically crowded" at prime times.

Volstead, The
20	21	20	E

E 50s | 125 E. 54th St., downstairs (bet. Lexington & Park Aves.) | 6/E to 51st-53rd Sts./Lexington Ave. | 212-583-0411 | www.thevolstead.com

"Classy but not snooty", this subterranean Midtown lounge named for the sponsor of Prohibition lures "tons of suits" into its "hidden-away", mahogany-lined lair; the pops are "pricey but potent", and the crowd says it's "much-needed" – "there's nothing else decent around."

Von
24	19	19	M

NoHo | 3 Bleecker St. (bet. Bowery & Elizabeth St.) | 6 to Bleecker St. | 212-473-3039 | www.vonbar.com

Vaunted as a "bearable hipster joint", this "relaxed" NoHo bar plies an "extensive selection" of wine and "impressive" imported brews in "cozy" verging on "sexy" quarters; the basement lounge has a "totally different vibe" with DJs and a "sweaty dance floor."

	APPEAL	DECOR	SERVICE	COST

NEW Vyne

G Village | 82 W. Third St., 2nd fl. (bet. Sullivan & Thompson Sts.) | A/B/C/
D/E/F/M to W 4th St. | 212-353-8963 | www.vynenewyork.com

- | - | - | E

NYU-land gets a touch of class via this Village wine bar that decants a
Euro-centric list with an emphasis on the usually neglected whites; located above Zinc Bar, the dark, industrial setting has lots of canoodling potential and few frat boys in evidence.

Ward III

24 | 22 | 24 | E

TriBeCa | 111 Reade St. (bet. Church St. & W. B'way) | 1/2/3 to
Chambers St. | 212-240-9194 | www.ward3tribeca.com

Mixology "reigns supreme" at this "invaluable" TriBeCan from some
Macao Trading Co. alums, a smoothly "welcoming" joint where tipplers order "from the list" or give the "expert" barkeeps particulars to
custom-craft a "bespoke cocktail" from scratch; thankfully, the "intimate yet awkward" space "contradicts the pretentious stereotype
of the neighborhood."

☑ Warren 77

20 | 20 | 17 | M

TriBeCa | 77 Warren St. (bet. Greenwich St. & W. B'way) | 1/2/3 to
Chambers St. | 212-227-8994 | www.warren77nyc.com

Brought to you by NY Ranger Sean Avery and Beatrice Inn proprietor
Matt Abramcyk, this TriBeCa sports bar is set in a "small", L-shaped
space done up in ancient locker room–style, equipped with vintage
boxing gloves and well-worn Hardy Boys mysteries; despite borderline "rude service" and an "overhyped" scene, it's usually "packed"
at prime times.

Washington Commons

- | - | - | M

Prospect Heights | 748 Washington Ave. (Park Pl.) | Brooklyn | 2/3/4 to
Grand Army Plaza | 718-230-3666

Laid-back is putting it mildly at this dog-friendly Prospect Heights store-
front where the relaxed mood draws a come-as-you-are crowd; a big,
no-nonsense backyard is stocked with picnic tables for alfresco drinking, while a rotating list of tap brews keeps suds enthusiasts happy.

Waterfront Ale House

20 | 15 | 20 | M

Murray Hill | 540 Second Ave. (30th St.) | 6 to 33rd St. |
212-696-4104

Brooklyn Heights | 155 Atlantic Ave. (bet. Clinton & Henry Sts.) |
Brooklyn | 2/3/4/5/N/R to Borough Hall | 718-522-3794
www.waterfrontalehouse.com

With a "strong beer list" and plenty of "neighborly pub appeal",
this Kips Bay/Brooklyn Heights duo attracts "many regulars" with
its "surprisingly decent" pub grub and "excellent" suds; "very
casual" – and well clear of any water – they're "reliable" refuges for
"low-key" imbibing.

Water Taxi Beach

22 | 16 | 14 | M

Governors Island | Governors Island (catch ferry at 10 South St.) | 1 to
South Ferry | no phone | www.watertaxibeach.com

"No shoes" are needed at this "man-made beach" on Governors
Island, a seasonal "oasis" of "picnic tables", "lit-up palm trees", "semi-
cheap beer" and "blasting music", topped off by a drop-dead Manhattan
view; siblings in LIC and at the Seaport have closed.

WCOU Radio ⌀
(aka Tile Bar)

–	–	–	M	

E Village | 115 First Ave. (7th St.) | L to 1st Ave. | 212-254-4317
Although diminutive and "divey", this East Village stalwart is still a "reliable" local joint owing to its budget pricing and "classic" rockin' juke; otherwise, it's on the "nothing-special" wavelength, but regulars find that a "relief."

NEW W Downtown Living Room

–	–	–	E	

Financial District | W Hotel Downtown | 123 Washington St., 5th fl. (Albany St.) | R to Rector St. | 646-826-8646 | www.wnewyorkdowntown.com
Boasting one of the most dramatic settings in town, this W Downtown Hotel lobby bar shoots for the stars with a way-out space-station look thanks to an undulating ceiling fitted out with white LED lighting; the cocktail menu comes via mixologist Charlotte Voisey (Rose Bar), while wraparound outdoor terraces with FiDi views ice the cake.

⊿ Weather Up

▽ 24	23	22	E	

NEW **TriBeCa** | 159 Duane St. (bet. Hudson St. & W. B'way) | 1/2/3 to Chambers St. | no phone
Prospect Heights | 589 Vanderbilt Ave. (bet. Bergen & Dean Sts.) | Brooklyn | C to Clinton/Washington Aves. | no phone
They mix a "mean cocktail" at this signless Prospect Heights class act where "skilled" protégés of mixologist Sasha Petraske concoct "potent" designer drinks in a dapper, white-tiled setting; though the potables come at a "premium price" ("especially for the neighborhood"), many "feel sexier just by walking through the door"; P.S. the TriBeCa branch opened post-Survey.

Webster Hall

18	16	14	E	

E Village | 125 E. 11th St. (bet. 3rd & 4th Aves.) | 4/5/6/L/N/Q/R to 14th St./Union Sq. | 212-353-1600 | www.websterhall.com
With "multiple levels" and dance floors to choose from, this ancient East Village club/music hall (established 1886) is so "gigantic" that it seems like "everyone in the city is in the building with you"; too bad critics pan it as a "low-class thrill" with "ridiculous prices" and "madly annoying" mobs of "teenyboppers" and "Staten Island weekend warriors."

Welcome to the Johnsons ⌀

15	13	15	I	

LES | 123 Rivington St. (bet. Essex & Norfolk Sts.) | F/J/M/Z to Delancey/Essex Sts. | 212-420-9911
Channeling "your creepy uncle's wood-paneled basement", this Lower East Side "dive to end all dives" serves "cheap PBR from a fridge" to a "surprisingly cool crowd" that awards it bonus points for a "rad jukebox"; but while an "interesting concept", its main "appeal" lies in boozing on a budget.

Wharf Bar & Grill

18	15	20	M	

Murray Hill | 587 Third Ave. (bet. 38th & 39th Sts.) | 4/5/6/7/S to 42nd St./Grand Central | 212-490-7270 | www.wharfnyc.com
This marine-themed Murray Hill watering hole may drift "under the radar", but it's still an "appealing" port in a storm for the "after-work

crowd" and "neighborhood" dudes in the mood to "watch sports"; if the interior seems "a little worn", there's a year-round deck out back.

Whiskey Blue
21 | 22 | 17 | E

E 40s | W New York Hotel | 541 Lexington Ave. (bet. 49th & 50th Sts.) | 6 to 51st St. | 212-407-2947 | www.gerberbars.com

"Traveling businessmen" and the "floozies who want to meet them" are part of the "elbow-to-elbow" "professional" scene at this Midtown hotel lounge, famed for its "pricey" pops, "pickup" potential and "smokin'" hot waitresses in "LBDs"; some call it a "late '90s redux" relic but admit that even the "wannabes are good-looking" here.

NEW Whiskey Brooklyn
- | - | - | M

Williamsburg | 44 Berry St., downstairs (N. 11th St.) | Brooklyn | L to Bedford Ave. | 718-387-8444 | www.thewhiskeybrooklyn.com

Like the name says, this new Williamsburg sports bar dispenses the same encyclopedic list of brown fluids as its Manhattan siblings, Whiskey Tavern and Whiskey Town; the brick-walled, cement-floored cellar setting may be pretty standard issue, but arcade games, shuffleboard tables, a stripper pole and a photo booth make it a destination for players.

Whiskey Park
20 | 21 | 19 | E

W 50s | Trump Parc | 100 Central Park S. (6th Ave.) | N/R to 5th Ave./ 59th St. | 212-307-9222 | www.gerberbars.com

Another Rande Gerber "guilty pleasure", this "swanky" lounge opposite Central Park caters to "black Amex" card holders with up-market vibes and stiff martinis that ensure there's "no problem mingling"; the "sexy" servers, "expensive" tabs and "pretension" may be all too familiar, but regulars say it's "more palatable now that it's not so hot."

Whiskey River
20 | 17 | 20 | M

Murray Hill | 575 Second Ave. (bet. 32nd & 33rd Sts.) | 6 to 33rd St. | 212-679-6799 | www.whiskeyrivernyc.com

"Cabin"-esque Murray Hill watering hole parked on a parched stretch of Second Avenue that floats "excellent drink prices" along with video games, "beer pong" and "Wii"; it can be a "bunch of fun" with a bunch of people, though it can also be a spell in "frat-boy hell."

Whiskey Tavern
20 | 19 | 23 | M

Chinatown | 79 Baxter St. (bet. Bayard & Walker Sts.) | 6/J/N/Q/Z to Canal St. | 212-374-9119 | www.whiskeytavernnyc.com

"*Cheers*" comes to Chinatown via this Whiskey Town spin-off where "locals", "cops and prosecutors" are among the "loyal customers" throwing back "interesting" variants on the eponymous spirit (think shots with a "pickle juice chaser"); "accommodating" service and "laid-back" atmospherics make for "great boozing" here.

Whiskey Town
17 | 12 | 17 | M

E Village | 29 E. Third St. (bet. Bowery & 2nd Ave.) | F to Lower East Side/ 2nd Ave. | 212-505-7344 | www.whiskeytownbar.com

"Small" and "super-casual", this East Village bar gets tipplers stoked with "reasonably priced" cans of brew "served in koozies", along with a 50-label whiskey lineup; a DJ spinning "*Footloose*" and patrons "belting out Journey" add to its "weird appeal."

	APPEAL	DECOR	SERVICE	COST

Whiskey Ward

▽ 23 | 15 | 22 | M

LES | 121 Essex St. (bet. Delancey & Rivington Sts.) | F/J/M/Z to Delancey/Essex Sts. | 212-477-2998 | www.thewhiskeyward.com

Ease those brown-liquor "hankerings" at this LES saloon where a "fine selection" of scotch, bourbon and "everything in between" is dispensed by "kind" barkeeps; anyone who digs a "dive-bar atmosphere" with free peanuts is bound to have an "awesome time."

White Horse Tavern ⊄

19 | 14 | 17 | M

W Village | 567 Hudson St. (11th St.) | A/C/E/L to 14th St./8th Ave. | 212-989-3956

Famed as the place where Dylan Thomas drank till he dropped, this circa-1880 West Village "relic" is also renowned as a former "bastion" of "beat poets and literary giants"; today, it's more popular with "tourists" and "drunken frat boys" "watching the world go by" from one of its sidewalk picnic tables.

NEW White Noise

- | - | - | M

E Village | 225 Ave. B, 2nd fl. (bet. 13th & 14th Sts.) | L to 1st Ave. | 212-539-0925 | www.whitenoiseny.com

This hidden, second-floor East Village perennial (fka Uncle Ming's, The Hose) is back on the scene, this time with a gritty rock 'n' roll sensibility that extends to its cheapish hooch and can't-be-bothered staff; the dim lighting and wide-open layout are the same as before, now dolled up with a paint-it-black color scheme.

White Rabbit

18 | 14 | 17 | M

LES | 145 E. Houston St. (bet. Eldridge & Forsyth Sts.) | F to Lower East Side/2nd Ave. | 212-477-5005 | www.whiterabbitnyc.com

"Affordable" and "chill", this minimalist Lower Eastsider draws a "mixed, unpretentious crowd" with "tight" DJ sets and video projections on the all-white walls; it's an "easy" door with "no cover", though elitists yawn "you've been to a hundred bars like this."

White Star

▽ 21 | 15 | 22 | E

LES | 21 Essex St. (bet. Canal & Hester Sts.) | F/J/M/Z to Delancey/Essex Sts.

This LES "hideaway" specializes in absinthe and straight spirits, though they also whip up "amazing" signature cocktails; despite "small" dimensions ("sardines have more room"), the "drinks make it worthwhile"; P.S. all-star mixologist Sasha Petraske is no longer involved.

Wicked Monk

21 | 18 | 21 | M

Bay Ridge | 8415 Fifth Ave. (85th St.) | Brooklyn | R to 86th St. | 718-921-0601 | www.wickedmonk.com

"Neighborhood" acolytes deem this Bay Ridge Irish fixture a "wicked awesome" place for pool, darts and beer, plus live "local bands"; the crowd skews "young on the weekends", but on school nights the patrons are "so old that you're surprised they still go to bars."

Wicked Willy's

17 | 15 | 17 | M

G Village | 149 Bleecker St. (bet. La Guardia Pl. & Thompson St.) | 6 to Bleecker St. | 212-254-8592

There's a "college thing" going on at this "pirate-themed" Villager near NYU, where "cheap" sauce, "beer pong tables", "drunken karaoke" and "random live music" keep all the mateys amused; aye, it's "nothing inspiring", but it can be a "good, rowdy time."

Wicker Park
17 | **14** | **17** | **M**

E 80s | 1469 Third Ave. (83rd St.) | 4/5/6 to 86th St. | 212-734-5600 | www.wickerparknyc.com

Post-college prepsters say this "typical UES hangout" (fka Martell's) does the trick for "relaxed" get-togethers after work, even if it's "nothing special by any means"; on weekends, it can be swamped with "noisy frat boys", but hey, "you live with it."

Wilfie & Nell
24 | **21** | **19** | **M**

W Village | 228 W. Fourth St. (bet. 7th Ave. S & W. 10th St.) | 1 to Christopher St. | 212-242-2990 | www.wilfieandnell.com

"Charming" Village Irish pub with a "rural" feel that draws "thick" throngs of "attractive" folks with a menu of "yummy drinks" and "way-above-par" pub grub; "word is out", however, so "get there early" or be prepared for "long waits" to get in.

NEW Windsor, The
- | **-** | **-** | **M**

W Village | 234 W. Fourth St. (W. 10th St.) | 1 to Christopher St./ Sheridan Sq. | 212-206-1208 | www.thewindsornyc.com

Last seen as the highfalutin resto Charles, this West Villager is back as a high-end sports bar, done up with burgundy leather booths and pin-striped fabric on the walls; a handful of flat-screens and upscale pub grub lure popped-collared athletic supporters.

Wine & Roses
22 | **20** | **21** | **E**

W 70s | 286 Columbus Ave. (73rd St.) | 1/2/3 to 72nd St. | 212-579-9463 | www.wineandrosesbar.com

A "perfect neighborhood wine bar", this "lively" Upper Westsider boasts a "carefully selected list" decanted by a "knowledgeable" crew; despite the "expensive" price tags, "roses on every table" make it a natural for "girls' night out" or as a "date destination."

Winebar
22 | **19** | **20** | **E**

E Village | 65 Second Ave. (bet. 3rd & 4th Sts.) | F to Lower East Side/ 2nd Ave. | 212-777-1608 | www.winebarnyc.com

The "lack of creativity in the name doesn't apply" to the "commendable" vinos vended at this East Village wine bar, a "dark", "intimate" place with an "all-European" list; "communal tables" and sidewalk seats make it "easy to relax" here.

Wined Up
22 | **19** | **20** | **E**

Flatiron | 913 Broadway, 2nd fl. (bet. 20th & 21st Sts.) | N/R to 23rd St. | 212-673-6333 | www.punchrestaurant.com

"Wind down" at this "sleek" Flatiron wine bar above the eatery Punch, where "excellent" varietals are poured by a "well-versed staff"; granted, it's "not cheap" and there's "not much of a scene", but the "inviting" space is "laid-back" and "quiet" enough for a "short date."

Wine Spot
- | **-** | **-** | **M**

G Village | 127 MacDougal St., downstairs (W. 3rd St.) | A/B/C/D/E/ F/M to W. 4th St. | 212-505-1248

A tea lounge by day, the basement level of this MacDougal Street duplex morphs into a wine-and-tapas dispenser after dark vending a tightly edited list of global vinos; the dimly lit, wood-lined setting has the cozy thing down pat, though basic (verging on plain) furnishings keep it from being truly transporting.

Winnie's

- | - | - | M

Chinatown | 104 Bayard St. (bet. Baxter & Mulberry Sts.) | 6/J/N/Q/ Z to Canal St. | 212-732-2384

Dubbed the "ultimate dive karaoke bar", this scruffy Chinatown warhorse is the venue of choice for low-budget slummers and bachelorettes eager to "belt out" their off-key renditions for a buck a song; drinks that "pack a punch" coax wallflowers up to the mike.

Wogies

15 | 10 | 18 | M

W Village | 39 Greenwich Ave. (Charles St.) | 1/2/F/L to 14th St./ 6th Ave. | 212-229-2171 | www.wogies.com

"What you see is what you get" at this ramshackle West Village "joint" known for its "cheap" pours, "decent cheesesteaks" and "affable" service; it "welcomes all Philly fans" when the Eagles are on the tube, managing to attract "more beer-soaked guys than the place can hold" on game days.

Woods, The

- | - | - | M

Williamsburg | 48 S. Fourth St. (bet. Kent & Wythe Aves.) | Brooklyn | L to Bedford Ave. | no phone

"Hipster" timber all the way, this South Williamsburg spot features "cheap" drinks, DJs spinning "without irony" and distressed industrial decor (think concrete floors, exposed wooden beams); given the "authentic" taco truck parked on the back patio, some say it could be the "new Union Pool."

Woodwork ⇗

- | - | - | M

Prospect Heights | 583 Vanderbilt Ave. (Dean St.) | Brooklyn | C to Clinton/Washington Aves. | 718-857-5777 | www.woodworkbk.com

Wide-open Prospect Heights taproom that lives up to its name with a rustic, woodworked interior reclaimed from an old Massachusetts barn; the flat-screens are soccer-centric, and the beer-and-wine offerings include lots of organic varieties, in keeping with its overall green feel.

Woody McHale's

∇ 20 | 16 | 25 | M

W Village | 234 W. 14th St., downstairs (bet. 7th & 8th Aves.) | 1/ 2/F/L to 14th St./7th Ave. | 212-206-0430 | www.woodymchales.com

This "casual" basement bar in the West Village is a "local" favorite, done up like a lumber-lined hunting lodge and tended by "friendly" if "somewhat salty" sorts; what with the HDTVs, Internet jukebox and "cheap beer specials", it's no surprise it's "populated by students."

Woody's

- | - | - | M

E Village | 31 Second Ave. (bet. 1st & 2nd Sts.) | F to Lower East Side/ 2nd Ave. | 212-777-0774

The latest incarnation of the revolving-door space that was formerly DTOX (and before that, Ice Bar), this big East Village gay bar still has its weekend go-go boys and Vegas-ey feel in place; yet despite lying between The Cock and The Urge, it's curiously underpopulated.

	APPEAL	DECOR	SERVICE	COST

World Bar
19 | 24 | 18 | VE

E 40s | Trump World Tower | 845 UN Plaza (1st Ave. & 47th St.) | 6 to 51st St. | 212-935-9361 | www.hospitalityholdings.com

"Worldly", "older" patrons unwind in style at this "elegant" East Side lounge opposite the U.N., an "upscale" lair proffering some of the "priciest drinks" in town; though it's "never crowded", the "sophisticated" ambiance alone should impress "someone special."

World Yacht
24 | 21 | 21 | VE

W 40s | Pier 81 (Hudson River & W. 41st St.) | A/C/E to 42nd St./Port Authority | 212-630-8100 | www.worldyacht.com

"Sublime" panoramas of NYC's "sparkling waterfront" are the hook at this harbor cruise offering a "delightful evening" of dinner, dancing and "sunset cocktails"; even though the "food's less than spectacular", those seeking "something different" say the ride "makes up for it" – so long as you arrive early to secure a "seat with a view."

W Times Square Living Room
23 | 24 | 19 | VE

W 40s | W Times Square Hotel | 1567 Broadway, 7th fl. (47th St.) | N/R to 49th St. | 212-930-7447 | www.gerberbars.com

"Surprisingly civilized for Times Square", this "chichi" hotel lounge is "always buzzing" with "tourists" and "businesspeople" throwing back "finely mixed cocktails"; the "posh" setup delivers exactly "what you'd expect" – and you'd better "expect to spend a lot."

W Union Square Living Room
22 | 23 | 20 | VE

Union Sq | W Union Square Hotel | 201 Park Ave. S. (17th St.) | 4/5/6/L/N/Q/R to 14th St./Union Sq. | 212-253-9119 | www.starwood.com

Certainly "not for the T-shirted", this "upscale" lobby lounge in the W Union Square is a "lively" option for "solid" cocktails served in an "open space with large windows"; natch, "you'll pay a pretty penny" for the privilege, but partisans say that's "normal in this environment."

WXOU Radio ⊄
▽ 22 | 15 | 24 | M

W Village | 558 Hudson St. (bet. Perry & W. 11th Sts.) | A/C/E/L to 14th St./8th Ave. | 212-206-0381

This West Village "bar's bar" is a "winning local" joint where fans tune in for "fairly priced drinks" and "classic rock" on the juke; "attentive" tapsters compensate for the no-plastic policy and "utter lack of decor."

Xai Xai Wine Bar
24 | 23 | 22 | E

W 50s | 369 W. 51st St. (bet. 8th & 9th Aves.) | C/E to 50th St. | 212-541-9241 | www.xaixaiwinebar.com

"Interesting" South African vinos are the hook at this "charming" Hell's Kitchen wine bar, a "simple neighborhood place" specializing in "terrific" varietals; expect a "helpful" expat staff and a "sexy little" space sporting cypress columns and exposed brick.

xes lounge
21 | 18 | 21 | M

Chelsea | 157 W. 24th St. (bet. 6th & 7th Aves.) | 1 to 23rd St. | 212-604-0212 | www.xesnyc.com

"Fab" Chelsea gay bar/lounge populated by locals, "PATH folks and everyone in between", all in search of "fun" and games; given a "great backyard" and prices that "won't break the wallet", it's no wonder that it can get "a little too crowded sometimes."

	APPEAL	DECOR	SERVICE	COST

Xicala
∇ 20 | 18 | 20 | E

Little Italy | 151 Elizabeth St. (bet. Broome & Kenmare Sts.) | 6 to Spring St. | 212-219-0599 | www.xicala.net

Spanish wines and a signature "strawberry sangria" are the lures at this "cute" Little Italy vino vendor that matches its potables with "yummy" tapas; "nice bartenders" complete the "cozy" picture.

NEW XIX
- | - | - | E

NoLita | 19 Kenmare St., downstairs (bet. Bowery & Elizabeth St.) | J/Z to Bowery | 212-966-1810

Under NoLita's Travertine restaurant lurks this under-the-radar, bottle service–ready lounge that plays the exclusivity card with an unmarked entrance guarded by serious bouncers; inside, the compact space has Roman Empire aspirations, with red leather banquettes and marble panels etched with images of ancient warriors.

NEW XVI
- | - | - | E

W 40s | Hilton Garden Inn | 251 W. 48th St., 16th fl. (bet. B'way & 8th Ave.) | C/E to 50th St. | 212-956-1300 | www.xviny.com

A reworking of the former Highbar, this new Hell's Kitchen rooftop is equipped with swanky modern furnishings meant to attract a high-spending crowd; it's accessed by the same obscure hallway as before, though the enclosed bar one floor below will be a separately named, stand-alone project with a speakeasy vibe and expertly shaken cocktails.

Yankee Tavern
20 | 15 | 18 | M

Bronx | 72 E. 161st St. (Gerard Ave.) | 4/B/D to Yankee Stadium | 718-292-6130

Get the "full Bronx experience" at this longtime tavern near the ballpark where the "truest of Yankee fans" congregate for "quick drinks" and "home-run service" before the game (offseason, it's a hangout for "courthouse employees"); in season, "they pack them in like the 4 train", so it's "not for anyone adverse to body contact."

Zablozki's ⊅
∇ 21 | 18 | 23 | M

Williamsburg | 107 N. Sixth St. (bet. Berry St. & Wythe Ave.) | Brooklyn | L to Bedford Ave. | 718-384-1903

"Not an ironic idea of a bar", this old-school "neighborhood" joint bucks the Williamsburg norm with a "real" taproom feel backed up by billiards, affordable sauce and a "convenient location"; in addition to its usual, down-to-earth regulars, there's "plenty of local color" too.

Zampa
23 | 21 | 24 | E

W Village | 306 W. 13th St. (bet. 8th Ave. & W. 4th St.) | A/C/E/L to 14th St./8th Ave. | 212-206-0601 | www.zampanyc.com

An "intimate" (read: "tiny") spot to zample Italian vinos, this West Village enoteca offers a "tasty, eclectic" selection that's "nice for the price" and decanted by a "fantastic" team; even better, it's "close to the Meatpacking but removed enough" to escape the mayhem.

Zebulon
23 | 21 | 18 | M

Williamsburg | 258 Wythe Ave. (bet. Metropolitan Ave. & N. 3rd St.) | Brooklyn | L to Bedford Ave. | 718-218-6934 | www.zebuloncafeconcert.com

A "little slice" of Parisian panache in Williamsburg, this world music venue showcases "excellent" acts nightly in a "chill" room with "lighting issues" (it's very "dark"); fans say it proves that the "Brooklyn musical scene is all it's hyped up to be", and even better, there's "never a cover."

Zinc Bar

19 | 17 | 18 | E

G Village | 82 W. Third St., downstairs (bet. Sullivan & Thompson Sts.) | A/B/C/D/E/F/M to W. 4th St. | 212-477-9462 | www.zincbar.com

There's "something cool" about this basement Village jazz club that books "great" performers with African, Latin and Brazilian leanings; regulars are still adjusting to new-ish digs that are "bigger" than the original Houston Street site but share the same "falling-apart" feel.

Zombie Hut

23 | 20 | 20 | M

Carroll Gardens | 273 Smith St. (Degraw St.) | Brooklyn | F/G to Carroll St. | 718-875-3433

"Beware of what's at the end of the straw" at this Smith Street "tiki hut" where the "wicked concoctions" virtually guarantee "you're gonna get sloshed"; the "seriously kitschy" decor and "awesome patio" have their "own charm" too.

INDEXES

Locations 172
Special Appeals 186

LOCATION MAPS

Manhattan Neighborhoods 183
Brooklyn Detail 184

Locations

Includes names and Appeal ratings.

Manhattan

CHELSEA

(26th to 30th Sts., west of 5th; 14th
to 26th Sts., west of 6th)

☒ Ace Hotel	25
Ainsworth	23
Amnesia	-
Avenue	23
Barracuda	19
☒ Bar Veloce	22
☒ Bateaux NY	26
Billymark's West	16
Black Door	19
Blarney Stone	14
Cabanas	22
Chelsea Brewing	20
NEW Chelsea Room	-
NEW Dbar	-
Drunken Horse	-
Eagle	21
Flight 151	16
☒ Frying Pan	26
g	21
Glass Bar	-
Gotham Comedy	20
Gstaad	19
GYM Sportsbar	20
Half King	20
Highline Ballrm.	21
Hiro	20
Hog Pit	14
Honey	19
Jake's Saloon	15
Juliet	23
La Pomme	19
Marquee	21
☒ 1 Oak	24
Peter McManus	21
Pierre Loti	23
Rare View	24
Rawhide	16
Rogue	17
Scores	18
Spirit Cruises	23
Suzie Wong	23
300 New York	21
Tillman's	23
Trailer Park	19
☒ 230 Fifth	23
xes lounge	21

CHINATOWN

(Canal to Pearl Sts., east of B'way)

☒ Apothéke	25
☒ Santos Party Hse.	25
Whiskey Tav.	20
Winnie's	-

EAST 40s

Annie Moore's	17
NEW Bar Downstairs	-
Beer Bar/Centro	20
NEW Bierhaus	-
Blarney Stone	14
Bookmarks	24
Calico Jack's	16
☒ Campbell Apt.	25
Connolly's	17
Lea	25
LQ	18
Mad46	24
Maggie's	18
McFadden's	15
925 Café/Cocktails	22
Overlook Lounge	18
Perfect Pint	20
☒ Top of the Tower	26
Uncle Charlie's	21
Vander Bar	-
Whiskey Blue	21
World Bar	19

EAST 50s

Beekman	24
Bill's Gay 90s	16
BlackFinn	16
Blackstone's	18
NEW Copia	-
Cornerstone Tav.	19
☒ Four Seasons/Bar	26
Haven	-
NEW Irish Exit	-
Jameson's	18
☒ King Cole Bar	27
☒ NEW Lavo	-
Le Bateau Ivre	21
NEW Lexicon	-
Lips	20
☒ Monkey Bar	23
Nikki Midtown	20
Opal	16
Pig N Whistle	18
☒ P.J. Clarke's	21

Redemption	21
Stag's Head	22
Sutton Place	17
T.G. Whitney's	16
Townhouse	20
Traffic	22
Turtle Bay	14
NEW Upstairs	-
Vero	22
Volstead	20

LOCATIONS

EAST 60s

Baker Street	17
Bar Italia	23
Club Macanudo	24
Z Feinstein's/Loews	26
O'Flanagan's	20
Z Plaza Athénée	27
Regency Library Bar	23
Subway Inn	18
Two E	-
Vino	22

EAST 70s

Bar Italia	23
Z Bar Pleiades	26
Z Bemelmans	27
Bounce	17
Z Brother Jimmy	17
Z Cafe Carlyle	27
David Copperfield	20
Doc Watson's	17
Finnegans Wake	19
Iggy's	15
Lexington Bar/Books	22
Session 73	17
Stir	18
Stumble Inn	20
Vero	22

EAST 80s

Auction House	22
BB&R	18
Brandy's	24
Comic Strip	20
Danny & Eddie's	-
NEW Delta House	-
Dorrian's	17
East End Tav.	17
Gaf Bar	16
Genesis	19
Jack Russell's	17
Johnny Foxes	15
Mad River	13
Molly Pitcher's	16

Rathbones	16
Ryan's Daughter	18
Saloon	18
Ship of Fools	15
Uptown Lounge	22
Wicker Park	17

EAST 90s & 100s
(90th to 110th Sts.)

Biddys Pub	-
Z Brother Jimmy	17
Kinsale	21
Manny's	19

EAST VILLAGE
(14th to Houston Sts., east of B'way, excluding NoHo)

Ace Bar	21
Against the Grain	28
Alphabet Lounge	18
Amsterdam Billiards	17
Angels & Kings	17
Z Angel's Share	26
Arrow	20
Babel Lounge	-
Banjo Jim's	20
Bar Carrera	21
Bar None	12
Bar on A	19
Z Bar Veloce	22
Beauty Bar	19
NEW Bedlam	-
Belgian Room	-
Big Bar	27
NEW Billy Hurricane's	-
Black/White	18
NEW Blind Barber	-
Blind Pig	18
Blue & Gold	16
Blue Owl	20
Boiler Room	18
Bourgeois Pig	23
Bowery Electric	18
Bowery Hotel	24
Bowery Wine Co.	19
Boxcar Lounge	18
B-Side	22
Bua	21
Burp Castle	21
Cabin/Below	-
Central Bar	19
Cherry Tavern	17
Cienfuegos	-
NEW Coal Yard	-
Cock	17
Common Ground	18

Continental	17
Coyote Ugly	15
Crocodile Lounge	19
Croxley Ales	19
☑ D.B.A.	22
☑ Death & Co	26
Decibel	24
Desnuda	21
Destination	-
Doc Holliday's	18
Double Down	-
Drop Off Service	21
Easternbloc	18
East Village Tav.	19
EastVille Comedy	-
11th St. Bar	20
Ella	20
Finnerty's	20
Forum	18
Grape & Grain	23
Grassroots	19
Heathers	-
Hi-Fi	20
Holiday Cocktail	18
Hop Devil Grill	18
NEW Idle Hands	-
NEW Immigrant	-
International Bar	20
In Vino	24
Joe's Pub	24
Karma	23
Keybar	19
KGB	20
King's Head	16
Klimat	-
Lakeside Lounge	21
Library	21
Lit	18
☑ Louis 649	27
Lovers/Today	-
Luca Bar/Lounge	17
Lucy's	20
Lunasa	21
Mama's Bar	-
Manitoba's	25
Mars Bar	19
☑ Mayahuel	26
☑ McSorley's	23
Nevada Smith's	16
Niagara	19
NEW Ninth Ward	-
No Malice Palace	21
Nowhere	21
Nublu	22

Nuyorican Poets	23
One & One	16
Otto's Shrunken	18
☑ PDT	27
Phoenix	21
Professor Thom's	19
Pyramid	18
NEW Queen Vic	-
Royale	21
Rue B	22
Ryan's Irish Pub	17
Scratcher	21
7B	19
Shoolbred's	19
Sing Sing	19
Solas	20
Sophie's	19
NEW Spanky & Darla's	-
Stay	-
St. Dymphna's	22
Stillwater	-
St. Marks Ale	18
Summit Bar	-
Sutra	19
Terroir	26
Thirsty Scholar	17
NEW 13th Step	-
NEW Trilby	-
12th St. Ale	19
2A	20
Urge	18
U2 Karaoke	-
V Bar	22
Velvet	21
Village Pourhouse	15
WCOU	-
Webster Hall	18
Whiskey Town	17
NEW White Noise	-
Winebar	22
Woody's	-

FINANCIAL DISTRICT

(South of Murray St.)

Bar Seven Five	-
Bayard's	-
Blarney Stone	14
Full Shilling	16
Jeremy's Ale	17
☑ P.J. Clarke's	21
17 Murray	19
☑ Ulysses	20
Vintry Wine	-
NEW W Downtown	-

FLATIRON

(14th to 26th Sts., 6th Ave. to Park Ave. S., excluding Union Sq.)

Boxers	-
Cabaret	-
Dewey's	14
Flatiron Lounge	22
☑ Flûte	23
☑ 40/40	19
☑ NEW Hurricane Club	-
Karaoke One 7	-
Lillie's	23
Lott	-
☑ Metropolitan Rm.	25
No Idea	15
Old Town Bar	21
Park Bar	23
☑ Raines Law Rm.	27
NEW Riff Raff's	-
Rye House	24
Slate	20
Spin New York	-
Splash	21
NEW Studio XXI	-
Taj II	17
VIP Club	23
Wined Up	22

GARMENT DISTRICT

(30th to 40th Sts., west of 5th)

Australian	20
NEW Bar on Fifth	-
Blarney Stone	14
☑ Brother Jimmy	17
NEW District 36	-
Empire Room	-
Escuelita	21
Fashion 40	18
Hammerstein	19
HK Lounge	19
Houndstooth	21
Katwalk	16
Local	19
Metro Grill Roof	23
Parlour	16
Rebel	-
Rick's Cabaret	23
Sky Room	-
Stitch	19
Stout	20
Tír na Nóg	18
☑ Top of the Strand	-

GRAMERCY PARK

(14th to 23rd Sts., east of Park Ave. S.)

Barfly	16
Belmont	19
Black Bear	18
☑ Brother Jimmy	17
Bull's Head	16
Cibar	22
Exchange B&G	-
Globe	20
☑ NEW Gramercy Terr.	-
Irving Plaza	19
Jade Bar	22
Molly's	23
Pete's Tavern	21
Pierre Loti	23
Plug Uglies	15
Revival	19
☑ Rose Bar	25
SideBar	18
Still	-
3 Steps	22

GREENWICH VILLAGE

(Houston to 14th Sts., west of B'way, east of 6th Ave.)

Amity Hall	-
Back Fence	19
Bar Carrera	21
Bar Six	21
Bitter End	20
NEW Blue Haven	-
☑ Blue Note	24
Bowlmor	20
NEW Buskers	-
Cafe Wha?	19
NEW Cayenne Lounge	-
Comedy Cellar	22
Dove	21
1849	17
8th St. Winecellar	23
Fat Black Pussycat	17
NEW GMT Tavern	-
Half Pint	21
Josie Wood's	17
Kenny's Castaways	19
La Lanterna	24
Le Poisson Rouge	20
Le Souk	22
MacDougal St. Ale	18
Madame X	17
Off the Wagon	17
124 Rabbit	22
Peculier Pub	20
Red Lion	20
Reservoir Bar	15
Shade	24
Sullivan Hall	21
Sullivan Room	18
Terra Blues	22

13	18
NEW 3 Sheets Saloon	-
Triona's	-
NEW Vault at Pfaff's	-
V Bar	22
Village Lantern	17
Village Underground	20
Vol de Nuit	22
NEW Vyne	-
Wicked Willy's	17
Wine Spot	-
Zinc Bar	19

HARLEM/ EAST HARLEM

(110th to 155th Sts., excluding Columbia U. area)

NEW Bier Int'l	-
El Morocco	20
Harlem Lanes	20
Lenox Lounge	23
Nectar	-
67 Orange St.	23
St. Nick's Jazz Pub	23

HUDSON SQUARE

(Canal to Houston Sts., west of 6th Ave.)

Anchor	18
Antarctica	17
City Winery	25
Ear Inn	23
Greenhouse	21
Kastel	-
S.O.B.'s	21
Sway	20

LITTLE ITALY

(Canal to Kenmare Sts., Bowery to Lafayette St.)

Z GoldBar	25
Z NEW Kenmare	-
NEW Lair	-
Z NEW Mulberry Project	-
Onieal's Grand St.	24
Randolph	-
Southside	20
Xicala	20

LOWER EAST SIDE

(Houston to Canal Sts., east of Bowery)

Above Allen	23
Arlene's Grocery	20
Back Room	23
Barramundi	21
Barrio Chino	22
Z NEW Beauty/Essex	-

Bob	21
Boss Tweed's	17
Bowery Ballroom	23
Box	24
Cake Shop	21
NEW Casa Mezcal	-
Chloe	23
Crash Mansion	15
NEW Culturefix	-
Dark Room	15
Delancey	19
Donnybrook	-
NEW Draft	-
Epstein's Bar	16
Fat Baby	17
Fontana's	21
GalleryBar	19
Happy Ending	18
Home Sweet Home	18
NEW Hotel Chantelle	-
Iggy's	15
Jadis	22
Katra	16
Kush	19
Libation	16
Living Room	23
Local 138	-
Local 269	-
Lolita	20
Loreley	22
Lucky Jack's	-
Magician	21
Marshall Stack	24
Max Fish	19
Mehanata	-
Mercury Lounge	21
Z Milk & Honey	25
Motor City	16
National Underground	-
Nurse Bettie	20
151	19
169 Bar	18
Painkiller	-
Panda	-
Parkside	-
Pianos	18
Pink Pony	17
Z Rockwood Music	26
Sapphire	18
Sixth Ward	20
Skinny	-
Stanton Public	22
St. Jerome's	-
NEW Tammany Hall	-
Tapeo 29	25

Ten Bells	24
200 Orchard	-
Uncle Charlie's	21
Verlaine	21
Welcome/Johnsons	15
Whiskey Ward	23
White Rabbit	18
White Star	21

MEATPACKING

(Gansevoort to 15th Sts., west of 9th Ave.)

Ara Wine Bar	20
Z Boom Boom	24
Brass Monkey	20
Z NEW Bunker	-
Cielo	23
Gaslight/G2	18
Griffin	21
Hogs & Heifers	18
Kiss & Fly	20
Z NEW Le Bain	-
Z Plunge	26
Z Provocateur	-
RDV	22
675 Bar	25
Z SL	23
Z Standard Biergarten	24
Tenjune	22
NEW Tzigan	-

MURRAY HILL

(26th to 40th Sts., east of 5th; 23rd to 26th Sts., east of Park Ave. S.)

Archive	-
Arctica	17
Bar 515	14
NEW Bar 29	-
Black Sheep	18
Z Brother Jimmy	17
Cask Bar	-
Failte	17
Fitzgerald's	-
Galway Hooker	18
NEW Gansevoort Park	-
Z Ginger Man	21
Hairy Monk	15
Hill	16
Z Jazz Standard	25
Joshua Tree	15
NEW Lex Bar	-
McCormack's	-
Mercury Bar	15
New York Comedy	18
NEW 1 Republik	-
Paddy Reilly's	-

NEW Park/Tavern	-
Patrick Kavanagh	-
Pine Tree Lodge	21
Polar	-
PS 450	20
Rare View	24
Rattle N Hum	-
Red Sky	17
Rodeo Bar	19
NEW Salon Millesime	-
Stone Creek	21
NEW Taproom No. 307	-
Third & Long	13
Tonic	16
Twelve	18
Van Diemens	19
Vertigo	20
Vig 27	17
Vino 313	22
Waterfront Ale Hse.	20
Wharf Bar & Grill	18
Whiskey River	20

NOHO

(Houston to 4th Sts., Bowery to B'way)

Agozar!	18
Bleecker St. Bar	17
Bowery Poetry	18
Z Madam Geneva	28
Sláinte	17
Soho Billiards	19
Swift	22
Temple Bar	23
3 Ten Lounge	15
Tom & Jerry's	21
Von	24

NOLITA

(Houston to Kenmare Sts., Bowery to Lafayette St.)

Botanica	20
Epistrophy	23
Monday Room	25
Z Pravda	22
R Bar	18
Spring Lounge	19
Sweet & Vicious	17
Vig Bar	23
NEW XIX	-

SOHO

(Canal to Houston Sts., west of Lafayette St.)

Bar 89	22
Broome St. Bar	17
Circa Tabac	24

Crosby Bar	24
Fanelli's	20
Grand Bar	23
Z NEW Jimmy	-
NEW Lani Kai	-
Merc Bar	22
Mercer Bar	22
Milady's	15
NEW Mister H	-
Naked Lunch	18
Z Pegu Club	25
Puck Fair	20
Red Bench	-
Room	25
SubMercer	24
Thom Bar	25

SOUTH STREET SEAPORT

Bin No. 220	20
NEW Keg No. 229	-
Paris	20

TRIBECA

(Canal to Murray Sts., west of B'way)

Anotheroom	22
Z Brandy Library	27
Z Bubble Lounge	21
Canal Room	21
Church Lounge	22
Eamonn's	17
Hideaway	18
M1-5 Bar	17
Nancy Whiskey	16
Patriot Saloon	16
Puffy's	14
Raccoon Lodge	18
Smith & Mills	21
Terroir	26
Z NEW Theater Bar	-
NEW Toro	-
Tribeca Tav.	17
Ward III	24
Z Warren 77	20
Z Weather Up	24

UNION SQUARE

(14th to 17th Sts., 5th Ave. to Union Sq. E.)

Underbar	21
Union Bar	17
W Union Sq.	22

WASHINGTON HTS./ INWOOD

(North of W. 155th St.)

United Palace	-

WEST 40s

Algonquin	23
Z Bar Centrale	26
Bar 41	23
Barrage	19
Bar-Tini	-
Z B. B. King Blues	21
Birdland	24
Blarney Stone	14
Bowlmor	20
Carolines	21
Cellar Bar	21
Connolly's	17
Croton Reservoir	17
Dave & Buster's	17
Don't Tell Mama	20
48 Lounge	26
Forty Four	22
Frames	23
Gaf Bar	16
Gift	28
Gossip	22
House of Brews	19
Hudson Terrace	21
Irish Rogue	18
Jimmy's Corner	21
Lansdowne Rd.	22
NEW Lantern's Keep	-
Latitude	15
Lucky Strike Lns.	22
M Bar	24
Mercury Bar	15
Morrell Wine	23
Z Oak Room	25
O'Flaherty's Ale	19
O'Lunney's	17
NEW On the Rocks	-
Pacha	17
Paramount Bar	-
Penthse. Exec. Club	23
Perdition	19
Perfect Pint	20
Pig N Whistle	18
Pony Bar	23
Z Press Lounge	-
NEW Réunion Surf Bar	-
Riposo	21
Ritz	23
Rudy's	20
Rum House	-
Smith's Bar	17
Social	16
St. Andrews	20
Swing 46	23
Tonic	16

Traffic	22
Village Pourhouse	15
World Yacht	24
W Times Sq.	23
NEW XVI	-

WEST 50s

NEW Above 6	-
Ardesia	-
Z Ava Lounge	23
Barcelona Bar	21
Bar Nine	18
Carnegie Club	23
Champagne Bar/Plaza	24
Coliseum Bar	15
Connolly's	17
'Disiac	23
Druids	21
Emmett O'Lunney's	21
Faces & Names	18
Flashdancers	21
Z Flûte	23
NEW Hash Fifty Five	-
Hooters	15
House of Brews	19
Z Hudson Hotel	24
Hustler Club	19
Iguana	20
NEW Industry Bar	-
Iridium	21
Jake's Saloon	15
Johnny Utah's	20
Mickey Mantle's	18
Moda Outdoors	-
Z Oak Bar	25
123 Burger	19
Palio Bar	23
P.J. Carney's	20
Posh	18
Rink Bar	21
Ritz-Carlton Star	26
Rose Club	22
Roseland	20
Russian Vodka Rm.	23
Z Salon de Ning	25
Terminal 5	19
Therapy	22
NEW Three Monkeys	-
Valhalla	22
Vintage	21
Vlada	21
Whiskey Park	20
Xai Xai	24

WEST 60s

Barcibo Enoteca	24
Z Dizzy's Club	27
Empire Hotel Bar	22
Z Empire Hotel Roof	24
Z MO Bar	24
Z P.J. Clarke's	21
Stone Rose	23

WEST 70s

Amsterdam Ale	-
Beacon Theatre	23
Bin 71	23
Blondies	18
Z Boat Basin	25
Bourbon St.	16
Columbus 72	17
Dive 75	19
Dublin House	17
P&G Cafe	21
Riposo	21
Shalel Lounge	23
Stand-Up NY	20
Wine & Roses	22

WEST 80s

Z Brother Jimmy	17
Dead Poet	20
420	18
George Keeley	21
Gin Mill	17
Jake's Dilemma	17
McAleer's Pub	15
Parlour	16
Prohibition	19

WEST 90s

Buceo 95	24
Cleopatra's Needle	19
Dive Bar	18

WEST 100s

(See also Harlem/East Harlem)	
Abbey Pub	21
Amsterdam Tavern	19
Broadway Dive	18
Ding Dong Lounge	18
Heights B&G	17
Lion's Head	19
Sip	-
Smoke	24
Suite	-
1020 Bar	17
Underground Lounge	15
Village Pourhouse	15

LOCATIONS

WEST VILLAGE

(Houston to 14th Sts., west of 6th
Ave., excluding Meatpacking)

NEW Anfora	-
NEW Aria Wine Bar	-
Art Bar	19
Arthur's Tavern	23
Automatic Slims	19
Barrow St. Ale	18
Bayard's Ale	19
Bleecker Heights	-
Z Blind Tiger	23
Blue Ribbon Bar	24
Bongo	22
NEW Brooklyneer	-
Cubby Hole	19
Daddy-O	21
Down the Hatch	16
Dublin 6	21
Duplex	20
Z Employees Only	23
Entwine	23
Fat Cat	21
Fiddlesticks	16
55 Bar	25
49 Grove	18
Galway Hooker	18
Garage	19
Henrietta Hudson	20
Highlands	24
Hudson Bar & Books	23
Z Jane Hotel	26
Jekyll & Hyde	18
Johnny's Bar	-
Julius	16
Kettle of Fish	19
LelaBar	22
Little Branch	24
Marie's Crisis	24
Monster	21
Mr. Dennehy's	20
NEW Orient Express	-
Otheroom	24
Pieces	17
RF Lounge	-
Riviera	19
Rockbar	-
Z Rusty Knot	20
Slaughtered Lamb	17
Z Smalls	26
NEW Snap	-
Stonewall Inn	16
Tortilla Flats	21
Upholstery Store	-

Z Village Vanguard	27
White Horse	19
Wilfie & Nell	24
NEW Windsor	-
Wogies	15
Woody McHale's	20
WXOU	22
Zampa	23

Bronx

An Béal Bocht	22
Stan's	21
Yankee Tav.	20

Brooklyn

BAY RIDGE

Delia's	24
Wicked Monk	21

BOERUM HILL

Boat	22
Brazen Head	20
Brooklyn Inn	25
Building/Bond	24
Camp	21
Pacific Standard	22

BROOKLYN HEIGHTS

Eamonn's	17
Floyd, NY	20
Waterfront Ale Hse.	20

BUSHWICK

Beauty Bar	19

CARROLL GARDENS

Abilene	23
Bar Great Harry	21
Black Mtn. Wine	28
Brooklyn Social	22
B61	-
Gowanus Yacht	22
JakeWalk	24
P.J. Hanley's	-
Zombie Hut	23

COBBLE HILL

Angry Wade's	16
Apt. 138	23
Clover Club	25
Last Exit	18
Sample	-

CONEY ISLAND

Peggy O'Neill's	20

DITMAS PARK

Castello Plan — _|

DUMBO

Galapagos — 21|
NEW Pub One — _|
Rebar — 24|

FORT GREENE

Brooklyn Public — 17|
Der Schwarze — _|
Stonehome — _|

GOWANUS

Z Bell House — 24|
Draft Barn — _|
Littlefield — _|

GRAVESEND

Draft Barn — _|

GREENPOINT

Black Rabbit — 24|
Diamond — _|
Enid's — 22|
Europa — 19|
Gutter — 19|
Manhattan Inn — _|
Matchless — 21|
Pencil Factory — 24|
NEW Spritzenhaus — _|
T.B.D. — _|

GREENWOOD HEIGHTS

Quarter — _|

PARK SLOPE

Barbès — 23|
Bar 4 — 19|
Z Beer Table — 22|
Black Horse — 16|
Brookvin — 23|
Buttermilk — 21|
Cherry Tree — _|
Commonwealth — 20|
Double Windsor — _|
Dram Shop — 18|
Excelsior — 19|
Fourth Ave. Pub — _|
NEW Freddy's Bar — _|
Gate — 20|
Ginger's — 18|
Great Lakes — 18|
High Dive — _|
Loki — 19|
Lucky 13 — _|

(PARK SLOPE cont.)

Z Mission Dolores — _|
Park Slope Ale — 19|
Rock Shop — _|
Sackett — _|
Sidecar — 24|
Southpaw — 20|
Tea Lounge — 22|
200 Fifth — 17|
Z Union Hall — 24|

PROSPECT HEIGHTS

NEW Branded Saloon — _|
Soda Bar — 16|
Washington Commons — _|
Z Weather Up — 24|
Woodwork — _|

RED HOOK

Fort Defiance — _|

WILLIAMSBURG

Abbey — 20|
Alligator — 19|
NEW Banter — _|
Barcade — 25|
Z Bembe — 26|
Berry Park — _|
Brooklyn Ale — 23|
Z Brooklyn Bowl — 27|
Brooklyn Brew. — 23|
NEW Brooklyn Wine — _|
Bushwick Country — 17|
Counting Room — _|
Daddy's — _|
Z D.B.A. — 22|
D.O.C. Wine — 24|
Dram — _|
Duff's — _|
Full Circle Bar — _|
Gibson — _|
NEW Good Co. — _|
Harefield Rd. — 25|
Hotel Delmano — 26|
Huckleberry — 24|
Iona — 23|
K & M Bar — _|
Knitting Factory — 21|
Larry Lawrence — 24|
Levee — _|
Loreley — 22|
Z NEW Maison Premiere — _|
Matt Torrey's — _|
Metropolitan — 18|
Mug's Ale — 20|
Music Hall — 23|
NEW Night of Joy — _|

LOCATIONS

Pete's Candy	25
Pinkerton	-
NEW Post Office	-
Public Assembly	-
Z Radegast	26
Richardson	-
Royal Oak	18
Satellite Lounge	-
Soft Spot	-
Spike Hill	18
Spuyten Duyvil	25
Sugarland	-
Teddy's	24
Trash	15
Trophy	19
Turkey's Nest	19
Union Pool	19
Velvet	21
NEW Whiskey Brooklyn	-
Woods	-
Zablozki's	21
Zebulon	23

Governors Island

Water Taxi Bch.	22

Queens

ASTORIA

Athens Café	18
Z Bohemian Hall	25
Z Cávo	26
Central	22
Grand Café	20
Hell Gate Social	-
Z Studio Square	25
Z Sweet Afton	25

FOREST HILLS

Bartini's	18

LONG ISLAND CITY

Creek & the Cave	-
Z Dutch Kills	26
L.I.C. Bar	22
Penthouse 808	-
NEW System	-

Staten Island

Beer Garden	21
Big Nose Kate's	19
Cargo	20
Full Cup	-

MANHATTAN NEIGHBORHOODS

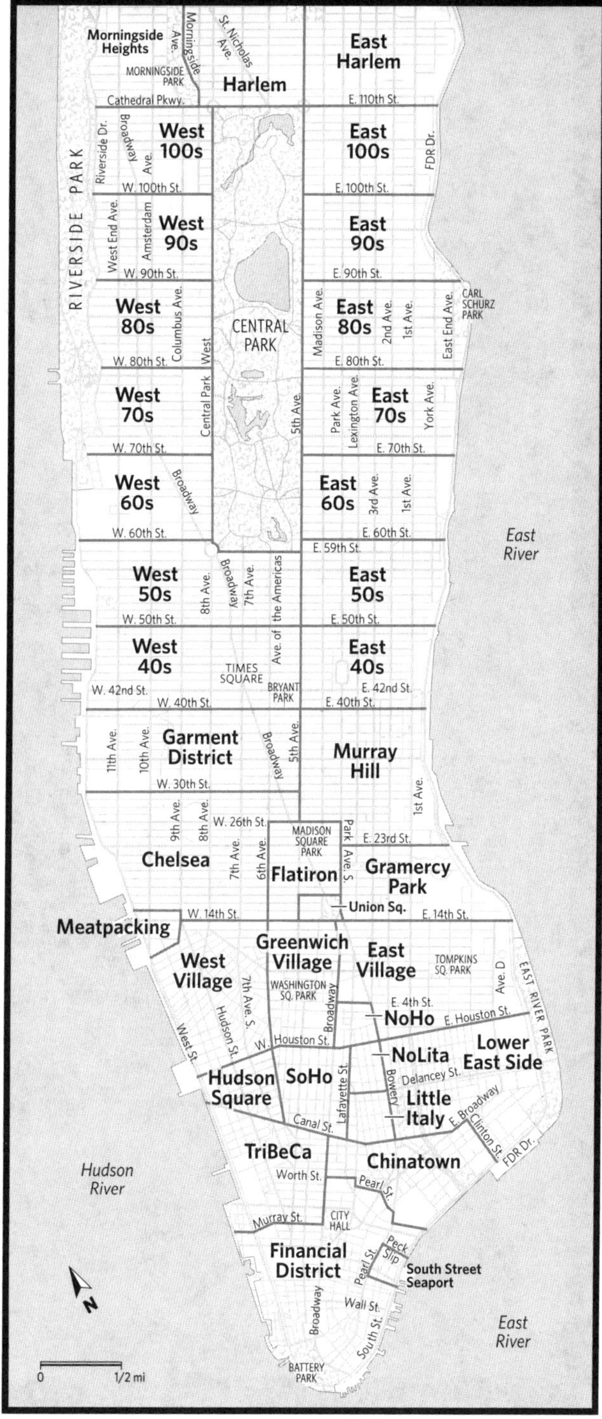

Morningside Heights
Morningside Ave.
St. Nicholas Ave.
MORNINGSIDE PARK
Harlem
East Harlem
Cathedral Pkwy.
E. 110th St.
West 100s
East 100s
Riverside Dr.
Broadway
Ave.
FDR Dr.
RIVERSIDE PARK
W. 100th St.
E. 100th St.
West 90s
East 90s
West End Ave.
Amsterdam
W. 90th St.
E. 90th St.
West 80s
East 80s
Columbus Ave.
CENTRAL PARK
Madison Ave.
2nd Ave.
1st Ave.
East End Ave.
CARL SCHURZ PARK
W. 80th St.
E. 80th St.
West
West 70s
East 70s
Central Park
5th Ave.
Park Ave.
Lexington Ave.
York Ave.
W. 70th St.
E. 70th St.
West 60s
East 60s
Broadway
3rd Ave.
1st Ave.
W. 60th St.
E. 60th St.
E. 59th St.
East River
West 50s
East 50s
8th Ave.
Broadway
7th Ave.
Ave. of the Americas
W. 50th St.
E. 50th St.
West 40s
East 40s
TIMES SQUARE
BRYANT PARK
W. 42nd St.
E. 42nd St.
W. 40th St.
E. 40th St.
Garment District
Murray Hill
11th Ave.
10th Ave.
Broadway
5th Ave.
1st Ave.
W. 30th St.
9th Ave.
8th Ave.
W. 26th St.
MADISON SQUARE PARK
Park Ave. S.
E. 23rd St.
Chelsea
7th Ave.
6th Ave.
Flatiron
Gramercy Park
Union Sq.
W. 14th St.
E. 14th St.
Meatpacking
Greenwich Village
East Village
TOMPKINS SQ. PARK
Ave. D
EAST RIVER PARK
West Village
7th Ave. S.
WASHINGTON SQ. PARK
Broadway
E. 4th St.
NoHo
E. Houston St.
Hudson St.
West St.
W. Houston St.
NoLita
Lower East Side
Hudson Square
SoHo
Lafayette St.
Bowery
Delancey St.
Little Italy
E. Broadway
Canal St.
Clinton St.
FDR Dr.
TriBeCa
Chinatown
Hudson River
Worth St.
Pearl St.
Murray St.
CITY HALL
Financial District
Peck Slip
Pearl St.
South Street Seaport
N
Broadway
Wall St.
South St.
East River
0
1/2 mi
BATTERY PARK

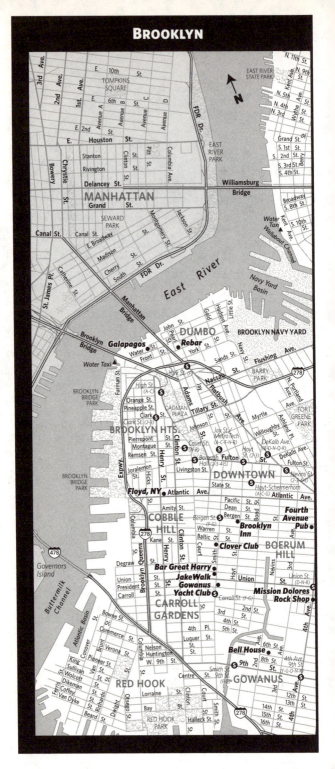

DETAIL

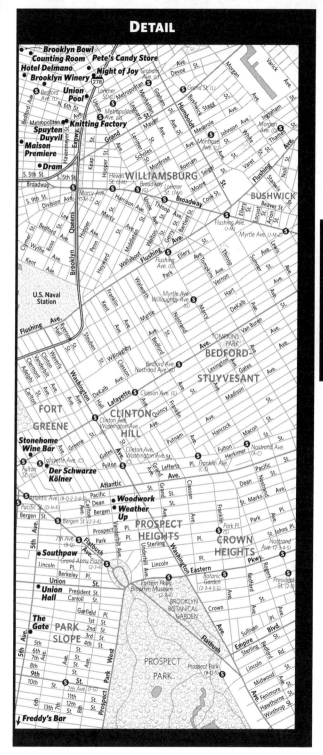

Brooklyn Bowl
Counting Room Pete's Candy Store
Hotel Delmano Night of Joy
Brooklyn Winery
Union Pool
Knitting Factory
Spuyten Duyvil
Maison Premiere
Dram

WILLIAMSBURG
BUSHWICK

U.S. Naval Station

BEDFORD STUYVESANT

FORT GREENE

CLINTON HILL

Stonehome Wine Bar

Der Schwarze Kölner

Woodwork
Weather Up

PROSPECT HEIGHTS

CROWN HEIGHTS

Southpaw

Union Hall

The Gate

PARK SLOPE

Brooklyn Museum

BROOKLYN BOTANICAL GARDEN

Freddy's Bar

PROSPECT PARK

Special Appeals

Listings cover the best in each category and include venue names, locations and Appeal ratings. Multi-location nightspots' features may vary by branch.

AFTER WORK

NEW Above 6	W 50s	-
Annie Moore's	E 40s	17
Archive	Murray Hill	-
Z Ava Lounge	W 50s	23
NEW Bar Downstairs	E 40s	-
Bar 515	Murray Hill	14
Bar Italia	E 70s	23
Bar Nine	W 50s	18
Bayard's	Financial	-
Beer Bar/Centro	E 40s	20
Z Bemelmans	E 70s	27
NEW Bierhaus	E 40s	-
BlackFinn	E 50s	16
Blackstone's	E 50s	18
Z Boat Basin	W 70s	25
Bookmarks	E 40s	24
Z Brandy Library	TriBeCa	27
Z Bubble Lounge	TriBeCa	21
Buceo 95	W 90s	24
Calico Jack's	E 40s	16
Z Campbell Apt.	E 40s	25
Church Lounge	TriBeCa	22
Connolly's	multi.	17
Croton Reservoir	W 40s	17
Dewey's	Flatiron	14
Eamonn's	multi.	17
Emmett O'Lunney's	W 50s	21
Empire Room	Garment	-
Faces & Names	W 50s	18
Fashion 40	Garment	18
Z Flûte	W 50s	23
48 Lounge	W 40s	26
Z Four Seasons/Bar	E 50s	26
Full Shilling	Financial	16
Gaf Bar	W 40s	16
Galway Hooker	Murray Hill	18
Z Ginger Man	Murray Hill	21
Houndstooth	Garment	21
Z Hudson Hotel	W 50s	24
NEW Industry Bar	W 50s	-
Jake's Saloon	multi.	15
Jameson's	E 50s	18
Jeremy's Ale	Financial	17
Katwalk	Garment	16
Z King Cole Bar	E 50s	27
Latitude	W 40s	15
Lea	E 40s	25
Mad River	E 80s	13
Maggie's	E 40s	18
M Bar	W 40s	24
McCormack's	Murray Hill	-
Mercury Bar	multi.	15
Moda Outdoors	W 50s	-
No Idea	Flatiron	15
Z Oak Bar	W 50s	25
O'Flaherty's Ale	W 40s	19
Old Town Bar	Flatiron	21
O'Lunney's	W 40s	17
123 Burger	W 50s	19
Opal	E 50s	16
Palio Bar	W 50s	23
Paramount Bar	W 40s	-
NEW Park/Tavern	Murray Hill	-
Park Bar	Flatiron	23
Perfect Pint	multi.	20
Pig N Whistle	multi.	18
P.J. Carney's	W 50s	20
Z P.J. Clarke's	E 50s	21
Pony Bar	W 40s	23
PS 450	Murray Hill	20
Rare View	Murray Hill	24
Redemption	E 50s	21
Rink Bar	W 50s	21
Shalel Lounge	W 70s	23
SideBar	Gramercy	18
Social	W 40s	16
Splash	Flatiron	21
St. Andrews	W 40s	20
Stitch	Garment	19
Sutton Place	E 50s	17
T.G. Whitney's	E 50s	16
NEW Three Monkeys	W 50s	-
Tír na Nóg	Garment	18
Turtle Bay	E 50s	14
Z 230 Fifth	Chelsea	23
Z Ulysses	Financial	20
Union Bar	Union Sq	17
NEW Upstairs	E 50s	-
Uptown Lounge	E 80s	22
Vander Bar	E 40s	-
Whiskey Blue	E 40s	21
Whiskey Park	W 50s	20
Wilfie & Nell	W Vill	24

ART BARS

Bowery Poetry	NoHo	18
Box	LES	24

NEW Casa Mezcal | **LES**	-
Creek & the Cave | **LIC**	-
NEW Culturefix | **LES**	-
NEW Freddy's Bar | **Park Slope**	-
Galapagos | **Dumbo**	21
GalleryBar | **LES**	19
Half King | **Chelsea**	20
KGB | **E Vill**	20
Littlefield | **Gowanus**	-
Nublu | **E Vill**	22
Nuyorican Poets | **E Vill**	23
Panda | **LES**	-
Public Assembly | **W'burg**	-
T.B.D. | **Greenpt**	-

BACHELOR PARTIES

Cabaret | **Flatiron**	-
Flashdancers | **W 50s**	21
Z 40/40 | **Flatiron**	19
Hogs & Heifers | **Meatpacking**	18
Hustler Club | **W 50s**	19
Penthse. Exec. Club | **W 40s**	23
Rick's Cabaret | **Garment**	23
Scores | **Chelsea**	18
VIP Club | **Flatiron**	23

BACHELORETTE PARTIES

Alphabet Lounge | **E Vill**	18
Automatic Slims | **W Vill**	19
Cafe Wha? | **G Vill**	19
Hogs & Heifers | **Meatpacking**	18
Johnny Utah's | **W 50s**	20
Lips | **E 50s**	20
Tortilla Flats | **W Vill**	21
Winnie's | **Chinatown**	-

BEAUTIFUL PEOPLE

Above Allen | **LES**	23
Avenue | **Chelsea**	23
Z Boom Boom | **Meatpacking**	24
Bowery Hotel | **E Vill**	24
Box | **LES**	24
Cellar Bar | **W 40s**	21
g | **Chelsea**	21
Z GoldBar | **L Italy**	25
Grand Bar | **SoHo**	23
Hiro | **Chelsea**	20
Z Hudson Hotel | **W 50s**	24
Z NEW Kenmare | **L Italy**	-
Z NEW Le Bain | **Meatpacking**	-
Z Madam Geneva | **NoHo**	28
Mercer Bar | **SoHo**	22
NEW Mister H | **SoHo**	-
Z NEW Mulberry Project | **L Italy**	-
Z 1 Oak | **Chelsea**	24

Z Plunge | **Meatpacking**	26
Z Provocateur | **Meatpacking**	-
RDV | **Meatpacking**	22
Z Rose Bar | **Gramercy**	25
Z Rusty Knot | **W Vill**	20
Z SL | **Meatpacking**	23
Z Standard Biergarten | **Meatpacking**	24
Stone Rose | **W 60s**	23
Tenjune | **Meatpacking**	22
Therapy | **W 50s**	22
Thom Bar | **SoHo**	25

BOTTLE SERVICE

(Bottle purchase sometimes required to secure a table)

Above Allen | **LES**	23
Z Apothéke | **Chinatown**	25
Avenue | **Chelsea**	23
Box | **LES**	24
NEW Chelsea Room | **Chelsea**	-
Cielo | **Meatpacking**	23
NEW District 36 | **Garment**	-
El Morocco | **Harlem**	20
Z 40/40 | **Flatiron**	19
49 Grove | **W Vill**	18
NEW Gansevoort Park | **Murray Hill**	-
Greenhouse | **Hudson Square**	21
Griffin | **Meatpacking**	21
NEW Hash Fifty Five | **W 50s**	-
Hiro | **Chelsea**	20
Hustler Club | **W 50s**	19
Kastel | **Hudson Square**	-
Z NEW Kenmare | **L Italy**	-
Kiss & Fly | **Meatpacking**	20
La Pomme | **Chelsea**	19
Z NEW Lavo | **E 50s**	-
Z NEW Le Bain | **Meatpacking**	-
Lott | **Flatiron**	-
LQ | **E 40s**	18
Lucky Strike Lns. | **W 40s**	22
Marquee | **Chelsea**	21
NEW Mister H | **SoHo**	-
Nikki Midtown | **E 50s**	20
Z 1 Oak | **Chelsea**	24
Pacha | **W 40s**	17
Penthse. Exec. Club | **W 40s**	23
Z Plunge | **Meatpacking**	26
Polar | **Murray Hill**	-
Z Provocateur | **Meatpacking**	-
RDV | **Meatpacking**	22
Rick's Cabaret | **Garment**	23
NEW Riff Raff's | **Flatiron**	-
Scores | **Chelsea**	18
Z SL | **Meatpacking**	23

NEW Studio XXI | **Flatiron**	-
SubMercer | **SoHo**	24
Suzie Wong | **Chelsea**	23
NEW System | **LIC**	-
Taj II | **Flatiron**	17
Tenjune | **Meatpacking**	22
NEW Tzigan | **Meatpacking**	-
NEW XIX | **NoLita**	-

CABARET

Box | **LES**	24
Z Cafe Carlyle | **E 70s**	27
Don't Tell Mama | **W 40s**	20
Duplex | **W Vill**	20
Z Feinstein's/Loews | **E 60s**	26
Joe's Pub | **E Vill**	24
Lips | **E 50s**	20
Z Metropolitan Rm. | **Flatiron**	25
Z Oak Room | **W 40s**	25

CELEB-SIGHTINGS

Avenue | **Chelsea**	23
Z Bar Centrale | **W 40s**	26
Z Boom Boom | **Meatpacking**	24
Box | **LES**	24
Z 40/40 | **Flatiron**	19
Z NEW Lavo | **E 50s**	-
Z NEW Le Bain | **Meatpacking**	-
NEW Mister H | **SoHo**	-
Z 1 Oak | **Chelsea**	24
Scores | **Chelsea**	18
Z SL | **Meatpacking**	23

CHEAP DRINKS

Angry Wade's | **Cobble Hill**	16
Antarctica | **Hudson Square**	17
Barfly | **Gramercy**	16
Billymark's West | **Chelsea**	16
Black Bear | **Gramercy**	18
Blarney Stone | **multi.**	14
Blue & Gold | **E Vill**	16
Boat | **Boerum Hill**	22
Z Bohemian Hall | **Astoria**	25
Boiler Room | **E Vill**	18
Boss Tweed's | **LES**	17
Boxcar Lounge | **E Vill**	18
Brooklyn Brew. | **W'burg**	23
Broome St. Bar | **SoHo**	17
Cherry Tavern | **E Vill**	17
NEW Coal Yard | **E Vill**	-
Continental | **E Vill**	17
NEW Delta House | **E 80s**	-
Doc Holliday's | **E Vill**	18
1849 | **G Vill**	17
Enid's | **Greenpt**	22

Finnerty's | **E Vill**	20
Floyd, NY | **Bklyn Hts**	20
NEW Freddy's Bar | **Park Slope**	-
Gowanus Yacht | **Carroll Gdns**	22
Grassroots | **E Vill**	19
Holiday Cocktail | **E Vill**	18
International Bar | **E Vill**	20
Jeremy's Ale | **Financial**	17
Johnny's Bar | **W Vill**	-
Josie Wood's | **G Vill**	17
Levee | **W'burg**	-
MacDougal St. Ale | **G Vill**	18
Mad River | **E 80s**	13
Manitoba's | **E Vill**	25
Mars Bar | **E Vill**	19
Milady's | **SoHo**	15
Motor City | **LES**	16
Mug's Ale | **W'burg**	20
Nancy Whiskey | **TriBeCa**	16
National Underground | **LES**	-
Off the Wagon | **G Vill**	17
123 Burger | **W 50s**	19
Parkside | **LES**	-
Patriot Saloon | **TriBeCa**	16
Pieces | **W Vill**	17
Plug Uglies | **Gramercy**	15
Pony Bar | **W 40s**	23
Raccoon Lodge | **TriBeCa**	18
Rudy's | **W 40s**	20
Ryan's Irish Pub | **E Vill**	17
7B | **E Vill**	19
Skinny | **LES**	-
Solas | **E Vill**	20
Sophie's | **E Vill**	19
NEW Spanky & Darla's | **E Vill**	-
St. Marks Ale | **E Vill**	18
Subway Inn | **E 60s**	18
Turkey's Nest | **W'burg**	19
12th St. Ale | **E Vill**	19
Welcome/Johnsons | **LES**	15

CLOSINGS (59)

Ace of Clubs
Aces & Eights
Alibi
Arlo & Esme
Back Page
Baddies
Bar 46: Athletic Club
Batista
BEast
Beer Island
Bogart's
Branch
Carnival
Cheap Shots

Citibar
Clo
Comix
CV
Divine Bar
Doghouse Saloon
Don Hill's
Eldridge, The
Element
ESPN Zone
Forbidden City
Gates, The
Glass
Hideout, The
High Bar
Imperial, The
Kemia Bar
Love
Mason Dixon
Metro 53
Moe's
M2
My Little Secret
Oasis
Obivia
119 Bar
Peter's
Pink
Pussycat Lounge
Quo
Revival
Rose Live Music
Sin Sin/Leopard Lounge
Star Lounge
Stoned Crow
Su Casa
Total Wine Bar
Touch
Town Tavern
Veloce Club
View Bar
Vintage Irving
Wet Bar
Yard, The
Zanzibar

COFFEEHOUSES

Athens Café | **Astoria**	18
Building/Bond | **Boerum Hill**	24
Cake Shop | **LES**	21
Full Cup | **SI**	-
Panda | **LES**	-
Sip | **W 100s**	-
Tea Lounge | **Park Slope**	22
Two E | **E 60s**	-

COMEDY CLUBS

(Call ahead to check nights, times, performers and covers)

Carolines | **W 40s**	21
Comedy Cellar | **G Vill**	22
Comic Strip | **E 80s**	20
EastVille Comedy | **E Vill**	-
Gotham Comedy | **Chelsea**	20
New York Comedy | **Murray Hill**	18
Stand-Up NY | **W 70s**	20

COMMUTER OASES

Grand Central
Annie Moore's | **E 40s**	17
Beer Bar/Centro | **E 40s**	20
NEW Bierhaus | **E 40s**	-
Blarney Stone | **E 40s**	14
Bookmarks | **E 40s**	24
Z Campbell Apt. | **E 40s**	25
Lea | **E 40s**	25
Maggie's | **E 40s**	18
Overlook Lounge | **E 40s**	18
Vander Bar | **E 40s**	-

Penn Station
Blarney Stone | **multi.**	14
Houndstooth | **Garment**	21
Local | **Garment**	19
Parlour | **Garment**	16
Rick's Cabaret | **Garment**	23
Stitch | **Garment**	19
Stout | **Garment**	20
Tír na Nóg | **Garment**	18

Port Authority
Bar 41 | **W 40s**	23
Croton Reservoir | **W 40s**	17
Fashion 40 | **Garment**	18
HK Lounge | **Garment**	19
Sky Room | **Garment**	-

COOL LOOS

Bar 89 | **SoHo**	22
Z NEW Beauty/Essex | **LES**	-
Z Boom Boom | **Meatpacking**	24
Gift | **W 40s**	28
Jekyll & Hyde | **W Vill**	18
Z P.J. Clarke's | **E 50s**	21
Smith & Mills | **TriBeCa**	21

DANCE CLUBS

Cielo | **Meatpacking**	23
Columbus 72 | **W 70s**	17
NEW District 36 | **Garment**	-
Escuelita | **Garment**	21
Europa | **Greenpt**	19
NEW Lexicon | **E 50s**	-
LQ | **E 40s**	18
Pacha | **W 40s**	17

Pyramid | **E Vill**	18
Saloon | **E 80s**	18
✷ Santos Party Hse. | **Chinatown**	25
Sapphire | **LES**	18
S.O.B.'s | **Hudson Square**	21
Swing 46 | **W 40s**	23
NEW System | **LIC**	-
Webster Hall | **E Vill**	18

DINNER CRUISES

✷ Bateaux NY | **Chelsea**	26
Spirit Cruises | **Chelsea**	23
World Yacht | **W 40s**	24

DIVES

Abbey | **W'burg**	20
Ace Bar | **E Vill**	21
Alligator | **W'burg**	19
Angry Wade's | **Cobble Hill**	16
Antarctica | **Hudson Square**	17
Arlene's Grocery | **LES**	20
Back Fence | **G Vill**	19
Barfly | **Gramercy**	16
Bar Great Harry | **Carroll Gdns**	21
Bar None | **E Vill**	12
Billymark's West | **Chelsea**	16
Black/White | **E Vill**	18
Blarney Stone | **multi.**	14
Blue & Gold | **E Vill**	16
Boat | **Boerum Hill**	22
Boiler Room | **E Vill**	18
Boss Tweed's | **LES**	17
Botanica | **NoLita**	20
Bourbon St. | **W 70s**	16
Broadway Dive | **W 100s**	18
B-Side | **E Vill**	22
Bull's Head | **Gramercy**	16
Bushwick Country | **W'burg**	17
Cherry Tavern | **E Vill**	17
NEW Coal Yard | **E Vill**	-
Cock | **E Vill**	17
Continental | **E Vill**	17
Coyote Ugly | **E Vill**	15
Crocodile Lounge | **E Vill**	19
Dark Room | **LES**	15
Ding Dong Lounge | **W 100s**	18
Dive Bar | **W 90s**	18
Doc Holliday's | **E Vill**	18
Double Down | **E Vill**	-
Down the Hatch | **W Vill**	16
Dublin House | **W 70s**	17
11th St. Bar | **E Vill**	20
55 Bar | **W Vill**	25
NEW Freddy's Bar | **Park Slope**	-
Gin Mill | **W 80s**	17
Grassroots | **E Vill**	19

Great Lakes | **Park Slope**	18
Hi-Fi | **E Vill**	20
Holiday Cocktail | **E Vill**	18
Iggy's | **E 70s**	15
International Bar | **E Vill**	20
Jake's Dilemma | **W 80s**	17
Jeremy's Ale | **Financial**	17
Jimmy's Corner | **W 40s**	21
Johnny's Bar | **W Vill**	-
King's Head | **E Vill**	16
Lakeside Lounge | **E Vill**	21
Levee | **W'burg**	-
Library | **E Vill**	21
Lit | **E Vill**	18
Local 269 | **LES**	-
Lucky 13 | **Park Slope**	-
Lucy's | **E Vill**	20
Mars Bar | **E Vill**	19
McAleer's Pub | **W 80s**	15
Mehanata | **LES**	-
Milady's | **SoHo**	15
Motor City | **LES**	16
Nancy Whiskey | **TriBeCa**	16
Nevada Smith's | **E Vill**	16
No Idea | **Flatiron**	15
O'Flanagan's | **E 60s**	20
151 | **LES**	19
NEW 1 Republik | **Murray Hill**	-
169 Bar | **LES**	18
Otto's Shrunken | **E Vill**	18
Parkside | **LES**	-
Patriot Saloon | **TriBeCa**	16
Peculier Pub | **G Vill**	20
Phoenix | **E Vill**	21
Pieces | **W Vill**	17
Plug Uglies | **Gramercy**	15
Pyramid | **E Vill**	18
Raccoon Lodge | **TriBeCa**	18
Rathbones | **E 80s**	16
Rawhide | **Chelsea**	16
Red Lion | **G Vill**	20
Reservoir Bar | **G Vill**	15
Rudy's | **W 40s**	20
Satellite Lounge | **W'burg**	-
7B | **E Vill**	19
Skinny | **LES**	-
Sophie's | **E Vill**	19
NEW Spanky & Darla's | **E Vill**	-
Spring Lounge | **NoLita**	19
Subway Inn | **E 60s**	18
Sugarland | **W'burg**	-
1020 Bar | **W 100s**	17
Trash | **W'burg**	15
Turkey's Nest | **W'burg**	19
WCOU | **E Vill**	-

Welcome/Johnsons	**LES**	15
Whiskey River	**Murray Hill**	20
Whiskey Ward	**LES**	23
Winnie's	**Chinatown**	-

DJs

Canal Room	**TriBeCa**	21
Cielo	**Meatpacking**	23
Columbus 72	**W 70s**	17
NEW District 36	**Garment**	-
Escuelita	**Garment**	21
Hiro	**Chelsea**	20
NEW Lexicon	**E 50s**	-
Marquee	**Chelsea**	21
Nublu	**E Vill**	22
Pacha	**W 40s**	17
Pianos	**LES**	18
Pyramid	**E Vill**	18
Saloon	**E 80s**	18
Z Santos Party Hse.	**Chinatown**	25
Sapphire	**LES**	18
S.O.B.'s	**Hudson Square**	21
Splash	**Flatiron**	21
Sullivan Room	**G Vill**	18
Swing 46	**W 40s**	23
NEW System	**LIC**	-
Webster Hall	**E Vill**	18

DRAG SHOWS

Barracuda	**Chelsea**	19
Escuelita	**Garment**	21
NEW Industry Bar	**W 50s**	-
Lips	**E 50s**	20
Monster	**W Vill**	21
Pieces	**W Vill**	17

DRINK SPECIALISTS

BEER
(* Microbrewery)

Against the Grain	**E Vill**	28
Amity Hall	**G Vill**	-
Amsterdam Ale	**W 70s**	-
Anotheroom	**TriBeCa**	22
Baker Street	**E 60s**	17
NEW Banter	**W'burg**	-
Barcade	**W'burg**	25
Bar Great Harry	**Carroll Gdns**	21
Barrow St. Ale	**W Vill**	18
Beer Bar/Centro	**E 40s**	20
Z Beer Table	**Park Slope**	22
Belgian Room	**E Vill**	-
Berry Park	**W'burg**	-
NEW Bierhaus	**E 40s**	-
NEW Bier Int'l	**Harlem**	-
Z Blind Tiger	**W Vill**	23
Z Bohemian Hall	**Astoria**	25
Boxcar Lounge	**E Vill**	18

Brass Monkey	**Meatpacking**	20
Brazen Head	**Boerum Hill**	20
Brooklyn Ale	**W'burg**	23
Brooklyn Brew.*	**W'burg**	23
Burp Castle	**E Vill**	21
Cask Bar	**Murray Hill**	-
Chelsea Brewing*	**Chelsea**	20
Croxley Ales	**E Vill**	19
David Copperfield	**E 70s**	20
Z D.B.A.	**multi.**	22
Der Schwarze	**Ft Greene**	-
Dewey's	**Flatiron**	14
Diamond	**Greenpt**	-
NEW Draft	**LES**	-
Draft Barn	**Gowanus**	-
East Village Tav.	**E Vill**	19
Fourth Ave. Pub	**Park Slope**	-
Gate	**Park Slope**	20
George Keeley	**W 80s**	21
Gibson	**W'burg**	-
Z Ginger Man	**Murray Hill**	21
Half Pint	**G Vill**	21
Harefield Rd.	**W'burg**	25
Hop Devil Grill	**E Vill**	18
House of Brews	**multi.**	19
NEW Idle Hands	**E Vill**	-
Iona	**W'burg**	23
Jake's Dilemma	**W 80s**	17
Jeremy's Ale	**Financial**	17
K & M Bar	**W'burg**	-
NEW Keg No. 229	**Seaport**	-
King's Head	**E Vill**	16
Kinsale	**E 90s**	21
Lillie's	**Flatiron**	23
Loreley	**multi.**	22
MacDougal St. Ale	**G Vill**	18
Matchless	**Greenpt**	21
Z McSorley's	**E Vill**	23
Z Mission Dolores	**Park Slope**	-
Mug's Ale	**W'burg**	20
O'Flaherty's Ale	**W 40s**	19
124 Rabbit	**G Vill**	22
Otheroom	**W Vill**	24
Pacific Standard	**Boerum Hill**	22
NEW Park/Tavern	**Murray Hill**	-
Park Slope Ale	**Park Slope**	19
Peculier Pub	**G Vill**	20
Pony Bar	**W 40s**	23
Puck Fair	**SoHo**	20
Z Radegast	**W'burg**	26
Rattle N Hum	**Murray Hill**	-
Room	**SoHo**	25
Sixth Ward	**LES**	20
Slaughtered Lamb	**W Vill**	17
NEW Snap	**W Vill**	-

Spike Hill | **W'burg**	18
NEW Spritzenhaus | **Greenpt**	-
Spuyten Duyvil | **W'burg**	25
Stag's Head | **E 50s**	22
Z Standard Biergarten | **Meatpacking**	24
St. Andrews | **W 40s**	20
St. Marks Ale | **E Vill**	18
Stout | **Garment**	20
Z Studio Square | **Astoria**	25
Swift | **NoHo**	22
NEW Taproom No. 307 | **Murray Hill**	-
NEW Three Monkeys | **W 50s**	-
Tír na Nóg | **Garment**	18
200 Fifth | **Park Slope**	17
Z Ulysses | **Financial**	20
Valhalla | **W 50s**	22
Village Pourhouse | **multi.**	15
Vol de Nuit | **G Vill**	22
Waterfront Ale Hse. | **multi.**	20
NEW Windsor | **W Vill**	-

CHAMPAGNE

Z Bubble Lounge | **TriBeCa**	21
Champagne Bar/Plaza | **W 50s**	24
Z Flûte | **multi.**	23
Morrell Wine | **W 40s**	23

COCKTAILS

Z Angel's Share | **E Vill**	26
Z Apothéke | **Chinatown**	25
Z Bar Pleiades | **E 70s**	26
Z Bemelmans | **E 70s**	27
Blue Owl | **E Vill**	20
Z Brandy Library | **TriBeCa**	27
Brooklyn Social | **Carroll Gdns**	22
Church Lounge | **TriBeCa**	22
Cibar | **Gramercy**	22
Clover Club | **Cobble Hill**	25
Z Death & Co | **E Vill**	26
Z Dutch Kills | **LIC**	26
Z Employees Only | **W Vill**	23
Flatiron Lounge | **Flatiron**	22
Z Flûte | **multi.**	23
Hotel Delmano | **W'burg**	26
JakeWalk | **Carroll Gdns**	24
Z King Cole Bar | **E 50s**	27
NEW Lani Kai | **SoHo**	-
NEW Lantern's Keep | **W 40s**	-
Little Branch | **W Vill**	24
Z Madam Geneva | **NoHo**	28
Z NEW Maison Premiere | **W'burg**	-
Z Milk & Honey | **LES**	25
Z Monkey Bar | **E 50s**	23
Z NEW Mulberry Project | **L Italy**	-

Z PDT | **E Vill**	27
Z Pegu Club | **SoHo**	25
Z Pravda | **NoLita**	22
Z Raines Law Rm. | **Flatiron**	27
Rum House | **W 40s**	-
Z Rusty Knot | **W Vill**	20
Sidecar | **Park Slope**	24
Z NEW Theater Bar | **TriBeCa**	-
Verlaine | **LES**	21
Ward III | **TriBeCa**	24
Z Weather Up | **multi.**	24
White Star | **LES**	21
World Bar | **E 40s**	19

MARTINIS

Z Angel's Share | **E Vill**	26
Bar 89 | **SoHo**	22
Bar 4 | **Park Slope**	19
Bar Nine | **W 50s**	18
Bartini's | **Forest Hills**	18
Bayard's | **Financial**	-
Z Bemelmans | **E 70s**	27
Carnegie Club | **W 50s**	23
Cellar Bar | **W 40s**	21
Cibar | **Gramercy**	22
Circa Tabac | **SoHo**	24
Delia's | **Bay Ridge**	24
Double Down | **E Vill**	-
Forty Four | **W 40s**	22
Z King Cole Bar | **E 50s**	27
Z MO Bar | **W 60s**	24
Onieal's Grand St. | **L Italy**	24
Z Pravda | **NoLita**	22
Rue B | **E Vill**	22
Russian Vodka Rm. | **W 50s**	23
Temple Bar | **NoHo**	23
Uptown Lounge | **E 80s**	22
Verlaine | **LES**	21
Vintage | **W 50s**	21

RUM

Cienfuegos | **E Vill**	-
Z NEW Hurricane Club | **Flatiron**	-
Painkiller | **LES**	-
NEW Riff Raff's | **Flatiron**	-

SAKE/SHOCHU/SOJU

Decibel | **E Vill**	24
Suzie Wong | **Chelsea**	23

SCOTCH/SINGLE MALTS

Barbès | **Park Slope**	23
Z Brandy Library | **TriBeCa**	27
Brazen Head | **Boerum Hill**	20
Carnegie Club | **W 50s**	23
Club Macanudo | **E 60s**	24
Z D.B.A. | **multi.**	22
Harefield Rd. | **W'burg**	25

Highlands | **W Vill**	24
Hudson Bar & Books | **W Vill**	23
Lexington Bar/Books | **E 70s**	22
Spike Hill | **W'burg**	18
St. Andrews | **W 40s**	20
Swift | **NoHo**	22
Terra Blues | **G Vill**	22
Tír na Nóg | **Garment**	18
Vintry Wine | **Financial**	-
Whiskey Ward | **LES**	23

TEQUILA

Barbès | **Park Slope**	23
Barrio Chino | **LES**	22
☷ D.B.A. | **multi.**	22
☷ Mayahuel | **E Vill**	26

VODKA

Barramundi | **LES**	21
Mama's Bar | **E Vill**	-
☷ Pravda | **NoLita**	22
Russian Vodka Rm. | **W 50s**	23
Temple Bar | **NoHo**	23
Vlada | **W 50s**	21

WHISKEY

Barbès | **Park Slope**	23
☷ D.B.A. | **multi.**	22
NEW Idle Hands | **E Vill**	-
JakeWalk | **Carroll Gdns**	24
Lillie's | **Flatiron**	23
NEW On the Rocks | **W 40s**	-
NEW Post Office | **W'burg**	-
Rye House | **Flatiron**	24
NEW Whiskey Brooklyn | **W'burg**	-
Whiskey Tav. | **Chinatown**	20
Whiskey Town | **E Vill**	17
Whiskey Ward | **LES**	23

WINE BARS

NEW Anfora | **W Vill**	-
Ara Wine Bar | **Meatpacking**	20
Ardesia | **W 50s**	-
NEW Aria Wine Bar | **W Vill**	-
Bar Carrera | **multi.**	21
Barcibo Enoteca | **W 60s**	24
Bar Italia | **E 70s**	23
☷ Bar Veloce | **multi.**	22
Bin No. 220 | **Seaport**	20
Bin 71 | **W 70s**	23
Black Mtn. Wine | **Carroll Gdns**	28
Blue Ribbon Bar | **W Vill**	24
Bowery Wine Co. | **E Vill**	19
NEW Brooklyn Wine | **W'burg**	-
Brookvin | **Park Slope**	23
Buceo 95 | **W 90s**	24
Castello Plan | **Ditmas Pk**	-

City Winery | **Hudson Square**	25
Counting Room | **W'burg**	-
Desnuda | **E Vill**	21
D.O.C. Wine | **W'burg**	24
Drunken Horse | **Chelsea**	-
8th St. Winecellar | **G Vill**	23
Entwine | **W Vill**	23
Epistrophy | **NoLita**	23
☷ Flûte | **multi.**	23
Grape & Grain | **E Vill**	23
NEW Immigrant | **E Vill**	-
In Vino | **E Vill**	24
Jadis | **LES**	22
Le Bateau Ivre | **E 50s**	21
LelaBar | **W Vill**	22
Monday Room | **NoLita**	25
Morrell Wine | **W 40s**	23
Nectar | **Harlem**	-
Pierre Loti | **multi.**	23
Pinkerton | **W'burg**	-
Riposo | **multi.**	21
Sample | **Cobble Hill**	-
Stonehome | **Ft Greene**	-
Tapeo 29 | **LES**	25
Ten Bells | **LES**	24
Terroir | **multi.**	26
Upholstery Store | **W Vill**	-
V Bar | **G Vill**	22
Vero | **multi.**	22
Vino | **E 60s**	22
Vino 313 | **Murray Hill**	22
Vintry Wine | **Financial**	-
Von | **NoHo**	24
NEW Vyne | **G Vill**	-
Wine & Roses | **W 70s**	22
Winebar | **E Vill**	22
Wined Up | **Flatiron**	22
Wine Spot | **G Vill**	-
Xai Xai | **W 50s**	24
Xicala | **L Italy**	20
Zampa | **W Vill**	23

WINE BY THE GLASS
(See also Wine Bars, above)

Anotheroom | **TriBeCa**	22
Bar Six | **G Vill**	21
Iridium | **W 50s**	21
Lexington Bar/Books | **E 70s**	22
☷ Louis 649 | **E Vill**	27
Otheroom | **W Vill**	24
Room | **SoHo**	25
Smoke | **W 100s**	24

EURO

Avenue | **Chelsea**	23
Bar Italia | **E 70s**	23

SPECIAL APPEALS

Bar Six | **G Vill**	21
Z Bar Veloce | **E Vill**	22
Cielo | **Meatpacking**	23
Circa Tabac | **SoHo**	24
Epistrophy | **NoLita**	23
Z Flûte | **multi.**	23
Forty Four | **W 40s**	22
Z GoldBar | **L Italy**	25
Grand Bar | **SoHo**	23
Z Hudson Hotel | **W 50s**	24
Kiss & Fly | **Meatpacking**	20
Z NEW Lavo | **E 50s**	-
Le Souk | **G Vill**	22
Mercer Bar | **SoHo**	22
Nikki Midtown | **E 50s**	20
Z 1 Oak | **Chelsea**	24
Z Provocateur | **Meatpacking**	-
RDV | **Meatpacking**	22
Thom Bar | **SoHo**	25

EXPENSE-ACCOUNTERS

Above Allen | **LES**	23
Z Ava Lounge | **W 50s**	23
Avenue | **Chelsea**	23
Bar Seven Five | **Financial**	-
Z Bateaux NY | **Chelsea**	26
Bayard's | **Financial**	-
Z Bemelmans | **E 70s**	27
Z Blue Note | **G Vill**	24
Z Boom Boom | **Meatpacking**	24
Bowery Hotel | **E Vill**	24
Z Brandy Library | **TriBeCa**	27
Z Bubble Lounge | **TriBeCa**	21
Z Cafe Carlyle | **E 70s**	27
Z Campbell Apt. | **E 40s**	25
Carnegie Club | **W 50s**	23
Cellar Bar | **W 40s**	21
Champagne Bar/Plaza | **W 50s**	24
NEW Chelsea Room | **Chelsea**	-
Church Lounge | **TriBeCa**	22
Club Macanudo | **E 60s**	24
Z Flûte | **multi.**	23
48 Lounge | **W 40s**	26
NEW Gansevoort Park | **Murray Hill**	-
Z GoldBar | **L Italy**	25
Grand Bar | **SoHo**	23
Z Hudson Hotel | **W 50s**	24
Z NEW Jimmy | **SoHo**	-
Z King Cole Bar | **E 50s**	27
Z NEW Lavo | **E 50s**	-
Z NEW Le Bain | **Meatpacking**	-
NEW Lex Bar | **Murray Hill**	-
Z MO Bar | **W 60s**	24
Z Monkey Bar | **E 50s**	23

Morrell Wine | **W 40s**	23
Z Oak Bar | **W 50s**	25
Z Oak Room | **W 40s**	25
Z Plaza Athénée | **E 60s**	27
Polar | **Murray Hill**	-
Z Provocateur | **Meatpacking**	-
Rose Club | **W 50s**	22
Z Salon de Ning | **W 50s**	25
NEW Salon Millesime | **Murray Hill**	-
Z SL | **Meatpacking**	23
Stone Rose | **W 60s**	23
Two E | **E 60s**	-
NEW Tzigan | **Meatpacking**	-
NEW W Downtown | **Financial**	-
World Bar | **E 40s**	19
NEW XIX | **NoLita**	-

EYE-OPENERS

(Serves alcohol starting at 8 AM on most days)

Billymark's West | **Chelsea**	16
Blarney Stone | **multi.**	14
Dublin House | **W 70s**	17
Jeremy's Ale | **Financial**	17
Rudy's | **W 40s**	20
Spring Lounge | **NoLita**	19

FIREPLACES

Amsterdam Ale | **W 70s**	-
Amsterdam Billiards | **E Vill**	17
Angry Wade's | **Cobble Hill**	16
Arctica | **Murray Hill**	17
Arlene's Grocery | **LES**	20
Art Bar | **W Vill**	19
Auction House | **E 80s**	22
Back Room | **LES**	23
Z Bar Veloce | **Chelsea**	22
Bayard's Ale | **W Vill**	19
Beekman | **E 50s**	24
Black Bear | **Gramercy**	18
Black Mtn. Wine | **Carroll Gdns**	28
Black Rabbit | **Greenpt**	24
Blackstone's | **E 50s**	18
Boat | **Boerum Hill**	22
Bookmarks | **E 40s**	24
Bowery Hotel | **E Vill**	24
Z Brandy Library | **TriBeCa**	27
Camp | **Boerum Hill**	21
Carnegie Club | **W 50s**	23
Central Bar | **E Vill**	19
Cherry Tree | **Park Slope**	-
Cibar | **Gramercy**	22
Clover Club | **Cobble Hill**	25
Delancey | **LES**	19
Delia's | **Bay Ridge**	24

Dorrian's | **E 80s**	17
Dove | **G Vill**	21
Dublin 6 | **W Vill**	21
☑ Empire Hotel Roof | **W 60s**	24
☑ Employees Only | **W Vill**	23
Entwine | **W Vill**	23
Faces & Names | **W 50s**	18
Failte | **Murray Hill**	17
Forty Four | **W 40s**	22
NEW Gansevoort Park | **Murray Hill**	–
Garage | **W Vill**	19
Gaslight/G2 | **Meatpacking**	18
Gin Mill | **W 80s**	17
Globe | **Gramercy**	20
Gossip | **W 40s**	22
☑ Hudson Hotel | **W 50s**	24
Iguana | **W 50s**	20
Jack Russell's | **E 80s**	17
Jekyll & Hyde | **W Vill**	18
☑**NEW** Jimmy | **SoHo**	–
Josie Wood's | **G Vill**	17
Keybar | **E Vill**	19
La Lanterna | **G Vill**	24
NEW Lani Kai | **SoHo**	–
Latitude | **W 40s**	15
Lexington Bar/Books | **E 70s**	22
L.I.C. Bar | **LIC**	22
Lion's Head | **W 100s**	19
Loki | **Park Slope**	19
Metropolitan | **W'burg**	18
Molly's | **Gramercy**	23
O'Flaherty's Ale | **W 40s**	19
169 Bar | **LES**	18
Raccoon Lodge | **TriBeCa**	18
Riviera | **W Vill**	19
☑ Rose Bar | **Gramercy**	25
Shoolbred's | **E Vill**	19
Slaughtered Lamb | **W Vill**	17
NEW Spritzenhaus | **Greenpt**	–
Teddy's | **W'burg**	24
T.G. Whitney's | **E 50s**	16
Tillman's | **Chelsea**	23
Turtle Bay | **E 50s**	14
☑ Union Hall | **Park Slope**	24
Velvet | **E Vill**	21
Vig 27 | **Murray Hill**	17
Whiskey River | **Murray Hill**	20
Woods | **W'burg**	–
Zombie Hut | **Carroll Gdns**	23

FIRST DATE

☑ Angel's Share | **E Vill**	26
Anotheroom | **TriBeCa**	22
Art Bar | **W Vill**	19
Bar 4 | **Park Slope**	19

☑ Bemelmans | **E 70s**	27
Black Door | **Chelsea**	19
☑ Boat Basin | **W 70s**	25
Bowlmor | **multi.**	20
☑ Bubble Lounge | **TriBeCa**	21
☑ Cafe Carlyle | **E 70s**	27
Cibar | **Gramercy**	22
Delia's | **Bay Ridge**	24
☑ Dizzy's Club | **W 60s**	27
D.O.C. Wine | **W'burg**	24
Grape & Grain | **E Vill**	23
☑ Jazz Standard | **Murray Hill**	25
☑ Louis 649 | **E Vill**	27
☑ MO Bar | **W 60s**	24
Onieal's Grand St. | **L Italy**	24
Otheroom | **W Vill**	24
Park Bar | **Flatiron**	23
☑ Raines Law Rm. | **Flatiron**	27
Red Bench | **SoHo**	–
Room | **SoHo**	25
Shade | **G Vill**	24
Stir | **E 70s**	18
Tea Lounge | **Park Slope**	22
Vero | **multi.**	22
Von | **NoHo**	24

FOREIGN FEELING

ASIAN

Decibel | **E Vill**	24
Suzie Wong | **Chelsea**	23

FRENCH

Barbès | **Park Slope**	23
Bar Six | **G Vill**	21
Le Bateau Ivre | **E 50s**	21
Rue B | **E Vill**	22
Zebulon | **W'burg**	23

GERMAN

NEW Bierhaus | **E 40s**	–
Loreley | **multi.**	22
☑ Radegast | **W'burg**	26
NEW Spritzenhaus | **Greenpt**	–

INDIAN

Sutra | **E Vill**	19
Taj II | **Flatiron**	17

IRISH

An Béal Bocht | **Bronx**	22
Annie Moore's | **E 40s**	17
Baker Street | **E 60s**	17
Biddys Pub | **E 90s**	–
Black Sheep | **Murray Hill**	18
Blackstone's | **E 50s**	18
Blarney Stone | **multi.**	14
Boss Tweed's | **LES**	17

SPECIAL APPEALS

Name	Rating
Brooklyn Public | **Ft Greene**	17
Bua | **E Vill**	21
Central Bar | **E Vill**	19
Cherry Tree | **Park Slope**	-
Coliseum Bar | **W 50s**	15
Connolly's | **multi.**	17
Dead Poet | **W 80s**	20
Doc Watson's | **E 70s**	17
Donnybrook | **LES**	-
Dorrian's | **E 80s**	17
Druids | **W 50s**	21
Dublin House | **W 70s**	17
Dublin 6 | **W Vill**	21
Eamonn's | **multi.**	17
11th St. Bar | **E Vill**	20
Emmett O'Lunney's | **W 50s**	21
Failte | **Murray Hill**	17
Fiddlesticks | **W Vill**	16
Finnegans Wake | **E 70s**	19
Finnerty's | **E Vill**	20
Fitzgerald's | **Murray Hill**	-
Full Shilling | **Financial**	16
Gaf Bar | **W 40s**	16
Galway Hooker | **multi.**	18
Genesis | **E 80s**	19
George Keeley | **W 80s**	21
Globe | **Gramercy**	20
Gossip | **W 40s**	22
Hairy Monk | **Murray Hill**	15
Half King | **Chelsea**	20
Harefield Rd. | **W'burg**	25
Iggy's | **multi.**	15
Iona | **W'burg**	23
NEW Irish Exit | **E 50s**	-
Irish Rogue | **W 40s**	18
Jake's Saloon | **multi.**	15
Jameson's | **E 50s**	18
Johnny Foxes | **E 80s**	15
Josie Wood's | **G Vill**	17
Kinsale | **E 90s**	21
Lansdowne Rd. | **W 40s**	22
Lillie's | **Flatiron**	23
Local 138 | **LES**	-
Lucky Jack's | **LES**	-
Lunasa | **E Vill**	21
Maggie's | **E 40s**	18
McAleer's Pub | **W 80s**	15
McCormack's | **Murray Hill**	-
McFadden's | **E 40s**	15
Z McSorley's | **E Vill**	23
Molly Pitcher's | **E 80s**	16
Molly's | **Gramercy**	23
Mr. Dennehy's | **W Vill**	20
O'Flaherty's Ale | **W 40s**	19
O'Flanagan's | **E 60s**	20
O'Lunney's | **W 40s**	17
One & One | **E Vill**	16
Paddy Reilly's | **Murray Hill**	-
Paris | **Seaport**	20
Parlour | **multi.**	16
Patrick Kavanagh | **Murray Hill**	-
Peggy O'Neill's | **Coney Is**	20
Perdition | **W 40s**	19
Perfect Pint | **multi.**	20
Peter McManus | **Chelsea**	21
Pig N Whistle | **multi.**	18
P.J. Carney's | **W 50s**	20
Z P.J. Clarke's | **multi.**	21
Plug Uglies | **Gramercy**	15
Puck Fair | **SoHo**	20
Ryan's Daughter | **E 80s**	18
Ryan's Irish Pub | **E Vill**	17
Scratcher | **E Vill**	21
Sixth Ward | **LES**	20
Sláinte | **NoHo**	17
Social | **W 40s**	16
St. Dymphna's | **E Vill**	22
Stout | **Garment**	20
Z Sweet Afton | **Astoria**	25
Swift | **NoHo**	22
T.G. Whitney's | **E 50s**	16
Thirsty Scholar | **E Vill**	17
Tír na Nóg | **Garment**	18
Z Ulysses | **Financial**	20
Wicked Monk | **Bay Ridge**	21
Wilfie & Nell | **W Vill**	24

LATIN

Name	Rating
Agozar! | **NoHo**	18
Barrio Chino | **LES**	22
NEW Casa Mezcal | **LES**	-
El Morocco | **Harlem**	20
Escuelita | **Garment**	21
LQ | **E 40s**	18
Nuyorican Poets | **E Vill**	23
S.O.B.'s | **Hudson Square**	21
Tapeo 29 | **LES**	25
Zinc Bar | **G Vill**	19

MOROCCAN

Name	Rating
Babel Lounge | **E Vill**	-
Bar Six | **G Vill**	21
Karma | **E Vill**	23
Katra | **LES**	16
Kush | **LES**	19
Le Souk | **G Vill**	22
Z Plaza Athénée | **E 60s**	27
Shalel Lounge | **W 70s**	23
Sway | **Hudson Square**	20
Zinc Bar | **G Vill**	19

RUSSIAN

KGB | **E Vill**	20
🏠 Pravda | **NoLita**	22
Russian Vodka Rm. | **W 50s**	23

FRAT HOUSE

Amity Hall | **G Vill**	-
Automatic Slims | **W Vill**	19
Bar 515 | **Murray Hill**	14
Bar Great Harry | **Carroll Gdns**	21
Bar None | **E Vill**	12
Barrow St. Ale | **W Vill**	18
NEW Bar 29 | **Murray Hill**	-
BB&R | **E 80s**	18
NEW Bierhaus | **E 40s**	-
NEW Billy Hurricane's | **E Vill**	-
Black Bear | **Gramercy**	18
BlackFinn | **E 50s**	16
Black Sheep | **Murray Hill**	18
Blackstone's | **E 50s**	18
Bleecker Heights | **W Vill**	-
Bleecker St. Bar | **NoHo**	17
NEW Blue Haven | **G Vill**	-
Bounce | **E 70s**	17
Bourbon St. | **W 70s**	16
🏠 Brother Jimmy | **multi.**	17
Bull's Head | **Gramercy**	16
Calico Jack's | **E 40s**	16
Croxley Ales | **E Vill**	19
NEW Delta House | **E 80s**	-
Dewey's | **Flatiron**	14
Dive Bar | **W 90s**	18
Doc Watson's | **E 70s**	17
Donnybrook | **LES**	-
Down the Hatch | **W Vill**	16
NEW Draft | **LES**	-
1849 | **W Vill**	17
Fiddlesticks | **W Vill**	16
Genesis | **E 80s**	19
Gin Mill | **W 80s**	17
Half Pint | **G Vill**	21
Hill | **Murray Hill**	16
Iggy's | **E 70s**	15
NEW Irish Exit | **E 50s**	-
Jake's Dilemma | **W 80s**	17
Jeremy's Ale | **Financial**	17
Joshua Tree | **Murray Hill**	15
Josie Wood's | **G Vill**	17
Lucky Jack's | **LES**	-
MacDougal St. Ale | **G Vill**	18
Mad River | **E 80s**	13
Manny's | **E 90s**	19
McFadden's | **E 40s**	15
Molly Pitcher's | **E 80s**	16
No Idea | **Flatiron**	15
Off the Wagon | **G Vill**	17

123 Burger | **W 50s**	19
Peculier Pub | **G Vill**	20
Professor Thom's | **E Vill**	19
Raccoon Lodge | **TriBeCa**	18
Rathbones | **E 80s**	16
Ryan's Daughter | **E 80s**	18
Saloon | **E 80s**	18
Ship of Fools | **E 80s**	15
SideBar | **Gramercy**	18
Sláinte | **NoHo**	17
NEW Snap | **W Vill**	-
Social | **W 40s**	16
Southside | **L Italy**	20
Spring Lounge | **NoLita**	19
Still | **Gramercy**	-
St. Marks Ale | **E Vill**	18
Stout | **Garment**	20
Stumble Inn | **E 70s**	20
Sutton Place | **E 50s**	17
Third & Long | **Murray Hill**	13
NEW 13th Step | **E Vill**	-
Tonic | **Murray Hill**	16
Tortilla Flats | **W Vill**	21
Traffic | **E 50s**	22
Turtle Bay | **E 50s**	14
12th St. Ale | **E Vill**	19
Whiskey River | **Murray Hill**	20
Wicker Park | **E 80s**	17
NEW Windsor | **W Vill**	-
Woody McHale's | **W Vill**	20

GAMES

BOARD GAMES

Abilene | **Carroll Gdns**	23
Amsterdam Tavern | **W 100s**	19
NEW Banter | **W'burg**	-
Bar Great Harry | **Carroll Gdns**	21
Barramundi | **LES**	21
BB&R | **E 80s**	18
🏠 Bell House | **Gowanus**	24
Biddys Pub | **E 90s**	-
Black Bear | **Gramercy**	18
Black Rabbit | **Greenpt**	24
Blue & Gold | **E Vill**	16
Broadway Dive | **W 100s**	18
Brooklyn Inn | **Boerum Hill**	25
B61 | **Carroll Gdns**	-
Buttermilk | **Park Slope**	21
Camp | **Boerum Hill**	21
Cherry Tree | **Park Slope**	-
Common Ground | **E Vill**	18
🏠 D.B.A. | **E Vill**	22
Dive 75 | **W 70s**	19
NEW Draft | **LES**	-
Dram Shop | **Park Slope**	18

Dublin 6	**W Vill**	21
Emmett O'Lunney's	**W 50s**	21
Fat Cat	**W Vill**	21
Heathers	**E Vill**	-
Hog Pit	**Chelsea**	14
Huckleberry	**W'burg**	24
Levee	**W'burg**	-
Lion's Head	**W 100s**	19
Lunasa	**E Vill**	21
🅩 Mission Dolores	**Park Slope**	-
Pacific Standard	**Boerum Hill**	22
NEW Réunion Surf Bar	**W 40s**	-
675 Bar	**Meatpacking**	25
NEW Snap	**W Vill**	-
Solas	**E Vill**	20
Tea Lounge	**Park Slope**	22
V Bar	**G Vill**	22
NEW W Downtown	**Financial**	-
Wogies	**W Vill**	15
World Bar	**E 40s**	19
Zombie Hut	**Carroll Gdns**	23

BOCCE BALL

Floyd, NY	**Bklyn Hts**	20
🅩 Union Hall	**Park Slope**	24

BOWLING

Bowlmor	**multi.**	20
🅩 Brooklyn Bowl	**W'burg**	27
Frames	**W 40s**	23
Gutter	**Greenpt**	19
Harlem Lanes	**Harlem**	20
Lucky Strike Lns.	**W 40s**	22
300 New York	**Chelsea**	21

DARTS

Ace Bar	**E Vill**	21
Amsterdam Billiards	**E Vill**	17
An Béal Bocht	**Bronx**	22
Angry Wade's	**Cobble Hill**	16
Barcelona Bar	**W 50s**	21
Barfly	**Gramercy**	16
Bar None	**E Vill**	12
Barrow St. Ale	**W Vill**	18
Beer Garden	**SI**	21
Berry Park	**W'burg**	-
Biddys Pub	**E 90s**	-
Billymark's West	**Chelsea**	16
Black Bear	**Gramercy**	18
Blackstone's	**E 50s**	18
Blarney Stone	**multi.**	14
Bleecker St. Bar	**NoHo**	17
Boss Tweed's	**LES**	17
Boxers	**Flatiron**	-
Brazen Head	**Boerum Hill**	20
Broadway Dive	**W 100s**	18

Brooklyn Ale	**W'burg**	23
Bull's Head	**Gramercy**	16
Cherry Tree	**Park Slope**	-
Coyote Ugly	**E Vill**	15
Danny & Eddie's	**E 80s**	-
David Copperfield	**E 70s**	20
Doc Watson's	**E 70s**	17
Dram Shop	**Park Slope**	18
Eamonn's	**multi.**	17
Fat Black Pussycat	**G Vill**	17
Fiddlesticks	**W Vill**	16
Finnerty's	**E Vill**	20
Fitzgerald's	**Murray Hill**	-
Gaf Bar	**multi.**	16
Galway Hooker	**Murray Hill**	18
Gate	**Park Slope**	20
George Keeley	**W 80s**	21
NEW Good Co.	**W'burg**	-
Grassroots	**E Vill**	19
GYM Sportsbar	**Chelsea**	20
Josie Wood's	**G Vill**	17
Kettle of Fish	**W Vill**	19
Lansdowne Rd.	**W 40s**	22
Lion's Head	**W 100s**	19
Loki	**Park Slope**	19
MacDougal St. Ale	**G Vill**	18
Manny's	**E 90s**	19
McAleer's Pub	**W 80s**	15
Molly Pitcher's	**E 80s**	16
O'Flaherty's Ale	**W 40s**	19
169 Bar	**LES**	18
Overlook Lounge	**E 40s**	18
Pacific Standard	**Boerum Hill**	22
Paddy Reilly's	**Murray Hill**	-
P&G Cafe	**W 70s**	21
Patriot Saloon	**TriBeCa**	16
Peggy O'Neill's	**Coney Is**	20
Puffy's	**TriBeCa**	14
Rock Shop	**Park Slope**	-
Ryan's Daughter	**E 80s**	18
Ship of Fools	**E 80s**	15
Southpaw	**Park Slope**	20
Stag's Head	**E 50s**	22
Stillwater	**E Vill**	-
Stout	**Garment**	20
1020 Bar	**W 100s**	17
T.G. Whitney's	**E 50s**	16
Thirsty Scholar	**E Vill**	17
Tonic	**Murray Hill**	16
Triona's	**G Vill**	-
Turkey's Nest	**W'burg**	19
Underground Lounge	**W 100s**	15
Union Pool	**W'burg**	19
Wicked Monk	**Bay Ridge**	21
Zablozki's	**W'burg**	21

Vote at ZAGAT.com

FOOSBALL

Amsterdam Billiards | **E Vill**	17
Apt. 138 | **Cobble Hill**	23
Bar 4 | **Park Slope**	19
B-Side | **E Vill**	22
Down the Hatch | **W Vill**	16
Fat Cat | **W Vill**	21
Finnerty's | **E Vill**	20
Hog Pit | **Chelsea**	14
Jake's Dilemma | **W 80s**	17
Luca Bar/Lounge | **E Vill**	17
Matchless | **Greenpt**	21
Off the Wagon | **G Vill**	17
Parkside | **LES**	-
Royal Oak | **W'burg**	18
675 Bar | **Meatpacking**	25
☒ Whiskey Brooklyn | **W'burg**	-

PINBALL

Ace Bar | **E Vill**	21
Amsterdam Billiards | **E Vill**	17
Bar Carrera | **E Vill**	21
Bar Great Harry | **Carroll Gdns**	21
Barracuda | **Chelsea**	19
☒ Bell House | **Gowanus**	24
Boat | **Boerum Hill**	22
Buttermilk | **Park Slope**	21
Daddy's | **W'burg**	-
Double Down | **E Vill**	-
Eamonn's | **TriBeCa**	17
Easternbloc | **E Vill**	18
Enid's | **Greenpt**	22
Fontana's | **LES**	21
Frames | **W 40s**	23
Hi-Fi | **E Vill**	20
Irish Rogue | **W 40s**	18
Kettle of Fish | **W Vill**	19
Levee | **W'burg**	-
Lucy's | **E Vill**	20
Max Fish | **LES**	19
☒ Mission Dolores | **Park Slope**	-
Motor City | **LES**	16
Mug's Ale | **W'burg**	20
Otto's Shrunken | **E Vill**	18
Pacific Standard | **Boerum Hill**	22
Rawhide | **Chelsea**	16
7B | **E Vill**	19
Southpaw | **Park Slope**	20
Zablozki's | **W'burg**	21

PING-PONG

B61 | **Carroll Gdns**	-
Fat Cat | **W Vill**	21
☒ Frying Pan | **Chelsea**	26
☒☒☒ Good Co. | **W'burg**	-
Iona | **W'burg**	23

Slate | **Flatiron**	20
Spin New York | **Flatiron**	-
☒ Standard Biergarten | **Meatpacking**	24
T.B.D. | **Greenpt**	-

POOL HALLS

Amsterdam Billiards | **E Vill**	17
Fat Cat | **W Vill**	21
Slate | **Flatiron**	20
Soho Billiards | **NoHo**	19

POOL TABLES
(See also Pool Halls)

Abbey | **W'burg**	20
Ace Bar | **E Vill**	21
Alligator | **W'burg**	19
Angry Wade's | **Cobble Hill**	16
Antarctica | **Hudson Square**	17
Apt. 138 | **Cobble Hill**	23
Arctica | **Murray Hill**	17
Barcade | **W'burg**	25
Barfly | **Gramercy**	16
Bar None | **E Vill**	12
Barracuda | **Chelsea**	19
Barrow St. Ale | **W Vill**	18
☒☒☒ Bar 29 | **Murray Hill**	-
BB&R | **E 80s**	18
Billymark's West | **Chelsea**	16
Blackstone's | **E 50s**	18
Blarney Stone | **multi.**	14
Bleecker St. Bar | **NoHo**	17
Blondies | **W 70s**	18
Blue & Gold | **E Vill**	16
Boiler Room | **E Vill**	18
Boss Tweed's | **LES**	17
Boxers | **Flatiron**	-
☒☒☒ Branded Saloon | **Prospect Hts**	-
Brooklyn Ale | **W'burg**	23
Brooklyn Inn | **Boerum Hill**	25
Brooklyn Social | **Carroll Gdns**	22
B61 | **Carroll Gdns**	-
Bull's Head | **Gramercy**	16
☒☒☒ Buskers | **G Vill**	-
Cargo | **SI**	20
Cherry Tavern | **E Vill**	17
Crash Mansion | **LES**	15
Creek & the Cave | **LIC**	-
Danny & Eddie's | **E 80s**	-
Dewey's | **Flatiron**	14
Dive Bar | **W 90s**	18
Doc Holliday's | **E Vill**	18
Doc Watson's | **E 70s**	17
Double Down | **E Vill**	-
Dram Shop | **Park Slope**	18
Eagle | **Chelsea**	21

SPECIAL APPEALS

Name	Rating
East End Tav. | E 80s	17
Europa | Greenpt	19
Failte | Murray Hill	17
Fat Black Pussycat | G Vill	17
Fiddlesticks | W Vill	16
Finnerty's | E Vill	20
Fontana's | LES	21
☑ 40/40 | Flatiron	19
Galway Hooker | multi.	18
Ginger's | Park Slope	18
GYM Sportsbar | Chelsea	20
Henrietta Hudson | W Vill	20
Hi-Fi | E Vill	20
Hog Pit | Chelsea	14
Hogs & Heifers | Meatpacking	18
☑ Hudson Hotel | W 50s	24
NEW Industry Bar | W 50s	-
Irish Rogue | W 40s	18
Jack Russell's | E 80s	17
Jake's Dilemma | W 80s	17
Josie Wood's | G Vill	17
Lansdowne Rd. | W 40s	22
Latitude | W 40s	15
Levee | W'burg	-
Loki | Park Slope	19
Lucky Jack's | LES	-
Lucky Strike Lns. | W 40s	22
Lucy's | E Vill	20
MacDougal St. Ale | G Vill	18
Manny's | E 90s	19
Matchless | Greenpt	21
Max Fish | LES	19
Metropolitan | W'burg	18
Milady's | SoHo	15
M1-5 Bar | TriBeCa	17
No Idea | Flatiron	15
Nowhere | E Vill	21
O'Flaherty's Ale | W 40s	19
O'Flanagan's | E 60s	20
169 Bar | LES	18
Overlook Lounge | E 40s	18
Paddy Reilly's | Murray Hill	-
P&G Cafe | W 70s	21
Parkside | LES	-
Parlour | multi.	16
Patriot Saloon | TriBeCa	16
Phoenix | E Vill	21
Pieces | W Vill	17
Plug Uglies | Gramercy	15
Prohibition | W 80s	19
Raccoon Lodge | TriBeCa	18
Rawhide | Chelsea	16
Reservoir Bar | G Vill	15
Rockbar | W Vill	-
Rock Shop | Park Slope	-
☑ Rose Bar | Gramercy	25
☑ Rusty Knot | W Vill	20
Ryan's Daughter | E 80s	18
Ship of Fools | E 80s	15
675 Bar | Meatpacking	25
Sixth Ward | LES	20
Skinny | LES	-
Slaughtered Lamb | W Vill	17
Sophie's | E Vill	19
Southpaw | Park Slope	20
Stillwater | E Vill	-
Stonewall Inn | W Vill	16
Stout | Garment	20
Sugarland | W'burg	-
1020 Bar | W 100s	17
Trash | W'burg	15
Tribeca Tav. | TriBeCa	17
Triona's | G Vill	-
Turkey's Nest | W'burg	19
200 Fifth | Park Slope	17
Uncle Charlie's | LES	21
Webster Hall | E Vill	18
Welcome/Johnsons | LES	15
Whiskey Park | W 50s	20
Whiskey Ward | LES	23
NEW White Noise | E Vill	-
Wicked Monk | Bay Ridge	21
Wicked Willy's | G Vill	17
Woody's | E Vill	-
Zablozki's | W'burg	21

SKEE-BALL

Name	Rating
Ace Bar | E Vill	21
☑ Brother Jimmy | multi.	17
Crocodile Lounge | E Vill	19
Dave & Buster's | W 40s	17
Full Circle Bar | W'burg	-

TRIVIA NIGHTS

Name	Rating
Abbey Pub | W 100s	21
An Béal Bocht | Bronx	22
Baker Street | E 60s	17
Bar Great Harry | Carroll Gdns	21
☑ Bell House | Gowanus	24
Black Rabbit | Greenpt	24
Blarney Stone | Garment	14
Cargo | SI	20
Dewey's | Flatiron	14
Double Down | E Vill	-
Excelsior | Park Slope	19
Flight 151 | Chelsea	16
Henrietta Hudson | W Vill	20
Iggy's | multi.	15
Johnny Foxes | E 80s	15
King's Head | E Vill	16
Last Exit | Cobble Hill	18

Otto's Shrunken | **E Vill**	18
Pete's Candy | **W'burg**	25
P.J. Hanley's | **Carroll Gdns**	-
Professor Thom's | **E Vill**	19
NEW Réunion Surf Bar | **W 40s**	-
SideBar | **Gramercy**	18
Skinny | **LES**	-
NEW Snap | **W Vill**	-
Soft Spot | **W'burg**	-
Stonewall Inn | **W Vill**	16
Third & Long | **Murray Hill**	13
Tortilla Flats | **W Vill**	21
Twelve | **Murray Hill**	18

VIDEO GAMES

Abbey | **W'burg**	20
Ace Bar | **E Vill**	21
Alligator | **W'burg**	19
Apt. 138 | **Cobble Hill**	23
Arrow | **E Vill**	20
Barcade | **W'burg**	25
Barcelona Bar | **W 50s**	21
Barfly | **Gramercy**	16
Bar 4 | **Park Slope**	19
Bar Nine | **W 50s**	18
Bar None | **E Vill**	12
Barrow St. Ale | **W Vill**	18
BB&R | **E 80s**	18
Beer Garden | **SI**	21
Big Nose Kate's | **SI**	19
Billymark's West | **Chelsea**	16
Black Bear | **Gramercy**	18
Blackstone's | **E 50s**	18
Blarney Stone | **multi.**	14
Bleecker Heights | **W Vill**	-
Bleecker St. Bar | **NoHo**	17
Boat | **Boerum Hill**	22
Z Bohemian Hall | **Astoria**	25
Boiler Room | **E Vill**	18
Boss Tweed's | **LES**	17
Broadway Dive | **W 100s**	18
Z Brother Jimmy | **multi.**	17
Bull's Head | **Gramercy**	16
Bushwick Country | **W'burg**	17
Buttermilk | **Park Slope**	21
Chelsea Brewing | **Chelsea**	20
Cherry Tavern | **E Vill**	17
Cherry Tree | **Park Slope**	-
Coyote Ugly | **E Vill**	15
Crash Mansion | **LES**	15
Crocodile Lounge | **E Vill**	19
Daddy's | **W'burg**	-
Danny & Eddie's | **E 80s**	-
Dave & Buster's | **W 40s**	17
David Copperfield | **E 70s**	20

Z D.B.A. | **W'burg**	22
Dead Poet | **W 80s**	20
Ding Dong Lounge | **W 100s**	18
Dive Bar | **W 90s**	18
Doc Holliday's | **E Vill**	18
Doc Watson's | **E 70s**	17
Double Down | **E Vill**	-
Down the Hatch | **W Vill**	16
Dublin House | **W 70s**	17
Duplex | **W Vill**	20
Eagle | **Chelsea**	21
East End Tav. | **E 80s**	17
Enid's | **Greenpt**	22
Europa | **Greenpt**	19
Failte | **Murray Hill**	17
Fat Black Pussycat | **G Vill**	17
Flight 151 | **Chelsea**	16
Fourth Ave. Pub | **Park Slope**	-
Frames | **W 40s**	23
Gaf Bar | **multi.**	16
George Keeley | **W 80s**	21
Ginger's | **Park Slope**	18
GYM Sportsbar | **Chelsea**	20
Harlem Lanes | **Harlem**	20
Hi-Fi | **E Vill**	20
Hog Pit | **Chelsea**	14
Hogs & Heifers | **Meatpacking**	18
Home Sweet Home | **LES**	18
Hop Devil Grill | **E Vill**	18
Iggy's | **multi.**	15
Iona | **W'burg**	23
Jack Russell's | **E 80s**	17
Jake's Dilemma | **W 80s**	17
Jekyll & Hyde | **W Vill**	18
Jeremy's Ale | **Financial**	17
Jimmy's Corner | **W 40s**	21
Johnny Foxes | **E 80s**	15
Johnny's Bar | **W Vill**	-
Josie Wood's | **G Vill**	17
Julius | **W Vill**	16
Kenny's Castaways | **G Vill**	19
Kettle of Fish | **W Vill**	19
Lakeside Lounge | **E Vill**	21
Levee | **W'burg**	-
Library | **E Vill**	21
Lion's Head | **W 100s**	19
Luca Bar/Lounge | **E Vill**	17
Lucy's | **E Vill**	20
Manny's | **E 90s**	19
McAleer's Pub | **W 80s**	15
Metropolitan | **W'burg**	18
Milady's | **SoHo**	15
Molly Pitcher's | **E 80s**	16
Motor City | **LES**	16
Nevada Smith's | **E Vill**	16

No Idea | **Flatiron**	15
Nowhere | **E Vill**	21
Otto's Shrunken | **E Vill**	18
P&G Cafe | **W 70s**	21
Paris | **Seaport**	20
Parkside | **LES**	-
Patriot Saloon | **TriBeCa**	16
Peculier Pub | **G Vill**	20
Peggy O'Neill's | **Coney Is**	20
Peter McManus | **Chelsea**	21
Phoenix | **E Vill**	21
Pine Tree Lodge | **Murray Hill**	21
Raccoon Lodge | **TriBeCa**	18
Rawhide | **Chelsea**	16
Reservoir Bar | **G Vill**	15
Rudy's | **W 40s**	20
Ryan's Daughter | **E 80s**	18
7B | **E Vill**	19
Ship of Fools | **E 80s**	15
Sidecar | **Park Slope**	24
675 Bar | **Meatpacking**	25
Skinny | **LES**	-
Slaughtered Lamb | **W Vill**	17
NEW Snap | **W Vill**	-
Sophie's | **E Vill**	19
Southpaw | **Park Slope**	20
Stanton Public | **LES**	22
Stillwater | **E Vill**	-
St. Marks Ale | **E Vill**	18
Subway Inn | **E 60s**	18
Sugarland | **W'burg**	-
Tea Lounge | **Park Slope**	22
T.G. Whitney's | **E 50s**	16
Trash | **W'burg**	15
Tribeca Tav. | **TriBeCa**	17
Turkey's Nest | **W'burg**	19
Underground Lounge | **W 100s**	15
Village Pourhouse | **W 100s**	15
Z Warren 77 | **TriBeCa**	20
Welcome/Johnsons | **LES**	15
Wharf Bar & Grill | **Murray Hill**	18
NEW Whiskey Brooklyn | **W'burg**	-
Whiskey River | **Murray Hill**	20
Wicked Monk | **Bay Ridge**	21
Wicked Willy's | **G Vill**	17
xes lounge | **Chelsea**	21
Yankee Tav. | **Bronx**	20

GAY

(See also Lesbian; * certain nights only)

Barracuda | **Chelsea**	19
Barrage | **W 40s**	19
Bar-Tini | **W 40s**	-
Boiler Room | **E Vill**	18

Boxers | **Flatiron**	-
Cock | **E Vill**	17
Eagle | **Chelsea**	21
Easternbloc | **E Vill**	18
Escuelita | **Garment**	21
Excelsior | **Park Slope**	19
g | **Chelsea**	21
GYM Sportsbar | **Chelsea**	20
NEW Industry Bar | **W 50s**	-
Julius | **W Vill**	16
Lips | **E 50s**	20
Marie's Crisis | **W Vill**	24
Metropolitan | **W'burg**	18
Monster | **W Vill**	21
Nowhere | **E Vill**	21
Phoenix | **E Vill**	21
Pieces | **W Vill**	17
Posh | **W 50s**	18
Pyramid* | **E Vill**	18
Rawhide | **Chelsea**	16
Ritz | **W 40s**	23
Rockbar | **W Vill**	-
Splash | **Flatiron**	21
Stonewall Inn | **W Vill**	16
Sugarland | **W'burg**	-
Suite | **W 100s**	-
Therapy | **W 50s**	22
Townhouse | **E 50s**	20
Uncle Charlie's | **multi.**	21
Urge | **E Vill**	18
Vig 27 | **Murray Hill**	17
VIP Club* | **Flatiron**	23
Vlada | **W 50s**	21
Woody's | **E Vill**	-
xes lounge | **Chelsea**	21

HAPPY HOUR

Abilene | **Carroll Gdns**	23
Agozar! | **NoHo**	18
Angry Wade's | **Cobble Hill**	16
Baker Street | **E 60s**	17
Bar None | **E Vill**	12
Barrage | **W 40s**	19
Barrow St. Ale | **W Vill**	18
Black Sheep | **Murray Hill**	18
Bleecker St. Bar | **NoHo**	17
Blondies | **W 70s**	18
Blue Owl | **E Vill**	20
Bob | **LES**	21
Boss Tweed's | **LES**	17
Botanica | **NoLita**	20
Bounce | **E 70s**	17
Bourbon St. | **W 70s**	16
Boxcar Lounge | **E Vill**	18
Brazen Head | **Boerum Hill**	20

Brother Jimmy | **multi.** — `17`
Bull's Head | **Gramercy** — `16`
Calico Jack's | **E 40s** — `16`
Continental | **E Vill** — `17`
Cornerstone Tav. | **E 50s** — `19`
David Copperfield | **E 70s** — `20`
Dead Poet | **W 80s** — `20`
Dewey's | **Flatiron** — `14`
Doc Holliday's | **E Vill** — `18`
Down the Hatch | **W Vill** — `16`
Drop Off Service | **E Vill** — `21`
East End Tav. | **E 80s** — `17`
Enid's | **Greenpt** — `22`
Epstein's Bar | **LES** — `16`
Fat Black Pussycat | **G Vill** — `17`
Flight 151 | **Chelsea** — `16`
420 | **W 80s** — `18`
Full Shilling | **Financial** — `16`
g | **Chelsea** — `21`
Gate | **Park Slope** — `20`
George Keeley | **W 80s** — `21`
Gin Mill | **W 80s** — `17`
Hairy Monk | **Murray Hill** — `15`
Heights B&G | **W 100s** — `17`
Houndstooth | **Garment** — `21`
Iggy's | **E 70s** — `15`
NEW Industry Bar | **W 50s** — `-`
Jake's Dilemma | **W 80s** — `17`
Jameson's | **E 50s** — `18`
Johnny Foxes | **E 80s** — `15`
Johnny's Bar | **W Vill** — `-`
Karma | **E Vill** — `23`
Katwalk | **Garment** — `16`
Kenny's Castaways | **G Vill** — `19`
Keybar | **E Vill** — `19`
Lakeside Lounge | **E Vill** — `21`
Latitude | **W 40s** — `15`
Lit | **E Vill** — `18`
Local 138 | **LES** — `-`
Lolita | **LES** — `20`
Mad River | **E 80s** — `13`
Manitoba's | **E Vill** — `25`
Metropolitan | **W'burg** — `18`
Nancy Whiskey | **TriBeCa** — `16`
Off the Wagon | **G Vill** — `17`
O'Flaherty's Ale | **W 40s** — `19`
Opal | **E 50s** — `16`
Paddy Reilly's | **Murray Hill** — `-`
Parlour | **W 80s** — `16`
Pieces | **W Vill** — `17`
Plug Uglies | **Gramercy** — `15`
Posh | **W 50s** — `18`
PS 450 | **Murray Hill** — `20`
Raccoon Lodge | **TriBeCa** — `18`
Rawhide | **Chelsea** — `16`

Riviera | **W Vill** — `19`
Russian Vodka Rm. | **W 50s** — `23`
Sapphire | **LES** — `18`
7B | **E Vill** — `19`
Shade | **G Vill** — `24`
Ship of Fools | **E 80s** — `15`
Sláinte | **NoHo** — `17`
Soft Spot | **W'burg** — `-`
Splash | **Flatiron** — `21`
St. Dymphna's | **E Vill** — `22`
Stitch | **Garment** — `19`
St. Marks Ale | **E Vill** — `18`
T.G. Whitney's | **E 50s** — `16`
Thirsty Scholar | **E Vill** — `17`
Tortilla Flats | **W Vill** — `21`
Turtle Bay | **E 50s** — `14`
Union Bar | **Union Sq** — `17`
Verlaine | **LES** — `21`
Vertigo | **Murray Hill** — `20`
Washington Commons | **Prospect Hts** — `-`
WCOU | **E Vill** — `-`
Welcome/Johnsons | **LES** — `15`
WXOU | **W Vill** — `22`
xes lounge | **Chelsea** — `21`

HOOKAHS

Babel Lounge | **E Vill** — `-`
NEW Hash Fifty Five | **W 50s** — `-`
Karma | **E Vill** — `23`
Katra | **LES** — `16`
Kush | **LES** — `19`
Le Souk | **G Vill** — `22`

HOTEL BARS

Ace Hotel
    Z Ace Hotel | **Chelsea** — `25`
Algonquin Hotel
    Algonquin | **W 40s** — `23`
    Z Oak Room | **W 40s** — `25`
Andaz 5th Avenue Hotel
    NEW Bar Downstairs | **E 40s** — `-`
Andaz Wall Street Hotel
    Bar Seven Five | **Financial** — `-`
Beekman Tower Hotel
    Z Top of the Tower | **E 40s** — `26`
Bowery Hotel
    Bowery Hotel | **E Vill** — `24`
Bryant Park Hotel
    Cellar Bar | **W 40s** — `21`
Carlton Hotel
    NEW Salon Millesime | **Murray Hill** — `-`
Carlyle Hotel
    Z Bemelmans | **E 70s** — `27`
    Z Cafe Carlyle | **E 70s** — `27`

SPECIAL APPEALS

Chelsea Hotel
  NEW Chelsea Room | **Chelsea** ⌐

Cooper Square Hotel
  NEW Trilby | **E Vill** ⌐

Crosby Street Hotel
  Crosby Bar | **SoHo** 24

Dream Hotel
  Z Ava Lounge | **W 50s** 23

Edison Hotel
  Rum House | **W 40s** ⌐

Elysée Hotel
  Z Monkey Bar | **E 50s** 23

Empire Hotel
  Empire Hotel Bar | **W 60s** 22
  Z Empire Hotel Roof | **W 60s** 24

Fashion 26 Hotel
  Rare View | **Chelsea** 24

Flatotel
  Moda Outdoors | **W 50s** ⌐

Four Seasons Hotel
  Z Four Seasons/Bar | **E 50s** 26

Gansevoort Hotel
  Z Plunge | **Meatpacking** 26
  Z Provocateur | **Meatpacking** ⌐

Gansevoort Park Hotel
  NEW Gansevoort Park | ⌐
  Murray Hill

Gramercy Park Hotel
  Z NEW Gramercy Terr. | ⌐
  Gramercy
  Jade Bar | **Gramercy** 22
  Z Rose Bar | **Gramercy** 25

Hilton Garden Inn
  NEW XVI | **W 40s** ⌐

Hotel 41 at Times Sq.
  Bar 41 | **W 40s** 23

Hudson Hotel
  Z Hudson Hotel | **W 50s** 24

Indigo Hotel
  Glass Bar | **Chelsea** ⌐

Ink48 Hotel
  Z Press Lounge | **W 40s** ⌐

Inn at Irving Pl.
  Cibar | **Gramercy** 22

Iroquois Hotel
  NEW Lantern's Keep | **W 40s** ⌐

James Hotel
  Z NEW Jimmy | **SoHo** ⌐

Jane Hotel
  Z Jane Hotel | **W Vill** 26

Kimberly Hotel
  NEW Upstairs | **E 50s** ⌐

Library Hotel
  Bookmarks | **E 40s** 24

Loews Regency Hotel
  Z Feinstein's/Loews | **E 60s** 26
  Regency Library Bar | **E 60s** 23

Mandarin Oriental Hotel
  Z MO Bar | **W 60s** 24

Mansfield Hotel
  M Bar | **W 40s** 24

Marcel at Gramercy Hotel
  Polar | **Murray Hill** ⌐

Maritime Hotel
  Cabanas | **Chelsea** 22
  Hiro | **Chelsea** 20

Marriott Fairfield Inn
  Sky Room | **Garment** ⌐

Mercer Hotel
  Mercer Bar | **SoHo** 22
  SubMercer | **SoHo** 24

Metro Hotel
  Metro Grill Roof | **Garment** 23

Mondrian Soho Hotel
  NEW Mister H | **SoHo** ⌐

Paramount Hotel
  Paramount Bar | **W 40s** ⌐

Peninsula Hotel
  Z Salon de Ning | **W 50s** 25

Pierre Hotel
  Two E | **E 60s** ⌐

Plaza Athénée Hotel
  Z Plaza Athénée | **E 60s** 27

Plaza Hotel
  Champagne Bar/Plaza | 24
  W 50s
  Z Oak Bar | **W 50s** 25
  Rose Club | **W 50s** 22

Pod Hotel
  Le Bateau Ivre | **E 50s** 21

Radisson Lexington Hotel
  LQ | **E 40s** 18

Ravel Hotel
  Penthouse 808 | **LIC** ⌐

Ritz-Carlton Central Park
  Ritz-Carlton Star | **W 50s** 26

Room Mate Grace Hotel
  Gift | **W 40s** 28

Roosevelt Hotel
  Mad46 | **E 40s** 24
  Vander Bar | **E 40s** ⌐

Royalton Hotel
  Forty Four | **W 40s** 22

Setai 5th Ave. Hotel
  NEW Bar on Fifth | **Garment** ⌐

Shelburne Murray Hill Hotel
  Rare View | **Murray Hill** 24

6 Columbus Hotel
  NEW Above 6 | **W 50s** ⌐

60 Thompson Hotel	
Thom Bar	**SoHo**	25
Smyth Hotel	
NEW Toro	**TriBeCa**	–
SoHo Grand Hotel	
Grand Bar	**SoHo**	23
Standard Hotel	
Z Boom Boom	**Meatpacking**	24
Z NEW Le Bain	**Meatpacking**	–
Z Standard Biergarten	**Meatpacking**	24
St. Giles Hotel, The Court	
NEW Lex Bar	**Murray Hill**	–
Strand Hotel	
Z Top of the Strand	**Garment**	–
St. Regis Hotel	
Z King Cole Bar	**E 50s**	27
Surrey Hotel	
Z Bar Pleiades	**E 70s**	26
Thompson LES Hotel	
Above Allen	**LES**	23
Tribeca Grand Hotel	
Church Lounge	**TriBeCa**	22
Trump Soho Hotel	
Kastel	**Hudson Square**	–
W Hotel Downtown	
NEW W Downtown	**Financial**	–
W New York Hotel	
Whiskey Blue	**E 40s**	21
W Times Square Hotel	
W Times Sq.	**W 40s**	23
W Union Square Hotel	
Underbar	**Union Sq**	21
W Union Sq.	**Union Sq**	22

JAZZ CLUBS

Arthur's Tavern	**W Vill**	23
Birdland	**W 40s**	24
Z Blue Note	**G Vill**	24
Cleopatra's Needle	**W 90s**	19
Z Dizzy's Club	**W 60s**	27
Fat Cat	**W Vill**	21
55 Bar	**W Vill**	25
Garage	**W Vill**	19
Iridium	**W 50s**	21
Z Jazz Standard	**Murray Hill**	25
Lenox Lounge	**Harlem**	23
Z Smalls	**W Vill**	26
Smoke	**W 100s**	24
St. Nick's Jazz Pub	**Harlem**	23
Swing 46	**W 40s**	23
Z Village Vanguard	**W Vill**	27
Zinc Bar	**G Vill**	19

JUKEBOXES

Abbey Pub	**W 100s**	21
Ace Bar	**E Vill**	21
Alligator	**W'burg**	19
Amsterdam Tavern	**W 100s**	19
Angels & Kings	**E Vill**	17
Angry Wade's	**Cobble Hill**	16
Antarctica	**Hudson Square**	17
Apt. 138	**Cobble Hill**	23
Art Bar	**W Vill**	19
Australian	**Garment**	20
Banjo Jim's	**E Vill**	20
Barcelona Bar	**W 50s**	21
Barfly	**Gramercy**	16
Bar None	**E Vill**	12
Barrow St. Ale	**W Vill**	18
NEW Bar 29	**Murray Hill**	–
Bayard's Ale	**W Vill**	19
Beer Garden	**SI**	21
Belgian Room	**E Vill**	–
Biddys Pub	**E 90s**	–
Big Nose Kate's	**SI**	19
Billymark's West	**Chelsea**	16
Black Bear	**Gramercy**	18
Black Sheep	**Murray Hill**	18
Blackstone's	**E 50s**	18
Blarney Stone	**multi.**	14
Bleecker Heights	**W Vill**	–
Blondies	**W 70s**	18
Blue & Gold	**E Vill**	16
Boat	**Boerum Hill**	22
Z Bohemian Hall	**Astoria**	25
Boiler Room	**E Vill**	18
Boss Tweed's	**LES**	17
Bowery Wine Co.	**E Vill**	19
Broadway Dive	**W 100s**	18
Brooklyn Ale	**W'burg**	23
Brooklyn Inn	**Boerum Hill**	25
Brooklyn Social	**Carroll Gdns**	22
Broome St. Bar	**SoHo**	17
B-Side	**E Vill**	22
B61	**Carroll Gdns**	–
Bull's Head	**Gramercy**	16
Buttermilk	**Park Slope**	21
Cargo	**SI**	20
Cherry Tavern	**E Vill**	17
NEW Coal Yard	**E Vill**	–
Coliseum Bar	**W 50s**	15
Common Ground	**E Vill**	18
Commonwealth	**Park Slope**	20
Connolly's	**multi.**	17
Continental	**E Vill**	17
Coyote Ugly	**E Vill**	15
Croton Reservoir	**W 40s**	17
Cubby Hole	**W Vill**	19

SPECIAL APPEALS

Daddy's | **W'burg**	-
Danny & Eddie's | **E 80s**	-
Dark Room | **LES**	15
David Copperfield | **E 70s**	20
Dead Poet | **W 80s**	20
Diamond | **Greenpt**	-
Dive Bar | **W 90s**	18
Dive 75 | **W 70s**	19
Doc Holliday's | **E Vill**	18
Doc Watson's | **E 70s**	17
Dorrian's | **E 80s**	17
Double Down | **E Vill**	-
Dram Shop | **Park Slope**	18
Drop Off Service | **E Vill**	21
Druids | **W 50s**	21
Dublin House | **W 70s**	17
Duff's | **W'burg**	-
Eamonn's | **multi.**	17
1849 | **G Vill**	17
Excelsior | **Park Slope**	19
Faces & Names | **W 50s**	18
Fat Baby | **LES**	17
Fat Black Pussycat | **G Vill**	17
Fat Cat | **W Vill**	21
Finnerty's | **E Vill**	20
Fitzgerald's | **Murray Hill**	-
Flight 151 | **Chelsea**	16
Floyd, NY | **Bklyn Hts**	20
Fontana's | **LES**	21
Fourth Ave. Pub | **Park Slope**	-
Gaf Bar | **multi.**	16
Gate | **Park Slope**	20
Genesis | **E 80s**	19
George Keeley | **W 80s**	21
☑ Ginger Man | **Murray Hill**	21
Ginger's | **Park Slope**	18
Gossip | **W 40s**	22
Grassroots | **E Vill**	19
Great Lakes | **Park Slope**	18
Hi-Fi | **E Vill**	20
High Dive | **Park Slope**	-
Hog Pit | **Chelsea**	14
Hogs & Heifers | **Meatpacking**	18
Holiday Cocktail | **E Vill**	18
Home Sweet Home | **LES**	18
Hop Devil Grill | **E Vill**	18
Iggy's | **multi.**	15
International Bar | **E Vill**	20
Jack Russell's | **E 80s**	17
Jake's Saloon | **multi.**	15
Jameson's | **E 50s**	18
Jeremy's Ale | **Financial**	17
Jimmy's Corner | **W 40s**	21
Johnny's Bar | **W Vill**	-
Joshua Tree | **Murray Hill**	15
Josie Wood's | **G Vill**	17
Julius | **W Vill**	16
Kenny's Castaways | **G Vill**	19
Kettle of Fish | **W Vill**	19
King's Head | **E Vill**	16
Kinsale | **E 90s**	21
Lakeside Lounge | **E Vill**	21
Lenox Lounge | **Harlem**	23
Levee | **W'burg**	-
Library | **E Vill**	21
Lion's Head | **W 100s**	19
Loki | **Park Slope**	19
Lucky 13 | **Park Slope**	-
Lucy's | **E Vill**	20
MacDougal St. Ale | **G Vill**	18
Magician | **LES**	21
Mama's Bar | **E Vill**	-
Manitoba's | **E Vill**	25
Manny's | **E 90s**	19
Mars Bar | **E Vill**	19
Marshall Stack | **LES**	24
Max Fish | **LES**	19
McAleer's Pub | **W 80s**	15
McCormack's | **Murray Hill**	-
Mercury Bar | **multi.**	15
Metropolitan | **W'burg**	18
Milady's | **SoHo**	15
☑ Mission Dolores | **Park Slope**	-
Molly Pitcher's | **E 80s**	16
Molly's | **Gramercy**	23
Mug's Ale | **W'burg**	20
Nancy Whiskey | **TriBeCa**	16
No Idea | **Flatiron**	15
Nowhere | **E Vill**	21
O'Flaherty's Ale | **W 40s**	19
Paddy Reilly's | **Murray Hill**	-
P&G Cafe | **W 70s**	21
Paris | **Seaport**	20
Parkside | **LES**	-
Patrick Kavanagh | **Murray Hill**	-
Patriot Saloon | **TriBeCa**	16
Peculier Pub | **G Vill**	20
Peggy O'Neill's | **Coney Is**	20
Perfect Pint | **multi.**	20
Peter McManus | **Chelsea**	21
Pete's Tavern | **Gramercy**	21
Phoenix | **E Vill**	21
Pine Tree Lodge | **Murray Hill**	21
Pink Pony | **LES**	17
P.J. Carney's | **W 50s**	20
☑ P.J. Clarke's | **multi.**	21
Plug Uglies | **Gramercy**	15
Quarter | **Greenwood Hts**	-
Raccoon Lodge | **TriBeCa**	18
Rawhide | **Chelsea**	16

Red Sky	**Murray Hill**	17
Reservoir Bar	**G Vill**	15
Rock Shop	**Park Slope**	-
Royale	**E Vill**	21
☑ Rusty Knot	**W Vill**	20
Ryan's Daughter	**E 80s**	18
Sackett	**Park Slope**	-
Satellite Lounge	**W'burg**	-
7B	**E Vill**	19
17 Murray	**Financial**	19
Ship of Fools	**E 80s**	15
Sidecar	**Park Slope**	24
Soda Bar	**Prospect Hts**	16
Sophie's	**E Vill**	19
Spring Lounge	**NoLita**	19
Spuyten Duyvil	**W'burg**	25
Stillwater	**E Vill**	-
St. Nick's Jazz Pub	**Harlem**	23
Stone Creek	**Murray Hill**	21
Sweet & Vicious	**NoLita**	17
Teddy's	**W'burg**	24
Tom & Jerry's	**NoHo**	21
Trash	**W'burg**	15
Tribeca Tav.	**TriBeCa**	17
Trophy	**W'burg**	19
Turkey's Nest	**W'burg**	19
Twelve	**Murray Hill**	18
12th St. Ale	**E Vill**	19
Underground Lounge	**W 100s**	15
☑ Union Hall	**Park Slope**	24
Valhalla	**W 50s**	22
WCOU	**E Vill**	-
Welcome/Johnsons	**LES**	15
Wharf Bar & Grill	**Murray Hill**	18
Whiskey River	**Murray Hill**	20
Whiskey Ward	**LES**	23
White Horse	**W Vill**	19
Wicked Monk	**Bay Ridge**	21
Wicker Park	**E 80s**	17
Woody McHale's	**W Vill**	20
WXOU	**W Vill**	22
Yankee Tav.	**Bronx**	20
Zablozki's	**W'burg**	21

KARAOKE BARS

(Call to check nights, times and prices)

Karaoke One 7	**Flatiron**	-
Sing Sing	**E Vill**	19
U2 Karaoke	**E Vill**	-
Winnie's	**Chinatown**	-

LESBIAN

(* Certain nights only; call ahead)

Cubby Hole	**W Vill**	19
Ginger's	**Park Slope**	18
Henrietta Hudson	**W Vill**	20
Nowhere*	**E Vill**	21
RF Lounge	**W Vill**	-

LIVE ENTERTAINMENT

(See also Cabaret, Comedy Clubs, Drag Shows, Jazz Clubs, Karaoke Bars, Music Clubs, Piano Bars, Spoken Word, Strip Clubs)

Agozar!	Latin	**NoHo**	18
Alphabet Lounge	bands	**E Vill**	18
Bar Nine	rock	**W 50s**	18
Bar on A	blues	**E Vill**	19
☑ Bateaux NY	jazz	**Chelsea**	26
☑ Bemelmans	piano	**E 70s**	27
Big Nose Kate's	bands	**SI**	19
☑ Bohemian Hall	bands	**Astoria**	25
☑ Bubble Lounge	bands	**TriBeCa**	21
Bull's Head	bands	**Gramercy**	16
☑ Campbell Apt.	jazz	**E 40s**	25
Carnegie Club	swing	**W 50s**	23
Connolly's	bands	**W 40s**	17
Continental	rock	**E Vill**	17
Doc Watson's	Irish	**E 70s**	17
☑ Flûte	jazz	**multi.**	23
Gowanus Yacht	jazz	**Carroll Gdns**	22
Great Lakes	bands	**Park Slope**	18
Iggy's	karaoke/bands	**E 70s**	15
King's Head	rock	**E Vill**	16
Lit	karaoke	**E Vill**	18
Nevada Smith's	karaoke	**E Vill**	16
O'Flaherty's Ale	rock	**W 40s**	19
Onieal's Grand St.	jazz	**L Italy**	24
Paddy Reilly's	Irish	**Murray Hill**	-
Parkside	spoken word	**LES**	-
Parlour	comedy	**W 80s**	16
Prohibition	R&B/soul	**W 80s**	19
Rodeo Bar	bands	**Murray Hill**	19
Rue B	jazz	**E Vill**	22
Russian Vodka Rm.	jazz/piano	**W 50s**	23
St. Andrews	Celtic	**W 40s**	20
Swift	Irish	**NoHo**	22
Teddy's	bands	**W'burg**	24
T.G. Whitney's	karaoke	**E 50s**	16

MATURE CROWDS

Algonquin	**W 40s**	23
☑ Bar Pleiades	**E 70s**	26
Beekman	**E 50s**	24
☑ Bemelmans	**E 70s**	27
Buceo 95	**W 90s**	24

☑ Cafe Carlyle	E 70s	27
☑ Campbell Apt.	E 40s	25
Carnegie Club	W 50s	23
Champagne Bar/Plaza	W 50s	24
City Winery	Hudson Square	25
Club Macanudo	E 60s	24
☑ Dizzy's Club	W 60s	27
☑ Feinstein's/Loews	E 60s	26
☑ King Cole Bar	E 50s	27
Lexington Bar/Books	E 70s	22
M Bar	W 40s	24
☑ Metropolitan Rm.	Flatiron	25
Morrell Wine	W 40s	23
☑ Oak Bar	W 50s	25
☑ Oak Room	W 40s	25
Palio Bar	W 50s	23
☑ Plaza Athénée	E 60s	27
☑ Top of the Tower	E 40s	26
Townhouse	E 50s	20
Two E	E 60s	-
☑ Village Vanguard	W Vill	27
World Bar	E 40s	19

MEAT MARKETS

Amnesia	Chelsea	-
Automatic Slims	W Vill	19
Bar 515	Murray Hill	14
Barrage	W 40s	19
☑ NEW Beauty/Essex	LES	-
Belmont	Gramercy	19
NEW Bierhaus	E 40s	-
Bounce	E 70s	17
Bourbon St.	W 70s	16
☑ Brother Jimmy	multi.	17
Calico Jack's	E 40s	16
NEW Chelsea Room	Chelsea	-
Church Lounge	TriBeCa	22
Cock	E Vill	17
Dorrian's	E 80s	17
Eagle	Chelsea	21
Forum	E Vill	18
NEW Gansevoort Park	Murray Hill	-
GYM Sportsbar	Chelsea	20
☑ Hudson Hotel	W 50s	24
Iguana	W 50s	20
NEW Industry Bar	W 50s	-
Joshua Tree	Murray Hill	15
Kiss & Fly	Meatpacking	20
☑ NEW Lavo	E 50s	-
Libation	LES	16
Mad River	E 80s	13
McFadden's	E 40s	15
Naked Lunch	SoHo	18
Nikki Midtown	E 50s	20
Opal	E 50s	16

Parlour	multi.	16
☑ Plunge	Meatpacking	26
PS 450	Murray Hill	20
Redemption	E 50s	21
Red Sky	Murray Hill	17
Revival	Gramercy	19
Saloon	E 80s	18
Splash	Flatiron	21
☑ Standard Biergarten	Meatpacking	24
Sutton Place	E 50s	17
Therapy	W 50s	22
13	G Vill	18
NEW 13th Step	E Vill	-
Tonic	Murray Hill	16
Tortilla Flats	W Vill	21
Traffic	E 50s	22
Turtle Bay	E 50s	14
2A	E Vill	20
☑ 230 Fifth	Chelsea	23
Underbar	Union Sq	21
Vlada	W 50s	21
Webster Hall	E Vill	18
Whiskey Blue	E 40s	21
Whiskey Park	W 50s	20
xes lounge	Chelsea	21

MUSIC CLUBS

(See also Jazz Clubs)

Arlene's Grocery	LES	20
Back Fence	G Vill	19
Banjo Jim's	E Vill	20
☑ B. B. King Blues	W 40s	21
Beacon Theatre	W 70s	23
☑ Bell House	Gowanus	24
Bitter End	G Vill	20
Bowery Ballroom	LES	23
Bowery Electric	E Vill	18
☑ Brooklyn Bowl	W'burg	27
Cafe Wha?	G Vill	19
Cake Shop	LES	21
Canal Room	TriBeCa	21
City Winery	Hudson Square	25
Delancey	LES	19
El Morocco	Harlem	20
Europa	Greenpt	19
Fat Baby	LES	17
Fontana's	LES	21
Galapagos	Dumbo	21
Hammerstein	Garment	19
Highline Ballrm.	Chelsea	21
Irving Plaza	Gramercy	19
Joe's Pub	E Vill	24
Knitting Factory	W'burg	21
Lakeside Lounge	E Vill	21
Le Poisson Rouge	G Vill	20

Littlefield | **Gowanus** ⎤

Mercury Lounge | **LES** 21

Music Hall | **W'burg** 23

Otto's Shrunken | **E Vill** 18

Pianos | **LES** 18

Public Assembly | **W'burg** ⎤

Rebel | **Garment** ⎤

Rock Shop | **Park Slope** ⎤

🄴 Rockwood Music | **LES** 26

Roseland | **W 50s** 20

🄴 Santos Party Hse. | **Chinatown** 25

Session 73 | **E 70s** 17

S.O.B.'s | **Hudson Square** 21

Sullivan Hall | **G Vill** 21

Terminal 5 | **W 50s** 19

🄴**NEW** Theater Bar | **TriBeCa** ⎤

Trash | **W'burg** 15

🄴 Union Hall | **Park Slope** 24

United Palace | **Wash. Hts** ⎤

Village Underground | **G Vill** 20

NEWCOMERS (90)

Above 6 | **W 50s** ⎤

Anfora | **W Vill** ⎤

Aria Wine Bar | **W Vill** ⎤

Banter | **W'burg** ⎤

Bar Downstairs | **E 40s** ⎤

Bar on Fifth | **Garment** ⎤

Bar 29 | **Murray Hill** ⎤

🄴 Beauty/Essex | **LES** ⎤

Bedlam | **E Vill** ⎤

Bierhaus | **E 40s** ⎤

Bier Int'l | **Harlem** ⎤

Billy Hurricane's | **E Vill** ⎤

Blind Barber | **E Vill** ⎤

Blue Haven | **G Vill** ⎤

Branded Saloon | **Prospect Hts** ⎤

Brooklyneer | **W Vill** ⎤

Brooklyn Wine | **W'burg** ⎤

🄴 Bunker | **Meatpacking** ⎤

Buskers | **G Vill** ⎤

Casa Mezcal | **LES** ⎤

Cayenne Lounge | **G Vill** ⎤

Chelsea Room | **Chelsea** ⎤

Coal Yard | **E Vill** ⎤

Copia | **E 50s** ⎤

Culturefix | **LES** ⎤

Dbar | **Chelsea** ⎤

Delta House | **E 80s** ⎤

District 36 | **Garment** ⎤

Draft | **LES** ⎤

Freddy's Bar | **Park Slope** ⎤

Gansevoort Park | **Murray Hill** ⎤

GMT Tavern | **G Vill** ⎤

Good Co. | **W'burg** ⎤

🄴 Gramercy Terr. | **Gramercy** ⎤

Hash Fifty Five | **W 50s** ⎤

Hotel Chantelle | **LES** ⎤

🄴 Hurricane Club | **Flatiron** ⎤

Idle Hands | **E Vill** ⎤

Immigrant | **E Vill** ⎤

Industry Bar | **W 50s** ⎤

Irish Exit | **E 50s** ⎤

🄴 Jimmy | **SoHo** ⎤

Keg No. 229 | **Seaport** ⎤

🄴 Kenmare | **L Italy** ⎤

Lair | **L Italy** ⎤

Lani Kai | **SoHo** ⎤

Lantern's Keep | **W 40s** ⎤

🄴 Lavo | **E 50s** ⎤

🄴 Le Bain | **Meatpacking** ⎤

Lex Bar | **Murray Hill** ⎤

Lexicon | **E 50s** ⎤

🄴 Maison Premiere | **W'burg** ⎤

Mister H | **SoHo** ⎤

🄴 Mulberry Project | **L Italy** ⎤

Night of Joy | **W'burg** ⎤

Ninth Ward | **E Vill** ⎤

1 Republik | **Murray Hill** ⎤

On the Rocks | **W 40s** ⎤

Orient Express | **W Vill** ⎤

Park/Tavern | **Murray Hill** ⎤

Post Office | **W'burg** ⎤

Pub One | **Dumbo** ⎤

Queen Vic | **E Vill** ⎤

RDV | **Meatpacking** 22

Réunion Surf Bar | **W 40s** ⎤

Riff Raff's | **Flatiron** ⎤

Salon Millesime | **Murray Hill** ⎤

Snap | **W Vill** ⎤

Spanky & Darla's | **E Vill** ⎤

Spritzenhaus | **Greenpt** ⎤

Studio XXI | **Flatiron** ⎤

System | **LIC** ⎤

Tammany Hall | **LES** ⎤

Taproom No. 307 | **Murray Hill** ⎤

🄴 Theater Bar | **TriBeCa** ⎤

13th Step | **E Vill** ⎤

Three Monkeys | **W 50s** ⎤

3 Sheets Saloon | **G Vill** ⎤

Toro | **TriBeCa** ⎤

Trilby | **E Vill** ⎤

Tzigan | **Meatpacking** ⎤

Upstairs | **E 50s** ⎤

Vault at Pfaff's | **G Vill** ⎤

Vyne | **G Vill** ⎤

W Downtown | **Financial** ⎤

Whiskey Brooklyn | **W'burg** ⎤

White Noise | **E Vill** ⎤

Windsor | **W Vill** ⎤

XIX | **NoLita**	—
XVI | **W 40s**	—

NIGHTCLUBS

Amnesia | **Chelsea**	—
Avenue | **Chelsea**	23
Ⓩ **NEW** Bunker | **Meatpacking**	—
NEW Chelsea Room | **Chelsea**	—
El Morocco | **Harlem**	20
Europa | **Greenpt**	19
Ⓩ 40/40 | **Flatiron**	19
49 Grove | **W Vill**	18
NEW Gansevoort Park | **Murray Hill**	—
Greenhouse | **Hudson Square**	21
Griffin | **Meatpacking**	21
Juliet | **Chelsea**	23
Ⓩ **NEW** Kenmare | **L Italy**	—
Kiss & Fly | **Meatpacking**	20
La Pomme | **Chelsea**	19
Ⓩ **NEW** Lavo | **E 50s**	—
Ⓩ **NEW** Le Bain | **Meatpacking**	—
LQ | **E 40s**	18
Marquee | **Chelsea**	21
NEW Mister H | **SoHo**	—
Nikki Midtown | **E 50s**	20
Ⓩ 1 Oak | **Chelsea**	24
Ⓩ Plunge | **Meatpacking**	26
Polar | **Murray Hill**	—
Ⓩ Provocateur | **Meatpacking**	—
NEW Riff Raff's | **Flatiron**	—
Ⓩ SL | **Meatpacking**	23
Suzie Wong | **Chelsea**	23
Tenjune | **Meatpacking**	22

NY STATE OF MIND

Arlene's Grocery | **LES**	20
Arthur's Tavern | **W Vill**	23
Ⓩ Bemelmans | **E 70s**	27
Bill's Gay 90s | **E 50s**	16
Bitter End | **G Vill**	20
Blue & Gold | **E Vill**	16
Ⓩ Blue Note | **G Vill**	24
Bowlmor | **W 40s**	20
Box | **LES**	24
Brooklyn Inn | **Boerum Hill**	25
Brooklyn Social | **Carroll Gdns**	22
Ear Inn | **Hudson Square**	23
Fanelli's | **SoHo**	20
Globe | **Gramercy**	20
Jeremy's Ale | **Financial**	17
K & M Bar | **W'burg**	—
Ⓩ King Cole Bar | **E 50s**	27
Lenox Lounge | **Harlem**	23
Ⓩ **NEW** Maison Premiere | **W'burg**	—
Marie's Crisis | **W Vill**	24

McAleer's Pub | **W 80s**	15
Ⓩ McSorley's | **E Vill**	23
Nuyorican Poets | **E Vill**	23
Ⓩ Oak Bar | **W 50s**	25
Old Town Bar | **Flatiron**	21
Pete's Tavern | **Gramercy**	21
Ⓩ P.J. Clarke's | **E 50s**	21
Roseland | **W 50s**	20
Rudy's | **W 40s**	20
Ⓩ Smalls | **W Vill**	26
Stan's | **Bronx**	21
St. Nick's Jazz Pub | **Harlem**	23
Ⓩ 230 Fifth | **Chelsea**	23
Ⓩ Village Vanguard | **W Vill**	27
Webster Hall | **E Vill**	18
White Horse | **W Vill**	19

OLD NEW YORK

(50+ yrs.; Year opened; * building)

1817 | Ear Inn* | **Hudson Square**	23
1827 | Julius* | **W Vill**	16
1847 | Fanelli's | **SoHo**	20
1851 | Bayard's* | **Financial**	—
1854 | McSorley's | **E Vill**	23
1855 | Vault at Pfaff's* | **G Vill**	—
1860 | Brooklyn Inn* | **Boerum Hill**	25
1864 | Pete's Tavern | **Gramercy**	21
1873 | Paris | **Seaport**	20
1874 | P.J. Hanley's | **Carroll Gdns**	—
1880 | Globe* | **Gramercy**	20
1880 | White Horse | **W Vill**	19
1884 | P.J. Clarke's | **E 50s**	21
1886 | Webster Hall* | **E Vill**	18
1887 | Teddy's* | **W'burg**	24
1892 | Old Town Bar | **Flatiron**	21
1904 | Salon Millesime* | **Murray Hill**	—
1906 | Hammerstein | **Garment**	19
1910 | Bohemian Hall | **Astoria**	25
1919 | 55 Bar | **W Vill**	25
1919 | Roseland | **W 50s**	20
1920 | Milady's | **SoHo**	15
1923 | Campbell Apt.* | **E 40s**	25
1923 | Yankee Tav. | **Bronx**	20
1924 | Molly's | **Gramercy**	23
1926 | Bill's Gay 90s | **E 50s**	16
1926 | 169 Bar | **LES**	18
1927 | P.J. Carney's | **W 50s**	20
1928 | Beacon Theatre | **W 70s**	23
1929 | Marie's Crisis | **W Vill**	24
1929 | Top of the Tower* | **E 40s**	26
1930 | United Palace* | **Wash. Hts**	—
1933 | Dublin House | **W 70s**	17

1933 | Rudy's | **W 40s**	20
1934 | Smith's Bar | **W 40s**	17
1934 | Subway Inn | **E 60s**	18
1935 | 7B | **E Vill**	19
1935 | Village Vanguard | **W Vill**	27
1936 | Peter McManus | **Chelsea**	21
1937 | Arthur's Tavern | **W Vill**	23
1938 | Bowlmor | **G Vill**	20
1939 | Lenox Lounge | **Harlem**	23
1940 | Sophie's | **E Vill**	19
1945 | Holiday Cocktail | **E Vill**	18
1945 | Oak Bar | **W 50s**	25
1945 | Puffy's | **TriBeCa**	14
1947 | Bemelmans | **E 70s**	27
1949 | King Cole Bar | **E 50s**	27
1950 | Kettle of Fish | **W Vill**	19
1952 | Duplex | **W Vill**	20
1953 | McAleer's Pub | **W 80s**	15
1955 | Cafe Carlyle | **E 70s**	27
1955 | Parkside | **LES**	-
1958 | Blue & Gold | **E Vill**	16
1960 | Dorrian's | **E 80s**	17

OUTDOOR SPACES

GARDEN

Apt. 138 | **Cobble Hill**	23
Black Rabbit | **Greenpt**	24
☑ Bohemian Hall | **Astoria**	25
Boxcar Lounge | **E Vill**	18
Brazen Head | **Boerum Hill**	20
Brookvin | **Park Slope**	23
☑ Cávo | **Astoria**	26
Central | **Astoria**	22
Cherry Tree | **Park Slope**	-
Cibar | **Gramercy**	22
Commonwealth | **Park Slope**	20
Croxley Ales | **E Vill**	19
Daddy's | **W'burg**	-
Danny & Eddie's | **E 80s**	-
☑ D.B.A. | **multi.**	22
Der Schwarze | **Ft Greene**	-
Diamond | **Greenpt**	-
'Disiac | **W 50s**	23
Doc Watson's | **E 70s**	17
Draft Barn | **Gravesend**	-
Dram Shop | **Park Slope**	18
Druids | **W 50s**	21
☑ Employees Only | **W Vill**	23
Entwine | **W Vill**	23
Excelsior | **Park Slope**	19
Fourth Ave. Pub | **Park Slope**	-
Ginger's | **Park Slope**	18
Gossip | **W 40s**	22
Gowanus Yacht | **Carroll Gdns**	22
Half King | **Chelsea**	20

Hell Gate Social | **Astoria**	-
Huckleberry | **W'burg**	24
International Bar | **E Vill**	20
Iona | **W'burg**	23
Last Exit | **Cobble Hill**	18
L.I.C. Bar | **LIC**	22
Loki | **Park Slope**	19
Loreley | **multi.**	22
Lunasa | **E Vill**	21
Madame X | **G Vill**	17
☑ **NEW** Maison Premiere | **W'burg**	-
Mug's Ale | **W'burg**	20
☑ **NEW** Mulberry Project | **L Italy**	-
NEW Ninth Ward | **E Vill**	-
No Malice Palace | **E Vill**	21
Nublu | **E Vill**	22
O'Flaherty's Ale | **W 40s**	19
Pete's Candy | **W'burg**	25
NEW Pub One | **Dumbo**	-
Quarter | **Greenwood Hts**	-
☑ Radegast | **W'burg**	26
☑ Raines Law Rm. | **Flatiron**	27
Revival | **Gramercy**	19
Royale | **E Vill**	21
Rue B | **E Vill**	22
Sixth Ward | **LES**	20
Soda Bar | **Prospect Hts**	16
Soft Spot | **W'burg**	-
Spuyten Duyvil | **W'burg**	25
☑ Standard Biergarten | **Meatpacking**	24
Stanton Public | **LES**	22
Stonehome | **Ft Greene**	-
☑ Studio Square | **Astoria**	25
Sweet & Vicious | **NoLita**	17
T.B.D. | **Greenpt**	-
NEW Trilby | **E Vill**	-
Trophy | **W'burg**	19
Whiskey Tav. | **Chinatown**	20

PATIO/TERRACE

Alligator | **W'burg**	19
Arctica | **Murray Hill**	17
Ardesia | **W 50s**	-
Barcade | **W'burg**	25
Barcibo Enoteca | **W 60s**	24
Bar 4 | **Park Slope**	19
Beer Bar/Centro | **E 40s**	20
Belmont | **Gramercy**	19
Big Nose Kate's | **SI**	19
Bin No. 220 | **Seaport**	20
☑ Boat Basin | **W 70s**	25
Boss Tweed's | **LES**	17
Boxcar Lounge | **E Vill**	18

Boxers | **Flatiron**	–
Ⓩ Brandy Library | **TriBeCa**	27
NEW Brooklyn Wine | **W'burg**	–
Ⓩ Brother Jimmy | **Gramercy**	17
Ⓩ Bubble Lounge | **TriBeCa**	21
Bushwick Country | **W'burg**	17
Camp | **Boerum Hill**	21
Cargo | **SI**	20
Castello Plan | **Ditmas Pk**	–
Ⓩ Cávo | **Astoria**	26
Chelsea Brewing | **Chelsea**	20
Cielo | **Meatpacking**	23
Creek & the Cave | **LIC**	–
Crocodile Lounge | **E Vill**	19
Crosby Bar | **SoHo**	24
Ⓩ D.B.A. | **E Vill**	22
'Disiac | **W 50s**	23
Double Down | **E Vill**	–
Druids | **W 50s**	21
Duff's | **W'burg**	–
Gate | **Park Slope**	20
Ginger's | **Park Slope**	18
NEW Good Co. | **W'burg**	–
GYM Sportsbar | **Chelsea**	20
Harefield Rd. | **W'burg**	25
High Dive | **Park Slope**	–
Hill | **Murray Hill**	16
HK Lounge | **Garment**	19
Hooters | **W 50s**	15
House of Brews | **W 50s**	19
Ⓩ Hudson Hotel | **W 50s**	24
Jekyll & Hyde | **W Vill**	18
Ⓩ**NEW** Kenmare | **L Italy**	–
Kiss & Fly | **Meatpacking**	20
Larry Lawrence | **W'burg**	24
Littlefield | **Gowanus**	–
Local | **Garment**	19
Loki | **Park Slope**	19
Metropolitan | **W'burg**	18
Ⓩ Mission Dolores | **Park Slope**	–
Moda Outdoors | **W 50s**	–
Monday Room | **NoLita**	25
Morrell Wine | **W 40s**	23
Nublu | **E Vill**	22
123 Burger | **W 50s**	19
Overlook Lounge | **E 40s**	18
P&G Cafe | **W 70s**	21
Park Slope Ale | **Park Slope**	19
Peggy O'Neill's | **Coney Is**	20
Perfect Pint | **W 40s**	20
Phoenix | **E Vill**	21
Pierre Loti | **Gramercy**	23
Pine Tree Lodge | **Murray Hill**	21
Ⓩ P.J. Clarke's | **Financial**	21
P.J. Hanley's | **Carroll Gdns**	–
Professor Thom's | **E Vill**	19
Richardson | **W'burg**	–
Rink Bar | **W 50s**	21
Ritz | **W 40s**	23
Royale | **E Vill**	21
Sackett | **Park Slope**	–
Sample | **Cobble Hill**	–
Ship of Fools | **E 80s**	15
Social | **W 40s**	16
St. Dymphna's | **E Vill**	22
Sugarland | **W'burg**	–
Ⓩ Sweet Afton | **Astoria**	25
Swing 46 | **W 40s**	23
T.G. Whitney's | **E 50s**	16
NEW Three Monkeys | **W 50s**	–
Tribeca Tav. | **TriBeCa**	17
Ⓩ Ulysses | **Financial**	20
Uncle Charlie's | **E 40s**	21
Underground Lounge | **W 100s**	15
Union Pool | **W'burg**	19
Vintage | **W 50s**	21
Vol de Nuit | **G Vill**	22
Washington Commons | **Prospect Hts**	–
NEW W Downtown | **Financial**	–
Ⓩ Weather Up | **Prospect Hts**	24
Wharf Bar & Grill | **Murray Hill**	18
Whiskey River | **Murray Hill**	20
Woods | **W'burg**	–
xes lounge | **Chelsea**	21
Zombie Hut | **Carroll Gdns**	23

ROOFTOP

Above Allen | **LES**	23
NEW Above 6 | **W 50s**	–
Ⓩ Ava Lounge | **W 50s**	23
Berry Park | **W'burg**	–
Bookmarks | **E 40s**	24
Brass Monkey | **Meatpacking**	20
Cabanas | **Chelsea**	22
Delancey | **LES**	19
Eagle | **Chelsea**	21
Ⓩ Empire Hotel Roof | **W 60s**	24
NEW Gansevoort Park | **Murray Hill**	–
Glass Bar | **Chelsea**	–
Ⓩ**NEW** Gramercy Terr. | **Gramercy**	–
Heights B&G | **W 100s**	17
HK Lounge | **Garment**	19
Ⓩ Hudson Hotel | **W 50s**	24
Hudson Terrace | **W 40s**	21
Hustler Club | **W 50s**	19
Ⓩ**NEW** Jimmy | **SoHo**	–
Latitude | **W 40s**	15
Ⓩ**NEW** Le Bain | **Meatpacking**	–

Local | **Garment**	19
Mad46 | **E 40s**	24
Metro Grill Roof | **Garment**	23
Penthouse 808 | **LIC**	-
🗷 Plunge | **Meatpacking**	26
🗷 Press Lounge | **W 40s**	-
Rare View | **multi.**	24
Red Sky | **Murray Hill**	17
Rick's Cabaret | **Garment**	23
Rock Shop | **Park Slope**	-
🗷 Salon de Ning | **W 50s**	25
Sky Room | **Garment**	-
Sutton Place | **E 50s**	17
Terminal 5 | **W 50s**	19
13 | **G Vill**	18
Thom Bar | **SoHo**	25
Tonic | **Murray Hill**	16
🗷 Top of the Strand | **Garment**	-
🗷 Top of the Tower | **E 40s**	26
🗷 230 Fifth | **Chelsea**	23
NEW Upstairs | **E 50s**	-
NEW XVI | **W 40s**	-

SIDEWALK

Abilene | **Carroll Gdns**	23
Agozar! | **NoHo**	18
Amsterdam Ale | **W 70s**	-
An Béal Bocht | **Bronx**	22
Anotheroom | **TriBeCa**	22
Athens Café | **Astoria**	18
Bar Carrera | **G Vill**	21
Bar 515 | **Murray Hill**	14
Barfly | **Gramercy**	16
Bar Italia | **multi.**	23
Bar Six | **G Vill**	21
Bayard's Ale | **W Vill**	19
NEW Bier Int'l | **Harlem**	-
Bin 71 | **W 70s**	23
Blind Pig | **E Vill**	18
Bowery Wine Co. | **E Vill**	19
Brass Monkey | **Meatpacking**	20
Brooklyn Public | **Ft Greene**	17
🗷 Brother Jimmy | **multi.**	17
Bua | **E Vill**	21
Buceo 95 | **W 90s**	24
Dive Bar | **W 90s**	18
Doc Watson's | **E 70s**	17
D.O.C. Wine | **W'burg**	24
Dublin 6 | **W Vill**	21
Duplex | **W Vill**	20
Epstein's Bar | **LES**	16
Exchange B&G | **Gramercy**	-
Fiddlesticks | **W Vill**	16
Finnegans Wake | **E 70s**	19
Garage | **W Vill**	19
Genesis | **E 80s**	19

Grand Café | **Astoria**	20
Gutter | **Greenpt**	19
Half King | **Chelsea**	20
Henrietta Hudson | **W Vill**	20
Honey | **Chelsea**	19
Hotel Delmano | **W'burg**	26
Irish Rogue | **W 40s**	18
Jake's Dilemma | **W 80s**	17
Jake's Saloon | **W 50s**	15
Johnny Foxes | **E 80s**	15
Joshua Tree | **Murray Hill**	15
K & M Bar | **W'burg**	-
Le Souk | **G Vill**	22
Mama's Bar | **E Vill**	-
McAleer's Pub | **W 80s**	15
Mickey Mantle's | **W 50s**	18
Molly Pitcher's | **E 80s**	16
One & One | **E Vill**	16
Onieal's Grand St. | **L Italy**	24
Opal | **E 50s**	16
Pencil Factory | **Greenpt**	24
Pete's Tavern | **Gramercy**	21
Pinkerton | **W'burg**	-
Prohibition | **W 80s**	19
Redemption | **E 50s**	21
Red Lion | **G Vill**	20
Riviera | **W Vill**	19
Rogue | **Chelsea**	17
Ryan's Irish Pub | **E Vill**	17
Session 73 | **E 70s**	17
Shoolbred's | **E Vill**	19
SideBar | **Gramercy**	18
Sláinte | **NoHo**	17
Slaughtered Lamb | **W Vill**	17
Stillwater | **E Vill**	-
Stumble Inn | **E 70s**	20
Teddy's | **W'burg**	24
Tortilla Flats | **W Vill**	21
Twelve | **Murray Hill**	18
Uptown Lounge | **E 80s**	22
Vero | **multi.**	22
Vino | **E 60s**	22
Vlada | **W 50s**	21
White Horse | **W Vill**	19
Wicker Park | **E 80s**	17
Winebar | **E Vill**	22
Wogies | **W Vill**	15
Xicala | **L Italy**	20

WATERSIDE

🗷 Bateaux NY | **Chelsea**	26
🗷 Boat Basin | **W 70s**	25
Chelsea Brewing | **Chelsea**	20
🗷 Frying Pan | **Chelsea**	26
🗷 P.J. Clarke's | **Financial**	21
Spirit Cruises | **Chelsea**	23

Water Taxi Bch. | **Governors Island**	22
World Yacht | **W 40s**	24

PHOTO BOOTHS

Abbey | **W'burg**	20
☑ Ace Hotel | **Chelsea**	25
Arrow | **E Vill**	20
Bar 4 | **Park Slope**	19
BB&R | **E 80s**	18
☑ Bell House | **Gowanus**	24
Bleecker St. Bar | **NoHo**	17
Bushwick Country | **W'burg**	17
Crash Mansion | **LES**	15
Crocodile Lounge | **E Vill**	19
Dave & Buster's | **W 40s**	17
GalleryBar | **LES**	19
Lakeside Lounge | **E Vill**	21
L.I.C. Bar | **LIC**	22
Living Room | **LES**	23
Niagara | **E Vill**	19
Otto's Shrunken | **E Vill**	18
7B | **E Vill**	19
Southpaw | **Park Slope**	20
Trailer Park | **Chelsea**	19
Union Pool | **W'burg**	19
NEW Whiskey Brooklyn | **W'burg**	-

PIANO BARS

Bill's Gay 90s | **E 50s**	16
Brandy's | **E 80s**	24
Don't Tell Mama | **W 40s**	20
Duplex | **W Vill**	20
Ella | **E Vill**	20
Manhattan Inn | **Greenpt**	-
Marie's Crisis | **W Vill**	24
Monster | **W Vill**	21
Rum House | **W 40s**	-
Townhouse | **E 50s**	20
Uncle Charlie's | **E 40s**	21

PUNK BARS

Ding Dong Lounge | **W 100s**	18
Double Down | **E Vill**	-
Duff's | **W'burg**	-
Lucky 13 | **Park Slope**	-
Manitoba's | **E Vill**	25
Mars Bar | **E Vill**	19
Trash | **W'burg**	15

QUIET CONVERSATION

☑ Angel's Share | **E Vill**	26
Anotheroom | **TriBeCa**	22
Ara Wine Bar | **Meatpacking**	20
Archive | **Murray Hill**	-
Ardesia | **W 50s**	-
Back Room | **LES**	23
☑ Bar Pleiades | **E 70s**	26
Bar Seven Five | **Financial**	-
☑ Bemelmans | **E 70s**	27
Bin No. 220 | **Seaport**	20
Bin 71 | **W 70s**	23
Black Mtn. Wine | **Carroll Gdns**	28
Blue Ribbon Bar | **W Vill**	24
Boxcar Lounge | **E Vill**	18
☑ Brandy Library | **TriBeCa**	27
Brooklyn Inn | **Boerum Hill**	25
Burp Castle | **E Vill**	21
Champagne Bar/Plaza | **W 50s**	24
Cibar | **Gramercy**	22
Decibel | **E Vill**	24
☑ Dutch Kills | **LIC**	26
Epistrophy | **NoLita**	23
☑ Flûte | **multi.**	23
Hudson Bar & Books | **W Vill**	23
☑ King Cole Bar | **E 50s**	27
Little Branch | **W Vill**	24
Magician | **LES**	21
M Bar | **W 40s**	24
☑ Milk & Honey | **LES**	25
Monday Room | **NoLita**	25
Onieal's Grand St. | **L Italy**	24
NEW On the Rocks | **W 40s**	-
Otheroom | **W Vill**	24
Park Slope Ale | **Park Slope**	19
☑ PDT | **E Vill**	27
☑ Plaza Athénée | **E 60s**	27
☑ Raines Law Rm. | **Flatiron**	27
Regency Library Bar | **E 60s**	23
Richardson | **W'burg**	-
Rose Club | **W 50s**	22
Tea Lounge | **Park Slope**	22
Temple Bar | **NoHo**	23
☑ Top of the Tower | **E 40s**	26
NEW Toro | **TriBeCa**	-
Upholstery Store | **W Vill**	-
Velvet | **E Vill**	21
Vino | **E 60s**	22
Vintry Wine | **Financial**	-
Von | **NoHo**	24
White Star | **LES**	21
Wined Up | **Flatiron**	22
World Bar | **E 40s**	19

ROADHOUSES

Bar None | **E Vill**	12
NEW Billy Hurricane's | **E Vill**	-
Billymark's West | **Chelsea**	16
Coyote Ugly | **E Vill**	15
Doc Holliday's | **E Vill**	18

Ear Inn | **Hudson Square** `23`
Hog Pit | **Chelsea** `14`
Hogs & Heifers | **Meatpacking** `18`
Lott | **Flatiron** `-`
Raccoon Lodge | **TriBeCa** `18`
Rockbar | **W Vill** `-`
Rodeo Bar | **Murray Hill** `19`
Trailer Park | **Chelsea** `19`

ROMANTIC

☑ Angel's Share | **E Vill** `26`
Anotheroom | **TriBeCa** `22`
☑ Apothéke | **Chinatown** `25`
Auction House | **E 80s** `22`
☑ Bateaux NY | **Chelsea** `26`
☑ Bemelmans | **E 70s** `27`
Black Mtn. Wine | **Carroll Gdns** `28`
Bookmarks | **E 40s** `24`
Bourgeois Pig | **E Vill** `23`
☑ Bubble Lounge | **TriBeCa** `21`
Cellar Bar | **W 40s** `21`
Cibar | **Gramercy** `22`
Decibel | **E Vill** `24`
Delia's | **Bay Ridge** `24`
Dove | **G Vill** `21`
Ella | **E Vill** `20`
Flatiron Lounge | **Flatiron** `22`
☑ Flûte | **multi.** `23`
Hudson Bar & Books | **W Vill** `23`
☑ 🆕 Jimmy | **SoHo** `-`
☑ King Cole Bar | **E 50s** `27`
Kush | **LES** `19`
La Lanterna | **G Vill** `24`
🆕 Lani Kai | **SoHo** `-`
Le Bateau Ivre | **E 50s** `21`
Lexington Bar/Books | **E 70s** `22`
Little Branch | **W Vill** `24`
Madame X | **G Vill** `17`
☑ Madam Geneva | **NoHo** `28`
☑ 🆕 Maison Premiere | **W'burg** `-`
M Bar | **W 40s** `24`
☑ Milk & Honey | **LES** `25`
Onieal's Grand St. | **L Italy** `24`
Park Bar | **Flatiron** `23`
☑ Pegu Club | **SoHo** `25`
Red Bench | **SoHo** `-`
Regency Library Bar | **E 60s** `23`
Richardson | **W'burg** `-`
Rue B | **E Vill** `22`
Shalel Lounge | **W 70s** `23`
Spirit Cruises | **Chelsea** `23`
Temple Bar | **NoHo** `23`
☑ Top of the Strand | **Garment** `-`
☑ Top of the Tower | **E 40s** `26`
Von | **NoHo** `24`

☑ Weather Up | **multi.** `24`
World Yacht | **W 40s** `24`

SMOKING PERMITTED

Carnegie Club | **W 50s** `23`
Circa Tabac | **SoHo** `24`
Club Macanudo | **E 60s** `24`
Hudson Bar & Books | **W Vill** `23`
Karma | **E Vill** `23`
Lexington Bar/Books | **E 70s** `22`
Velvet | **E Vill** `21`

SPEAKEASY-STYLE

☑ Angel's Share | **E Vill** `26`
☑ Apothéke | **Chinatown** `25`
Back Room | **LES** `23`
Bill's Gay 90s | **E 50s** `16`
Black Door | **Chelsea** `19`
🆕 Blind Barber | **E Vill** `-`
Blue Owl | **E Vill** `20`
Brooklyn Social | **Carroll Gdns** `22`
☑ Death & Co | **E Vill** `26`
Dram | **W'burg** `-`
☑ Dutch Kills | **LIC** `26`
☑ Employees Only | **W Vill** `23`
☑ Flûte | **W 50s** `23`
Hotel Delmano | **W'burg** `26`
Huckleberry | **W'burg** `24`
JakeWalk | **Carroll Gdns** `24`
Little Branch | **W Vill** `24`
Lovers/Today | **E Vill** `-`
Manhattan Inn | **Greenpt** `-`
☑ Milk & Honey | **LES** `25`
☑ 🆕 Mulberry Project | **L Italy** `-`
124 Rabbit | **G Vill** `22`
Onieal's Grand St. | **L Italy** `24`
☑ PDT | **E Vill** `27`
☑ Raines Law Rm. | **Flatiron** `27`
Richardson | **W'burg** `-`
67 Orange St. | **Harlem** `23`
Smith & Mills | **TriBeCa** `21`
Volstead | **E 50s** `20`
☑ Weather Up | **multi.** `24`
White Star | **LES** `21`

SPOKEN WORD

An Béal Bocht | **Bronx** `22`
Back Fence | **G Vill** `19`
Barbès | **Park Slope** `23`
Bowery Poetry | **NoHo** `18`
🆕 Freddy's Bar | **Park Slope** `-`
Half King | **Chelsea** `20`
Joe's Pub | **E Vill** `24`
KGB | **E Vill** `20`
Le Poisson Rouge | **G Vill** `20`

SPECIAL APPEALS

Nuyorican Poets | E Vill	23
Pacific Standard | Boerum Hill	22
Pink Pony | LES	17
🅩 Union Hall | Park Slope	24

SPORTS BARS

Ainsworth | Chelsea	23
Angry Wade's | Cobble Hill	16
Australian | Garment	20
Baker Street | E 60s	17
Bar 515 | Murray Hill	14
Barfly | Gramercy	16
Bar None | E Vill	12
BB&R | E 80s	18
Beer Garden | SI	21
BlackFinn | E 50s	16
Black Sheep | Murray Hill	18
Blackstone's | E 50s	18
Bleecker Heights | W Vill	-
Bleecker St. Bar | NoHo	17
Blondies | W 70s	18
Bounce | E 70s	17
Bourbon St. | W 70s	16
Boxers | Flatiron	-
🅩 Brother Jimmy | multi.	17
Central Bar | E Vill	19
Cornerstone Tav. | E 50s	19
Croxley Ales | E Vill	19
Down the Hatch | W Vill	16
NEW Draft | LES	-
Dram Shop | Park Slope	18
East End Tav. | E 80s	17
Fitzgerald's | Murray Hill	-
🅩 40/40 | Flatiron	19
Genesis | E 80s	19
Gin Mill | W 80s	17
GYM Sportsbar | Chelsea	20
Hairy Monk | Murray Hill	15
Hill | Murray Hill	16
Irish Rogue | W 40s	18
Jack Russell's | E 80s	17
Jake's Dilemma | W 80s	17
Joshua Tree | Murray Hill	15
Kinsale | E 90s	21
Lansdowne Rd. | W 40s	22
Lion's Head | W 100s	19
Manny's | E 90s	19
McAleer's Pub | W 80s	15
McCormack's | Murray Hill	-
McFadden's | E 40s	15
Mercury Bar | multi.	15
Mickey Mantle's | W 50s	18
Molly Pitcher's | E 80s	16
Nevada Smith's | E Vill	16
Off the Wagon | G Vill	17

O'Flanagan's | E 60s	20
123 Burger | W 50s	19
Overlook Lounge | E 40s	18
Peggy O'Neill's | Coney Is	20
Professor Thom's | E Vill	19
Rathbones | E 80s	16
Red Lion | G Vill	20
Reservoir Bar | G Vill	15
Riviera | W Vill	19
Rogue | Chelsea	17
Ship of Fools | E 80s	15
SideBar | Gramercy	18
NEW Snap | W Vill	-
Social | W 40s	16
Stan's | Bronx	21
St. Marks Ale | E Vill	18
Third & Long | Murray Hill	13
NEW Three Monkeys | W 50s	-
NEW 3 Sheets Saloon | G Vill	-
Tonic | multi.	16
Triona's | G Vill	-
Turtle Bay | E 50s	14
Twelve | Murray Hill	18
200 Fifth | Park Slope	17
Village Pourhouse | multi.	15
🅩 Warren 77 | TriBeCa	20
NEW Whiskey Brooklyn | W'burg	-
NEW Windsor | W Vill	-
Yankee Tav. | Bronx	20

STRIP CLUBS

Cabaret | Flatiron	-
Flashdancers | W 50s	21
Hustler Club | W 50s	19
Penthse. Exec. Club | W 40s	23
Rick's Cabaret | Garment	23
Scores | Chelsea	18
VIP Club | Flatiron	23

SUITS

Annie Moore's | E 40s	17
NEW Bar Downstairs | E 40s	-
Bar Seven Five | Financial	-
Bayard's | Financial	-
Beer Bar/Centro | E 40s	20
🅩 Brandy Library | TriBeCa	27
🅩 Campbell Apt. | E 40s	25
Carnegie Club | W 50s	23
Cellar Bar | W 40s	21
Church Lounge | TriBeCa	22
Club Macanudo | E 60s	24
Full Shilling | Financial	16
🅩 Ginger Man | Murray Hill	21
🅩 NEW Lavo | E 50s	-
Lea | E 40s	25

MO Bar | **W 60s**	24
Moda Outdoors | **W 50s**	_
Nikki Midtown | **E 50s**	20
Oak Bar | **W 50s**	25
P.J. Clarke's | **E 50s**	21
Rink Bar | **W 50s**	21
Scores | **Chelsea**	18
Stone Rose | **W 60s**	23
Sutton Place | **E 50s**	17
Top of the Tower | **E 40s**	26
Townhouse | **E 50s**	20
Ulysses | **Financial**	20
NEW Upstairs | **E 50s**	_
Volstead | **E 50s**	20
Whiskey Blue | **E 40s**	21
World Bar | **E 40s**	19
W Times Sq. | **W 40s**	23

SWANKY

Above Allen | **LES**	23
Ava Lounge | **W 50s**	23
Avenue | **Chelsea**	23
NEW Bar on Fifth | **Garment**	_
Bar Pleiades | **E 70s**	26
Bar Seven Five | **Financial**	_
Beekman | **E 50s**	24
Boom Boom | **Meatpacking**	24
Bowery Hotel | **E Vill**	24
Brandy Library | **TriBeCa**	27
Cafe Carlyle | **E 70s**	27
Campbell Apt. | **E 40s**	25
Carnegie Club | **W 50s**	23
Cellar Bar | **W 40s**	21
Champagne Bar/Plaza | **W 50s**	24
NEW Chelsea Room | **Chelsea**	_
Church Lounge | **TriBeCa**	22
Cibar | **Gramercy**	22
Club Macanudo | **E 60s**	24
Empire Hotel Bar | **W 60s**	22
Empire Room | **Garment**	_
Feinstein's/Loews | **E 60s**	26
Flûte | **multi.**	23
48 Lounge | **W 40s**	26
40/40 | **Flatiron**	19
Forty Four | **W 40s**	22
NEW Gansevoort Park | **Murray Hill**	_
GoldBar | **L Italy**	25
Grand Bar | **SoHo**	23
Griffin | **Meatpacking**	21
Haven | **E 50s**	_
Hudson Hotel | **W 50s**	24
Jade Bar | **Gramercy**	22
Jane Hotel | **W Vill**	26
NEW Jimmy | **SoHo**	_
Juliet | **Chelsea**	23

Kastel | **Hudson Square**	_
King Cole Bar | **E 50s**	27
NEW Lavo | **E 50s**	_
Lucky Strike Lns. | **W 40s**	22
M Bar | **W 40s**	24
NEW Mister H | **SoHo**	_
MO Bar | **W 60s**	24
Monkey Bar | **E 50s**	23
Nikki Midtown | **E 50s**	20
1 Oak | **Chelsea**	24
Pegu Club | **SoHo**	25
Plunge | **Meatpacking**	26
Polar | **Murray Hill**	_
Press Lounge | **W 40s**	_
Provocateur | **Meatpacking**	_
RDV | **Meatpacking**	22
Rose Bar | **Gramercy**	25
Rose Club | **W 50s**	22
Salon de Ning | **W 50s**	25
NEW Salon Millesime | **Murray Hill**	_
SL | **Meatpacking**	23
Stone Rose | **W 60s**	23
Suzie Wong | **Chelsea**	23
Thom Bar | **SoHo**	25
230 Fifth | **Chelsea**	23
NEW Tzigan | **Meatpacking**	_
NEW W Downtown | **Financial**	_
Whiskey Park | **W 50s**	20
World Bar | **E 40s**	19
NEW XIX | **NoLita**	_

THEME BARS

Barcade | **W'burg**	25
Beauty Bar | **E Vill**	19
Big Nose Kate's | **SI**	19
Black Bear | **Gramercy**	18
Bourbon St. | **W 70s**	16
Camp | **Boerum Hill**	21
Exchange B&G | **Gramercy**	_
Flight 151 | **Chelsea**	16
Gstaad | **Chelsea**	19
Jekyll & Hyde | **W Vill**	18
Johnny Utah's | **W 50s**	20
KGB | **E Vill**	20
Pine Tree Lodge | **Murray Hill**	21
Polar | **Murray Hill**	_
Rodeo Bar | **Murray Hill**	19
Slaughtered Lamb | **W Vill**	17
Trailer Park | **Chelsea**	19
Wicked Monk | **Bay Ridge**	21
Wicked Willy's | **G Vill**	17

TIKI BARS

NEW Hurricane Club | **Flatiron**	_
NEW Lani Kai | **SoHo**	_

SPECIAL APPEALS

217

Otto's Shrunken | **E Vill** 18
Painkiller | **LES** -
NEW Riff Raff's | **Flatiron** -
Zombie Hut | **Carroll Gdns** 23

TOUGH DOORS

Avenue | **Chelsea** 23
Z Boom Boom | **Meatpacking** 24
Z NEW Bunker | **Meatpacking** -
Cabin/Below | **E Vill** -
Z NEW Kenmare | **L Italy** -
Z NEW Lavo | **E 50s** -
Z NEW Le Bain | **Meatpacking** -
NEW Mister H | **SoHo** -
Z NEW Mulberry Project | -
  L Italy
Z 1 Oak | **Chelsea** 24
Z Provocateur | **Meatpacking** -
Z SL | **Meatpacking** 23

TRENDY

Z Ace Hotel | **Chelsea** 25
Ainsworth | **Chelsea** 23
NEW Anfora | **W Vill** -
Avenue | **Chelsea** 23
Z NEW Beauty/Essex | **LES** -
NEW Bedlam | **E Vill** -
Bell House | **Gowanus** 24
NEW Blind Barber | **E Vill** -
Z Boom Boom | **Meatpacking** 24
Bowery Hotel | **E Vill** 24
Box | **LES** 24
Z Brooklyn Bowl | **W'burg** 27
Z NEW Bunker | **Meatpacking** -
Cabin/Below | **E Vill** -
Z Dutch Kills | **LIC** 26
Z Empire Hotel Roof | **W 60s** 24
NEW Gansevoort Park | -
  Murray Hill
Hotel Delmano | **W'burg** 26
Z NEW Hurricane Club | **Flatiron** -
Z Jane Hotel | **W Vill** 26
Z NEW Jimmy | **SoHo** -
Z NEW Kenmare | **L Italy** -
Z NEW Lavo | **E 50s** -
Z NEW Le Bain | **Meatpacking** -
Lillie's | **Flatiron** 23
Z Madam Geneva | **NoHo** 28
Z NEW Maison Premiere | -
  W'burg
NEW Mister H | **SoHo** -
Z NEW Mulberry Project | -
  L Italy
NEW Ninth Ward | **E Vill** -
Z 1 Oak | **Chelsea** 24
Z Provocateur | **Meatpacking** -

Z Raines Law Rm. | **Flatiron** 27
RDV | **Meatpacking** 22
Z Rusty Knot | **W Vill** 20
Rye House | **Flatiron** 24
Z Santos Party Hse. | **Chinatown** 25
Z SL | **Meatpacking** 23
NEW Spritzenhaus | **Greenpt** -
Z Standard Biergarten | 24
  Meatpacking
Z Studio Square | **Astoria** 25
Z NEW Theater Bar | **TriBeCa** -
Z 230 Fifth | **Chelsea** 23
Z Warren 77 | **TriBeCa** 20
Wilfie & Nell | **W Vill** 24

VIEWS

Above Allen | **LES** 23
NEW Above 6 | **W 50s** -
Z Ava Lounge | **W 50s** 23
Z Bateaux NY | **Chelsea** 26
Berry Park | **W'burg** -
Z Boat Basin | **W 70s** 25
Bookmarks | **E 40s** 24
Z Boom Boom | **Meatpacking** 24
Brass Monkey | **Meatpacking** 20
B61 | **Carroll Gdns** -
Cabanas | **Chelsea** 22
Chelsea Brewing | **Chelsea** 20
Z Dizzy's Club | **W 60s** 27
Z Empire Hotel Roof | **W 60s** 24
NEW Gansevoort Park | -
  Murray Hill
Glass Bar | **Chelsea** -
Z NEW Gramercy Terr. | -
  Gramercy
Heights B&G | **W 100s** 17
Z Hudson Hotel | **W 50s** 24
Hudson Terrace | **W 40s** 21
Z NEW Jimmy | **SoHo** -
Z NEW Le Bain | **Meatpacking** -
Mad46 | **E 40s** 24
Metro Grill Roof | **Garment** 23
Penthouse 808 | **LIC** -
Z P.J. Clarke's | **Financial** 21
Z Plunge | **Meatpacking** 26
Z Press Lounge | **W 40s** -
Rare View | **Murray Hill** 24
Z Salon de Ning | **W 50s** 25
Sky Room | **Garment** -
Spirit Cruises | **Chelsea** 23
Stone Rose | **W 60s** 23
Sutton Place | **E 50s** 17
Z Top of the Strand | **Garment** -
Z Top of the Tower | **E 40s** 26
Z 230 Fifth | **Chelsea** 23
NEW Upstairs | **E 50s** -

Water Taxi Bch. | **Governors Island**	22
World Yacht | **W 40s**	24
NEW XVI | **W 40s**	–

WIFI ACCESS

Amsterdam Ale | **W 70s**	–
Amsterdam Tavern | **W 100s**	19
Angels & Kings | **E Vill**	17
Arctica | **Murray Hill**	17
Barcelona Bar | **W 50s**	21
Bar Great Harry | **Carroll Gdns**	21
Black Horse | **Park Slope**	16
Black Rabbit | **Greenpt**	24
Bleecker Heights | **W Vill**	–
Z Blind Tiger | **W Vill**	23
Bowery Poetry | **NoHo**	18
Brass Monkey | **Meatpacking**	20
Brazen Head | **Boerum Hill**	20
Brooklyn Ale | **W'burg**	23
Z Brother Jimmy | **Murray Hill**	17
Bua | **E Vill**	21
Z Bubble Lounge | **TriBeCa**	21
Building/Bond | **Boerum Hill**	24
Cake Shop | **LES**	21
Cherry Tree | **Park Slope**	–
Coliseum Bar | **W 50s**	15
Crash Mansion | **LES**	15
Der Schwarze | **Ft Greene**	–
Dive Bar | **W 90s**	18
Dive 75 | **W 70s**	19
Donnybrook | **LES**	–
Epistrophy | **NoLita**	23
NEW Gansevoort Park | **Murray Hill**	–
Gibson | **W'burg**	–
Gift | **W 40s**	28
Grand Café | **Astoria**	20
Harefield Rd. | **W'burg**	25
Heathers | **E Vill**	–
Huckleberry | **W'burg**	24

Hudson Bar & Books | **W Vill**	23
Z Hudson Hotel | **W 50s**	24
Kiss & Fly | **Meatpacking**	20
Lakeside Lounge | **E Vill**	21
Lion's Head | **W 100s**	19
Lolita | **LES**	20
Loreley | **multi.**	22
Molly Pitcher's | **E 80s**	16
169 Bar | **LES**	18
NEW Park/Tavern | **Murray Hill**	–
Perdition | **W 40s**	19
Pete's Candy | **W'burg**	25
Z Plunge | **Meatpacking**	26
Rebar | **Dumbo**	24
NEW Réunion Surf Bar | **W 40s**	–
Rick's Cabaret | **Garment**	23
Rodeo Bar | **Murray Hill**	19
Royale | **E Vill**	21
NEW Salon Millesime | **Murray Hill**	–
Session 73 | **E 70s**	17
SideBar | **Gramercy**	18
Sip | **W 100s**	–
675 Bar | **Meatpacking**	25
NEW Snap | **W Vill**	–
St. Dymphna's | **E Vill**	22
Sweet & Vicious | **NoLita**	17
Swift | **NoHo**	22
T.B.D. | **Greenpt**	–
Tea Lounge | **Park Slope**	22
Teddy's | **W'burg**	24
Underground Lounge | **W 100s**	15
Valhalla | **W 50s**	22
V Bar | **G Vill**	22
Village Pourhouse | **E Vill**	15
White Rabbit | **LES**	18
White Star | **LES**	21
Wilfie & Nell | **W Vill**	24
Woody McHale's | **W Vill**	20
Zablozki's | **W'burg**	21
Zebulon † | **W'burg**	23

SPECIAL APPEALS

Wine Vintage Chart

This chart is based on our 0 to 30 scale. The ratings (by U. of South Carolina law professor **Howard Stravitz**) reflect vintage quality and the wine's readiness to drink. A dash means the wine is past its peak or too young to rate. Loire ratings are for dry whites.

Whites	95	96	97	98	99	00	01	02	03	04	05	06	07	08	09
France:															
Alsace	24	23	23	25	23	25	26	23	21	24	25	24	26	25	25
Burgundy	27	26	22	21	24	24	24	27	23	26	27	25	26	25	25
Loire Valley	-	-	-	-	-	-	26	21	23	27	23	24	24	26	
Champagne	26	27	24	23	25	24	21	26	21	-	-	-	-	-	-
Sauternes	21	23	25	23	24	24	29	24	26	21	26	24	27	25	27
California:															
Chardonnay	-	-	-	-	22	21	25	26	22	26	29	24	27	25	-
Sauvignon Blanc	-	-	-	-	-	-	-	-	26	25	27	25	24	25	
Austria:															
Grüner V./Riesl.	22	-	25	22	25	21	22	25	26	25	24	26	25	23	27
Germany:	21	26	21	22	24	20	29	25	26	27	28	25	27	25	25

Reds	95	96	97	98	99	00	01	02	03	04	05	06	07	08	09
France:															
Bordeaux	26	25	23	25	24	29	26	24	26	25	28	24	23	25	27
Burgundy	26	27	25	24	27	22	24	27	25	23	28	25	25	24	26
Rhône	26	22	23	27	26	27	26	-	26	25	27	25	26	23	26
Beaujolais	-	-	-	-	-	-	-	-	-	27	24	25	23	27	
California:															
Cab./Merlot	27	25	28	23	25	-	27	26	25	24	26	23	26	23	25
Pinot Noir	-	-	-	-	-	-	25	26	25	26	24	23	27	25	24
Zinfandel	-	-	-	-	-	-	25	23	27	22	24	21	21	25	23
Oregon:															
Pinot Noir	-	-	-	-	-	-	26	24	26	25	24	23	27	25	
Italy:															
Tuscany	25	24	29	24	27	24	27	-	25	27	26	26	25	24	-
Piedmont	21	27	26	25	26	28	27	-	24	27	26	25	26	26	-
Spain:															
Rioja	26	24	25	-	25	24	28	-	23	27	26	24	24	-	26
Ribera del Duero/ Priorat	26	27	25	24	25	24	27	-	24	27	26	24	26	-	-
Australia:															
Shiraz/Cab.	24	26	25	28	24	24	27	27	25	26	27	25	23	-	-
Chile:	-	-	-	-	25	23	26	24	25	24	27	25	24	26	-
Argentina:															
Malbec	-	-	-	-	-	-	-	-	-	25	26	27	25	24	-

ZAGATMAP

Manhattan Subway Map

Most Popular Nightlife

Map coordinates follow each name. Sections A–H lie south of 34th Street (see adjacent map). Sections I–P lie north of 34th Street (see reverse side of map).

1. 230 Fifth (A-4)
2. Campbell Apartment (P-5)
3. 1 Oak (B-2)
4. Brother Jimmy's † (L-5)
5. Four Seasons Hotel Bar* (N-5)
6. P.J. Clarke's (G-3, N-3, O-5)
7. McSorley's (C-5)
8. Hudson Hotel Bar (N-3)
9. Boat Basin Cafe (L-1)
10. Ginger Man (P-4)
11. B. B. King Blues Club (P-3)
12. Algonquin Blue Bar (P-4)
13. Pegu Club (D-4)
14. W Union Square Living Room (B-4)
15. Brandy Library (E-3)
16. Employees Only (D-2)
17. Flûte (B-4, O-3)
18. Whiskey Blue (O-5)
19. Angel's Share (C-5)
20. Apothéke* (F-5)
21. King Cole Bar (O-4)
22. Empire Hotel Rooftop (N-3)
23. PDT (C-5)
24. Blue Note (D-3)
25. D.B.A./D.B.A. Brooklyn (D-5, D-7)
26. Ulysses (H-4)

27. Bemelmans Bar (L-4)
28. Cafe Carlyle (L-4)
29. W Times Square Living Room (O-3)
30. Bubble Lounge (E-4)
31. Bar Veloce (B-3, C-5)
32. Flatiron Lounge* (B-3)
33. Death & Co (C-5)
34. Frying Pan* (A-1)
35. Oak Bar (N-4)
36. Blarney Stone (A-2, A-3, H-4, O-3, P-5)
37. Jekyll & Hyde* (D-3)
38. Monkey Bar* (O-4)
39. Rose Bar* (B-4)
40. Ritz-Carlton Star Lounge (N-4)
41. 40/40 (B-4)
42. Blind Tiger Ale House (D-3)
43. Milk and Honey (E-5)
44. Dizzy's Club Coca-Cola (N-3)
45. Pravda (D-4)
46. Ava Lounge (O-3)
47. Stone Rose* (N-3)
48. Stout (A-3)
49. Pete's Tavern (B-4)
50. Ace Hotel Lobby Bar (A-3)

---

*Indicates tie with above   † Indicates multiple branches